Social Formations of Early South India

Social Formations of Early South India

Rajan Gurukkal

OXFORD
UNIVERSITY PRESS

OXFORD
UNIVERSITY PRESS

Oxford University Press is a department of the University of Oxford.
It furthers the University's objective of excellence in research, scholarship,
and education by publishing worldwide. Oxford is a registered trademark of
Oxford University Press in the UK and in certain other countries

Published in India by
Oxford University Press
22 Workspace, 2nd Floor, 1/22 Asaf Ali Road, New Delhi 110002, India

First published 2010
Oxford India Paperbacks 2012
24th impression 2021

ISBN-13: 978-0-19-808939-1
ISBN-10: 0-19-808939-2

Typeset in Adobe Garamond Pro 10.5/13
by Le Studio Graphique, Gurgaon 122 002
Printed in India by Manipal Technologies Limited, Manipal

To

Professor R. Champakalashmi

Contents

Preface

This volume consists of revised versions of my essays, written over the last two decades and mostly published in their original form in certain national/international journals or books. The essays deal, broadly, with the socio-economic and political processes of the Tamil South in the period from the earliest to the early medieval. Thematically and spatio-temporally interconnected, the essays pertaining to aspects such as economy, technology, social relations, institutions, agrarian structure, political processes, state, writing, and so on, have culminated into this volume.

The essays are grouped into four sections: Historiography and Method, Early Social Formations, Social Transformations, and The New Social Formation. The first section seeks to delineate aspects such as sources, historiography, and methodology. The second group of essays deals with the various aspects of the ancient society from its pre-historic beginnings, traced from the archaeological relics in the form of cave paintings and etchings of a few rock shelters in the southern Western Ghats as delineated in the first essay. The rest of the collection examines human development at a later phase represented by the tribal social formation in the forested environment of the Tamil macro region as understood in the light of allusions in the ancient Tamil heroic poems, the productive forms and forces of change in the ancient society, the characteristics of its economy, their limiting impact on plough agriculture, the spread of writing and literacy, the features and dynamic of the ancient social formation, and the discursive processes in it, as construed using all the available sources in the perspective of people and landscape.

The third section includes essays that probe the processes of transformation of the social formation. Starting with the discussion of the transition from the ancient to early medieval in the Tamil macro region with a closer look at the historical processes of the formation of the state, the socio-economic processes of the transition from clan and lineage through hereditary occupations and caste, and the transformational implications of the spread of writing have also been discussed. There is an essay specifically dealing with the series of radical transformations of the various aspects of the social formation of ancient Kerala, which deserve the prefix 'great'.

The final section covers the structural and institutional features of the new social formation, namely, the agrarian social formation into which the ancient, that is, the agro-pastoral social formation dissolved itself. The first essay delineates the temple that was the pivotal institution of the agrarian social formation in the Tamil South as well as Kerala. The next essay, examining the experience of Kerala, takes on the historical antecedents of the birth of the caste system, the most crucial institution that subsumed the relations of production and strategies of labour realization of the agrarian social formation. The next essay through a case study of the Pandya Country, deals with the instituted character of the reservoir system of irrigation and its technology, a significant aspect of the agrarian social formation.

The essays despite their temporal disparateness and thematic divergence do converge on the central thesis of social formation that has been the methodology and framework of understanding for me all these years. They are independent individually but remain interconnected and amenable to ordering with a sense of sequence about the historical social development, thanks to their methodological consistency. Some of the properties of these essays are their integration of multiple sources and application of analytical tools like structuralism and semiology for heuristic purpose, social theoretical approach, systemic understanding, explanatory nature, thrust on the characterization of interfaces, and exploration of forces and processes of structural transformations. Each essay being a highlight of its own topic but pursued along the track of social formation constrained its author to discuss 'the part' as a fraction of 'the whole', notwithstanding the defect of repetition. The agro-pastoral social formation being the 'whole' for several essays, the 'part' discussed as the topic in each had to be shown as 'a part of the whole' for leaving every essay an accomplished stand-alone piece. A collection of such free-standing essays suffers from the fault of repetition *ad nauseam*. I, therefore, crave for the indulgence of my readers.

These essays are relevant in the context of representation of South Indian history catching up and the course on 'social formation' being introduced both at the undergraduate and postgraduate levels as a widely addressed theme of explanatory history. They cater to the academic requirements of students graduating in the discipline, and teachers as well as researchers engaged in South Indian history. That there is no book available on social formations in early south India as yet, is a reason worth stating by way of justification for the volume. I shall be delighted if it succeeds in serving the purposes of its readers.

I am indebted to many for my studies. M.G.S. Narayanan, who taught me what research means; R. Champakalakshmi, who guided my studies; and Romila Thapar, who showed me the depth of historical explanation, are the foremost among them. I acknowledge my indebtedness to each one of them. I am grateful to Raghava Varier, my sole research mate and Kesavan Veluthat, my critic friend who patiently went through the draft and helped improving it. I put on record the benefits of the discussions I had with Y. Subbarayalu, Noburu Karashima, Shereen F. Ratnagar, K. Rajan, and K.N. Ganesh. Bindu, O.M. helped me out with checking the diacritical marks throughout the manuscript. Jalaja has been the absent cause of all the research I have done and Krishnaraj its destination. I owe the professional quality of the book to the editors of the Oxford University Press. My gratitude to them is beyond words.

RAJAN GURUKKAL

Acknowledgements

I join the publisher to gratefully acknowledge the publishers of the journals and publications cited below for permission to publish the following articles in part or in full:

The Popular Prakashan

'The Beginnings of Early Historic Period: The Case of the Tamil South, Up to c. AD 500', in Romila Thapar (ed.), *Recent Perspectives of Early Indian History* (Mumbai, 1995), pp. 237–61.

Sage Publications

'Forms of Production and Forces of Change in Ancient Tamil Society', *Studies in History*, vol. 2, ns (New Delhi, 1989), pp. 159–75.

'Writing and Its Uses in the Ancient Tamil Country', *Studies in History*, vol. 12, ns 1 (New Delhi, 1996), pp. 67–81.

'Aspects of the Reservoir System of Irrigation in the Pandya State', *Studies in History*, vol. 2, no. 2, ns (New Delhi, 1986), pp. 155–62.

Indian History Congress

'Aspects of Early Iron Age Economy: Problems of Agrarian Expansion in Tamilakam', *Indian History Congress Proceedings* (Delhi, 1981). Reproduced in B.D. Chattopadhyaya (ed.), *Ancient Indian Economic History* (Delhi, 2003), pp. 220–9.

'Characterising Ancient Society: The Case of South India', Sectional Presidential Address, Ancient India, *Indian History Congress Proceedings* (Delhi, 1998).

Indian Council of Historical Research

'From Clan and Lineage to Hereditary Occupations and Caste in Early South India', *Indian Historical Review*, vol. XXII, nos 1–2, 1993–4, pp. 22–33.

'Shift of Trust from Words to Deeds: Implications of the Proliferation of Inscriptions in the Tamil South', *Indian Historical Review*, vol. XXXIV, no. 2 (New Delhi, 2007), pp. 16–35.

Manohar

'Tribes, Forest and Social Formation', in B.B. Chaudhuri and A. Bandopadhyaya (eds), *Tribes, Forest and Social Formation in India* (New Delhi, 2005), pp. 65–80.

Cosmo Books

'Antecedents of the State Formation in South India', in Champakalakshmi, *et al.* (eds), *State and Society in Pre-modern South India*, Current Books Publications (Thrissur, 2002), pp. 39–59.

Cultural Publications, Government of Kerala

'The Great Transformations', in Rajan Gurukkal and Raghava Varier (ed.), *Cultural History of Kerala*, vol. I (Thiruvananthapuram, 1999), pp. 235–74.

Indian Institute of Advanced Studies

'The Edakal Rock Engravings: Morphology and Meanings', *Studies in Humanities and Social Sciences*, vol. IV, no. 1 (Shimla, 1997), pp. 43–60.

Rawat Publications

'Formation of Caste Society in Kerala: Historical Antecedents', in K.L. Sharma (ed.), *Caste and Class in Indian States* (Delhi, 1994), pp. 395–410.

Pearson Longman Publications

'Temples as Sites of Social and Religious Interaction', in B.D. Chattopadhyaya (ed.), *A Social History of Early India* (Delhi, 2009), pp. 199–210.

Introduction
Conceptual Preliminaries

The essays in this volume overtly endeavour to depend on the theoretical framework of social formation, in identifying and piecing together meaningful clues from the sources so as to interpret the character of the societies under review. According to the framework, understanding historically existing landscapes and people, starts with inquiries into the material processes of social appropriation of nature and the social processes of distribution of the material appropriated. This basic understanding helps us inquire into the level of technology and nature of social relations against the background of which we are able to make sense of the political ideas, institutions, and cultural practices of the people. Social formation is, therefore, the structured and interconnected aggregate of a people's relations, socio-political institutions, customs, rituals, and other cultural practices engendered by a given level of technology and economy of subsistence and survival in time. The primacy of the economic is insisted upon as determinant 'in the last instance' but to be the least mechanical about it. The concept of social formation is not new to Indian historiography, thanks to the book by R.S. Sharma, which conceptualizes the historical processes of ancient Ganga valley, ingenuously harping on historical materialism.[1] Conceptualization of formation processes of ideas and institutions in the Ganga valley is familiar too, thanks to the studies by Romila Thapar, creatively engaging the riches of social theory.[2]

SOCIAL FORMATION THEORY

Social formation owes its theory to historical materialism, which makes the expression technical, signifying Marx's theory of the stages of social development as well as a society in any of the stages in time. Marx used the term 'social formation' (*gesellschaftsformen*) first in his economic manuscript to mean society as a system constituted by the economic, political, and ideological aspects in their interconnection.[3] Marx and Engels used the term to designate society in terms of its mode of production. Social formation is, therefore, generally defined as a concept of the social whole consisting of the same structural levels that figure as part of the characteristics of the mode of production.[4] Historical materialism, the actual 'science of history' constructed through the use of Marxist categories of knowledge derived through dialectical materialism, is distinct for the teleology of social developmental sequences and the dynamic of change unfolded through the theory of mode of production. Mode of production may be briefly defined as a systemic combine of forces and relations of production presupposing given labour processes and institutional forms of appropriation.[5] Broadly, it means a combination of structures or levels or instances such as the economic, juridico-political, ideological, and theoretical, determined 'in the last instance' by the economic. The theory of mode of production presupposes three things: the economic base, the juridico-political superstructure, and the ideological super-structure. The economic encompasses the social strategies of subsistence and survival, and the ideological, the entire gamut of cultural aspects including religion. Base–superstructure correlation and the schema of sequential stages, often made undeservedly rigid, the former to the extent of mistaking the analogy and the latter, the illustration, for theory.

Any attempt at defining the concept of social formation should begin with the oft-quoted passage in Marx's preface to *The Critique of Political Economy* which is the ever best expression about it. Marx says,

> An aggregate of human beings constitutes a society when, and only when, the people are in some way related. The essential relation is not kinship, but much wider; namely, that developed through production and mutual exchange of commodities. The particular society is characterised by what it regards as necessary; who gathers or produces the things, by what implements; who lives of the production of others, and by what right, divine or legal—cults and laws are social by-products; who owns the tools, the land, sometimes the body and soul of the producer; who controls the disposal of the surplus, and regulates quantity and form of the supply. Society is held together by bonds of production.

The term society in the passage stands for social formation. This is clear when he says,

> In the social production of their means of existence, men enter into definite, necessary relations which are independent of their will, productive relationships

> which correspond to a definite stage of development of their material productive forces. The aggregate of those productive relationships constitute the economic structure of the society, the real basis on which a juridical and political superstructure arises and to which definite forms of social consciousness correspond. The mode of production of the material means of existence conditions the whole process of social, political, and intellectual life.

The nature and basis of human relations are made clear by Engels in his remark that the most common feature of all social formations is 'surplus labour' (labour beyond the time required for the labourer's own maintenance), and appropriation of the products of this unpaid surplus labour.[6]

Structuralist Marxist theorists endeavoured to restate the theory of mode of production by putting its science first, and its knowledgeable application as a powerful instrument of analysis primary, in order to check its uninformed usage for mechanical typological reduction. What has been brought to the fore by these theorists is the strength of the theory as the theory of theory. It was structuralist Marxist theorists like Louis Althusser, Balibar, Barry Hindess, Paul Q. Hirst, Maurice Godelier, Nicos Poulantzas, and a few others who gave the expression 'social formation' a more specific technical connotation.[7] In *Reading Capital*, Althusser and Balibar define social formation as a 'totality of "instances" articulated on the basis of a determinate mode of production,' which is an explanation of complex associations in a society.[8] They specify three 'instances': the economic, political, and ideological, signifying 'practices' as essential constituents of a social formation since they refer to basic 'functions without which human social existence cannot be conceived.' The economic practice refers to 'the transformation of natural resources into socially useful products,' political practice to 'the reproduction and administration of collective social relations and their institutional forms,' and ideological practice to 'the constitution of social subjects and their consciousness.' These 'instances' are themselves distinct structural levels of 'social relations' and 'practices', each of which possesses a functional unity across more specific structures. Practice is central to the concept of every 'instance', for all levels of social existence are based on social practices, but this hardly implies autonomy of human agency. It is not the human agency that is decisive about 'instances' and 'practices', for they are relations determined 'in the last instance' by the economic.[9] This is opposed to the humanist readings of Marx offered by Lukács, Gramsci, and others, which on the contrary stress the role of human agency in the history of social development.

A variety of diverse practices exists for all time in the 'complex unity' of any given social formation. The economic, political, and ideological 'instances' function as a system of interrelated and interdependent 'practices' and institutions as an 'articulation', of unified relations of domination and subordination. Althusser calls this homologous unity of distinct and uneven manners of determination, 'structural causality'. Nevertheless, he is sure of the 'relative autonomy' of 'instances' in the case of particular social formations of any region, which have unique patterns of development, thanks to the specific historical matrix and cultural conditions of existence. While Althusser recognizes the decisive role of the mode of production in determining the nature of the social formation, he rejects the mechanical presumption that the economic instance invariably determines the exact nature of other instances like superstructures, because of the relative autonomy of each instance as exemplified and illustrated by the difference in empirical experiences across regions. He maintains that each instance has its own relative autonomy securing a place and function in the complex unity of the social formation. The 'instances' are invariably 'uneven' and the consequences of contradictions inherent in the assemblage of the variety of articulations are beyond prediction. At the same time the theoretically accessible link between the two and the primacy of the economic in 'the last instance' cannot be overlooked. Althusser's argument is that there exists a structured hierarchy of determinations in relatively autonomous institutions and practices, and that therefore, we cannot characterize social formation as a system in which everything causes everything else. We cannot characterize it in a structuralist–essentialist totality where every practice as a part signifies the whole either. Althusserian 'structural causality' thus makes typological reduction of social formation unacceptable for its mechanistic determinism, but not in any way by implying eclectic indeterminacy, valid.

Social relations are manifestations of concrete relations engendered by the economic practice that is realized, reproduced, and transformed through a relatively autonomous process. In economic practice, contradictions exist within and between subsistence strategies of social groups, in spite of the fact that the dominance of one or the other in terms of productivity is explicit. In political practice, contradictions exist within and between relations of representation and relations of hegemony expressed in the antagonistic interests of those who effectively control the institutions of collective social organization, and the social groups within the social formation lacking such control. In ideological practice, contradictions exist within and between relations that empower and enable individuals as social subjects and relations of subjection, which restrict individuals to specific roles and capacities. Althusser emphasizes 'the contradictions between and within the structured relations and practices that constitute human beings as social subjects, and places, positions, and roles as the social space within which all human practice necessarily occurs'. In short, any social formation is 'a complex hierarchy of functionally organized institutions or instances whose unity can be neither ignored altogether nor reduced to a single closed system.'[10]

Godelier makes a distinction between the concepts of 'social formation' and 'mode of production'. He argues that 'in defining a social formation, one must produce a synthetic definition of the precise nature of the diversity and unity of the economic and social relations which characterize a society at a given epoch.' He prescribes the following scientific steps to produce such a synthetic definition: First of all, it is important to 'identify the number and character of the various modes of production which are found combined in a particular way within a specific society and which constitute its economic base at a specific period.' The next step is to 'identify the various elements in the social and ideological superstructure whose origin and function correspond to these various modes of production.' The final step is to 'define the exact form and content of the articulation and combination of these various modes of production in a hierarchical order, in so far as one mode of production dominates the others, and in some way subjects them to the needs and logic of its own mode of functioning, and integrates them, more or less, in the mechanism of its own reproduction.'

In Godelier's formulation a social formation is a combination of more than one mode of production, of which one dominates. Any social formation therefore, presupposes at least one mode of production to be subordinate. Godelier points out that when a mode of production, whether dominant or subordinate, is surrounded by the limiting forces of other modes of production within the social formation, its functioning necessarily differs from what it would have been, had the mode of production existed in autonomy. The argument is that any mode of production is a constituent element of a social formation and therefore, it is determined by the properties of the ensemble in which it is situated. According to him what we find in empirical research are not modes of production, but social formation, the structure of which is the result of the combination of at least two distinct modes of production, one of which is dominant and the other subordinate. He argues that it is in this way 'the concept of social formation is most useful in the analysis of particular, concrete, historical realities captured in the real, irreversible time of given period of history.' Structuralist Marxists like Nicos Poulantzas, Pierre-Philippe Rey, Emmanuel Terray, and Claude Meillassoux presume that in pre-capitalist social formations an alternative source of contradiction originates from the universality about the co-existence of the several unevenly evolved modes of production that are imperfectly articulated rather than integrated.[11] They codify the special relationship between the forces and relations of production by arguing that the former were determinants and the latter, dominant.

Poulantzas observes that it is through the study of the structure, constitution, and functioning of various modes of production and social formations, and the forms of their transition from one type to another, that historical materialism 'has its object, namely the concept of history.' He shows how concepts like mode of production and social formation in historical materialism are effective in analysing particular situations of regional history through the study of 'the elemental structures and practices whose specific combinations constitute a mode of production and a social formation.' It has been pointed out that 'only impure social formations actually exist, and these will contain several coexisting modes of production with all their constituent levels or even several relatively autonomous fragments of modes of production.' Poulantzas maintains that it is the dominant mode of production that confers fundamental unity on a social formation.

Pierre-Philippe Rey maintains that a mode of production is dominant within a social formation when it subjects the functioning of other modes of production represented in the social formation to the requirements of its own reproduction.[12] Foster-Carter opines that the precise definition of the social formation therefore, depends upon one's understanding of mode of production and articulation, that is, the exact combination of forces and relations of production or the connections among structural levels or the connection of a mode of production to a social formation or the connections among modes of production within a social formation.[13] According to E. Terray, a social formation cannot be understood except by beginning with an analysis of the relations of production, which form its base, influencing the system as a whole. He establishes the decisive importance of productive relations by showing the crucial role that the institutional form of labour expropriation plays in the functioning of the social formation. He argues that to understand the structure of relations of production, it is necessary to begin the analysis not only from the mode of production but also from the social formation of which it is a part. Not only the economic infrastructure but also the political and ideological superstructures must be taken into account. Althusser's application of the Freudian concept of over-determination that refers to the complex set of elements and associations in the context of causation, in fact, precludes the question as to whether the relations or the forces have primacy in a social formation. Nevertheless, he maintains that in any given historical epoch, one of the three structural levels that is, the economic, the political, and the ideological in a social formation, may have greater influence and determinacy than the rest.

We draw a lot of practical insights from the recuperation of the concept of social formation by Structuralist Marxists, especially Althusser and some of the leading anthropological theorists among them, done in the light of their empirical experience. There are far more theoretical insights to be drawn from the writings of Marx himself, which help deeper probing into historical social formations. Marx's observation that at the level of features and manifestations of any social formation we see coexistence of the old and the new is an example. His contention that no social formation ever perishes before all the productive forces have developed for which it is wide enough; and, new, higher productive forces never come into being before the material conditions of their existence have matured in the womb of the old society itself, is another example. A very significant lesson that a historian has to draw from Marx is what Althusser has noted as 'a central epistemological premise of Marx's social theory, that is, the cognitive insistence up on the difference between phenomenal appearances and the basic underlying reality—"the difference between surface appearances and underlying theoretical truth"'.[14] Likewise, it is essential for a historian to bear in mind Marx's distinction between the universality of economic, political, and ideological practices, and the variety of determinate institutional forms, which can be located historically. Re-reading Marx, we learn to avoid the mistaken notion that there exists a single institutional form within every social formation that will correspond to the European historical experience. Also we recognize that while there are differences of economic relations across social formations, there is theoretically accessible universality about the interconnection between every social formation and its set of economic relations. The point is that concrete historical social formations are composed of elements whose inner structural logic is theoretically determined, while historical processes simply break up and recombine these elements in various ways. Theoretically, the number of instances in a social formation is open rather than closed, and it is not the specifications of distinct practices thereof, which are the historian's interest, however important it is heuristically, for the principal objective should be the hermeneutics of the structural truth. It is important that such features of the social formation are borne in mind at the time of historical analysis of a given period and place.

The central theoretical insight that the historian seeking to analyse the transformation of a social formation is Marx's 'primacy thesis' that theorizes the process of one mode of production dissolving into another, impelled under the dynamic of incompatibility between forces and relations of production.[15] Cohen observes that over a period of time the productive forces with the inherent potential go on developing as long as the relations of production are compatible. For the forces of production to develop further from the point of incompatibility, the relations of production should change. If there is an objective interest in transforming the relations of production to restore compatibility with forces of production, the capacity for bringing that change about will ultimately be brought into being. When forces and relations of production are incompatible, the relations change in such a way that compatibility between forces and relations of production is restored.[16] The social formation cannot be more advanced than its forces of production. Similarly, the forces of production cannot be more advanced than what their relations of production can support. Forces of production in any social formation require from time to time alterations in the relations of production ensuring development-compatibility, the absence of which sets in use-incompatibility and production crisis and the subsequent dissolution of the social formation.[17]

The historiographical advantage of the concept of social formation is its capacity to provide a framework of comprehension enabling holistic perception of history. It helps us view past life as a totality without its being compartmentalized into aspects such as the social, economic, political, cultural, religious, and so on. Althusser's definition of 'social formation' as the total complex of economic infrastructure and superstructure renders plausible a very powerful framework of comprehension for understanding historical societies. It encourages us to focus on the interfaces of well-represented social systems, especially their transitional phases with greater significance, a practice not often followed in the textbooks of history. The perspective enables incorporation of insights from cognate disciplines and auxiliary branches of history. There is the possibility of maintaining a better integration of historical narrative with social theory, a method that provides the discipline intellectual depth.

THE SUBJECT MATTER

The subject matter of the present collection is historical analysis of social formations in the region consisting of the modern linguistic states called Tamil Nadu and Kerala, dating back from the early medieval down to the ancient times, done in a somewhat theoretical way as the task demands. The definition and framework of the concept of social formation adopted in the essays are derived from the theory of mode production restated by the structuralist–theorists and anthropologists of Marxian tradition, noted in the above section. Instead of viewing social formation as a combination of 'modes of production', we seek to define it as an ensemble of a few unevenly evolved 'forms of production' interconnected to one another and structured by the dominance of one form that need not necessarily be superior to the rest in terms of technology and productivity. Since the expression 'mode of production' is widely in use to mean a specific social totality of epochal identity almost on a par with 'social formation', we accept 'forms of production' appropriate in order to avoid confusion. The concept of social formation is to illustrate and exemplify in the light of the theory of mode of production, how the regional particular history in terms of specific concrete details, in their interconnections constitute the abstract totality, the system, and render concrete knowledge possible. Historical analysis can, then, reach out beyond mere description and classify the combinations of forms of production and fragments of forms of production, which go into the making of any given social formation. Kosambi's observation is relevant here:

> ... no single mode prevailed uniformly over the whole country at any one time; so it is necessary to select for treatment that particular mode which, at any period, was the most vigorous, most likely to dominate production, and which inevitably spread over the greater part of the country, no matter how many of the older forms survived in outward appearance.[18]

We underline the centrality of productive forces in productive forms that join together to accomplish the social formation and go about examining specific practices, relations, ideas, and institutions attached to each form as well as those that dominated the rest and characterized the social totality through the articulated features, processes, and dynamic thereof involving the tension of incompatibility between forces and relations of production.

The earliest point in the time line of the essays is that of the pre-historic covering the Mesolithic Kerala as a case and the Iron Age South India as a close look at the entire region under review, several centuries and hence presupposing more than one social formation. The sample spot-lighting of the pre-historic for a general understanding is justified, for transformation of life in the hoary past was tremendously slow. Life in the Stone Age and early Iron Age, often designated pre-historic, had certainly undergone a major change involving a radical shift in the strategies of subsistence from hunting–gathering to agriculture, but without much of socio-cultural differences from each other, since the pre-historic economies such as hunting–gathering, primitive agriculture, and a combination of the two, despite their varying levels of technology of subsistence as well as survival, were subsumed by relations of tribal kinship. Apart from stone tools, rock-art constitutes the rare source for imagining pre-historic life, the contours of cultures and transformations of which in the light of clues in the rock-art of Kerala, point to the process in a larger region, perhaps the whole of peninsular India, for pre-historic social formations are comparable across vast regions, unlike those of later times noted for their strikingly unique and locale-specific features. That was a social formation with instances and practices unarticulated and hence remaining a single whole in which the cultural or ideological dominated, subsuming even the economic.

The social formation identified and analysed at length in the book is the agro-pastoral whose structure and composition as a totality along with its features, forces, relations, institutions, practices, and processes form the subject matter for a few essays. An account of the forms of production and forces of change in ancient Tamil society is given at the outset, identifying in the light of clues in the multiple sources especially the ancient Tamil heroic texts, the instances and practices of agro-pastoral social formation as a combination of several uneven forms of production such as hunting–gathering, crafts production, fishing cum salt-making, and plough agriculture structured by the dominance of millet farming and cattle-keeping. An analysis of the productive relations, their basis of clan-kin-ties, and the pattern of circulation of resources through institutions like prestations, gifts, predatory exaction, and redistribution, has been done for understanding the primary instance of the social formation. Interpreting the negative impact of instances and practices of the dominant form on the most potential form of production, the built-in contradictory dynamic of kinship based production relations, and redistributive economy blocking the development of productive forces characterized by the technology of iron, the logic of transformation is worked out. A specialized assessment of problems of agrarian expansion provides various details of institutions, customary practices and exchanges that characterized the social formation, which were utterly uncongenial for the expansion of plough agriculture, the form of production waiting for domination. The details of kin-based relations of production, the culture of clan ties, and formation of the lineage system and incompatibility of all these with the productive forces, which provided the context of the subsequent emergence of the institution of caste have been examined. There is close focus on the processes and antecedents of the formation of the state out of the juridico-political ideas, institutions, structures, and practices of unevenly evolved chiefdoms that distinguished the social formation.

One of the main aspects of the social formation, discussed at length, using theoretical insights, is the issue of structural transformation. Identifying and analysing the processes and dynamic of productive forces and relations, characterizing institutional and structural manifestations and, interpreting the pattern of change in the form of a series of transitions from the pre-existing to the new, the great transformations that the social formation underwent in time, are presented in detail, recounting the series of transitions: the transition from kin-labour to non-kin labour, from thrust hoe to plough, from millet to paddy, from clans to hereditary occupation groups and caste, chiefdom to monarchy, heterodox ideology to Brahmanism, and from pre-rice landscape to wet-rice landscape. These transformations leading to the total dissolution of the social formation have been discussed in detail as illustrated and exemplified by the experiences of the Tamil macro region as well as those of the Kerala micro region, under the schema of the processes of transition from the ancient to early medieval social formation.

A few essays delineate the instances of the new social formation of the Tamil south, by drawing closer to the specific features of productive forces represented by the plough and technology of water management, relations based on subjected labour of hereditary specialisation diversified into multiple arts and crafts and their permanent occupation groups, institutions of extra-economic coercion, structures of hegemonic control, and processes of expropriation of unpaid surplus. The institutional manifestation of wet-rice expansion in the form of *brahmadēya* and *dēvadāna*, the rise of the temple as the headquarters integrating agrarian relations, proliferation of land-rights through re-distribution of endowments, generation of services based on tenemancy in land, accommodation of hereditary service groups into the system of caste, hierarchical arrangement of surplus appropriation, ideological legitimization of social relations, emergence of class-structured society, divinization of monarchy, and formation of the state were the specific developments that characterized the new social formation. Some of the essays focus on the experience of the Tamil south while others, on that of the Kerala region. There is a specialized study of the technology of irrigation and institutions of water management, particularly the cascaded reservoir system, and the community practice of prioritized distribution.

As regards conceptual consideration of the category of the social formation, the first framework available to examine is the 'Asiatic Mode', which characterizes the mode of production of pre-colonial Asia, a petrified system of long continuity from the agrarian past, distinct for features such as the existence of an absolute state-power keeping the village communities in complete subjugation, made possible through the construction and maintenance of irrigation sources.[19] The existence of a large class of administrative staff assisting the state in extracting the surplus from the village settlements, absence of private ownership of land, lack of commercial centres, and the isolated and localized existence of the village communities, prompted some scholars to categorize it as Asiatic Mode Production (AMP). Nevertheless, the AMP categorization hardly has many protagonists among historians inclined to conceptualization, who by and large, prefer to characterize the society, feudal. The Marxist sequential model of transformation of the classical ancient into the medieval feudal acquired a strong presence as the accepted paradigm in the historiography of northern India with the work of R.S. Sharma.[20] However, in the absence of classical society in South Indian history, the direct application of the model became difficult.

The question, as to whether or not the social formation that emerged out of the dissolution of the ancient can be called feudal has been raised by several scholars looking at its features. According to Marxist perspective the feudal model being the most relevant to a formation resultant of the dissolution of primitive modes, historians subscribed to it took feudalism, the point of reference for their exercise in typology. Noticing the empirical differences of features of the social formation in northern India, made out from sources, prompted a few historians to seek the possibility of developing an Indian variety of the feudal mode of production, notwithstanding dissimilarities in their characterization. D.D. Kosambi, a historian committed to anti-deterministic stance with 'sources first' approach, called the social totality of early India feudal, but as introduced 'from above' for the process 'from below' only to follow.[21] R.S. Sharma without taking issues with Kosambi for the concept of feudalism from above and below, went about characterizing Indian feudalism, keeping in view of the features identified by Marc Bloch as fundamental, showing the growth of individual ownership of land at the cost of royal and communal ownership, the existence of landed intermediaries, subjection of the peasantry through sub-infeudation, eviction, and imposition of non-customary taxes and forced labour, conversion of income from trade and crafts into benefices and, the existence of a self-sufficient economy buttressed by lesser use of coins and comparative absence of trade.[22] Marc Bloch defined the system, 'a subject peasantry; widespread use of the service tenemant (that is, the *fief*) instead of salary; the supremacy of a class of specialized warriors; ties of obedience and protection which bind man to man; fragmentation of authority; and, in the midst of all this survival of other forms of association, family and state.'[23] Marx had emphasized the hierarchical system of land ownership and serf labour chained to it.[24] The ruling class structure is shown crucial in the system in Joseph R. Strayer and Rushton Coulborn.[25] To some scholars *seigniorial* and serf elements are fundamental. However, the particular ties between large estates and small farms; the institution of serfdom and the *seigniorial* taxation seem to be the fundamental features of European feudalism.[26]

Several historians objected to the application of the feudal model in the Indian context soon after the thesis was put forward. The objections acquired theoretical grounds only recently with the onset of a controversy among historians, triggered by an essay of Harbans Mukhia challenging the thesis of Indian feudalism.[27] His major objections are: Feudalism, unlike Capitalism was not a universal system and it defies a universal definition. All pre-capitalist societies were characterized by a primarily agricultural economy, appropriation of the surplus by the ruling class through extra-economic methods, and so on, and the application of the term 'feudal' in a broad sense cannot distinguish them against one another on the basis of the specific economic process involved in each one of them. Feudalism in Europe has been shown emerging out of a crisis of the production relations caused by the catastrophic collision of the primitive and ancient modes of production. Since R.S. Sharma's proposition ascribes the establishment of feudalism to administrative and legal procedures, Mukhia wonders as to how a new mode of production can be the result of a state policy. He argues that it has yet to be proved in the context of India that the dependence of the peasantry on the landlords involved an extraneous control over the peasants' process of production.

Recent historical scholarship creatively responding to the auxiliary questions and criticisms, has further strengthened the concept of Indian feudalism, a process in which R.S. Sharma himself played a pivotal role, involving efforts at theoretical upgradation of the original proposition of Indian feudalism.[28] Certain theoretical inadequacies of the model of Indian feudalism, such as the ascription of external causes to the origins of the social formation with the involuntary implication that the ancient Indian society lacked any built-in potential for change, prompted R.S. Sharma himself to have new thoughts on the problem. The reinterpretation of the 'Kali Age' as a period of 'production-crisis' and the emergence of the institution of land grants as an outcome of the crisis proved to be a major historiographical advance that resulted from the theoretical criticism levelled against the presages of Indian feudalism.[29] The absence of manorial system and serfdom, the two fundamental aspects that unify the variations of feudalism observed in different parts of Europe, a criticism paused against the labelling of early medieval social formations in India feudal, has been explained afresh, maintaining that beneath such institutional manifestations, existed servitude in India, perhaps in a more severe form than that of 'serfdom'. The existence of a servile class of primary producers, subjected to immobility, has been proved beyond doubt in the light of sources. It is natural that the institutional manifestation of the mode of labour expropriation and the level of servitude would vary from place to place, for their nature is culturally and historically determined. It has been rightly pointed out by R.S. Sharma that feudalism has to be seen as a mode of the distribution of the means of production and of the appropriation of the surplus, in which the relationship between the class of landlords expropriating the unpaid surplus labour and the category of primary producers is of crucial importance. The basis of circulation of the produce under the system was extra-economic coercion as in the case of feudalism despite the variations with which it existed. R.S. Sharma maintains that one cannot discern more fundamental universals than these minimum across the variants identified at various places in time the world over.

The particularities of the 'Indian feudal model' are not pan-Indian, as the case of the agrarian social formation in the Tamil South exemplifies. The land of the Tamils which lay outside the pale of the Mauryan Empire had not passed through the mode of production that characterized the latter. The social formation of the Tamil Nadu and Kerala region in fact, was the structured outcome of the contradictory relations that fettered the forces of production represented by the plough under conditions of use-incompatibility and the entailing production crisis. The empirical experience of structural transformation of the immediate post-Gupta society had no resemblance with the instances, practices, and relations of contemporary south India. Nevertheless, it is true that the historical conditions of the Tamil region and Kerala were influenced by the socio-economic processes of the north from time to time. Many of the ideas and institutions of the north spread to the south adding on to the internal contradictions of the material milieu of the age.

The following are the features of the social formation of the early medieval period in the Tamil South as distinguished from those of the north: the emergence of numerous agrarian settlements as administratively autonomous constituents, managed by the temple-based corporations of the landholders; the growth of many of the warrior households as the seats of the lineage of chiefs, ruling over small localities; the organization of the entire political structure on the basis of the rights over land; and the persistence of the heads of pastoral groups as warrior leaders in the agrarian villages in addition to the numerous specialized warrior groups existing throughout the region. The records preserved in the temples, mainly dealing with the activities of the temple-centred local body called *sabha* carry information about these features. The social formation in question is of a predominantly agrarian economy in which a class of non-cultivating land-owners expropriated unpaid surplus labour from the primary producers through extra-economic methods. Keeping in view of the features and properties of the social formation, several historians have preferred to call the social formation a variant of 'Indian feudalism'.[30] They had to somehow defend the proposition in opposition to the objections raised by Burton Stein to the 'feudal model' in the context of medieval South India and his application of the 'Segmentary State Model' as an alternative.

Burton Stein's objections to the application of the term feudal are not raised on theoretical grounds, and they do not involve the question of universals and particularities in the economic processes. His alternative—the 'Segmentary State' is an adapted version of what Aiden Southall, an anthropologist formulated to illustrate the state organization in a tribal society of segmentary and lineage system.[31] The following are characteristics of the segmentary state according to Stein: a central government with absolute authority at the centre and a ritual sovereignty over the similar and mutually exclusive peripheral constituents; a specialized administrative staff for the centre and its repetition on a small scale in the peripheral constituents, organized into a hierarchy in relation to the centre; the power of the centre repeated at each level in a descending order; and the flexibility of the political relation of the remote points of the territory to the centre. After reviewing the various aspects of Southall's formulations Stein reduces the conception of the 'Segmentary State' as follows:

In the segmentary state there may be numerous 'centres' of which one has primacy as a source of ritual sovereignty, but all exercise actual political control over a part, or segment, of the political system encompassed by the state ... subordinate levels, or 'zones' of the segmentary state may be distinguished and the organisation of these is 'pyramidal'. That is the relationship between the centre and the peripheral units of any single segment are the same—in reduced form—as the relationship between the prime centre and all peripheral focuses of power....

Stein describes the states under the Cōḻas and the Vijayanagara rulers, with the help of the 'segmentary state' model. It is significant that the model is applied to a tribal polity, an advanced agrarian polity and a further developed one. This would suggest that the political structure under the 'segmentary state' model has no relation with the economic base. The political structure remains the same under different modes of production. There is no attempt in Stein to probe into the processes and relations of production behind the 'segmentary state' formation. To him the model seems to be a substitute for the method of analysing the mode of production in order to understand the political ideas and institutions. The model as such has only a descriptive value and is hardly a scientific tool of analysis. It is true that some of the features of the political organization we have taken up for study, resemble certain characteristics of the 'segmentary state' conception. It is not uncommon that certain elements in the political superstructures of diverse social formations are apparently comparable. Their external description through a model without ascertaining the correlation between the actual political structure and its economic base is an unscientific exercise.

NOTES AND REFERENCES

1. R.S. Sharma, 1983, *Material Culture and Social Formations in Ancient India*, New Delhi. See the introduction for details of the perspective. pp. xv–xxiii.
2. Most of Romila Thapar's articles and books vouch for it. However, see particularly chapters of her, *Ancient Indian Social History*, New Delhi, 1978. Also her, *From Lineage to State*, New Delhi, 1984.
3. Karl Marx, 1953, *Grundrisse*, Introduction, Berlin, p. 104. See the relevant extracts in E.J. Hobsbawm (ed.), 1964, *Pre-capitalist Economic Formations*,

London, p. 12; Barry Hindess and Paul Q. Hirst, 1977, *Pre-capitalist Modes of Production*, London, pp. 10–11; G.A. Cohen, 1978, *Karl Marx's Theory of History: A Defense*, Princeton, p. 7; Perry Anderson, 1983, *In the Tracks of Historical Materialism*, London, p. 14. See the discussion in Jon Elster, 1985, *Making Sense of Marx*, Cambridge, pp. 1–41; E.O. Wright *et al.*, 1992, *Reconstructing Marism*, London, pp. 62–7.

4. Dominique Legros, 1979, 'Economic Base, Mode of Production, and Social Formation: A Discussion of Marx's Terminology', in *Dialectical Anthropology*, Amsterdam, 4: 243–9.
5. For details of the theory of mode of production, see Hindess and Hirst, *Pre-capitalist Modes of Production*. Also see, Anderson, *In the Tracks of Historical Materialism*.
6. See the discussion in Engels, 1969, *Anti-Duhring*, pp. 52–4.
7. For details of conceptualization see, Etienne Balibar, 'The Fundamental Concepts of Historical Materialism', in Louis Althusser and E. Balibar, 1970, *Reading Capital*, London, pp. 31–3.
8. See discussion in Althusser and Balibar, *Reading Capital*, p. 2. Also see, Robert Paul, 1992, *Althusser and the Renewal of Marxist Social Theory*, Oxford, pp. 61–4.
9. See details of 'Various Levels and Instances of Social Formation', see Althuser, 1969, *For Marx*, London, p. 101, 166. Also, Althusser and Balibar, *Reading Capital*, p. 58.
10. See, Althusser, *For Marx*, pp. 87–128. Also E. Terray, 1974, *Marxism and Primitive Society*, London, p. 79.
11. Nicos Poulantzas, 1973, *Political Power and Social Classes*. NLB, pp. 42–5. Also his, *State, Power, Socialism*, 1978, NLB, pp. 64–7; Pierre-Phillippe Rey, 1975, 'The Lineage Mode of Production', *Critique of Anthropology*, 3(1): 27–79. Also his, 1979, 'Class Contradiction in Lineage Societies', *Critique of Anthropology*, 4(13–14): 41–60. Emmanuel Terray, *Marxism and Primitive Society*, pp. 13–16; C. Meillassoux, 1978, 'Kinship Relation and Relations of Production', in David Seddon, (ed.), *Relations of Production*, London, pp. 231–5.
12. See Pierre-Philippe Rey, 'The lineage Mode of Production'. Also his, 'Class Contradiction in Lineage Societies'.
13. See Aidan Foster-Carter, 1978, 'The Modes of Production Controversy', *New Left Review*, London, no. 107, pp. 52–4. Also see, Ralph Miliband, 1977, *Marxism and Politics*, London, pp. 117–19.
14. See the idea highlighted in Louis Althusser, 1971, 'Ideology and Ideological State Aparatuses', in his *Lenin and Philosophy*, London, p. 17. Also, E.O. Wright, *et al.*, *Reconstructing Marxism*, p. 11.
15. For a brilliant analysis of 'the primacy thesis' see, G.A. Cohen, 1978, *Karl Marx's Theory of History: A Defence*, London, pp. 151–92. Also see the discussion in E.O. Wright *et al.*, *Reconstructing Marxism*, pp. 19–23.

16. For a fresh interpretation of the process and specific illustration see Cohen, *Karl Marx's Theory of History*, pp. 152, 158, 171, and 198. Also see the discussion in E.O. Wright *et al.*, *Restructuring Marxism*, pp. 19–46.
17. See the analysis and diagrammatic representation of Cohen's interpretation in E.O. Wright *et al.*, *Restructuring Marxism*, London, pp. 19–32.
18. D.D. Kosambi, 1976, *Culture and Civilisation of Ancient India in Historical Outline*, New Delhi, p. 14.
19. Perhaps the best theoretical rejection of AMP is in Hindess and Hirst, *Pre-capitalist Modes of Production*, London, pp. 178–200. Similarly the best rejection through historical empiricism is in Perry Anderson, 1974, *Lineages of the Absolutist State*, London. Several historians have dismissed the mode as inapplicable to Indian history. See, D.D. Kosambi, 'The Basis of Despotism', *Economic and Political Weekly* (*EPW*), vol. ix, pp. 1417–19; R.S. Sharma, 1975, 'The Socio-economic Base of Oriental Despotism in Early India', in *International Congress of Human Sciences in Asia and North Africa*, Mexico. Irfan Habib, 1977, 'An Examination of Wittfogel's Theory of Oriental Despotism', *Enquiry*: Old Series, no. 6, pp. 54–73. Romila Thapar, 1978, *Ancient Indian Social History*, New Delhi, pp. 1–23. However, there have been a couple of attempts at validating the AMP in the context of early South Indian history. See, Burton Stein, 1985, 'Politics, Peasants, and Deconstruction of Feudalism in Medieval India', in *Journal of Peasant Studies*, xii(2–3), New York; Also, Kathleen Gough, 1980, 'Modes of Production in Southern India', in *EPW*, 15(5–7), Mumbai. The notion of changelessness characteristic of AMP influences Sivathamby, 1974, 'Early South Indian Society and Economy', *Social Scientist*, vol. 29, New Delhi.
20. R.S. Sharma, 1968, *Indian Feudalism*, Calcutta.
21. D.D. Kosambi, 1975, *An Introduction to the Study of Indian History*, rpt, Bombay, pp. 24–43.
22. R.S. Sharma, *Indian Feudalism*.
23. Marc Bloch, 1975, *Feudal Society*, vol. I, London, p. 9.
24. Marx viewed it as the immediate pre-capitalist mode of production characterized by the power of the ruling class rested on the control of arable land, leading to a class society based on the exploitation of the peasants facilitated by the military elite. For fundamentals of Marx's interpretation, see, *Grundrisse*, pp. 451–500.
25. Joseph R. Strayer defined it as 'public power in private hands'. See his *Feudalism*, Princeton, 1956, p. 12; R. Colbourn, 1956, *Feudalism in History*, Princeton, p. 4.
26. See P. Anderson, 1974, *Passages from Antiquity to Feudalism*, London, pp. 69–74. Also his, 1974, *Lineages of the Absolutist State*, London, pp. 66–71.
27. Harbans Mukhia, 1979, 'Was there Feudalism in India?' first published in *Indian History Congress Proceedings*, Delhi and subsequently in *Journal of Peasant Studies*, 12(2–3), New York, 1981.

28. To Marx it was a hierarchical system of landownership with serf labour chained to it. See excerpts in Bottomore and Rubel (eds), 1979, *Karl Marx*, Penguin, rpt, pp. 120–30. The ruling class structure is taken as fundamental in R. Coulborn, 1956, *Feudalism in History*, Princeton, p. 4. It was a closed estate economy to Henry Pyrenne, 1958, *Economic and Social History of Medieval Europe*, London, pp. 7–12. *Seignorial* and serf elements are emphasized in certain studies. See P. Anderson, *Lineages of Absolutist State*, p. 408; Moris Dobb, 1970, *Capitalism, Development and Planning*, New York, rpt, pp. 2–3; R.H. Hiltion, 1976, *Peasants, Knights and Heretics*, Cambridge, p. 4. Spread of service tenements and the rise of a class of full-time warriors are considered central in Marc Bloch, *Feudal Society*, p. xiv; R.S. Sharma, 1984, 'How Feudal was Indian Feudalism?', *Social Scientist*, no. 129, pp. 16–28. Also reproduced in *Journal of Peasant Studies*, special issue of feudalism debates, edited by T.J. Byres and Harbans Mukhia, vol. 12 nos 2 and 3, 1985.
29. See, R.S. Sharma, 1978, 'The Kali Age: A Period of Social Crisis', *Indian History Congress Proceedings*, Delhi; B.N.S. Yadava, 1978–9, 'The Accounts of the Kali Age and the Social Transition from the Antiquity to the Middle Ages', *Indian Historical Review*, V(1 and 2). B.N.S. Yadava, 1980, 'The Problem of the Emergence of Feudal Relations in Early India', Presidential Address, *Indian History Congress Proceedings*, Delhi. Also see, R.S. Sharma 'How Feudal was Indian Feudalism?'
30. See, Kesavan Veluthat, 1976, *Brahman Settlements in Kerala*, Calicut. Also his, 'Royalty and Divinity: Legitimisation of Monarchical Power in South India', *Indian History Congress Proceedings*, Delhi, 1978. Also his, 'The Temple Base of the Bhakti Movement', *Indian History Congress Proceedings*, Delhi, 1979. The joint paper by M.G.S. Narayanan and Kesavan, V., 'Bhakti Movement in South India', S.C. Malik (ed.), *Indian Movements: Some Aspects of Dissent, Protest and Reform in Indian Tradition*, Shimla, 1989. Kesavan, V., 'The South Indian Temple', Seminar Paper, Indian History Congress, Bodh Gaya, 1981.
31. Aidan Southall, 1988, 'The Segmentary State in Africa and Asia', *Comparative Studies in Society and History*, 30(1): 52–82. For the application of the model in the context of medieval South India, see, Burton Stein, 1980, *Peasant State and Society in Medieval South India*, New Delhi.

Section I

Historiography and Method

1

Early Social Formations

A Historiographic Review*

This chapter attempts a historiographic analysis of the works on early south India, published during the last few decades. It begins with observations on how historians have been variously characterizing Iron Age society. The shift from the practice of identifying cultures and ethnic groups according to each major source category to that of the integrated utilization of varied source categories is a significant historiographic development. This leads to a closer look at the ancient Tamil anthologies, one of the major sources, to highlight the modern methods of textual analysis by historians. An interpretative aspect of the anthologies, the *tiṇai* concept (physiographic divisions), which has been evoking insightful responses from modern historians, is examined. Subsequently the question of kinship, its dissolution, emergence of the institution of caste, and the social division of labour is reviewed. The nature of contemporary exchange, both internal and external, and its impact on the society has also been analysed. This is followed by a discussion on the institutions of gift and redistribution in the context of collective appropriation of resources. The chapter then examines how in the light of the concept of redistribution, cattle raids and plunder are reinterpreted. The effects of plunder on agricultural production are discussed as the first step towards the characterization of contemporary social formation. The development of interest among historians in the characterization of social formation and political structure is examined, followed by observations on

* This chapter is a revised version of, 1995, 'The Beginnings of Early Historic Period: The Case of the Tamil South, Upto *c.* A.D. 500' in Romila Thapar (ed.), *Recent Perspectives of Early Indian History*, (Popular Prakashan: Mumbai), pp. 237–61.

the question of prime movers that brought about the dissolution of the social formation.

The dawn of history in the Tamil south as elsewhere in peninsular India, is marked by the diffusion of diverse strands of the Black and Red Ware (BRW), noted for the use of a variety of iron artefacts. Identified as megalithic culture, this has been treated as a specific single culture type in the past writings on early south Indian history. New excavations and case studies of the region over the last three decades have considerably widened our knowledge about the different strands of culture and their pattern of distribution.[1] Several questions transcending the usual typological, stratigraphical, and chronological issues have been raised and attempts made at identifying the forms of subsistence, material culture, and social organization.[2] Social organizations are assumed to have become widespread in the Tamil south by the middle of the first millennium BC, bringing about homogeneity and linguistic identity in the region.[3]

The recently excavated sites are mostly burials and very rarely, habitation centres. Apart from the usual pottery types, beads, bangles, terracotta items, and iron artefacts, copper and bronze objects have been recovered from the sites. Similarly, a few ploughshares are now added to the list of agricultural implements, which included only hoes, shovels, sickles, and spades. However, hunting tools generally dominate and agricultural implements are not only marginal but almost entirely primitive, except in the case of the few ploughshares of a relatively later period. This marginal status of agrarian tools tends to belie the earlier assumption that it represented the culture of sedentary agriculturists. The alternative argument now put forth is that it could have been the culture of pastoralists and subsistence farmers.[4] Some scholars still continue to associate the culture with irrigated agriculture,[5] which is not altogether unlikely at a slightly later phase of its development. There is no consensus on the principal form of subsistence adopted by the people behind the relics.

Evidence of craft production, structural activity in brick, and a kind of barter at certain sites has prompted some historians to associate them with the first phase of urban development in the south.[6] The manifold iron artefacts, pottery types, beads of gold, silver, copper, hornblendes, bone, glass, paste, terracotta, semi-precious stones, bangles of shell show a specialization in craft production and some kind of exchange. Excavations at Kanchipuram, Kunnattur, Kaveripattinam, Uraiyur, and Tirukkampuliyur attest to the beginning of brick constructions in the initial decades of the Christian era. All these sites seem to have grown from the BRW level and some of them have yielded material denoting Roman contacts. The terracotta spindle whorls and dye-vats recovered from certain sites indicate the manufacture of textiles and the level of textile technology. Excavations have exposed dye-vats and relics of glass which suggest that the place was a centre for the manufacture of textiles and glass objects, although this is a disputed point. Controversies as to whether or not it was a manufacturing centre revolves round the identification of dye-vats and the existence of a local glass industry. In the absence of a convincing alternative, the earlier identification still holds good. Similarly, excavations at Nattamedu prove it to be a centre of a glass industry. These were clearly Indo-Roman trading enclaves and appear to be more like stations of foreign merchants than urban centres with local bases.[7] Compared to the Deccan, the number of trade stations in the Tamil regions is marginal and there is a marked difference in the urban character of the centres in the two regions.[8] However, the nature of urban development and its link with the hinterland is not very clear.

The tendency in the past writings on the early historic period in south India was to identify cultures and ethnic groups in association with the major source categories. Hence the identification of the megalithic and Iron Age people and culture is based on archaeological sources, heterodox religious groups are associated with the early epigraphical sources, the discovery of a maritime civilization relies on the Graeco-Roman sources and numismatic evidence, and idea of the Sangam society and people is based on the ancient Tamil anthologies. The archaeological source comprising a variety of burial types and funerary deposits like BRW and iron artefacts signified a specific ethnic group and culture known after the megaliths in earlier writings. Similarly, the earliest post-Mauryan epigraphical material, that is, the Tamil brāhmi cave inscriptions signified the Jain and Buddhist people.[9] The Graeco-Roman accounts and Roman coins at once indicated a civilized people engaged in long-distance overseas trade.[10] Ancient Tamil heroic poems represented a people and culture known after the Sangam, which was an academy of scholars who collected and redacted the poems into anthologies.[11] Even while using evidence from various sources, the fact that all of them contain clues to the different phases of one and the same social formation, was not properly understood. The integrated utilization of the various categories of sources in broad anthropological perspectives, is now gaining currency.[12] This approach is made possible by the corroboration of data in the varied sources, such as archaeology and literature.[13]

A category among the sources that has received significant attention over the period under review is that of the ancient Tamil anthologies, popularly known as the Sangam literature, constituting a mine of information on the conditions of life around the beginning of the Christian era. *Eṭṭuttokai* (The Eight Anthologies) and *Pattupāṭṭu* (The Ten Idylls) are the two major groups of texts included in the corpus of Sangam literature. Some scholars have included *Tolkāppiyam*, the Tamil grammatical treatise, *Patinenkīḻkkaṇakku*, the eighteen didactical texts, and *Cilappatikāram* and *Maṇimēkalai*, the twin epics in the *Sangam* corpus[14] Though the precise chronology of the literature is still an unsettled problem, there is a greater clarity about the time of the different anthologies.[15] It has now become fairly well established that the poems are not contemporaneous with the Sangam Age and that there is a time lag of three or four centuries between the composition of the poems and their compilation into anthologies.[16] This has proved that expressions such as 'Sangam Age' and 'Sangam Culture', used for denoting the period and culture, respectively, of the poems are misnomers.

Some scholars, however, still use these terms, while a few have tried to substitute the expressions with the term 'classical' in their writings with little or no explanation.[17] Of the whole corpus of literature, the *Eṭṭuttokai* collection, excluding *Kalittokai* and *Paripāṭal*, is considered the most archaic, belonging as they do to around the third century BC to AD third century. (Some of the idylls of *Pattupāṭṭu* collection, particularly the *āṟṟuppaṭai* literature and the *tiṇaippāṭṭu*,[18] are also of closer antiquity.[19] As regards the contents, contexts, and historical veracity of the poems, modern researchers have also made a substantial contribution. The methods and concepts tested and found valid elsewhere for analysing the structure and composition of comparable literature, have revolutionized our understanding of the anthologies.[20] It has been recognized that the anthologies are heroic poems that are not free from the tradition of oral compositions characterized by formulaic diction, stock phrases, stylized expressions, and the use of symbols for unconscious meaning.[21] Modifying this view of treating the whole corpus of heroic poems as part of an oral tradition, it has been argued that the megalithic oral poetry preceded the ancient Tamil poems.[22]

Historians are now aware that they can hardly go by the apparent contents of the poems for writing history since the genuine meaning of the poems is shrouded in symbols and codes, which carry hidden meanings that are not apparent in a superficial reading. The hidden meanings relate not to the level of consciousness but to that of the unconscious and require the help of modern methods in folkloristics for decoding them. However, what the overall social context and the poetic contents signify is historical and, therefore, attempts are being made to identify signifiers in them. The most useful signifiers are those rendering clues to the subsistence pattern and social relations which are extremely important for the reconstruction of the historical process of early society.

A notable achievement in the attempts at identifying signifiers from anthologies is the insightful interpretation of the concept of *tiṇai*, according to which *Tamilakam* consisted of five tiṇais or physiographic divisions, namely, *kuṟiñji* (hilly backwoods), *pālai* (parched zone), *mullai* (pastoral tract), *marutam* (wet land), and *neital* (the littoral). It involves the description of inhabitants and their modes of adaptation in each tiṇai. This has been understood in the past as a mechanical compartmentalization of nature into five divisions, symbolically denoting the historical evolution from the primitive to the civilized in south India.[23] Following the commentators of the poems, historians had debated the actual sequential order of the five tiṇais and thought that the order denoted the human evolution in world history. Pioneering scholars like S.K. Aiyangar, P.T. Srinivasa Iyengar, and K.V. Subrahmania Aiyer are among such historians.[24] Modern studies do not follow the versions of the commentators far removed from the period of the anthologies, but view the concept in a realistic perspective and take it as a reflection of reality, drawing support from the *āṟṟuppaṭai* literature and the existing physiography of the Tamil region.[25] Commentators writing on the compositions after many centuries, certainly had serious lexical problems with a large number of terms and expressions, apart from their real context. They could view things only through a grammarian's eye, searching for the rules and principles of poetics. What are socially symbolic in the poetics were beyond their comprehension. Without caring for these limitations of the commentators, historians often followed the interpretations given by them and lost sight of historical reality. The fivefold physiographic division, which was a mere poetic concept to the commentators, therefore, hardly made any realistic sense to the historians even though they sought to make it historical. The division is now understood as part of the continuum in nature with the tiṇais that are interspersed and scattered in the region as overlapping segments with no point of beginning or end.

The realistic interpretation of the *tiṇai* concept and the poetic specifications about the nature, people, and products of each *tiṇai* has generated ideas regarding contemporary economic activities.[26] Taking *tiṇais* as micro-eco-zones of given modes of human adaptation, attempts have been made to ascertain the process of interaction and formation of macro-eco-zones.[27] With a view to characterizing contemporary social formation, efforts have been made to identify the forms and forces of production in the *tiṇai*s and to corroborate the inferences with clues in the other categories of sources.[28] From the poetic specifications such as hunting and gathering of the *kuṟiñji*, plundering and cattle lifting of the *pālai*, animal husbandry and shifting agriculture of the *mullai*, agriculture of the *marutam*, and fishing-cum-salt manufacturing of the *neital*, we can presume the forms of subsistence adopted by the peoples of the time. It has been understood that in the areas where *tiṇai*s merged, the social groups as well as the forms of subsistence made a mixed appearance. People in the areas of *mullai-marutam* are found to have adopted a variety of crafts as their means of subsistence. Leaving aside the primitive forms of subsistence such as fishing and plundering, it has become clear that there were four forms of material production, namely, animal husbandry, shifting cultivation, petty commodity production, and plough agriculture.[29] There are archaeological pointers to all these forms of production, albeit without any precise dating of each one's commencement. The antiquity of plough agriculture, in the absence of clear dating for the sites that have yielded ploughshares, is an elusive problem in the south. However, it has been argued that in the light of the *Koḻuvaāṇikan* of the Tamil *brāhmi* label-inscription at the Mankulam cave referring to a dealer in *koḻu* (ploughshares), we are able to push the antiquity of the plough, at least in the Vaigai valley, to the second century BC.[30] The use of the plough during the period of the poems is well attested to by the numerous references in them.

In addition to the concept of tinai, the broad physiographical division of the region into *vanpulam* (non-agrarian tracts) and *menpulam* (agrarian wetland) conceived by the poet and recognized by the people, is also well taken in recent writings on ancient Tamil society as a pointer to the nature and extent of contemporary agriculture.[31] It is now clear that the extent of wetland agriculture in the days of the poems was very limited and confined to small pockets of menpulam surrounded by large vanpulam tracts of inhospitable conditions.[32] There is a consensus that a large majority of contemporary people took to dryland agriculture and animal husbandry. It is presumed that craft production was by and large associated with pastoral agriculturists. However, centres of plough agriculture must have sustained their own artisans and craftsmen on the fringes of wetland.

Studies of kinship and its bearing on the relations of agricultural production have generated concepts providing insights into problems of social relations in the past.[33] This has stimulated attempts to explore the nature of kinship and its role as the basis of production relations in the society during the time of the poems.[34] Clues within the poems show that the basis of contemporary relations of production was kinship. Primitive agriculture and animal husbandry, which characterized society, resorted only to the cooperative labour of affinal or agnatic kins, presupposing no evolved social division of labour. Even in plough agriculture, the framework of kinship though the forces of production presuppose some kind of social division of labour. However, reference in the poems to potters performing ritual functions and bards following certain magico-religious rites, indicate that the division of labour was altogether different since *brāhmaṇa* households in the period of the poems represented a new production system involving relations transcending the network of kinship. The novelty of the production system was that it was based on the relations between a group of non-cultivating people and cultivating clansmen. Kinship ceased to exist as the organizing factor since *brāhmaṇas* who had their own *gōtras* and *pravaras* were obviously outside the kinship nexus of local clansmen. Their alien status is indicated in the poems, which address them as *vaṭamar*, literally, the people from the north.

The question of caste in early south Indian society has been looked at afresh against the background of findings on the nature of contemporary social division of labour. Historians have always been trying to associate the institution of caste with the society during the time of the poems, scarcely approving the *varṇa* system. The tendency has been to show that the caste systems of the early Tamil society were not based on the concept of the four *varṇas*, but on its own norms. It was argued that the four *kuṭis*: *pāṇan, paṛaiyan, tuṭiyan*, and *kaṭampan* mentioned in a poem, constituted the four castes of the region. However, in the poems the term kuti means a settlement. The poet is not referring to the general situation in the region, but only to that of the particular village where he was singing. *Pārppār* (seers), *aracar* (kings), *iṭaiyar* (cowherds), and *kuṛavar* (hunters) are the four castes according to a commentator of the anthologies. The reference in the *Tolkappiyam-porul* to the four castes as *antaṇar*, aracar, *vaṇikar*, and *vēḷāḷar* has been shown as not corresponding to the four divisions in the varṇa system in order to establish the distinctive features of the Tamil caste system. The confusion results from taking clan surnames for caste suffixes and juxtaposing them with the varṇa system. It has been clarified that the institution of caste was yet to characterize early Tamil society and what has been listed as castes by scholars in the past are clan names.[35] The poems show that *brāhmaṇas* were considered to be the high-born in contemporary society, but there is no evidence of their total distancing from others as the purest group in those days.[36] Paranar, a scholarly *brāhmaṇa* bard (*pulavar*) mentions that on his way to the court of Kantira-ko, a hill chief, he had his food with the people of the forest and their hunter chief. Like ordinary bards (*pāṇar*), *brāhmaṇas* also freely moved with the folk, participating in collective dining and drinking.

The nature of interaction among social segments and the process of subsequent integration of the largely self-sustaining eco-zones have received some serious attention.[37] There are numerous references in the poems to the interaction of the tinais against one another in terms of material goods. Poems show that there were certain fixed points of exchange known as *āvaṇam* or *ankāṭi* where people from far-off places came for exchange (*An.* 93: 10, *Prp.* 68: 10).[38] The exchange was based on a kind of barter system, referred to in the poems as *noṭuttal*, which involved only the use-value of goods. Paddy was the medium of barter in most cases and it was exchanged for salt. By and large, the circulation of goods was through hawkers and pedlars, besides the manufacturers themselves, who exchanged their products at the production centres. *Umaṇar*, the dealers in salt, had to cart the loads to distant places through difficult and inhospitable terrain and, therefore, moved in caravan troops mentioned in the poems as *cāttu* (*sārtha*) (*An.* 39:10; 167; 291:15). The Tamil region was part of the network of long-distance exchange as well. Many specialist merchants frequented the region to collect and exchange goods. At important markets like Madurai and Puhar, merchants from distant regions and different cultures gathered for exchanges as described in *Maduraikkāñci* and *Paṭṭiṇappālai*. The role of the local merchants in long-distance trade is not very clear since the evidence is quite scanty. A label inscription in the cave at Mankulam refers to *nikamattōr*, the members of *nikamam* at Vellarai (near Tiruchirappalli), probably a body of traders located there. But this is hardly enough evidence to speak about local merchants and the nature of trade carried out by them. With the evidence of the hoards of coins, references to the *kalinkam* variety of silk in the poems, mention of the *māturam* variety of textiles and the *pāṇḍyakavāṭakam* type of pearls in the *Arthaśāstra*, historians have been focusing too much on the inland trade of south India, without examining sufficiently the nature of contemporary exchanges. Modern writings referring to the question of exchanges during the period, cast serious doubts on the relevance of the term 'trade' in the context of exchange involving no notion of exchange-value and profit.[39]

This is particularly noticeable in the writings on the overseas exchange of the Tamils, often referred to as the extensive foreign trade of Tamilakam. Inspired by the notices of the Graeco-Roman coins, historians of south India imagined a civilization of the Tamils as old as 1,800 years. The archaeological data from excavations and the literary references to *yavanas* bringing gold supported modern imaginative reconstruction. The implicit presumption has been that the Tamils benefited the most in these relations since the drain of gold from Rome to India had been in proportions alarming to the Romans, as noted by Pliny. However, the absence of clear evidence of the Tamils organizing overseas trade and controlling the traffic of goods, has been a problem. The silence of archaeology about the huge urban complexes described in *Maduraikkāñci* and *Paṭṭiṇappālai* has been another vexing problem. This has led to the assumption that south India prior to the inception of Roman trade was not a seat of civilization. On the contrary, Roman trade acted as the catalyst for the genesis of its civilization).[40] The generally unimpressive layers of the pre- and post-Roman periods and the evidence for structural activity, petty commodity production, and foreign occupation in the evidence relating to the Roman period at excavation sites seem to support the assumption.

With the publication of a body of literature specializing in discussions of the organization, operation, and functions of trade, the perspectives on trade have undergone drastic modifications.[41] There is now considerable awareness of the overall context of trade in the historical process of social development. We are fairly sure of what necessitates and makes trade possible, as well as how and when. The major prerequisites for a society to forge ahead in organizing trade are defined through a variety of comparative studies.[42] These developments in the realm of knowledge about the mechanisms of early trade have necessitated a thorough re-examination of the whole question of the so-called foreign trade of south India. Attempts have been made to re-examine the sources for the extent of generalizations and assumptions around the nature of foreign trade by south India.

The focus of the re-examination is on questions such as: what were the goods shipped from the Tamil region? Were they mainly raw materials or manufactured goods? Who organized and controlled the traffic of goods? What was the role of the Tamil merchants? What was the exact nature of exchange? We know that aromatics, pepper, ginger, cardamoms, cloves, a variety of wild fauna, timber such as teak and sandal, certain cotton fabrics, precious stones, gems, and pearls were the items shipped from the Tamil region. Obviously, most of these goods were obtained from nature. The goods that reached the Tamil coast from the Mediterranean were: Roman coins, topaz, fine clothing, antimony, coral, crude glass, copper, tin, lead, and some quantity of wine and wheat, besides ceramics. Wine, wheat, and ceramics were brought for the traders who had to stay back for some time since the sailing of ships depended on the monsoon winds. Most of the trading centres had settlements of foreign merchants who stayed for longer durations. The Peutingarian Tables[43] mention a temple of Augustus situated on the west coast, but this has not been corroborated by archaeological evidence or any other source. Of the incoming goods, it is well known that Roman gold ranked foremost and no doubt, was a luxury object. Similarly, fine cloth, coral, and topaz suggest the existence of a wealthy section requiring goods that conferred prestige. Depending on literary references, the dates of which are uncertain, attempts have been made to identify *paratavar*, the fishing and salt manufacturing people, as a consumer class.[44] However, the families of the chiefs could certainly have afforded luxury goods. Crude glass, tin, copper, and lead were evidently raw materials for the local beads and bronze industries. But such items came in marginal quantities compared to the gold and silver coins.

The question of who organized and controlled the traffic of goods has been discussed in relation to the level of contemporary social development and the nature of political power.[45] It was a transitional society of diverse clans slowly dissolving into households, with a political organization not basically different from that of chiefdoms. Long-distance trade is not normally the affair of an economy of clans and households, but the activity of a society with surplus production, economic specialization, multiplicity of crafts, and a group of full-time traders. There is neither direct evidence nor indirect reason to believe that contemporary set-up satisfied any of these attributes. This would lead us to the presumption that local merchants had a very small role in the organization of foreign trade. Evidence supports the arrival of foreign merchants with their own domestic requirements and security arrangements for the collection and shipping of goods.

It has been argued that the Tamils in those days had a fairly developed technology of shipbuilding.[46] The early anthologies refer only to small boats like *pahri, ōṭam, timil, paṭagu*, and *ampi*, which were used for local transport and fishing. References to sea-going vessels called *marakkalam* are found only in later texts of about the AD sixth century onwards. The reference in the *Periplus* to large ships called *colandia*, which made voyages to '*Chryse*' and to the '*Ganges*' has often been cited as evidence for advanced shipbuilding in south India.[47] However, these are hardly sufficient indicators for assuming that local merchants had a significant role in the overseas trade of the time.

The question of the exact nature of overseas exchange has been examined in relation to the nature of inland exchanges in the region.[48] What has been fascinating to historians was the commendable quantity of the pre-Mauryan punch-marked and Roman coins discovered in hoards at different parts of the region. They have viewed the coins in terms of money and exchange in terms of profit. This accounts for the characterization of contemporary exchange as imbalanced trade with south India at an advantage. Pliny's reference to the anxiety of the Senate over the drain of gold owing to the demand for eastern goods emphasizes this. Pliny has made another reference[49] to goods from India being sold at a hundred times their original cost, which would mean that the quantum of gold that reached India was a hundred times less than what the traders got. It should be noted that the traders were mostly Egyptians, Greeks, Arabs, Abyssinians, and Persians. However, what is crucial is not the quantity of coins, but the value attributed to them. It is anachronistic to presume that the Tamils in those days attributed money value to the coins since the very nature of their modes of exchange precluded it. Being use-value-based exchanges of the barter type involving no notion of price and profit, they provided scope neither for the coins to function as a means of payment nor as a measure of value.[50]

Historians have assessed the impact of overseas exchange on the Tamil society in varying degrees. Some believe that the impact was substantial, leading to important changes in society, and others, just the contrary. With the presumption that overseas exchange could be a catalyst for major social developments, it has been surmised that in south India it triggered off the spark of civilization.[51] It has been assumed that along with certain other internal factors, the overseas exchange relations of the period also had a significant role in the stabilization of the urban process, class formation, and emergence of the state.[52] Arguments against this position reside on the character of exchange that precluded the circulation of labour and capital.[53] Such exchange relations would hardly lead to any significant socio-economic or political changes. There is no evidence to show that the overseas exchange stimulated the transformation of contemporary economy and social relations.

The inland merchants and manufacturers continued to be subsumed with the network of clan ties and kinship. They do not seem to have acted as middlemen between the foreign merchants and the chiefs in the transaction of goods. The foreign merchants freely made use of the Tamil ports for the traffic of goods from the south-east Asian world as well, with no involvement of native traders as middlemen.[54] Without clear indications for the development of a trading group on equal footing with contemporary foreign merchants or for the growth of at least a group of competent middlemen, how do we consider the overseas exchange as exerting a transforming impact on Tamil society? The overseas demand for south Indian muslin, beryl, and pearls must certainly have stimulated their production, but we do not know to what extent. We are in the dark about who organized the production and what relations emerged. Certain clues in the poems would have us believe that the overseas demand for goods was hardly enough for generating relations of non-kin labour in the manufacturing sector. This defies the assumption of any serious impact of overseas exchange on the society of the time.

Anthropological and historical studies on early forms of exchange have led to the increasing realization of the importance of certain institutions like gift giving, as a means of distribution.[55] The institution of gift giving (*koṭai*) which is celebrated in the anthologies has been examined in the context of the social distribution of resources. Since the resources were first pooled by the chiefs who subsequently reallocated them to their dependents, the concept of redistribution has been applied to explain the implications of the institution. The chiefs redistributed the resources among their kinsmen, bards, merchants, and dependents. It involved a determinate pattern of social relationships based on kinship and interpersonal relationships beyond kinship. Cattle and grain were the main resources that were redistributed, though bards claim to have received gifts of gold, elephants, chariots, gems, and muslin. These claims are poetic motifs for extolling the munificence of heroes.[56] But it is not unlikely that on rare occasions, the scholarly bards (*pulavar*) received such prestige goods as gifts. Lesser bards (*pāṇar*) normally received a meal, grain, or used clothes as a reward for their recitation.

Developing the concept of redistribution, the context and meaning of raids by the chieftains of the time are reinterpreted.[57] In past writings, *veṭci* has been taken for a pre-war routine of protecting the enemy's cattle by lifting them. This understanding, based on the description of *ātamtōmpal* in *Tolkāppiyam-poruḷ* has been rightly re-interpreted as cattle raids, pure and simple.[58] Veṭci signifies all plunder raids in a society that was predominantly pastoral in character and it makes much sense in the context of redistribution because plunder was the instituted means for the chiefs to pool resources. Plunder as an essential economic function in a redistributive society has been well recognized by historians and anthropologists.[59] The anthologies are full of evidence of plunder raids that the chiefs used to replenish their coffers, which were constantly drained due to the incessant demands of redistribution. It has been shown that plunder and raids were fundamental to the maintenance of contemporary redistributive economy.[60] Poetic concepts such as *veṭci* (cattle raid), *karantai* (cattle recovering), *vañji* (chieftains' attack), *kāñji* (defending), and *tumpai* (preparing for a raid) clearly illustrate the institutionalization of raids in contemporary society.

Some attempts have been made to assess the effects of plunder on agricultural production during this period. Destruction of settlements (*cēri*) and cultivated fields (*kaḻani*) was part of the scorched-earth policy in raids. The burning of agricultural settlements (*eriparanteṭuttal*) and crops was a routine act of the raiding chief. Plunder raids, destruction of agricultural settlements, dominance of the ideology of war, and booty redistribution were utterly uncongenial to the development of wetland agriculture. Naturally, this type of agriculture failed to expand beyond small pockets of river plains and remained confined to the large non-agrarian tracts. Despite the availability of iron and knowledge of its technology, advanced farming made no significant progress during the period. The need for frequent redistribution and the strain of raids should have acted as a compulsion on the chiefs to intensify production. But there is no evidence of any initiative taken by chiefs in the intensification of production, except the tradition of Karikala *Cōḻa* building an *anicut*.[61] Actually, the political organization of the time was rooted in the economy of primitive agriculture and animal husbandry, which hardly suited advanced farming. This would suggest that wetland agriculture was yet to develop and expand.

It is now being recognized through increasingly well-known studies in economic anthropology that social history has to be viewed in terms of social formation, which is a theoretical notion of development.[62] The concept of social formation presupposes conceiving historical societies in terms of their systems of production relations and structures of domination as discussed in the introduction. In short, it means social analysis in terms of the concept of modes of production. Though it accepts established modes of production as marked stages of reference for identifying the level of social development, there is no quest for discovering them in any pure form. The focus is on the forces and relations of production and the resulting structure of society. Any rigorous analysis of a past society has to focus on the material process of production and the social process of appropriation so as to know how the society is structured and dominated. Material process means the process of appropriation of nature and the social process of appropriation refers to the system of the distribution of produce. Tamil society of the early historic period has been viewed from the perspective of social formation and by way of examining its material and social processes of production and distribution, it has been discovered that there existed a combination of several forms of subsistence and a complex redistributive relationship of collective appropriation.[63]

Primitive agriculture, animal husbandry, petty commodity production, and plough agriculture have been identified as the principal forms of production, whose relations dominated and structured the social formation. Any social formation in the past may be viewed as a combination of different forms of production structured by the dominance of one over the rest. The relations of the dominant form of production characterize the social formation through the process of interaction. The situation of diverse economies coexisting and interacting has also been conceived and described without the framework of social formation, where the notion of uneven development based on the potential for ecological adaptations is the guideline.[64] Here, the concept of coexistence and interaction of several forms of production dominated and structured by the relations of one among them does not provide an explanation. The notion of ecological zones and their suitability to resource development is the alternative framework adopted here.

There is a developing interest in the characterization of the political level within the social formation of early south India, an interest that has been kindled by the revealing studies on the process of state formation in early societies.[65] Now the problem can be approached with a vast range of ideas about the preconditions, mechanisms, and processes of the formation of state power in a pre-state society. The earliest phase in the process of the state formation in the Tamil South has been identified in the proto-historic period, with the emergence of micro-eco-zones or primary habitats of communities depending on the subsistence forms possible there, where the existence of clan-based chieftains is envisaged.[66] The five varieties of terrains (*tiṇais*) mentioned in the ancient Tamil poems have been recognized as the basic eco-zones or macro-eco-zones. The formation of macro-eco-zones through the interaction of the micro-eco-zones is the next phase, characterized by the emergence of larger chiefdoms. The final stage has been associated with the gradual integration of several macro-eco-zones into a larger primary region (*nādu*) in the early historic period, witnessing the formation of the pristine state.[67] The forces at work in the process of the formation of macro-regions and their integration have been identified as both internal and external, the former being economic and cultural factors and the latter, the influence of the Mauryan State and the northern socio-religious ideas and institutions. The influence of the Mauryan State on Tamil society has been established in the light of literary evidence, particularly from the anthologies,[68] but it is striking that there is virtually no Mauryan presence in the archaeology of the region.[69] The intrusion of northern social ideas and institutions is well attested to again by the literary evidence. However, the role of such external factors in the process of state formation can hardly be significant when compared to the role of internal factors since the state is primarily the result of the internal dynamic.[70]

It remains uncertain whether the period really witnessed the whole process of transformation from pre-state to state society. Clues in the anthologies point more or less to a chiefdom-level society with three categories of political powers; *Kiḷār* (village headman), *Vēḷir* (hill chiefs), and *vēntar* (low-land chiefs). An *ūr-kiḻān* of the pristine type was a clan-based headman who had kinship ties with his people. Velir were the hill chiefs who sometimes subjugated the neighbouring *ūr-kiḻār* for predatory exaction, but confined their domain to the respective hills and peoples with whom they had clan ties. The *vēntar* were the biggest chiefs and held control over larger areas through the subordination of the Kilār who fought for and shared the booty with them. They were the three lineages: Cēra, Cōḻa, and Pāṇḍya with their domains in the *kuṛiñji*-dominated zones from the Western Ghats to the Arabian Sea, the Kaveri basin, and *mullai-pālai*-dominated south-central zones, including the sea coast. But there was no notion of the precise boundary of each one's domain or the practice of periodic exaction in fixed tithes or rent. Similarly, there is no evidence to show that the allegiance of lesser chiefs in the border zone was perpetual in the case of any of the *vēntar*. Absence of territoriality is implicit here and it makes one suspicious of the assumption about the existence of a state during the early historic period.[71] The nature of political power as reflected in the anthologies has been characterized in an entirely different manner, which is not very different from the conventional one, equating the chieftain to a king and emperor.[72]

Some efforts have been made to identify the prime movers of the social formation, which subsequently brought about structural transformation.[73] Though not in terms of prime movers, all major developments in the early historic Tamil society have been viewed as consequences of the dialectics of socio-economic change.[74] This dialectics refer to the totality of the dynamics of interaction among peoples. The formation of macro-eco-zones and the development of chiefdoms in such zones can be attributed to the economic interaction among the social groups of different micro-eco-zones. It has been argued that the process of socio-economic interaction between the relatively backward hill tracts and the developed alluvial plains generated enormous forces of change that had far-reaching consequences.[75] The argument is that the backward zones remained as they were owing to the contradictions immanent in their economic infrastructure, but interactions with developed zones generated the forces of their transformation. It is this process of interaction which has been characterized as dialectical. The mode of human adaptation in each micro-eco-zone had its own limitations in terms of technology and productivity. There were environmental as well as social contradictions, in the sense that certain terrains were uncongenial and the means of livelihood inadequate. Sometimes the mode of human adaptation itself was contradictory. The variety of forms of subsistence and the modes of social appropriation proved contradictory within themselves as well as against one another. Certain zones had more of these contradictions and remained relatively more backward. It has been suggested that the forces of their development were generated through their interaction with developed zones. In addition, there were forces released by the external dynamic, particularly long-distance trade. All such factors would only account for the formation of what we identify as the early historic Tamil society and the implicit premise, therefore, is a view of gradual development without any breakthrough.

The alternative argument is based on the characterization of diverse forms of production and the complex redistributive system.[76] Of the different forms of production, plough agriculture was the superior one in terms of technology and productivity, but it was yet to secure its conditions of domination. The superior forms of production need not always be dominant and require certain conditions to exert an overriding influence on the co-existing forms of production and ensure their expansion and development. Here, plough agriculture was still in the process of securing domination over animal husbandry and primitive farming. This was the basic contradiction within the social formation. Moreover, the complex redistributive system was incapable of improving its low labour productivity and facilitating economic reproduction. The limitations of kinship-based production in terms of surplus, the low level of economy, and the destructive effects of predatory exaction were other handicaps of the system. A quest for the identification of prime movers had to centre itself on these contradictions and the alternative evolving out of them. The *brāhmaṇa* households using non-kin labour have been viewed as the nuclei of the evolving alternative.[77]

The *brāhmaṇa* households with their dependence on non-kin labour represented a new system of relations in production as distinct from the prevailing one based on kinship. The novelty of the system was that it involved the relationship between two different classes: the *brāhmaṇa* landholders and the non-*brāhmaṇa* labourers. However, it was established as a simple hierarchy with no intermediaries on land, a class totally unknown to the anthologies. There is no direct evidence for a precise assessment of the strength of the *brāhmaṇa* households during the period, which was obviously not great enough to characterize the society, as implied by the main features of the economy. But the influence of brahmanical culture on the anthologies is remarkably strong,[78] although the reverse has also been argued,[79] maintaining that the influence of Sanskrit on ancient Tamil was quite marginal and the archaic stratum of the anthologies represents an essentially non-Sanskritic culture.

Disintegration of kinship as the basis of production has been viewed as a perceptible manifestation of change in the prevailing system.[80] Apart from what is explicit in the case of developing *brāhmaṇa* households where formation of relations transcending kinship is inevitable, there could be certain other contexts that also facilitated the disintegration process. Predatory marches and migrations could have caused it to an extent, though we do not get information about it straight from the sources. The anthologies do refer to the context of warrior leaders getting *ūr* (primary settlement) as reward for helping the bigger chiefs in their plunder campaigns. Developing on such references, it has been argued that several warrior settlements were coming up through the process during the period.[81] The warrior settlements have been visualized as proto-feudal villages with localized services and obligations presupposing organization of local clansmen for production. It is important that the warrior leaders receiving ūr in lieu of their obligatory services (viṭutolil) to ruling chiefs, were often alien to the people of such *ūr*. The founding of settlements by warrior leaders in areas often beyond their original *ūr* would mean formation of relations transcending kinship. But it is unlikely that the warrior leaders were given the right over the land of the *ūr*.

Instead, what had been granted to them could be the right to some kind of exaction from the concerned ūr.

We do not have any direct evidence for a total crisis, but there are indications of a major change during the closing decades of the AD third century, marked by the disappearance of certain institutions and economic activities. The eclipse of the *vēntar* and Vēlir categories of chiefs, their bards and their plunder-based redistribution is a very conspicuous change. A decline in the post-Roman layer of the archaeological sites corresponds to this period.[82] The well-known Indo-Roman trading centres such as Arikamedu, Nattamedu, Karaikkadu, and Vāsavasamudram seem to have been deserted at the close of the AD second century. However, the sites with Buddhist associations show signs of continued occupation until the fifth century. The relics of a Buddhist shrine and a few *stūpas* at Kanchipuram and the Buddhist monastery at Kaveripattinam, belonging to the AD fourth–fifth centuries are some examples. Certain sites such as Uraiyur, Tirukkampuliyur, and Atiyamankottai have also yielded evidence of structures in brick in the AD third–fourth centuries, while Tirukkampuliyur and Atiyamankottai indicate signs of continued occupation and development without the usual break at the immediate post-Roman levels. But the archaeological excavations are too limited and incomplete to draw any reasonable inference. Moreover, since the link between the sites and the hinterlands are elusive, there is little chance for direct archaeological indications for or against a social crisis.

The tradition about the evils of the *Kaḷabhra* inroads has been interpreted as a social crisis, which led to the disappearance of the characteristic institutions of the time. The *Kaḷabhras* were a predatory people belonging to the uplands of Karnataka, and were believed to have entered the Tamil region and caused the eclipse of the Cēra, Cōḻa, and Pāṇḍya chiefs. *Vinayavinicchaya*, a Buddhist work in Pali, probably composed at the monastery of Kaveripattinam, mentions a certain Achuta Vikanta of the *Kalabhra-kula* as the patron ruler of the period. It appears that the predatory marches continuing from earlier times culminated in the *Kaḷabhra* inroads and brought about a total crisis, the memory of which survived to later times, as evidenced by references in a few copper plates of the Pallava and Pāṇḍya kings. The *brāhmaṇas* who seem to have been the worst affected, remembered the crisis of the days as the evils of the Kali age. This has encouraged thoughts about the relevance of the interpretation of Kaliyuga in the context of a social crisis[83] to the situation in Tamil society. However, the *Kaḷabhra* episode can hardly be so fundamental as to provide an explanation for changes of a substantial nature. The prime movers of social change were the contradictions within the system, which were possibly accentuated by the inroads of the *Kaḷabhras*.

A class of literature called the *Kīḻkkaṇakku* belonging to the AD fourth–fifth centuries emphasizes the significance of peace, obedience, loyalty, and morality in the society. This presupposes the existence of a situation which called for such aspects of social morality or conduct. These didactic texts have been associated with the period of the *Kaḷabhra* invasion and the aftermath.[84]

Whatever the nature of the crisis that followed the *Kaḷabhra* inroads was, the end of the period of chaos was marked by the steady growth of wetland agriculture, which meant the growth of a new system of social relations. The process was characterized by the proliferation of *brahmadēya* villages. It has been argued that the new system evolved out of its microcosm present in the *brāhmaṇa* households of the time of the heroic poems. A *brahmadēya* is never referred to in the actual text of the poems, but their colophons which date to a later period, do refer to it. The recent discovery of a rock inscription at Pulankurichchi near Ponnamaravati (Manamadurai), probably of late fourth century or early fifth century AD has confirmed the existence of *brahmadēya* villages during the period.[85] Like the colophons, the inscription also uses the term *pirammatāya*, perhaps suggesting the chronological proximity of the two. The *brahmadēya* village, represented by the Pulankurichchi inscription, is a fully evolved agrarian unit with structured land relations and service-bound settlers. Obviously, it presupposes a long development from the days of the heroic poems, the process of which is virtually unknown to us. Some of the early copper plates, while referring to the previous history of the villages donated, mention that they were originally *ēkabhōga brahmadēyas* and lost in the wake of the *Kaḷabhra* raids. Subsequently, when the lost villages were restored to the heir of the original donee, they were converted into corporate *brahmadēyas*. This would suggest that a crucial phase in the developmental process was that of the transformation of individual *brāhmaṇa* households into corporate settlements. The Pallava and Pāṇḍya kings had a leading role in the creation of such corporate *brahmadēyas* whose proliferation in their turn, led to the establishment of a new kingship of *cakravartin* status.

The formation of corporate agrarian settlements has been understood as a process of the development of close cooperation between the peasant cultivators and *brāhmaṇas*, virtually amounting to that of an alliance.[86] This view has been challenged, emphasizing the actual processes of the formation of institutions, groups, and relations in the field of production.[87] The institutional, organizational, and ideational means required for mobilizing people so as to satisfy the needs of the labour process in wetland agriculture were already with the *brāhmaṇa* landholders. What has been pointed out as crucial in the process of the formation of the new agrarian society was, therefore, the deployment of the institutional organizational apparatuses by the *brāhmaṇas* for managing agricultural people by means of a variety of social instruments rather than the result of a formal alliance. The corporate body, caste, and *bhakti* were the major means that the *brāhmaṇas* devised for the integration of the agrarian society. It appears that such a society of systematized relations and functions, reinforced by the institution of caste and the cult of bhakti, began to take shape with the close of the AD fifth century. *Tolkāppiyam-porul*, the well-known grammatical treatise, probably of the early sixth century, represents the efflorescence of a society with these features. Here, the genesis of a new social formation, structured by the dominance of relations peculiar to wetland agriculture becomes complete, anticipating further institutional manifestations during the ensuing period.

By and large, historians who were engaged in the study of south India had evinced little interest in the socio-economic life of the past. A few historians did focus on economic aspects. K.M. Gupta, who took up the study of the land-system of south India, was one of them. It was indeed a potential departure from the hackneyed historiography of dynasties though the output remained largely a compilation of literary and epigraphical data, precluding the possibility of attempting an historical explanation of contemporary land relations and tenurial structure. A. Appadurai, another historian of deviation who dealt with the economic conditions of the Cōḻa period, produced a compilation of data relating to trade and agriculture. T.M. Sreenivasan who studied the irrigation and water supply of the Pāṇḍya country also deviated from the norm. His work covers a long span of time that is too vast and unmanageable for a deeper analysis of the systems, practices, relations, and the socio-economic context.

From the mid-1960s, the historiography of south India began to face attacks at its basic methodological concepts and design, with the writings of Burton Stein and his fellow researchers, whose historiographic perspectives were distinct with the striking feature of conceptual presupposition drawn from cognate disciplines like sociology and anthropology. The conceptual ground of their historical explanations was set by a group of sociologists and anthropologists such as C.G. Diehl, Louis Dumont, E.R. Leach, and others who had analysed various aspects of the socio-cultural milieu of south India. McKing Marriott, B.S. Cohn, J. Middleton, R. Cohen, and others had further enriched the field through their conceptual models applicable in the historical context of South Asia in general and south India in particular. Burton Stein and his associates found the research works on south India stunted because they were narrative compilations bereft of conceptualization and ideological presupposition. Of these historians of the new school of thought, the most significant was Burton Stein himself. Clarence Maloney, George L. Hart, George W. Spencer, Kenneth R. Hall, F.W. Clothey, K. Zvelebil, Arjun Appadorai, C.A. Breckenridge, Brenda Beck, S.A. Barnet, Nicholas Dirks, David Ludden, Dennis Hudson, Friedhem Hardy, James Heitzman, and David Schulman are some of the notable names in the new historiography of south India opened up by Stein. Several edited volumes appeared, comprising the results of their investigations into the manifold aspects of south Indian history, under the initiative of scholars such as Frykenberg, R.G. Fox, J.F. Richards, John Parker, A. Sjoberg, M. Schneider, Kathleen Gough, Burton Stein, and others. The notable contributions by these scholars to the historiography of south India are: application of anthropological and sociological models for historical explanation; demonstration of the importance of studying systems, structures, ideas, and institutions of the past societies; presentation of an interdisciplinary approach; and introduction of scientific and sophisticated methods of analysis of the source material as computerization of inscriptional terms and the statistical analysis of their contexts and occurrences would exemplify.

Except for a few like Reverend Houtat and Lemercinier, who combine the concept of mode of production with structural anthropology, and Kathleen Gough, who reviews the relevance of the concept of 'mode of production' itself to the history of south India and seeks to discover the paradigm in an idealistic perspective, all the above writers use their models as substitutes for historical materialism. She identifies the early medieval social formation of the Tamil south as based on the Asiatic mode of production. However, some of the anthropological and sociological models introduced by these scholars in the field of historical studies are really useful in understanding the nature of certain ideas, institutions, structures, relations, and processes of the past societies. The 'centre and net-works' model of B.S. Cohn and McKing Marriot, the 'reciprocity—redistribution' model of Karl Polanyi, and the 'segmentary state' model of Southall are examples, to mention only a few. But none of these models helps us understand a social formation in its entirety. The models describe the structures but do not explain the mechanisms of their formation–transformation continuum, which is the fundamental part of any historical enquiry, particularly to those insisting upon materialistic prime movers. Raising such questions of historical changes is beyond their problematique.

Noburu Karashima's contribution, in association with Y. Subbarayalu, B. Sitaraman, and P. Shanmugham, to the field of scientific analysis of the epigraphs, classification of their contents, and quantification of the variables, is of great help for the students of south Indian history. His distribution chart and notes on the revenue terms occurring in the Tiruchchirappalli district and the former Pudukkottai state, though of a later period, are of some help in understanding the socio-economic history. David Ludden's thesis on the Tirunelvely district, though covering a wider span of time, contains certain aspects of the economy and culture of the early medieval period.

Among the modern scholars, the able research of Y. Subbarayalu on the political geography and the nature of state power in general, and on the territorial units of Pandi-Mandalam in particular, are directly related to the politico-economic aspects of the problem under study, both factually and conceptually. The research of R. Champakalakshmi on the Iron Age habitats, processes of early trade, urbanization, ideology, political structure, Jainism, and the bhakti movement in south India tremendously help the present study. M.G.S. Narayanan's reinterpretations of the institutional and organizational aspects of the early medieval south Indian society, the temple-centred agrarian economy, and the bhakti ideology provide very valuable insights. I. Mahadevan's contributions to the study of the *brāhmi* inscriptions deserve special mention here. So also do M.R. Raghava Varier's articles on the early historic socio-economic history of Tamilakam. Among the relatively young generation of researchers in the socio-economic history of early medieval south India, Veluthat Kesavan ranks foremost. His studies on the ideas, organizations, and institutions of the *brāhmaṇa* settlements, the temple base of the bhakti movement, and the political structure of monarchy enable a better understanding of the socio-political aspects of the period under study.

There were several critical, corrective, and dismissive responses to the American modes of perception by Indian historians such as Y. Subbarayalu, Champakalakshmi, M.G.S. Narayanan, D.N. Jha, Vijaya Ramaswamy, and Kesavan Veluthat, to mention those in the forefront.[88] A major contribution by way of mustering the epigraphical data base for the socio-economic studies of early south India was made by Noburu Karashima of Japan. His publications mainly pertain to the post-Cōḷa period, but do take issues with the conclusions by Burton Stein and other on the Cōḷa period as well.[89] All of them, albeit in differing degrees of vehemence, attacked Stein's rejection of the Indian feudalism thesis, imposed several factual corrections on his text, and dismissed his alternative model of the segmentary state. The entire details of these works do not matter here since we are primarily concerned about what a review of recent historiographic dimensions would require us to recapitulate. The two most pertinent questions in the context are: the beginning of the early medieval socio-economic system; and its conceptual categorization.

There are two categories of propositions about the beginnings of the early medieval socio-economic system that manifested itself by eighth and ninth centuries; one 'the Brahman peasant alliance' presented by Burton Stein and the other that of alternatives presented by his critics. The concept of the *brāhmaṇa*-peasant alliance postulates the early medieval agrarian system as an outcome of a voluntary alliance between *brāhmaṇas* and dominant peasants for mutual benefits.[90] It maintains that the dispersed peasant societies and *brāhmaṇas* closely cooperated each other in the historical process of manifestation of the socio-economic system in which an asymmetrical relationship was fundamental. But social asymmetry was not powerful enough for the kings to appropriate the agrarian surplus, unlike their counterpart in northern India. Burton Stein argues that the close co-operation between the peasant cultivators of south India and the *brāhmaṇas* who coexisted with them as spiritual preceptors can best be understood as an alliance. The criticisms against the concept are varied and relative to different issues ranging from empirical facts to conceptual generalizations.

D.N. Jha, one of the critics of the 'alliance thesis' has ably demonstrated its invalidity in the light of the extant historiographic research on south India and conceptual researches on the world peasant societies.[91] But there is no alternative proposition in the critique which mainly yearns to show the unfounded nature of Stein's assumptions such as the predominance of peasant economy, relative social symmetry, the *brāhmaṇa* patronage of the dominant peasantry. His focus is primarily on the inapplicability of the concepts of 'peasant economy' and 'segmentary state' rather than on the origins of the agrarian system differently. Similarly, M.G.S. Narayanan, another critic, is also primarily concerned about the historically unfounded state of Stein's 'peasant society' and 'segmentary state' categorization.

M.G.S. Narayanan visualizes the origins of what he calls feudal society through an alternative concept of 'the Brahman ruler alliance'.[92] According to him, the process was that of a close co-operation between the chieftains and *brāhmaṇas*, meaning that the alliance was not with the peasants but with the rulers. He maintains that the alliance and close co-operation between the *brāhmaṇas* on the one side and the chieftains of the Pāṇḍya, Cēra, and Cōḻa lineages on the other were based on mutual benefits. As protectors of the *brāhmaṇas* and the Vedic rituals, the chiefs or ruling lineages acquired the *kshatriya* status through their ancestry being linked up with the Purāṇic genealogy. In short, the *brāhmaṇas* secured royal patronage and the rulers, better status and ranking of *varṇa* legitimacy. This alliance in M.G.S. Narayanan's view, drove a wedge between the local bards, namely the panas and the patron chieftains eulogized by them in heroic compositions. According to him, the *brāhmaṇas*, cleverly assuming the role of the bards and composing the bardic eulogies that constituted the principal means to the chieftans' legitimacy, succeeded in replacing the *pāṇas*. This led to the elevation of the *brāhmaṇa* priest to the position of a royal preceptor and the eventual growth of *brāhmaṇa* settlements. Simultaneously, various factors like the decline of Roman trade, distribution of *brāhmaṇa* settlements, and the impact of brahmanical culture, according to him conspired to promote the feudal social order and new form of state. He argues that already, in, the Tamil heroic society of cattle raids and politics of plunder, several proto-feudal settlements had emerged as a result of land gifts to warriors.[93] So the growth of those settlements and the subsequent proliferation of *brāhmaṇa* settlements through extensive royal land grants gradually led to the establishment of what is called the south Indian feudal system.

Basically, both the above propositions are gradualist in approach, according to which change is slow. The gradualist viewpoint is tantamount to recourse to natural laws and precludes theory. It needs no causation since change is viewed as a natural evolutionary process postulating no disjunction between the pre-existing system and the changed reality which would mean continuity. Systemic differentiation and continuity represent contradictory positions difficult to maintain simultaneously. Burton Stein clearly makes systemic differentiation and calls the new system the 'peasant society' 'segmentary state'. The '*brāhmaṇa*-peasant alliance' in his view, is the causation of the genesis of the system. M.G.S. Narayanan, on the contrary, does not make a similar differentiation since according to his proposition, it is a gradual process of the proto-feudal evolving as feudal.

He criticizes Stein primarily not for his characterization of the genesis, but for the categorization of the socio-economic system as 'peasant society' under 'segmentary state', though he seeks to replace '*brāhmaṇa*-peasant alliance' with the '*brāhmaṇa*-ruler alliance'. D.N. Jha criticizes Stein for both. He rejects the '*brāhmaṇa*-peasant alliance' thesis as well as the 'peasant society' 'segmentary state' models to defend the feudal model albeit without a theoretically apposite alternative to explain its origins.

Subbarayalu, Champakalakshmi, and Vijaya Ramaswamy criticize Stein for his factual errors so the charges are empirical rather that theoretical. Kesavan's criticism of Stein pertains to the 'peasant society' 'segmentary state' model and overtly seeks to vindicate the feudal model.[94] As regards the conceptual categorization of the early medieval socio-economic system as feudal, there is a relatively better exponential development in south Indian historiography. Subbarayalu, Champakalakshmi, and Vijaya Ramaswamy, with a strong anchor in empiricism, tended to be neutral without any overt commitment in defence of the feudal model. Karashima pushes the period to the thirteenth century and strongly defends the case of feudal categorization.[95] D.N. Jha, M.G.S. Narayanan, and Kesavan Veluthat unremittingly argue for the validity of the feudal model through theoretical empiricism. They have successfully contested the 'peasant society' 'segmentary state' model which is based on a weak anthropological framework. The invalidity of the model is explicit in its explanatory impotency and anachronistic applicability. An anthropological model drawn out in the context of tribal society and adapted to be applicable in the context of peasant societies is static and hence ahistorical. In the social scientific perspective, the model is useless since it cannot explain change nor accommodate it.

Generally speaking, the critics have by and large abstained from putting up a theoretical rebuttal of Stein's characterization of the beginning of the 'peasant society'. Consequently, all of them happened to accept either consciously or inadvertently the gradualist/evolutionist view of the origins of what they categorized as feudal society. Having rejected the 'peasant society' 'segmentary state' model for affirming the feudal model without a concomitant framework characterizing the genesis of feudalism, the critics of Stein are in a situation of theoretical self-contradiction. That the critics rejected the '*brāhmaṇa*-peasant alliance' with or without alternatives hardly helps them escape the trap of theoretical self-contradiction implicit in the acceptance of the gradualist perception. They virtually united an ideographic account with a theoretical category notwithstanding the inconsistency of harnessing a phenomenological description to a materialistic interpretation and divested themselves of the primary task of theoretical encounter. It is significant too that the rejection of the 'segmentary state' model depended mainly on Stein's factual errors rather than on a sustained theoretical engagement. That the task of a total theoretical rebuttal received no primacy, even though any critique in defence of a theoretical model like feudalism has to be inevitably theoretical, is a serious lack.

Categorization of a socio-economic system as feudal presupposes the historical materialist approach, which is a schematic use of the theory of mode of production to explain the structure and direction of epochal changes in history. It is a totalizing project. Though there is no rule that the use of mode of production theory has to follow the epochal schema, its use has to be theoretical. The categorization exercise of historians is not always theoretical, but comparative in terms of a general taxonomy of socio-economic systems distinguished on the basis of the characteristic features rather than according to the mode of production paradigm. The critics of Stein have looked for what D.D. Kosambi and R.S. Sharma have identified as the characteristic feature of Indian feudalism, a model that has been debated by the historians over some time.[96] The debate was primarily of the empiricist kind and was seldom theoretical. Harban Mukhia's criticism of R.S. Sharma's Indian feudalism thesis did not transcend the premises of checking the empirical ground of categorization. The debate led to discovering historiographic ways more successfully by approximating the Indian situation to European feudalism. The most vital discovery was of the possibility of unravelling the presages of Indian feudalism through the interpretation of the Kali Age.[97] It did strengthen the categorization with some scope of ascribing historical materialist origins to Indian feudalism.

A similar advance has not taken place in south Indian historiography. This curious historiography situation precluded thoughts about systems, structures, and processes *sui-generis* to south India. How north Indian forms evolved here and with what modifications was the central historiographic concern. The diffusionist preoccupation of historians constrained them always to look for an external dynamic in order to explain socio-economic changes in south India.[98] The gradualist view did not necessitate any attempt at exploring the deeper leaves of socio-economic processes. Diffusion of ideas and transplanting of institutions alone would not do for effecting radical socio-economic changes. Fundamental structure changes as a result of internal dynamics and to socio-cultural transplant works only if internal materiality registers corresponding growth. In the case of feudal categorization, the gradualist view goes well with the diffusionist assumptions. Neither the socio-economic unevenness nor the time lag seems to have bothered the historians of south India in pushing a north-south homology for feudalism. Views about Aryanization, the Mauryan effect, the impact of long-distance trade, and the Jain Buddhist expansion served only to represent south India as the north's socio-cultural transplant. It is true that historical evidences of contacts between the two are substantial. But it is equally true that the socio-economic development was never homologous in the two zones. The question of a region's built-in potential for structural transformation, therefore, did not arise, closing the door of the historiography to the exponential wealth of its counterpart in the north. This is not to underscore the serious socio-economic writings that enrich the historiography of early medieval south India. The purport is only to try and understand how the historiographic dimension happened to exclude certain questions that are fundamental to a conceptualization of the categorization of socio-economic structures. The most fundamental question in this context pertains to the material processes of the birth of south Indian feudalism.

However, marginal it is, there has been an earnest effort to problematize the material processes of the birth of what is called the early medieval socio-economic system of south India.[99] It proceeds on the basic assumptions of the theory of the mode of production, but not by swearing to vouch for the schematic sequential stages imposed on history. The concept of social formations and insight of critical theory that jointly render the mode of production theory plausible, constitute the basis of the effort. Accordingly, the Tamil society of the early historic period has been viewed as a social formation resulting from a combination of several unevenly evolved forms of subsistence and a complex redistributive relationship of collective appropriation.[100] Of the different forms of production, plough agriculture was the superior one in terms of technology and productivity, but it was yet to secure compatible social relations ensuring conditions of development and domination. This was the basic contradiction within the social formation. Moreover, the complex redistributive system was incapable of improving its low labour productivity and facilitating economic reproduction. The reciprocally limiting slash-and-burn technology and kin-based productive relations, the low level of productivity besides the destructive effects of predatory exaction were the major handicaps of the system.[101] Theoretically, it was the problem of incompatibility between the system of kin-based relations of production with little scope for expansion on the one side and plough technology with enormous potential of development on the other, causing the latter to fret.[102]

The quest for the material processes of the birth of a new socio-economic order centres itself around these contradictions and the evolving alternative system of productive relations compatible to plough technology. The *brāhmaṇa* households as units of production based on non-kin labour represented the beginning of a compatible system of productive relations. Theoretically, the shift from kin labour to non-kin labour would destabilize the pre-existing social order and head for an inevitable crisis. Disintegration of kinship in the wake of the horizontal expansion of *brāhmaṇa* households, incessant predatory marches, and the migrations and emergence of new settlements indicated the dissolution of the dominant social order.[103] Though there is no direct evidence for a total crisis which the material conditions anticipated, we have indications of a major change during the closing decades of the third century.

A disjunction is explicit in the sources, both archaeological as well as literary which in their spatio-temporal contexts would have us believe that by the close of the AD third century many of the characteristic features of the social formations had phased out. There is a marked decline in the post-third-century layers of the major archaeological sites with the exception of a couple of Buddhist centres that continued to flourish.[104] The three ruling lineages of the Cēras, Cōḻas, and Pāṇḍyas went into oblivion together with their politics of plunder, redistributive economy, and the heroic compositions of typical bardic diction. Historians have been associating this phenomenon with the inroads of the *Kaḷabhras* from the uplands of Karnataka, who are said to have swept through the domains of the Tamil chieftains and caused their eclipse.

The *Kaḷabhra* episode does not really provide any intelligible causation for a fundamental change which requires a better explanation. What is to be emphasized as a social scientific explanation is the role of the contradictory dynamic of the social formation that was maturing over the years. It is not unlikely that the predatory marches of the *Kaḷabhras* accentuated the culmination process, which seemingly had evil effects on the *brāhmaṇa*, households. The hardships of the days, transmitted as dreadful memories across generations of people, find allusions equating the sufferings to those of the Kali Age, in a few copper plates of the eighth to ninth centuries.[105]

NOTES AND REFERENCES

1. See also F.R. Allchin, 1963, *Neolithic Cattle Keepers of South India*, Eiden; S.B. Deo, 1973, *Problem of South Indian Megaliths*, Dharwar; L.S. Leshnik, 1974, *South Indian Megalithic Burials: The Pandukal Complex*, Wiesbaden; A. Sundara, 1975, *Early Chamber Tombs of South India*, Delhi; B. Narasimahaiah, 1980, *Neolithic and Megalithic Cultures in Tamilnadu*, Delhi. The literature on the Iron Age/megaliths produced by a number of eminent archaeologists till late 1970 constitutes an impressive body of reference. See K.S. Ramachandran, 1971, *A Bibliography on Indian Megaliths*, Madras. Several new studies, both empirically and conceptually important, followed: B.K. Gururaja Rao, 1972, *Megalithic Culture in South India*, Mysore. Also, Sundara, and S. Gurumurthy, 1981, *Ceramic Traditions in South India*, Madras. A. Sundara, 1975, *Early Chamber Tombs of South India*, Delhi. The study is based on the generally accepted assumption that the distribution of iron-smelting and iron-using cultures spread from the northwest to the Vidarbha area and subsequently, to the farther south. See C.V.F. Haimendorf, 1954, 'When, How and Where from did the Dravidians Come?' *Indo-Asian Culture*, 17(3): 238–48; K.N. Dikshit, 1969, 'The Origin and Distribution of Megaliths in India', *Culture and Archaeology*, no. 3, pp. 66–9, Banaras Hindu University. The megalith building practice seems to have reached India in many waves. The port-hole dolmens must have come from the Caucasus through Iran; rock-cut caves from Palestine and Ethiopia across the sea; and the *kuṭakkal* type of Kerala came from Indonesia. See Balakrishnan Nair, 1977, *The Problem of Dravidian Origins: A Linguistic, Anthropological and Archaeological Approach*, Madras, pp. 54 ff.
2. L.S. Leshnik, 1974, *South Indian Megalithic Burials: The Pandukal Complex*, Wiesbaden.
3. C. Maloney, 1970, 'The Beginnings of Civilisation in South India', *Journal of Asian Studies*, 29(3). Also his, 1976, 'Archaeology of South India: Accomplishments and Prospects', in Burton Stein (ed.), *Essays in South India*, New Delhi.
4. Leshnik, *South Indian Megalithic Burials: The Pandukal Complex.*
5. B.K. Gururaja Rao, *Megalithic Culture in South India.*
6. S.H. Ritti (ed.), 1978, *A Decade of Archaeological Studies in South India*, Dharwar; R. Champakalakshmi, 1981, 'Urban processes in Early Medieval Tamil Nadu', *Indian History Congress Proceedings* (*IHCP*), New Delhi.
7. Ibid.
8. R.S. Sharma, 1987, *Urban Decay in India*. New Delhi, pp. 84–6.
9. For details about the Tamil *brāhmi* inscriptions see, T.V. Mahalingam, 1974, *South Indian Palaeography*, Madras, rpt, pp. 201 ff. The decipherment and the related studies have been thoroughly revised by I. Mahadevan. For the updated reading and interpretation of the inscriptions, see his, 'Corpus of the Tamil Brahmi Inscriptions', in R. Nagaswami (ed.), *Seminar on Inscriptions*, Madras, 1966. Also his, *Tamil Brahmi Inscriptions*, Madras, 1970. pp. 3–6.

The latest version is given in his, 2003, Early Tamil Epigraphy, Harward University.

10. See, W. Elliot, 1886, *Coins of Southern India*, Trubner; R. Sewell, 1904, 'Roman Coins Found in India', *Journal of the Royal Asiatic Society*, vol. XXIII, pp. 200–12. Also his *List of Antiquities* vol. I. pp. 66–8. M. Mattingly, 1960, *Roman Coins*, London. Details of roman coins and their find-spots are given in K.V.S. Aiyer, 1917, *Historical Sketches of the Dekhan*, vol. I. Madras, pp. 86–7. The Roman coins recovered from the various places of Kerala are discussed in P.L. Gupta, 1965, *The Early Coins from Kerala*, Trivandrum. For the recent additions see, Sashibhushan, 1987, 'Roman Coins from Kerala', *Malayalam Literary Survey*, Trichur, pp. 75–80.
11. The three main anthologies *Eṭṭuttokai, Pattuppaṭṭu*, and *Patinenkīḻkkaṇakku* and the grammatical treatise *Tolkāppiyam* constitute what is popularly called the corpus of Sangam texts. The chronology of the texts is largely uncertain. The early stratum of the corpus, *Ettuttokai* except *Kalittokai* and *Paripāṭal*, is dated between *c.* 200 BC and AD 300. Similarly, excepting a few, the compositions in *Pattuppattu* are of *c.* AD 300–400. *Patinenkilkkanakku* texts mostly belong to fourth–fifth centuries. *Tolkāppiyam* is of a still later period. For the traditional views, see Kanakasabhai Pillai, 1904, *The Tamils 1800 Years Ago*, Madras; S.K. Iyengar, 1918, *Beginnings of South Indian History*, Madras. P.T. Srinivasa Iyengar, 1929, *History of the Tamils*, Madras; N. Subrahmanian, 1966, *Sangam Polity*, Delhi. For recent studies on the texts and chronology see, K. Kailasapathy, 1968, *Tamil Heroic Poetry*, London; J.R. Marr, 1987, *The Eight Anthologies: A Study in Early Tamil Literature*, Institute of Asian Studies, Madras; George L. Hart, 1975, *The Poems of Ancient Tamil: Their Milieu and their Sanskrit Counterparts*, Berkley. Also see, George L. Hart, 1979, *Poets of Tamil Anthologies: Ancient Poems of Love and War*, Princeton; V. Kamil Zvelebil, 1986, *Literary Conventions in Akam Poetry*, Institute of Asian Studies, Madras. Also his, 'The Earliest Account of the Tamil Academies', *Indo-lranian Journal*, vol. xv, Leiden, pp. 109–35. For an excellent analytical comprehension, see, Takanobu Takahashi, 1989, *Poetry and Poetics: Literary Conventions of Tamil Love Poetry*, Japan.
12. Maloney, 1970, 'The Beginnings of Civilization in South India'; R. Gurukkal, 1989a, 'Forms of Production and Forces of Change in Ancient Tamil Society', *Studies in History*, 5(2); S. Seneviratne, 1989, 'Pre-state Societies to State Societies: Transformations in the Political Ecology of South India with Special Reference to Tamil Nadu', Seminar on State in Pre-colonial South India, New Delhi.
13. R. Champakalakshmi, 1975–6, 'Archaeology and Tamil Literary Tradition', *Purātatva*, no. 8, Delhi.
14. Subrahmanian, 1966, *Sangam Polity*, Madras.
15. K. Kailasapathy, 1968, *Tamil Heroic Poetry*, London; Zvelebil, 1973a; Hart, *The Poems of Ancient Tamil*; Marr 1987.
16. Kailasapathy, *Tamil Heroic Poetry*.

17. K. Zvelebil, 1973a, *The Smile of Murugan*, Leiden. Also his, 1973b, 'The Earliest Account of the Tamil Academies', Indo-Iranian Journal, XV(2); B. Stein, 1980, *Peasant State and Society in Medieval South India*, New Delhi.
18. *Aṛruppaṭai* songs are songs of bards and itinerant people. These songs contain description of routes. *Ciṛupāṇāṛruppaṭai* (short) and *Perumpāṇāṛruppaṭai* (long) songs are well known examples. *Tiṇaippāṭṭu* is the song on the tiṇai (ecotype). *Mullaippāṭṭu* and *Kuṛiñjippāṭṭu* are famous examples.
19. Zvelebil, 1973a, *The Smile of Murugan* and 1973b, 'The Earliest Account of the Tamil Academies'; K. Sivathamby, 1974, 'Early South Indian Society and Economy: The *Tinai* Concept', *Social Scientist*, no. 29; Marr 1987.
20. Chadwick and Chadwick, 1932–40, *The Growth of Literature*; C.M. Bowra, 1966, *Heroic Poetry*, London; V. Propp, 1979, *Morphology of the Folktale*, Berkeley.
21. Kailasapathy, *Tamil Heroic Poetry*, Alexander M. Dubianski, 1980, 'An Analysis of the *Mullai-Palai* Fragment of Ancient Poetry', *Journal of Tamil Studies*, No. 17, Madras. Also his, 1981, 'A Motif of Messenger in the *Mullaittinai*', *Journal of Tamil Studies*, No. 19, Madras.
22. George L. Hart, 1978, *The Poems of Ancient Tamil*, New Delhi.
23. The terms 'primitive' and 'civilized' are used here to indicate primeval and evolved stages respectively, in the process of social development. See the discussions in S.B. Deo, 1985, 'The Vidarbha Megaliths', *Bulletin of the Deccan College of Postgraduate and Research Institute*, vol. 41. pp. 27–32. Also, 'The Megaliths', in S.B. Deo and Paddayya (eds), *Recent Advances in Indian Archaeology*, Pune, 1985. pp. 89–99.
24. N. Subrahmanian, *Sangam Polity*.
25. K. Sivathamby, 1974, 'Early South Indian Society and Economy: The *Tinai* Concept'; Gurukkal, 'Forms of Production and Forces of Change in Ancient Tamil Society'.
26. K. Sivathamby, 'Early South Indian Society and Economy: The *Tinai* Concept'.
27. S. Seneviratne, 'Pre-state Societies to State Societies: Transformations in the Political Ecology of South India with Special Reference to Tamil Nadu'.
28. Gurukkal, 'Forms of Production and Forces of Change in Ancient Tamil Society'.
29. Ibid.
30. Nair, *The Problem of Dravidian Origins*; Gurukkal, 'Forms of Production and Forces of Change in Ancient Tamil Society'.
31. Hart, *The Poems of Ancient Tamil*; Gurukkal, 'Forms of Production and Forces of Change in Ancient Tamil Society'.
32. Hart, *The Poems of Ancient Tamil*; Stein, *Peasant State and Society in Medieval South India*.
33. C. Levi Strauss, 1969, *The Elementary Structure of Kinship*, London; Trautman, 1974, *Kinship and History in South Asia*, Michigan; C. Meillassoux, 1973,

'The Social Organisation of the Peasantry: Economic Basis of Kinship', *Journal of Peasant Studies*, 1(1).

34. Hart, *The Poems of Ancient Tamil*; Gurukkal 1980a, 'The Socio-economic Milieu of the Kerala Tample: A Functional Analysis, *c.* 800–1200 AD', Studies in History, 2(1).
35. Hart, *The Poems of Ancient Tamil.*
36. Gurukkal, 'Forms of Production and Forces of Change in Ancient Tamil Society'.
37. Sivathamby, 'Early South Indian Society and Economy: The *Tinai* Concept'; Sivathamby 1976; Gurukkal, 'Forms of Production and Forces of Change in Ancient Tamil Society'.
38. *Pn.* = *Purananuru*; *An.* = *Akananuru*; *Prp* = *Patirruppattu.*
39. Gurukkal, 'Forms of Production and Forces of Change in Ancient Tamil Society'.
40. Maloney, 'The Beginnings of Civilization in South India'.
41. Meillassoux 1971; C.C. Lamberg-Karlovsky and J.A. Sabloff (eds), 1975, *Ancient Civilization and Trade*, Albuquerque.
42. Meillassoux 1971; S. Ratnagar, 1981, *Encounters: The Westerly Trade of Harappa Civilization*, New Delhi.
43. See *Malabar Manual*, vol. I.
44. Maloney, 'The Beginnings of Civilization in South India'.
45. Gurukkal, 'Forms of Production and Forces of Change in Ancient Tamil Society'; Also his, 1989b, 'Social Formation and Political Processes in Early Tamilakam', Seminar on State in Pre-colonial South India, New Delhi.
46. Subrahmanian, *Sangam Polity*; S. Singaravelu, 1966, *The Social Life of the Tamils: The Classical Period*, Kuala Lumpur; K.K. Pillai, 1979, *The Social History of the Tamils*, Madras.
47. Subrahmanian, *Sangam Polity.*
48. Gurukkal, 'Forms of Production and Forces of Change in Ancient Tamil Society'.
49. *Natural History*, VI. 26.
50. Gurukkal, 'Forms of Production and Forces of Change in Ancient Tamil Society'
51. Maloney, 'The Beginnings of Civilization in South India'.
52. Seneviratne, 'Pre-state Societies to State Societies: Transformations in the Political Ecology of South India with Special Reference to Tamil Nadu'.
53. Gurukkal, 'Forms of Production and Forces of Change in Ancient Tamil Society'.
54. C. Maloney, 1976, 'Archaeology of South India: Accomplishments and Prospects', in Burton Stein (ed.), *Essays in South India*, New Delhi.
55. Thapar, 1978, '*Dana* and *Dakshina* as Forms of Exchange', in Ancient Indian Social History, New Delhi; C.A. Gregory, 1983, *Gifts and Commodities*, London.

56. Kailasapathy, *Tamil Heroic Poetry.*
57. Gurukkal, 1981; Gurukkal, 'Forms of Production and Forces of Change in Ancient Tamil Society'.
58. Narayanan, 1977, *Re-interpretations in South Indian History*, Trivandrum.
59. E. Terray, 1972, *Marxism and Primitive Societies*, New York; R.S. Sharma, 1983, *Material Culture and Social Formations in Ancient India*, New Delhi.
60. Gurukkal, 'Forms of Production and Forces of Change in Ancient Tamil Society'.
61. *Anicut* is an ancient dam built by Karikala during the AD 2nd century over the river Cauvery. The dam was made of stone and mud, with outer granite layers in lime mortar.
62. Terray, *Marxism and Primitive Societies*; Godelier, 1977, *Perspectives in Marxist Anthropology*, Cambridge; Friedman and Rowlands, 1977 (ed.), *The Evolution of Social Systems*, London.
63. Gurukkal, 'Forms of Production and Forces of Change in Ancient Tamil Society'.
64. Seneviratne, 'Pre-state Societies to State Societies: Transformations in the Political Ecology of South India with Special Reference to Tamil Nadu'.
65. L. Krader, 1968, *The Formation of the State*, London; E.R. Service, 1975, *Origins of the State and Civilization: The Process of Cultural Evolution*, New York; H.J.M. Claessen and P. Skalnik, 1978, *The Early State*, The Hague; Thapar, 1984, *From Lineage to State*, New Delhi; Claessen and Velde, 1987, *Early State Dynamics*, Leiden.
66. Seneviratne, 'Pre-state Societies to State Societies: Transformations in the Political Ecology of South India with Special Reference to Tamil Nadu'.
67. Ibid.
68. M.G.S. Narayanan, 1975a, 'The Mouryan Problem in Sangam Literature, Journal of Indian History, 53(2): 243–54.
69. R. Thapar, 1973, *Asoka and the Decline of the Mauryas*, London. Also, *The Mauryas Revisited*, Calcutta, 1988.
70. Krader, *The Formation of the State*; Service, *Origins of the State and Civilization: The Process of Cultural Evolution*; Thapar, *From Lineage to State*.
71. Gurukkal, 'Forms of Production and Forces of Change in Ancient Tamil Society'.
72. R.S. Kennedy, 1976, 'King in Early South India as Chieftain and Emperor', *Indian Historical Review*, 3(1), New Delhi, pp. 1–15.
73. Gurukkal, 'Social Formation and Political Processes in Early Tamilakam'.
74. Seneviratne, 'Pre-state Societies to State Societies: Transformations in the Political Ecology of South India with Special Reference to Tamil Nadu'.
75. Ibid.
76. Gurukkal, 'Forms of Production and Forces of Change in Ancient Tamil Society'.
77. Ibid.

78. M.G.S. Narayanan, 1975b, 'The Vedic–Puranic-Shastraic Element in Tamil Sangam Society and Culture', in Essays in Indian Art, Religion, and Society, p. 128.
79. Hart, *The Poems of Ancient Tamil.*
80. Gurukkal, 'Forms of Production and Forces of Change in Ancient Tamil Society'.
81. M.G.S. Narayanan, 1982, 'The Warrior Settlements in the Sangam Age, *Indian History Congress Proceedings*, Kurukshetra.
82. Sharma, *Urban Decay in India.*
83. B.N.S. Yadava, 1978–9, 'The accounts of the Kali age and the Social Transition from the Antiquity to the Middle Ages', *IHR*, 5(1–2): 31–63, New Delhi; R.S. Sharma, 1982, 'The Kali Age: A Period of Social Crisis', in B.N. Mukherjee (ed.), *History and Thought: Essays in Honour of A.L. Basham*, New Delhi.
84. Arunachalam, M. 1979, 'The Kalabhras in the Pandiya Country and their Impact on the Life and Letters There' *Journal of the Madras University*, vol. 51(1): 33–45, Madras.
85. R. Nagaswamy, 1981, 'An Outstanding Epigraphical Discovery in Tamil Nadu', Proceedings of the Fifth International Conference Seminar on Tamil Studies, Madurai.
86. Stein, *Peasant State and Society in Medieval South India.*
87. D.N. Jha, 1984, 'Validity of the "Brahmana Peasant Alliance" and the "Segmentary State" in Early Medieval South India', *Social Science Probings*, 4(1): 1–26, New Delhi.
88. Y. Subbarayalu, 1982, 'The Cōḷa State', *Studies in History*: 4(2): 265; R. Champakalakshmi, 1981, 'Peasant State and Society in Medieval South India: A Review Article', *Indian Economic and Social History Review*, 18(3–4): 411–26; Vijaya Ramaswamy, 1982, 'Peasant State and Society in Medieval South India: A Review Article', *Studies in History*, 4(2): 307–319; Kesavan Veluthat, 1993, *The Political Structure of Early Medieval South India*, New Delhi, pp. 250–6.
89. Noburu Karashima, 1980, *South Indian History and Society: Studies from Inscriptions AD 850–1800.* New Delhi 1980. pp. xxv–xxxiii.
90. See Burton Stein, *Peasant State and Society in Medieval South India.*
91. D.N. Jha, 1989–91, 'Relevance of Peasant State and Society to Pallava-Cola Times', *IHR*, 8(1–2): 74–94.
92. M.G.S. Narayanan, 1988, 'The Role of Peasants in the Early History of Tamilakam in South India', *Social Scientist*, 16(9): 17–34.
93. M.G.S. Narayanan, 1982, 'Warrior Settlements in the Sangam Age', *Indian History Cogress Proceedings*, Delhi.
94. Kesavan Veluthat, 1993, *The Political Structure of Early Medieval South India*, New Delhi, pp. 250–6.
95. Noburu Karashima, *South Indian History and Society*, pp. xxx–xxxxii.

96. For a detailed discussion of the features of Indian feudalism, see R.S. Sharma, 1980, *Indian Feudalism*, rpt, New Delhi. The criticism is well represented in Harbans Mukhia, 1981, 'Was there feudalism in Indian History?', *Journal of Peasant Studies*, 8(3): 273–310. See a comprehensive response to the debate to the issues in R.S. Sharma, 1984, 'How Feudal was Indian Feudalism?' *Social Scientist*, no. 124, pp. 16–24, New Delhi.
97. See discussion on the Kali Age in Yadava, 'The Kali Age and the Social Transition'. Also see, R.S. Sharma, 1982, 'The Kali Age: A Period of Social Crisis', in S.N. Mukherji (ed.), *History and Thought: Essays in Honour of A.L. Basham*, Calcutta.
98. M.G.S. Narayanan, 'The Mauryan Problem in Sangam Works in Historical Perspective', *Journal of Indian History*, Trivandrum, L. iii, p. ii. Also Sudarsan Seneviratne, 1989, 'The Pre-State Societies to State Societies: Transformations in the Political Ecology of South India with special Reference to Tamil Nadu', Seminar Paper, Jawaharlal Nehru University, New Delhi.
99. See Rajan Gurukkal, 'Forms of Production and Forces of Change in Ancient Tamil Society'.
100. Ibid.
101. Ibid.
102. See the discussion in Bary M. Hindess and Paul Q. Hirst, 1979, *Pre-capitalist Modes of Production*, London, pp. 73–9. Also the discussion in R. Cohen, 1978, *Karl Marx's Theory of History: A Defense*, Princeton, pp. 18–23. For insights in kin-labour economy, C. Meillassoux, 1972, 'From Reproduction to Production', *Economy and Society*, 1(1). E. Terray, 1972, *Marxism and Primitive Societies*, New York, pp. 96–9. Also see the discussion on the economic implications of kin-labour in C. Meillassoux, 'The social organization of Peasantry: Economic Basis of kinship, '*Journal of Peasant Studies*', 1(1): 81–8, London.
103. Gurukkal, 'Forms of Production and Forces of Changes in Ancient Tamil Society'.
104. See T.V. Mahalingam. 1970, *Report on the Excavations in the Lower Kaveri Valley*, University of Madras. Also *Indian Archeology: A Review*, 1964–5, Archaeological Survey of India, New Delhi. For an assemblage of empirical data on the post-third century decline in the archaeological sites, see, R.S. Sharma, *Urban Decay in India*, pp. 84–6.
105. The illusion in the Velvikkuti copper plates is a good example. See the discussion in Gurukkal, 'Forms of Production and Forces of Changes in Ancient Tamil Society'. Long before the debate was set in the land system and socio-political conditions of early medieval period had been closely scrutinized. See M.G.S. Narayanan, 1996, *Perumals of Kerala: Political and Social Conditions of Kerala Under the Cēra Perumals of Makotai (c. AD 800–1124)*, Calicut. The first major empirical intervention into the debate is in R. Champakalakshmi, 1981, 'Peasant State and Society in Medieval

South India: A Review Article', *Indian Economic and Social History Review*, 18(3–4): 411–26; Y. Subbarayalu, 1982, 'The Cōḷa State', *Studies in History*, 4(2): 265; Vijaya Ramaswamy, 1982, 'Peasant State and Society in Medieval South India: A Review Article', *Studies in History*, 4(2): 307–19; Noburu Karashima, 1980, *South Indian History and Society: Studies from Inscriptions AD 850–1800*, New Delhi, 1980, pp. xxv–xxxiii; Kesavan Veluthat, 1993, *The Political Structure of Early Medieval South India*, New Delhi, pp. 250–6; M.G.S Narayanan, 1988, 'The Role of Peasants in the Early History of Tamilakam in South India', *Social Scientist*, 16(9): 24–7, New Delhi; D.N. Jha, 'Relevance of Peasant State and Society to Pallava–Cola Times'; D.N. Jha, 'Validity of the "Brahmana Peasant Alliance" and the "Segmentary State" in Early Medieval South India'.

2

The Course of Social Historiography of Kerala

Social history is history of society done in social scientific perspective often made out to be in contradistinction to political history. Ibn Khaldun's *Muqaddima*, the introduction to his great history of the Arabs and Berbers, the *Kitab al-'ibar*, may be perhaps the landmark in historiography for any one who conceives history with social processes at the centre but without losing sight of the interconnections of the economic and political. Khaldunian insights into linkages across different social groups, such as townspeople, nomads and traders, in discussing history with focus on processes of nomadism, urbanization, and oppression, prompt us to consider him the founder of holistic social history. That kind of history, basically theoretical in approach was not practised till eighteenth century that saw the writings of Adam Ferguson who identified the class factor in society, John Millar who wrote about the 'origin of the distinction of ranks', and a few others. Hegel philosophizing the past brought social phenomena central to historical analysis and Marx inverting the perception laid the ever strong methodological foundation for doing social history with intellectual depth. It gave rise to a commendable body of profound writings in the domain of the social history in Europe. In India, social history had a long gestation period in the cocoon of colonial anthropology before it stretched its wings as productions of creative depth and scientific rigour. Scientific social history caught scholarly attention under the methodological inspiration of historical materialism and hence the perception of the past used to be a socio-economic combine. D.D. Kosambi spearheaded the application of the methodology in Indian history and R.S. Sharma, Irfan Habib, and Bipan Chandra, to mention the most widely known names, extended it to analysing socio-economic processes. Amidst historians of pre-eminence, Romila Thappar remains distinct for her judicious use of social theory in supplementing the methodology of scientific social history.

In Kerala too the course of social historiography started off more as a part of colonial anthropology rather than of history. In fact, it began as community studies narrating upon one caste or the other as the writings of Charles Metcalf, Henry Maine, Thomas Munroe, William Logan, and Fawcett.[1] As specific portraits of the caste or community of the region, these works highlight what are the socially and culturally unique points about their objects and their surroundings, in terms of the physical feature, racial composition, kinship system, linguistic identity, and village economy. They are descriptive accounts of communities and caste-cultural practices largely intended to report the state of affairs to a readership not accustomed to them. It was an executive requirement for the administrators to understand the life and culture of the land and people to administer. Most writings were so designed as to be catering to the needs of those who were curious about the 'alien culture'. Nevertheless, a few writings are really academic and far beyond their original intent. For instance, William Logan's *Malabar*, at once quite scholarly and comprehensive, is far more than a manual that the colonial administration required. As regards the local scholars such as K.M. Panicker, L.A. Krishna Iyer, and L.A. Ravi Varma, the overall purpose was almost the same but at a different level.[2] In general what inspired all these writers was the exotic in their objects that they sought to describe, rather than their social historical context. It was the contrast between the civilized and the primitive, the urban and the rural, the citizens and the folk that they sought to come to terms with, but of course with a sense of social history that their contemporary consciousness allowed. The overall intent of anthropological writings continued to be more or less the same for a few more decades.

Quite detached from contemporary anthropology K.P Padmanabha Menon was the first among the professional historians to think in terms of a comprehensive history of the land and people of Kerala, as early as in the twenties. He had a perspective of social development, with which he tried to trace, as far as possible, a continuous history. Unlike his predecessors who had understood history as dynastic chronicle, Padmanabha Menon sought to bring territory and people as the core of the subject matter of history, as his *Kochi Rajya Charitram* exemplifies. Among historians, he was certainly the icebreaker to conceive something close to social history of the Malayalam speaking people. Nonetheless, the people whose history that Padmanabha Menon attempted to focus were that of the settlers in the agrarian plains of midland Kerala and not those in the forest and the sea coast.

In the early fifties some efforts were made to understand the historical background of the land-tenures and the entailing social relations in terms of castes and communities in Kerala.[3] Social anthropology drew very close to analytical social history as evidenced by the writings of Kathleen Gough on the changing kinship usages and implications of more basic transformations among the Nayars,[4] their ancestral worship,[5] institution of marriage,[6] and matrilineal kinship.[7] The studies by Gough were too specialized about one community alone, to be holistic. It was in the sixties that social anthropology could assume almost entirely the *genre* of social history. Joan P. Mencher pursued the study of the Nayar community in the north Malabar in the same perspective with a special focus on the family organization and ritual beliefs.[8] She also made a comparative study of the same community by reviewing the situation in south Malabar.[9] Her studies never acquired a holistic perspective of the larger society in terms of relations, structures, and processes even when she sought to analyse social change and the elitist social position of the Namputiri *brāhmaṇas*.[10]

L.A. Krishna Iyer published his two volumes of *Social History of Kerala* in 1968. Though conceived as a comprehensive social history of the whole of Kerala in terms of the land and people, the focus was the ancient peoples and their cultures as reconstructed ethnographically out of the studies of the Pre-Dravidians and Dravidian speaking hill tribes, communities, and castes of the plains. It was basically an assemblage of independent narratives on peoples and cultures rather than the pattern of interaction and coexistence. His problematique did not include questions relating to the nature of division of labour, labour process, system of appropriation, structure of the village community, and forces of transformation. He does not probe into the nature of communal property, emergence of a differentiated economy, and formation of the caste system. However, it was Krishna Iyer who tried to view people of Kerala as a whole in social historical perspective with a lot of insights into the phenomenon of cultural interaction, transformation, and persistence by taking the cues from the surviving ethnic groups, their landscapes and archaeological monuments there.[11]

There seems to have taken place no considerable dialogue between anthropologists and historians even though anthropologists themselves were very much archaeologists and historians in their own rights. The main reason was the basic difference in the subject matter that engaged the professional historians and anthropologists of those times. Historians were basically royal chroniclers engaged in rebuilding and updating the genealogy of kings while anthropologists were ethnologists unfolding the customs and practices of tribes and castes. It was this mutual exclusiveness of their professional interests far more than the growing disciplinary insularity or sense of academic territoriality that precluded dialogues between anthropologists and historians. Hardly had the knowledge produced by one supplemented what the other did, foreclosing the possibility of any exchange of ideas between the two.

Though Padmanabha Menon did show some interest in social affairs, the historiography of Kerala owed the *genre* of socio-economic history to Elamkulam Kunhan Pillai, a scholar in literature and linguistics. Kunhan Pillai did study dynastic history primarily to lay the foundation of chronology to social affairs, though incidentally his contributions to political history too turned out to be substantial. He was the first scholar who tried to conceive the past society in terms of a system.[12] Historical studies were problem oriented investigations and hence explanatory exercises for him. They led him to the fundamental aspects of social life such as land relations and system of inheritance. One can easily say that Elamkulam was the first scholar in Kerala who understood that social history should be discussed in the light of the material base of institutions, relations, and structures. His critical consciousness about social dominance, control, and exploitation made his historical narratives passionate and hence provocative.

Following the path of Elamkulam with much more positivistic methodological rigour M.G.S Narayanan strengthened the chronological foundation of social history with the help of new evidence as well as re-interpretation. His reinterpretations sharpened the knowledge about social institutions, their origins, contexts, functions, relations, and structures. He was the first to demonstrate in the historiography of Kerala the primacy of socio-economic structure as the determinant of the nature of political power.[13] Kesavan Veluthat added to the strength of Kerala's socio-economic historiography in the late seventies by specifically focusing on the *brāhmaṇa* settlements, their temple-centred institutional composition, and socio-economic power structure.[14]

An assessment of social anthropological studies shows that their overall understanding about the Kerala society in the medieval period (between fifteenth to the close of nineteenth century) was flat bereft of insights into differences in nuances and niceties of social affairs in time. Probably due to the predominance of synchronic perception about the themes such as kinship and marriage or the caste and community, anthropologists were least interested in probing the vertical depth of historical process. With the result they were hasty in clubbing several centuries into an epoch and generalizing the social characteristics thereof as illustrated by their notion of 'the medieval' which equated contemporary Kerala society to a Nayar dominated structure with several Namputiri landlords enjoying a higher status.[15] Nevertheless, the synchronic studies on the caste system and sub-caste proliferation have yielded good results. The studies covered the Christians, their family organization, social customs, beliefs, and cultural practices.[16]

In the late seventies social anthropological studies took a different turn dwelling upon transformational processes seminal to social history. It was in 1976 that Robin Jeffrey put up his explanatory thesis on the decline of the Nayar dominance.[17] Though centred around the Nayar community the study sought to capture the social dynamics of the community in the larger society and it was indeed a major social historical study of the circumstances of the dominance and the decline of the community. The state of affairs of the community in the contemporary Kerala attracted social historical analysis, historical backdrops, as well as the past proper of the region.[18] Some of the anthropologists and sociologists tried to identify the past of the caste and community in terms the social system, mostly by way of categorizing their medieval history as part of the feudal society in which the Nayar *taṛavāds* and Namputiri *illams* dominated as landed magnates with seigniorial jurisdiction over their localities.[19] However, the limitations of generalization persisted even in such instances of conceptual categorization. Preoccupied with the synchronic social affairs, the historical background has always been a matter of hazy generalization notwithstanding the lurking danger of anachronisms, anthropologists and sociologists missed the entire diachronic processes especially of the remote past. The question of organized social mobilization and transformation of relations, figured prominently in a subsequent study.[20] A close-up view of the transformational process in a caste has been attempted in social historical background.[21]

From the mid-1960s the historiography of South India began to face attacks at its basic methodological concepts and design, with the writings of Burton Stein and his fellow researchers, whose historiographic perspectives were distinct with the striking feature of conceptual presupposition drawn from cognate disciplines like sociology and anthropology. The conceptual ground of their historical explanations was set by a group of sociologists and anthropologists like C.G. Diehl, Louis Dumont, E.R. Leach, and others who had analysed various aspects of the socio-cultural milieu of South India. Mckim Marriott, B.S. Cohn, J. Middleton, R. Cohen, and others had further enriched the field through their conceptual models applicable in the historical context of South Asia in general and South India in particular. Burton Stein and his associates found the research works on South India, to a great extent, stunted at the state of being narrative compilations bereft of conceptualization and ideological presupposition. Of these historians of the new school of thought, the most significant was Burton Stein himself. Clarence Maloney, George L. Hart, George W. Spencer, Kenneth R. Hall, F.W. Clothey, K. Zvelebil, Arjun Appadorai, C.A. Breckenridge, Brenda Beck, S.A. Barnet, Nicholas Dirks, David Ludden, Dennis Hudson, Friedhem Hardy, James Heitzman, and David Schulman are some of the notable names in the new historiography of South India opened up by Stein. Several edited volumes appeared comprising the results of their investigations into the manifold aspects of South Indian history, under the initiative of scholars such as Frykenberg, R.G. Fox, J.F. Richards, John Parker, A. Sjoberg, M. Schneider and Kathleen Gough, Burton Stein, and so on. The notable contributions by these scholars and their volumes to the historiography of South India are: application of anthropological and sociological models for historical explanation; demonstration of the importance of studying systems, structures, ideas, and institutions of the past societies; presentation of interdisciplinary approach; and introduction of scientific and sophisticated methods of analysis of the source material as computerization of inscriptional terms and the statistical analysis of their contexts and occurrences would exemplify. The critical application of some of these got carried forward to the historiography of Kerala too.[22]

The researches of R.Champakalakshmi on Jainism and the *Bhakti* movement in South India tremendously helped trace social history of the Tamil South.[23] M.G.S. Narayanan's reinterpretations of the institutional and organizational aspects of the early medieval South Indian society, the temple centred agrarian economy and the bhakti ideology provided valuable insights for those interested in social history.[24] Mahadevan's contributions to the study of the *brāhmi* inscriptions deserve special mention here. So also do M.R. Raghava Varier's occasional articles in the early socio-economic history of Kerala. Kesavan Veluthat studying the ideas, organizations, and institutions of the *brāhmaṇa* settlements, the temple base of the bhakti movement and the political structure of monarchy, provided greater clarity about the systemic understanding of the social history of early medieval Kerala.[25]

The methodological impact of Burton Stein on South Indian historiography was quite significant though most of the conservative historians remained least affected. Stein's cognitive encounters with the logical contradictions in the accepted historiography of South India and his alternative historiographical propositions together with its conceptual language worked as a transforming influence on the young generation of historians, though most of them sought to be critical of his framework of comprehension and interpretation. Generally speaking, the critics of Stein have by and large abstained from putting up a theoretical rebuttal of Stein's characterization of the beginnings of the 'peasant society'. Consequently, all of them happened to accept either consciously or inadvertently the gradualist/evolutionist view of the origins of what they categorized as feudal society. Having rejected the peasant society segmentary state model for affirming the feudal model without a concomitant framework characterizing the genesis of feudalism the critics of Stein are in a situation of theoretical self-contradiction. That the critics rejected the 'brahman-peasant alliance' with or without alternatives hardly helps them escape the trap of theoretical self-contradiction implicit in the acceptance of the gradualist perception. They virtually united an ideographic account with a theoretical category notwithstanding the inconsistency of harnessing a phenomenological description to a materialistic interpretation and divested themselves of the primary task of theoretical encounter. It is significant too that the rejection of the 'segmentary state' model depended mainly on Stein's factual errors rather than on a sustained theoretical engagement. That the task of a total theoretical rebuttal received no primacy even though any critique in defence of a theoretical model like feudalism has to be inevitably theoretical is, a serious lack.

This is not to say that conceptual presuppositions and explanatory models stimulated all the subsequent studies in Kerala's social history. In fact, they largely remained unaffected by the historian's art and craft of conceptualization, auxiliary questions, historiographical critiques, alternative propositions and debates promoted by the convergence of sociological and anthropological studies in historical research. K.S. Mathew's study on the medieval society is an example of a plain ideographic narrative recounting the customs and practices of Kerala as alluded to in the northern ballads.[26]

The theoretical debates about feudalism had made a few researchers to think about the socio-economic processes that preceded the so-called feudal social formation. This on the one side led to an integrated use of sources and application of the concept of social formation on the other. The integrated utilization of the varied categories of sources of ancient Tamilakam in theoretical perspectives, has resulted in gaining more clarity in the social history of Kerala.[27]. This approach was made possible by efforts on the corroboration of data in the varied sources, such as archaeology and ancient Tamil literature.[28] One category among the sources that has received significant attention is that of the ancient Tamil anthologies, popularly known as the Sangam literature, constituting a mine of information on the conditions of life around the beginning of the Christian era as discussed previously.[29]

A poetic concept that is extremely useful for social history is that of the *aintiṇai*, delineated in the earlier chapters highlighting the realistic interpretation of the five *tiṇai*s in the light of poetic specifications about the nature, peoples, and products of each tiṇai which help generate ideas regarding contemporary economic activities.[30] Taking tiṇsais as micro-eco-zones of given modes of human adaptation, attempts have been made to ascertain the process of interaction and formation of macro-eco-zones. The studies in this perspective, identifying the forms and forces of production in the tinais as corroborated by the clues in other categories of sources and characterizing contemporary social formation of the Tamil south, have rendered the reconstruction of ancient and early historic society of Kerala plausible.[31] The kinship and its bearing on the relations of agricultural production, which have become clear in the studies provided a lot of insights into problems of social relations in contemporary Kerala too. This has stimulated attempts at exploring the nature of kinship and its role as the basis of production relations in the social formation of ancient Tamil poems.

The question of caste in early historic society in Kerala has to be looked at in the light of ancient social division of labour. Historians have associated the institution of caste with the society of the heroic poems, but without approving the *varṇa* system. Tendency has been to show that the caste system of Tamilakam was not based on the concept of the four varṇas, but on something different and *sui-generis*. It was argued that the four *kuṭis*, *pāṇar*, *paṛaiyar*, *tuṭiyar* that is and *kaṭampar* mentioned in a poem, constituted the four castes of the region. However in the poem the term kuṭi means a settlement of people. The poet is not referring to the general situation in the region, but only to that of the particular village where he was singing. The *pārppār* (seers), *aracar* (kings), *iṭaiyar* (cowherds), and *kuṟavar* (hunters) are the four castes according to a commentator of the anthologies. The reference in the *Tolkāppiyam-porul* to the four castes as *antanār, aracar, vāṇikar,* and *veḷḷālar* has been shown as not corresponding to the four categories in the varṇa system for establishing the distinctive feature of the Tamil caste, compared to that of the northern India. Historians have confused the characterization of the institution of caste by taking clan surnames for caste suffixes and by juxtaposing them with the varṇa system. It has been shown what scholars in the past interpreted as castes are clan names.

Several Maxist anthropological studies urge to view social history in terms of social formation.[32] Some efforts have been made by them to examine ancient social histoy of Kerala in the light of the conceptual framework of social formation.[33] The concept of social formation presupposes conceiving historical societies in terms of their systems of production relations and structures of domination. In short, it means social analysis in terms of the concept of modes of production. Though it accepts established modes of production as marked stages of reference for identifying the level of social development, there is no quest for discovering them in any pure form. The focus is on the forces and relations of production and the resulting structure of society. Any rigorous analysis of a past society has to focus on the material process of production and the social process of appropriation so as to know how the society is structured and dominated. Material process means the process of appropriation of nature and social process of appropriation refers to the system of the distribution of produce. Tamil society of the early historic period has been viewed from the perspective of social formation and by way of examining its material and social processes of production and distribution, it has been discovered that there existed a combination of several forms of subsistence and a complex redistributive relationship of collective appropriation. Primitive agriculture, animal husbandry, petty commodity production, and plough agriculture have been identified as the principal forms of production, whose relations dominated and structured the social formation. Any social formation in the past may be viewed as a combination of different forms of production structured by the dominance of one over the rest as explained in the introduction. The relations of the dominant form of production characterize the social formation through the process of interaction. The situation of diverse economies coexisting and interacting, has been conceived and described without the framework of social formation also, where the notion of uneven development based on the potential for ecological adaptations, is the guideline. In this the concept of coexistence and interaction of several forms of production dominated and structured by the relations of one among them does not provide the basis of explanation. The notion of ecological zones and their suitability to resource development is the alternative framework adopted here.

Some efforts have been made to identify the prime movers of the social formation, which subsequently brought about structural transformation of ancient social formation of Tamilakam in general and Kerala in particular.[34] It has been shown that among contemporary economic forms plough agriculture was the most superior in terms of technology and productivity, but it was yet to secure its socio-political and cultural conditions of domination. This was the basic contradiction within the social formation. Moreover, the complex redistributive system was incapable of improving its low labour productivity and facilitating economic reproduction. The limitations of kinship-based production in terms of surplus, the low level of economy and the destructive effects of predatory exaction were other handicaps of the system. A quest for the identification of prime movers was made centring around the contradictions and the alternative evolving out of them. The *brāhmaṇa* households using non-kin labour have been viewed as the nuclei of the evolving alternative. Disintegration of kinship as the basis of production has been viewed as a perceptible manifestation of change in the prevailing system. Apart from what is explicit in the case of developing *brāhmaṇa* households where formation of relations transcending kinship is inevitable, there could be certain other contexts also that facilitated the disintegration process. Predatory marches and migrations could have caused it to an extent, though we do not know about it straight from the sources. The anthologies do refer to the context of warrior leaders getting *ūr* (primary settlement) as reward for helping the bigger chiefs in their plunder campaigns. Developing on such references, it has been argued that several warrior settlements were coming up through the process during the period.[35] The warrior settlements have been visualized as proto-feudal villages with localized services and obligations presupposing organization of local clansmen for production. It is important that the warrior leaders receiving ūr in lieu of their obligatory services *(viṭutoḻil)* to ruling chiefs, were alien to the people of such *ūr*. The founding of settlements by warrior leaders in areas beyond their original *ūr* would mean formation of relations transcending kinship. But it is unlikely that the warrior leaders were given the right over the land of the *ūr*. What had been granted to them could be the right to some kind of exaction from the *ūr* concerned.

The concept of social formations and insight of critical theory that jointly render mode of production theory plausible, constitute the basis of the aforesaid effort. Accordingly, the Tamil society of early historic period has been viewed as a social formation resulting from a combination of several unevenly evolved forms of subsistence and a complex redistributive relationship of collective appropriation as elaborated in earlier chapters. Of the different forms of production, plough agriculture was the superior one in terms of technology and productivity, but it was yet to secure compatible social relations ensuring conditions of development and domination. This was the basic contradiction within the social formation. Moreover, the complex redistributive system was incapable of improving its low labour productivity and facilitating economic reproduction as noted in the earlier chapter. The reciprocally limiting slash-and-burn technology and kin-based productive relations, the low level of productivity besides the destructive effects of predatory exaction were the major handicaps of the system. Theoretically, it was the problem of incompatibility between the system of kin-based relations of production with little scope for expansion on the one side and plough technology with enormous potential of development on the other, causing the latter's fretting.

The quest for the material processes of the birth of a new socio-economic order centres itself around these contradictions and the evolving alternative system of productive relations compatible to plough technology. The *brāhmaṇa* households as units of production based on non-kin labour represented the beginning of a compatible system of productive relations. Theoretically, the shift from kin labour to non-kin labour would destabilize the pre-existing social order and head for an inevitable crisis. Disintegration of kinship in the wake of the horizontal expansion of *brāhmaṇa* households, incessant predatory marches, migrations, and emergence of new settlements indicated the dissolution of the dominant social order. Though there is no direct evidence for a total crisis which the material conditions anticipated, we have indications of a major change during the closing decades of the third century. Then there is a big gap of at least five centuries without sources until the temple inscriptions begin from ninth century.

A very significant gap in the social history of Kerala relates to the process between the close of the chiefdom level society and the consolidation of the agrarian social formation. It is only very recently that some attempt has been made to extrapolate the gap between the two well studied periods by using insights form social theory and environmental history. Efforts to extrapolate the gap with insights of social theory have given social history some continuity from the ancient to early medieval.[36] Being a non-cultivating group by themselves the brahmans had to depend upon the familial labour of the neighbouring clans for the cultivation of their land. The brahman land as an independent unit of production required working families attached to it for ensuring permanency of labour. So naturally families of clansmen must have become tied up with brahman households for providing labour. What exactly was the nature of arrangements in the incipient stages is not known. It was anyway a spontaneous process of institutional evolving out of the continuous interaction between brahmans and the neighbouring clans at the instance of land-operation. Naturally, one of the major processes in the social formation was the emergence of non-kin labour in the agrarian sector through the interaction between brahman households and the neighbouring clannish folk. The process of transformation of the social formation in Kerala was linked to this process of interaction. It was the making of paddy fields that tuned out to be crucial in the process. It was a long process involving transformation of clans into hereditary occupation groups of artisans and craftsmen, and subsequently into endogamous castes.

As already pointed out brahman households existed adjacent to clan settlements, as independent production units as early as the closing centuries before Christ. They sprang up on their own as sparsely distributed households along the red soil fringes of the alluvial ecosystem, using clan labour in the neighbourhood. How they spread to the wetland ecosystem and converged into temple centred corporate settlements when, are conjectures. What was crucial about the new formation was its binary basis between landholding and landlessness which eventually got mediated by intermediaries to form a complex structure. Specialized division of labour, its crystallization into hereditary occupations, and their non-economic coercive modes of social realization were the main characteristics.

As agrarian expansion advanced, human settlements (*ūr*) originally bound by kinship got integrated as agrarian localities (*nādu*) which subsequently acquired great political significance in the monarchical system. The role of caste in the integration of the agrarian society whose mechanisms of appropriation were based on extra-economic coercion, was extremely crucial. The formation of agrarian localities was an ongoing process, and everywhere it accomplished a uniform structure of social relations. The social structure was a hierarchy with landlords who consisted of the local ruling class (*paṭanāyar* who varied as *Nāḍuvāzhi*s of degree of prominence) on the top, the *brāhmaṇa*s as individuals and the corporate body (*ūr*/*sabha*), their leaseholders (*kārāḷar*) who were mainly artisans and craftsmen, in the middle, placed over the primary producers (*aṭiyāḷar*) who were at the bottom. Almost parallel to the leaseholders there were many who held small strips of land as hereditary holdings (*kāṇi*) which were also tilled by primary producers. The circulation of the produce in given shares thus took a structured path through all these categories enjoying different levels of entitlement. The most benefited were the landholders who were ensured goods and services by the settlers in their land while the most exploited were the primary producers. As part of the social mechanisms of ensuring goods and services to the landholders through the notion of obligation, all artisans and craftsmen were subjected to immobility. The conditions of subjection together with the objective reality of the producers being stripped off their produce constituted the major contradiction in the system.

The society in Kerala had become highly complex incorporating into it several indigenous and foreign elements of culture among which Christianity had a place of some importance. The cultural history of Christianity can be constructed only on the basis of very limited number of sources. Quite often one has no other option but to fall back on what is claimed as tradition in the form of legends, folksongs, and oral traditions probably of a later date. There have been very little attempts at doing the social history of Islam in Kerala, upon which Miller continues to be the authority as yet.[37] Apart from a few articles the study of the social history of the Jews and Arabs is a desideratum too.

With the advances in social historiography comprising fresh researches in the social processes, institutions and relations of the ancient and early medieval periods, a substantial part of the historical assumptions and generalizations of anthropological studies has gone obsolete. Anthropological studies continue with focus on family organization and kinship, certainly with better conceptualization, but with a poor grasp of the historical processes, mainly due to the paucity of serious studies on late medieval and early modern social history. Early modern history of Kerala received theoretical insights quite incidentally through the writings of K.N. Panikkar who delved deep into the socio-economic situation of the poor share-croppers of Malabar under British colonialism.[38]

A few studies in Malayalam shed new light in the social history of Kerala, of which the book by P.K. Balakrishnan deserves special mention despite its glaring obsolescence and poor methodology, for the set of non-conventional but commonsensical historiographical questions that it raised about the overall historical backwardness of the region's economy, society, polity, and culture. Focusing on the caste system with its instituted ideas, relations, traditions, customs, practices, and so on, the book seeks to expose the poor material status of the Namputiris who constituted the hegemonic caste of highest ritual and social rank. It provoked and to a great extent compelled the historians to do a critical revisit to sources and re-examine their 'taken for granted language of exaggeration' of the socio-economic, political, and cultural status of the region in the past. Several works have enriched social history of modern Kerala through researches in the perspectives of women studies. G. Arunima, Praveena Kodoth, J. Devika, and Susan Thomas are only some of the names.[39] Arunima examining the changes in the family organization and property relations with insights of studies of sexuality, gender, and caste against the historical background of the abolition of the matrilineal system in Kerala, has studied alongside the equally important phenomenon of the evolution of an Anglo-Indian legal morality, which legitimized these changes. Praveena's study relates to the patriarchal structure of the family and the discriminatory nature of property rights of women in the context of the land reforms. Devika, studying the engendering and individualization processes in the early modern language of social reform, highlights the gender discriminatory features of modernity. Susan's study is on the disintegration of the joint-family system and the nature of property rights among the Christian women. A significant study in social anthropology that enriches social history of modern Kerala is that of Philippos Ossella and Caroline Ossella on the Ezhava community.[40] The researches in the history of social processes of the marginal communities in Kerala have acquired a higher level of conceptualization heralding a breakthrough from the hackneyed anthropology of untouchables and tribes with the study of low castes' experience of colonial modernity by Sanal Mohan.[41]

To conclude, the social historiography of Kerala shows a long course of development in the field of historical scholarship about social groups, relations, institutions, structures and processes of transformation from colonial ideographic community anthropology through analytical social anthropology, descriptive social history, nomothetic anthropology to social theoretical history. Conceptualization of the social history in terms of macro systems, structures and formations, and their transformations is set aside by micro situations and experiences for a while in the wake of phenomenological reading of the ontology of specific experiences of gender discrimination and enslavement close-focused against features of colonial modernity.

NOTES AND REFERENCES

1. E. Fawcett, 1901, 'Nayars of Malabar', *Government Museum Bulletin*, 3(3), Madras.
2. K.M. Panikkar, 1918, 'Some Aspects of Nayar Life', *Journal of the Royal Anthropological Institute*, London, 48: 254–93; L.A. Krishna Iyer, 1926, *The Anthropology of the Syrian Christians*, Ernakulam; L.A. Ravi Varma, 1932, 'Castes of Malabar', *Kerala Society Papers*, 2(9): 171–204, Trivandrum; A. Ayyappan, 1947, *Nayadi-s of North Malabar*, Madras; Eric J. Miller, 1954, 'Caste and Territory in Malabar', *American Anthropologist*, 56(3): 410–20, New York. Also see his 1955, 'Village Structure in North Kerala', in M.N. Srinivas (ed.), *India's Villages*, London.
3. Adrian C. Mayer, 1952, *Land and Society in Malabar*, Oxford.
4. E. Kathleen Gough, 1952, 'Changing Kinship Usages in the Setting of Political and Economic Change among the Nayars of Malabar', *Journal of the Royal Anthropological Institute*, London, 82: 71–88.
5. E. Kathleen Gough, 1959, 'Cults of the Dead among the Nayars', in Milton Singer (ed.), *Traditional India: Structure and Change*, Philadelphia, pp. 446–78.
6. E. Kathleen Gough, 1959, 'The Nayars and the Definition of Marriage', *Journal of the Royal Anthropological Institute*, 89: 23–34, London, Also her 1956, 'Visiting Husbands in Malabar', *Journal of the M.S. University of Baroda*, 5:.37–56, Baroda. Also see K. Raman Unni, 1959, 'Caste in Southern Malabar', unpublished PhD thesis, M.S. University, Baroda.
7. E. Kathleen Gough and D.M. Schneider (eds), 1961, *Matrilineal Kinship*, Berkeley; J.J. Puthenkalam, 1962, 'Marriage and Family in Kerala', PhD thesis, Bombay University.
8. Joan P. Mencher, 1962, 'Changing Familial Roles among South Malabar Nayars', *Southwestern Journal of Anthropology*, 8(3): 230–45, New York. Also her, 1963, 'Growing up in South Malabar', *Human Organization*, 22: 54–65 London. Also, her 1964, 'Possession, Dance, and Religion in North Malabar, Kerala, India', *International Congress of Anthropological and Ethnological Sciences*, 9: 340–5, London. Also see M. Abraham, 1963, 'Nayars of Kerala', PhD thesis, Lucknow University.
9. Joan P. Mencher, 1965, 'The Nayars of South Malabar', in M.F. Nimkoff, (ed.), *Comparative Family Systems*, Boston, pp.163–91.
10. Joan Mencher, 1964, 'Social and Economic Change in India: The Namboodiri Brahmins', in *American Philosophical Society Yearbook 1964*,

pp. 398–402, Philadelphia; Also her, 'Kerala and Madras: A Comparative Study of Ecology and Social Structure', *Ethnology*, 5(2): 135—72; and her, 1966, 'Namboodiri Brahmins: An Analysis of a Traditional Elite in Kerala', *Journal of Asian and African Studies*, 1(3): 183–96; Joan P. Mencher and H. Goldberg, 1967, 'Kinship and Marriage Regulations among the Namboodiri Brahmans of Kerala', *Man*, 2(1): 87–106; J. Puthenkalam,1966, 'Marriage and the Family in Kerala', *Journal of Comparative Family Studies*, Calgary.

11. L.A. Krishna Iyer, 1961, *Kerala and Her People*, Palghat. Also his, 1968, *Social History of Kerala: Vol. I, The Pre-Dravidians*, Madras. Also, 1970, *Social History of Kerala: Vol II—The Dravidians*, Madras.
12. *Janmi Sampradayam Keralathil*, Kottayam, 1957. There is a consolidated form of his researches in, Elamkulam Kunjan Pillai, 1970, *Studies in Kerala History*, Kottayam.
13. M.G.S. Narayanan, 1972, 'Political and Social Conditions of Kerala Under the Kulasekhara Empire (*c*. AD 800 to AD 1124)', unpublished PhD dissertation, University of Kerala. Subsequently published as *Perumals of Kerala* (Calicut, 1996). Also his 1973, *Aspects of Aryanisation in Kerala*, Trivandrum.
14. Kesavan Veluthat, 1978, *Brahman Settlements in Kerala: Historical Studies*, Calicut. A further specialization of the socio-economic functions of the temple followed. See Rajan Gurukkal, 2002, *The Kerala Temple*, Vallathol Vidyapittham, Sukapuram.
15. See an assessment of social research in Joan P. Mencher and K. Raman Unni, 1975, 'Anthropological and Sociological Research in Kerala: Past Present, and Future Directions', in Burton Stein (ed.), *Essays on South India*, Honolulu.
16. After L.A. Krishna Iyer's study of the Christian community published in 1926 several studies on the Christians of Kerala followed. George Kurian, 1961, *The Indian Family in Transition: A Case Study of Kerala Christians*, The Hague; S.G. Pothan, 1963, *The Syrian Christians of Kerala*, Bombay.
17. R. Jeffrey, 1976, *The Decline of Nayar Dominance*, Sussex.
18. C.J. Fuller, 1976, *The Nayars Today*, Cambridge.
19. Even when Asiatic Mode of Production was the model used for the systemic characterization of the society of medieval India in general, Kerala was viewed as different for its medieval turned out to be feudal. E. Kathleen Gough, 1980, 'Modes of Production in Southern India', *Economic and Political Weekly*, 15(5, 6 & 7): 337–64, Mumbai.
20. J.W. Gladstone, 1985, 'Caste, Religion and People's Movements in Keralawith Particular Reference to South Kerala', *Religion and Society*, 32(1): 24–35.
21. A.K.B. Pillai, 1987, *The Culture of Social Stratification/Sexism: The Nayars*, Acton, MA.

22. Rajan Gurukkal, 1978, 'The Socio-economic Role of the Kerala Temple—*c.* AD 800—1200', Jawaharlal Nehru University. See the published version, *The Kerala Temple* (Sukapuram, 2002).
23. 'Urban Processes in Early Medieval Tamil Nadu', Proceedings of the Indian History Congress (here after IHC), Bodh Gaya, 1981; 'The Bhakti Movement and Religious Persecution in Tamil Nadu', IHC, Calicut, 1976; 'Kurandi Tirukkattampalli: An Ancient Jain Monastery of Tamil Nadu', in *Studies in Indian Epigraphy*, vol. II, Mysore, pp. 84–9; R. Champakalakshmi, 1996, *Trade, Ideology and Urbanisation, South India 300 BC to AD 1300*, New Delhi.
24. M.G.S. Narayanan, 1977, *Reinterpretations in South Indian History*, Trivandrum; Kesavan Veluthat, 1978, 'Bhakti Movement in South India', in S.C. Malik (ed.), *Indian Movements: Some Aspects of Dissent, Protest and Reform*, Shimla, pp. 51, 64.
25. Veluthat, *Brahman Settlements in Kerala*, Calicut; Royalty and Divinity: Legitimisation of Monarchical Power in South India', IHC, Hyderabad, 1978; 'The Temple Base of the Bhakti Movement', IHC, Waltair 1979; Veluthat, 1993, *The Political Structure of Early Medieval South India*, New Delhi.
26. K.S. Mathew, 1979, *Society in Medieval Malabar*, Kottayam.
27. Clarence Maloney, 1976, '"Archaeology in South India" Accomplishments and Prospects', in Burton Stein (ed.), *Essays on South India*, New Delhi; Rajan Gurukkal, 1989, 'Forms of Production and Forces of Change in Ancient Tamil Society', *Studies in History*, 5(2): 160–75.
28. K.R. Srinivasan, 1947, 'The Megalithic Burial and Cairn Fields of South India in the Light of Tamil Literature and Tradition', *Ancient India*, No. 2, pp. 9–16; R. Champakalakshmi, 1975–6, 'Archaeology and Tamil Literary Tradition', *Purātatva*, No. 8, Delhi.
29. Tamil Literature refers to what is popularly known as the Corpus of Sangam Literature here. The Corpus include in its most archaic stratum some of the anthologies grouped under *Eṭṭuttokai* and *Paṭṭuppattu* roughly belonging to second century BC and AD third century. Label inscriptions consist of the Tamil *brāhmi* labels belonging to *c.* third century BC to AD fourth century. The foreign notices comprise mainly the Graeco-Roman writings.
30. K. Sivathamby,1974, 'Early South Indian Society and Economy: The *Tinai* Concept', *Social Scientist*, No. 29, pp. 20–37.
31. Rajan Gurukkal, 'Forms of Production ...'.
32. E. Terray, 1972, *Marxism and Primitive Societies* (trans. Mary Kolpper), New York; M. Godelier, 1977, *Perspectives in Marxist Anthropology*, Cambridge; J. Friedman and M.J. Rowlands (eds), 1977, *The Evolution of Social Systems*, London.
33. K. Sivathamby, 'Early South Indian Society and Economy: The *Tinai* Concept'; Rajan Gurukkal, 'Forms of Production ...'.

34. Rajan Gurukkal, 'Forms of Production...; Gurukkal and M.R.R. Varier (eds), 1999, *Cultural History of Kerala*, Vol. I. Thiruvananthapuram.
35. M.G.S Narayanan, 1982, 'Warrior Settlements in the Sangam Age', *IHC Proceedings*, Delhi.
36. R. Gurukkal and M.R.R. Varier, *Cultural History*.
37. Ronald E. Miller, 1976, *Mappila Muslims of Kerala; A Study in Islamic Trends*, New Delhi.
38. K.N. Panikkar, 1990, *Against Lord and State*, New Delhi.
39. G. Arunima, 2003, *There Comes Papa: Colonialism and the Transformation of Matriliny in Kerala, Malabar c. 1850–1940*, New Delhi; Praveena Kodoth, 2001, 'Gender, Family and Property Rights: Questions from Kerala's Land Reforms', *Indian Journal of Gender Studies*, 8(2): 291–306; J. Devika,1999, 'En-gendering Individuals: A Study of Gender and Individualisation in Reform Language in Modern Keralam, 1880–1950', Mahatma Gandhi University, Kottayam, subsequently published in 2006 as *Engendering Individuals: The Language of Re-forming in Early 20th Century Keralam*, Hyderabad; Susan Thomas, 2004, 'Property Relations and Family Forms in Colonial Kerala', Unpublished PhD thesis, Mahatma Gandhi University.
40. Philippo Osella and Caroline Osella, 2000, *Social Mobility in Kerala: Modernity and Identity in Conflict*, London.
41. Sanal Mohan, 2005, 'Imagining Equality: Modernity and Social Transformation of Lower Castes in Colonial Kerala', Unpublished PhD thesis, Mahatma Gandhi University.

3

Semiotics of Ancient Tamil Poetics

A Methodological Consideration

This chapter discusses the semiotics of the homologous relationship between nature and the culture[1] of ancient Dravidians who inhabited the southern half of the Indian peninsula, as self-sustaining descent groups adapted to different ecosystems that characterized the landscape during a couple of centuries before and after the Christian era. '*Dravid*' becomes Tamil in the regional rendering, making Dravidians and Tamils interchangeable terms in the present context. A large body of ancient Tamil heroic poems broadly belonging to oral tradition and roughly dating back to the turn of the Christian era, has come down to us as edited, redacted, and anthologized collections.[2] These collections of heroic poems have plenty of proof showing the fundamental semiotic relationships of ancient Dravidians to ecotypes of their subsistence and survival.[3] The poems also abound in evidence of ecosemiotic aspects unique to the Dravidian culture.[4] The texts of the poems, their classificatory syntactics, and cultural semantics embody several characteristic signs drawn from specific ecosystems upon which the ancient Dravidians intimately depended for subsistence. They show how signs and processes of semiosis express the way humans interact with their environment for existence. Therefore, the prime area of analytical focus in the chapter is the intertextuality of the Tamil heroic poems/poetics and contemporary socio-cultural practices. It is the signal character of the cultural behaviour of nature-dependent peoples that constitutes the central concern of this discussion, while an appraisal of ecosemiosis in the various cultural contexts and situations of everyday life of the ancient Dravidians is the objective.

This chapter examines the homologous formation of ecological signs out of ecosystems and their subsequent cultural signification in linguistic and aesthetic practices of peoples adapted to different ecosystems.[5] The main focus is on the characteristic signs that spontaneously evolved from the processes of the subsistence or survival dependence of people on specific ecosystems, which are indicative of the holistic view of the universe, emphasizing the unity of human beings with their natural environment. It examines correspondences between the objects of the ecosystem and aspects of the culture.

ECOTYPES AND HUMAN ADAPTATIONS

The hillocks of Venkatam in the north, the cape of Kanyakumari in the south, and the long seashore in the east and west demarcated the geographical core of the Dravidian culture in the Indian peninsula. It has been a landscape of multiple ecotypes such as the coast, river basins, forested hills, grassy highlands, and dry zones, interspersed with one another. This geophysical reality is ecosemiotically encoded in the topography of the Dravidian poetics, whose *locus classicus* embodies the concept of the five terrains (*aintiṇai*), according to which the Tamil macro region (*Tamilakam*) consisted of five distinct ecotypes. These were the forested hills (*kuṛiñji*), dryland (*pālai*), pastoral tracts (*mullai*), wetlands (*marutam*), and littoral (*neital*)[6]. Among these ecotypes, the dry land is viewed as a seasonal phenomenon along parts of hilly backwoods and pastoral tracts. The poetics conceive of pālai as an ephemeral eco-situation contingent upon seasonal changes that lead to kuṛijñji and *mullai* tracts going dry. This would suggest that only four ecotypes (*nanilam*) existed as permanent features. There is no rigidity in the topology about its physiographic compartmentalization into five independent segments. While the parts of nature are perceived as five discontinuous segments, the whole is viewed as a continuum too. Where exactly an ecotype begins and where it ends cannot be demarcated since each one merges with the other.

Prescriptions in the poetics comprise specifications of the people inhabiting each landscape ecotype and the mode of human adaptation there. In the forested hill tracts (*kuṛiñji*), forest tribes such as *kuṛavar*, *paṛayar*, *vēṭṭuvar*, *kaṭampar*, and *vēṭar* are mentioned as the main inhabitants and hunting and gathering their mode of adaptation. They practised shifting cultivation too.

In the dryland ecotype (*pālai*), a marauding tribe called *maṛavar* were the inhabitants and cattle lifting their principal means of subsistence. Certain localities with a parched eco-system as their permanent character, especially in the summer, remained non-productive throughout the year, attracting hardly any settlements. The poems show that the absence of settlements and dearth of drinking water, as well as wild beasts and fire added to the adversity of the terrain. However, wayfarers had to cross these inhospitable tracts, which became a congenial situation for marauders or armed clans such as the *maṛavar* who plundered them. This precarious situation necessitated the services of armed personages to protect travellers from robbers, which meant that both plunder and protection were the means of subsistence in the pālai ecotype.

Pastoral tribes such as the *iṭaiyar* lived in the grassland ecotypes (*mullai*), with animal husbandry and shifting cultivation as the means of living, while clans such as *uḻavar* and *toḻuvar* inhabited the wetland ecotype (*marutam*) with plough agriculture as their means of existence. The fishing clan called *paratavar* were the inhabitants of the ecotype (*neital*) along the coastal tracts and the banks of inland waterbodies, fishing and salt extraction being their means of subsistence. A tribe called the *pāṇar*, who were wandering bards, are mentioned as inhabitants in all the ecotypes, making their living through singing and dancing, as did a group called *pulavar*, scholarly bards who could be found in all terrains too. Another group, mostly of functionaries associated with chiefly houses were the *porunar*, who assumed multiple functions such as those of the bard, actor, singer, warrior, and even of a chieftain. Similarly, a clan called the *kāṇi*, who took to astrology, was to be seen everywhere irrespective of geographical differences. In the pastoral and agrarian ecotypes, there were several bonded labourers (*vinaivalar*) placed at the service of chiefly households. In the areas where ecotypes merged, the inhabitants as well as their forms of subsistence were mixed.

HISTORICITY

Prescriptions in the poetics have been found true to contemporary life in the light of allusions in the heroic poems.[7] We may not see a one to one correspondence between an ecotype with its pattern of human adaptation as prescribed in the poetics and the historical milieu of the times because reality cannot be an orderly format, unlike its theoretical abstraction found in the poetics. Nonetheless, there is a great deal of historicity about what the poetics abstracted, as numerous allusions in the poems corroborate. Just as the ecotypes in their natural settings did not have clearly drawn boundaries, the patterns of human adaptation to them were mutually overlapping.

The poems provide a broad grouping of the five ecotypes into two: the small agrarian zone (*menpulam*), which produced paddy and sugarcane as the main crops and the large non-agrarian zone (*vanpulam*) with pulses and dryland grains such as millet, sesame, and horse-gram as the main crops. Apart from allusions in the poems, the historicity is further established by the fact that most of the tribal or clan names of the inhabitants mentioned in the poems have survived to our times in the region, as caste names with anthropological and ethnographic veracity show.

Judging from the songs pertaining to the *kuṛiñji* tract, the most important agricultural activity of the people was the slash-and-burn cultivation of millet on the hill slopes. A large number of songs refer to this cultivation and the various stages of it. One of the stages frequently mentioned in the poems is preparation of the soil by the slash-and-burn method. Other stages are tilling the land with an iron-tipped stick, channelling water to the millet field, and scaring off birds and animals from the crop. Millet was the staple food of the *kuṛiñji* people though paddy was not unknown, for its cultivation is attested by poems. Tubers, sugarcane, and peas were also cultivated along the hill tracts.

The allusions in the poems corroborate the prescriptions about the *mullai* terrain and the pattern of human adaptation in the ecotype. They refer to the pastoral people called *iṭaiyar* who were sheep/goat farmers as well as cattle-keepers. However, there were no full-time pastoral nomads in any of the *mullai* ecotypes of the Tamil region. The people in this ecosystem were by and large agro-pastoralists of brief or temporary transhumance, adapted to the slash-and-burn mode of cultivation but not without instances of repeated tilling, sowing, and reaping in the same plots. Interestingly, some poems refer to herdsmen as tillers as well. It is learnt from the poems that millet was extensively cultivated in the mullai tract. Both *kuṛiñji* and *mullai* had cultivable slopes at their merging zones that enabled inhabitants to take to shifting cultivation. Similarly, people in the *mullai-marutam* blending zones seem to have practised spinning and weaving and those in the *neital-marutam* blending zones, pot-making. Metal smelting seems to have been important in both the zones.

There are plenty of allusions in the poems to *marutam* as well-irrigated agrarian tracts fit for the cultivation of sugarcane and paddy, confined to small pockets of natural wetlands or river plains surrounded by large tracts of other ecotypes. The poems refer to ploughmen (*uḻavar*), hard labourers (vinaivalar), tillers (toḻuvar), and other agricultural people who constituted the main settlers of the terrain engaged in rice and sugarcane cultivation. As advanced agricultural areas, the *marutam* tracts attracted people from other ecotypes. Since *marutam* was the ecosystem of plough agriculture, it required the services of various artisans and craftsmen, whose existence in the terrain is attested by the poems. We have enough evidence in the poems to show that surplus in the ecotype was large enough to sustain a variety of socially necessary functionaries such as preceptors, bards, dancers, magicians, physicians, and astrologers.

In the poems, the sea-coast alone is not the terrain recognized as neital, but it denotes landscapes around natural water sources like lakes, rivers, and backwaters. The Tamil macro landscape is blessed with its extensive coastline rich in lagoons, backwaters, and estuaries and quite naturally, the poems refer to peoples who inhabited this area pursuing economic activities appropriate to the natural resources. A feature of the southern coastlines of the Indian peninsula is that the water levels are relatively low. In most places this shallowness facilitated the movements of tiny boats, though it prevented large vessels from entering the ports. Poems mention *paratavar*, the main inhabitants, engaged in fishing and salt manufacturing in the terrain and they are mentioned in the poems as pearl-divers as well. Apart from the main activities, some of the *paratavar* were engaged in gathering conch-shells. It is relevant to recall here that bangles made of conch-shells are reported from south Indian megalithic burials and poems allude to their production as among the major economic activities of the terrain. A group of full-time salt merchants, who frequented the neital with kith and kin to cart salt to the interior, finds frequent mention in the poems. The most archaic and basic geographical unit in the region was *ūr*, which meant a kin-based settlement consisting of a few families (*kuṭis*) living in small huts (*kurampu*) in a cluster, whose archaeology goes back to the Neolithic times. We understand from the poems that each ūr was too small to be clearly seen from a distance, though they were distinguished as big and small as well as old and new, spread across the diverse ecosystems. Settlements rose in the river valley and wetland ecosystems near other waterbodies. The poems mention numerous small but prosperous settlements in the marutam ecotypes. There are references in the poems to such settlements located in the neital and mullai ecosystems as well, though not abundantly. Each ūr was under the *kiḻār*, the headman of the descent group, who lived in a slightly bigger hut. Numerous settlements along the multiple eco-types around a hill constituted a macro geographical entity called *nādu* as a culturally constructed spatiality within the forest (*kāṭu*). However, this cultural spatiality was not yet clearly distinct from the forest since the former remained subsumed by the latter. In the agrarian wetland ecotypes, the contrast with the forest was explicit.

HISTORIOGRAPHY

So far, the ecosemiotics of the topology enunciated in the Tamil heroic poetics has not been a topic of hermeneutic interest in historiography or literary criticism. The author of *Tolkāppiyam*, the earliest of Tamil grammatical treatises, focuses only on the aspect of literary conventions apparent in the poetics, for obvious reasons. Likewise, his medieval commentators also confine themselves solely to its linguistic and literary aspects as the scope of their task warrants. Some modern scholars did evince an interest in the social and cultural implications of the topological aesthetics mentioned in the Tamil heroic poetics. It was Pandit Raghava Iyengar,[8] a Tamil scholar of the early twentieth century, who made an effort to establish a connection between the behavioural pattern prescribed for the landscape ecotype (*tiṇai*) in the poetics and contemporary social needs, viewing the latter as causing the genesis of aesthetic conventions. P.T. Srinivasa Iyengar,[9] another early scholar, thought that the topological concept in the poetics was an illustration of the evolution of the Dravidian civilization. To him it revealed the spread of the Tamils from the hills and mountains to the low-lying plains. According to V.R. Ramachandra Dikshitar,[10] yet another scholar of the early twentieth century, the landscape-based poetic conventions related to the pre-history of the Tamils. Several others, including geographers and anthropologists, held that the fivefold landscape types threw light on the origins and development of human culture.[11] Kamil Zvelebil, a recent authority in the subject, takes the landscape division as reflecting the historical migration of pre- and proto-Dravidian Tamil population from the hills and jungles to the fertile plains and to the seaboard. In other words, it meant the development from the Neolithic hunter, through the intermediate stage of the keeper of the flocks, to the settled tiller of the soil and fisherman.[12] N. Subrahmanian, a specialist on the socio-economic and political history of the ancient Tamil poems, takes the fivefold geographical division-based behavioural prescriptions in the poetics, as an allusion to 'stages of evolution' in the world proto-history. He found no sense in importing the concept into the history of the Tamil region.[13] These views clearly vouch for the fact that the previous scholars followed the general perspective of a unilinear development of society and culture, and hardly ever bothered to adhere rigorously to social theoretical insights. K. Sivathampi, a Tamil scholar of Sri Lanka, has argued in a recent study that the poetic prescriptions about the contexts, moods, and human-nature situations relate to contemporary socio-economic and cultural reality.[14]

A few scholars like Blanka Knotková-Capkova, A. Dubiansky, E. Wilden, and J. Vacek, have studied the encoded presence of nature in the ancient Tamil poetic canon, analysing the symbolism, especially of metaphorical representations of nature in aesthetic practices.[15] Their studies have encountered problems of identification of plants, their proper designations, alternatives, and multiple meanings and appraised some of the features of the semiotic system embedded in the Tamil heroic poems. The present discussion embodies the pioneering attempt at exploring the ecosemiotics of the Tamil heroic poetics and the historical context of homology between ecotypes and ancient Dravidian culture. It is the first time an endeavour has been made to study the ancient Dravidian ecosemiosis through the juxtaposition of the history of the Tamil peoples' dependence on the environment with their literary and aesthetic conventions.

ECOSYSTEM SIGNIFIERS

The construal of a twofold division of the ecosemiotic plane into primary and secondary parts emerges out of the preceding discussion of the landscape ecosystems and their characteristic plants. In the primary semiosic plane, it is a syntagmatic or straight-line semantic schema of direct symbolization of nature in terms of the ecosystem through a characteristic plant endemic to it.[16] The names of the previously mentioned five ecotypes, which are names of their characteristic plants, exemplify this. In the secondary semiosic plane, it is a paradigmatic or metaphorical semantic schema of indirect symbolization of culture through the characteristic features of human adaptation to the ecosystem.[17] One has to examine these syntagmatic and paradigmatic levels of signification in detail to know the ecosemiosic context under review.

As already noted, each of the five terrains or ecotypes conceived in the Tamil heroic poetics derives its name from a plant endemic to the ecosystem. The terrain of hilly backwoods derived its name from *kuṛiñji*, a species of shrub vegetation (*Strobilanthus*), which blooms once in twelve years. The plant is considered symbolic of an ecosystem abounding in forest-clad hills and slopes, with streams and tiny waterfalls. Landscapes with hills, open terraces, and high altitude grasslands were called *mullai*, which is a species of a tree (*Perris brevipis*) symbolic of the ecosystem. The name *marutam* given to the terrain of the wet-rice ecosystem, generally characterized by the alluvial tracts along the riverbanks, is derived from a tree in the wetlands often called *nirmarutu* (*Terminalia paniculata*) that is symbolic of the ecosystem. In the Tamil region, the term denotes well-irrigated agrarian tracts fit for the cultivation of sugarcane and paddy. *Neital* is a flowering plant, a kind of water lily (*Nymphaea stellata*), endemic to waterlogged and marshy tracts and, therefore, symbolic of the ecosystem. The seacoast alone is not the terrain recognized as *neital*, but also landscapes around natural water sources such as rivers and backwaters. *Pālai* is the name of a tree (*Alstonia scholaris*), which is typical of the parched zones and therefore, considered symbolic of the ecosystem.

It is not just the landscape ecotype alone that the plant signs are symbolic of but the culture as a whole that subsumes the human relationship to ecological existence and the ecological relationship to human existence, as the homologically intertwined nexus. This ecosemiotic dimension of the larger cultural whole is evident in the poetics' prescriptive attribution of certain features as specific to every landscape-ecosystem. The attributions in the poetics consist of three aspects: of space and time (*mutal*), of subsistence activities, food, deity, flora, fauna, musical instruments, and such other matters (*karu*), and of social behaviour (*uri*) involving the situations of love (*akam*) and combat (*puṛam*). In short, they encompassed the entire universe of human life. The implicit processes are those of socio-economic and cultural reality carried forward to poetics and subsequently stipulated as prescriptions for literary and aesthetic practice.

ECO-AESTHETIC CODING

A section (*Poruḷatikāram*) in the earliest Tamil grammatical treatise (*Tolkāppiyam*) clearly shows that an elaborate syntactic convention was in vogue among poets and singers all over the Tamil region in the early centuries of the Christian era that marked the prevalence of oral versification by bards. Generally, bards displayed a mastery over a vast repertoire of elements of poetic composition, consisting of set phrases, allegorical expressions, and ready-made rhymes with which they made instant verses by literally piecing together constituents almost like garland making. The Tamil bards (*pāṇar*) were full-time singers of heroic exploits, extolling the might and mien of warriors and chieftains. The term *pāṇar* literally meant a singer but it indicated a hereditary community that possessed, preserved, and transmitted the resources and craft of oral compositions. On the whole, the bard was a poor man, his life was solitary and devoted to roaming around settlements in diverse ecosystems singing praises of the headmen. The situation of scholarly *brāhmaṇa* poets, who moved like professional bards too, was not far different. This comparability accounts for the prevalence of a common ecosemiosic field in contemporary cultural semantics. The scholars who collected, redacted, grouped, and anthologized the bardic compositions could easily constitute a classificatory syntactic system for their tasks. Nonetheless, it is not reasonable to presume that the syntactic codes as a formally enunciated system preceded the compositions, enabling all the bards to be cohesive about the structure and composition of their verses. Just as prescriptive articulation of grammatical rules is a sequel to spontaneously evolved practices, syntactic codes of poetics must have been theoretical prescriptions abstracted out of conventions.

The formation of ecological signs as a direct outcome of the interrelationship between nature and processes of human subsistence or survival strategies, which is eminently durable and substantial, transcends its metonymic structure and enters a higher cognitive process of allegorical relations. Here the dyadic relation becomes triadic through metaphorical extensions to the regime of aesthetic practices, heralding a fertile field of ecosemiotics.[18] Each ecotype metaphorically symbolized a specific emotion in the aesthetics of romanticism, as its overall ecological setting would spontaneously inspire. For instance, *kuṛiñji* is symbolic of the libidinal passion of lovers enjoying the undisturbed union that the ecological setting of the forest quite naturally evokes; the *mullai* represents patient waiting for the lover, a mood that the pastoral expanse conjures up; the *marutam* is symbolic of hatred coming out of distrust, a temperament that agrarian tracts excite; the *pālai* stands for the frustration with which the dryland fills the mind; and the *neital* is symbolic of anxiety that the littoral fuels up. The classificatory syntactics of the Tamil heroic poetics, applied for dividing, sorting out, and arranging the poems into anthologies of specific features of identity, profusely exemplifies it. The syntactics embody the ecosemiotic sign system carrying features of nature into cultural semantics through linguistic and aesthetic practices. It is necessary here to subject the classificatory syntactics to further probing.

CLASSIFICATORY SYNTACTICS

In order to group the Tamil heroic poems in terms of the nature of their content, context, and mood, two broad classificatory categories were adopted: one based on the dual concept of inside (*akam*) and outside (*puṛam*), and the other based on the dual concept of terrain (tiṇai) and port (*tuṛai*). The first duality, made up of the two metaphors literally meaning the 'inside' and the 'outside', figuratively signified the feelings in the mind and heart and actions or activities out there as part of contemporary life, respectively. It is metasemiotic. The second, made up of the two metaphors literally meaning the 'terrain' and 'port' figuratively signified 'the situation' and 'context' respectively, which is ecosemiotic. Here the ecosemiotic duality alone deserves elaboration, for obvious reasons. The ecosemiotic dual concept of *tiṇai* and *tuṛai* has given rise to several sign-combinations, each as a sub-category accommodating poems of specific thematic identity.

Eleven sub-categories of ecosemiotic signs have evolved from the concept of the *tiṇai.* These include: (a) *tumpaittiṇai* (the terrain of the plant, *tumpai,* or *Leucas aspera*) accommodating the poems versifying the situation of warriors getting ready for a raid; (b) *vañjittiṇai* (the terrain of the plant, *vanji,* or *Salix tetrasperma*) accommodating poems in praise of warriors arriving to raid the enemy's settlement; (c) *kāñjittiṇai* (the terrain of the plant, *kānji,* or *Scolopia schreberi*) encompassing poems singing the defence against a raid; (d) *noccittiṇai* (the terrain of the plant, *nocci,* or *Vitex trifolia*) including poems praising warriors guarding the wall; (e) *veṭcittiṇai* (the terrain of the plant *veṭci* or *Ixora coccinea*) accommodating poems in praise of the cattle raid; (f) *karantaittiṇai* (the terrain of the plant, *karantai,* or *Anisomeles malabarica*) including poems in praise of the fight to recover raided cattle; (g) *vākaittaiṇi* (the terrain of the plant, *vākai,* or *Albezia lebbek*) containing poems extolling the devastation and martial rejoicing after a cattle raid; and (h) *uḻiñjaittiṇai* (the terrain of the plant, *uḻiñjai,* or *Cardiospermum halicacabum*) including poems in praise of warriors returning after a raid. All these are instances of invoking the dyadic relation between ecotypes and plants common in them. The relation is carried forward to the metaphorical plane of ecosemiosis as evident in the cultural practice of the warriors wearing the flower of the aforementioned plants symbolically on their heads: namely, tumpai (*Leucas aspera*), *vañji* (*Salix tetrasperma*), *kāñji* (*Scolopia schreberi*), *nocci* (*Vitex trifolia*), *veṭci* (*Ixora coccinea*), *karantai* (*Anisomeles malabarica*), *vākai* (*Albezia lebbek*), and *uḻinjai* (*Cardiospermum halicacabum*). The warriors wore the flowers as the avowal signs of the actions and moods glorified in the poems. Two sub-categories namely, *kaikkiḷaittiṇai* and *perumtiṇai,* accommodate poems dealing with one-sided love and incompatible love, respectively. There are two instances of using tiṇai as an ecosemiotic classificatory syntagm in a generic sense as seen in the category of the terrain of bards (*pāṭāntiṇai*) accommodating poems praising a hero's might, mien, and munificence, and the other, the terrain of common traits (*potuviyalttiṇai*) containing poems dealing with traits common to all the *tiṇai*s.

The number of sub-categories of the classificatory syntagm evolved under the ecosemiotic sign *tuṛai,* is almost six times larger than those under the sign *tiṇai*. They can be grouped into the following seven clusters of closely related meanings:

1. The *tuṛai*s accommodating the poems in praise of individual heroism, such as *aracavākaittuṛai* with poems praising a heroic chief; *tānainilaitturai* with poems extolling the heroism shown by the fighters as well as the fought; *ceṛumalaitaltturai* with poems in praise of a hero's fierce fight against the cattle lifters; *nallicaivanjitturai* with poems praising a hero's march with an intrinsic potential of devastation; *aḷilaṭṭutturai* with poems telling the tale of a hero destroying the enemies with a spear pulled out from his own chest; *piḷḷaippeyarcittuṛai* with poems extolling a hero's courage in ignoring evil omens; *makaṭpārkañjittuṛai* with poems praising a small chief's courage in denying his daughter even to a chieftain of the highest order (*vēntar*) seeking to marry her; *makanmaruttaltturai* with poems praising the courage of lower-ranked chief in saying no to a hero asking for his daughter; *erumaimaṛamtuṛai* with poems applauding a hero's single-handed fight against his enemies; *veṭṭiyaltturai* with poems on the heroes praising the chief; and *vāḻttiyaltturai* with poems in praise of the chief.
2. The *tuṛai*s including poems extolling the family tradition and heritage of a hero, such as *ēṛānmullaittuṛai* with poems praising the family tradition of a hero; *kuṭinilaiyuraittaltturai* with poems praising the heroic tradition of a warrior family; *mutalvañjittuṛai* with poems praising a warrior's ancestral tradition of heroic exploits; *vallānmullaittuṛai* with poems praising the place and family of a hero; *neṭumoḻitturai* with poems on a hero in praise of his achievements; and *mutinmullaittuṛai* with poems praising the warrior-families by depicting even their womenfolk as innately courageous.
3. The *tuṛai*s accommodating poems extolling the virtues of raids for plunder, such as *malapuḻavañjittuṛai* with poems versifying the raid and devastation of settlements; *koṛṛavaḷḷaittuṛai* with poems expressing grief in the plight of the devastated as an indirect way of praising a hero for his cattle raid; *ērkaḷavuruvakamtuṛai* with poems singing of battlefields with agricultural imagery; *marakkaḷavaḻittuṛai* with poems allegorically extolling the chief as a ploughman and; *vānmankalamttuṛai* with poems praising the power of a hero's sword.

4. The *tuṟai*s accommodating the poems on the collective passion of the communities for raids, such as *unṭāṭṭutuṟai* with poems versifying the context of collective drinking and dining by the warrior folk before setting out for a raid; *peruncōṟṟunilaittuṟai* with poems praising the rice feast offered to the warrior folk; *talaittōrramtuṟai* with poems on the context of collective rejoicing at the news of a hero bringing cattle as booty; *uvakaikkaluḻccittuṟai* with poems in praise of a wife shedding tears of joy as she feels proud of his bravery; *anantappaiyulttuṟai* with poems condoling the widow on the death of her heroic husband; *mutuppālaittuṟai* with poems condoling the loneliness of the widow; *tāpanilaittuṟai* with poems condoling the death of a woman's husband.
5. The *tuṟai*s accommodating the poems glorifying the heroic death of chiefs, such as *ceṟuviṭaiviḻttaltturai* with poems praising the heroic defence by warrior chiefs; *pānpāṭṭutturai* with poems versifying the bards' death song for the deceased hero.
6. The *tuṟai*s containing the poems extolling the chief's generosity in giving gifts, such as *iyanmoḻivāḻttutturai* with poems praising the munificence of a chief; *pāṇāṟṟuppaṭaitturai* with poems praising the generosity of a chief and urging the bard to go to him; *viṟaliyāṟṟuppaṭaitturai* with poems praising the generosity of a chief and persuading a female bard (*viṟali*) to go to him; *pulavarāṟṟuppaṭaitturai* with poems praising a chieftain's generosity in order to secure specific gifts; *vāḻttutturai* with poems in praise of the generosity of the chief.
7. The *tuṟai*s accommodating poems containing pieces of advice in higher values and virtues stressing the need for peace, security, and welfare of the people, such as *ceviyaṟivuṟutuṟai* with poems offering advice to the chieftain for the maintenance of peace, order, and security; *porunmoḻikkañcitturai* with poems versifying the context of advice to the chieftain about the secret of strength; *perunkāñjitturai* with poems appraising the chieftain about the transient nature of the worldly life; *mutumoḻikkāñjitturai* with poems conversing on ethics (*puruṣārtha*s like *dharma*, *artha*, and *kāma*); *manaiyaṟamtuṟai* with poems distinguishing between ascetic and domestic lives; *tāpatavākaitturai* with poems singing about the routine of an ascetic; *kaṭavulvāḻttutturai* with poems praising god, and *pārppanavākaitturai* with poems praising *brāhmaṇa*s and their rituals.

THE ECOSEMIOSIC REFERENT

The central semiosic referent here is the cultural milieu of the Tamil heroic society characterized by predatory marches of chieftains, booty-capture, redistribution, and roaming of bards singing the heroic exploits. All cultural practices, ideas, and institutions revolved round heroism and everything was subservient to the glorification of heroism. All institutional forms and cultural practices of the period vouch for the hegemony of the heroic ideology. The nature of deities and modes of worship in the various tiṇais is a pointer to the hegemony of the heroic ideology. The principal object of worship in the dominant ecotypes was the hero-stone erected on the wayside on the spot where a hero was killed in battle and which the local people and wayfarers decorated with peacock feathers and red flowers and worshipped. Other deities were *Cēyōn* or *Murukan* (the hunter god) of the *kuṟiñji*, *Māyōn* (the cowherd god) of the mullai, *Vēntan* (the warrior god) of the marutam and *Kaṭalōn* (the sea god) of the *neital*, all signifying, in varying degrees, the values of heroic ideology. The peoples believed in *ananku*, an evil spirit, and tried to propitiate it through various rites. They followed various magico-religious practices, such as soothsaying, observance of omens, and a variety of fasting. A large number of brahmanical customs also go back to the period. In fact, the brahmanical and non-brahmanical rites had a comingled existence during the period, often making it difficult to distinguish them. The dress and ornaments of the peoples varied from tiṇai to *tiṇai*. In *kuṟiñji*, the costume was *taḻayuṭai* made up mainly of leaves, bark, and flowers. Even chieftains wore bark and leaves on the body and head. Most of the people wore garlands made of flowers. Poems mention peacock feathers, tender leaves, and flower garlands as ornaments of both the living and the dead in the *kuṟiñji* and *mullai* tracts. The peoples of the other *tiṇai*s seem to have used cotton but generally its use must have been marginal. Similarly, they knew of ornaments made of gold and studded with precious stones and pearls, though the most common ones were those made out of conch shells, horns, bones, and glass.

To conclude, the central argument of this discussion is that the aesthetic prescriptions of the ancient Tamil heroic poetics vouch for a distinct homology between nature and contemporary Dravidian culture. The next argument is that the homology can be historicized in the light of allusions of the poems, which show the cultural milieu of the Tamil heroic society, the central semiosic referent. The subsequent argument is that the sign process has a trajectory starting with the homologous formation of ecological signs out of ecosystems and their subsequent cultural signification in linguistic and aesthetic practices. What emerges out of the analysis of the trajectory is the construal of a two-fold division of the ecosemiosic plane into primary and secondary parts: the primary semiosic plane of a syntagmatic or straight-line semantic schema of direct symbolization of nature in terms of the ecosystem and the secondary semiosic plane of a paradigmatic or metaphorical semantic schema of indirect symbolization of culture. The last point is that this approach is a fruitful historiographic exercise.

NOTES AND REFERENCES

1. The central interest of ecological semiotics may be *organismus semioticus* rather than *homo semioticus*, but in this chapter, the nature–culture homology is treated as more fundamental. See W. Enninger and W. Karl-Heinz, 1984, 'Language ecology revisited: From language ecology to sign ecology', in W. Enninger and L.M. Haynes (eds), *Studies in Language Ecology*, Wiesbaden, pp. 29–50; Yrjo Haila, 1986, 'On the semiotic dimension of ecological theory', *Biology and Philosophy*, 1: 377–87; Paul Bouissac, 1989, 'What is a human? Ecological semiotics and the new animism', *Semiotica*, 77: 497–516. Also see Paul Bouissac, 1993, 'Ecology of semiotic space', *American Journal of Semiotics*, 10: 145–65. For a comprehensive appraisal of all dimensions, see the discussions in the special issue on *Nature, Environment, and Signs* of *Zeitschrift für Semiotik*, 1996, 18.1; Winfried Noth, 1998, 'Ecosemiotics', *Sign Systems Studies*, 26: 332–43.
2. U.V. Swamynatha Iyer has edited and published the texts of idylls and anthologies belonging to the Tamil heroic poems during 1955–7. *Kuṛuntokai* (1955), *Kuṛiñjippāṭṭu* (1956), *Maduraikkānchi* (1956), *Malaippaṭukādam* (1956), *Mullaippāṭṭu* (1956), *Nedunalvādai* (1956), *Paripādal* (1956), *Paṭṭiṇappālai* (1956), *Perumpān Āttuppadai* (1956), *Porunar Attuppadai* (1956), *Puṛānanūṛu* (1956), *Ciṛupān Āttuppaḍai* (1956), *Padirruppattu* (1957), *Ainkuṛunūṛu* (1957) are the main texts belonging to the *Pattuppāṭṭu* and *Eṭṭuttokai* groups that he edited and published by the Saivasidhanta Kazhakam, Madurai.
3. K. Kailasapathy, 1968, *Tamil Heroic Poetry*, London. Also see George L. Hart, 1979, *Poets of the Tamil Anthologies: Ancient Poems of Love and War*, Princeton.
4. S. Bavanandan Pillai, 1916, *Tolkāppiyam. Poruḻatikāram*, Madras.
5. Kalevi Kull, 1998, 'Semiotic Ecology: Different Natures in the Semiosphere', *Sign Systems Studies*, vol. 26, pp. 344–71.
6. S. Bavanandan Pillai, *Tolkāppiyam. Poruḻatikāram.*
7. Rajan Gurukkal, 1989, 'Forms of Production and Forces of Change in Ancient Tamil Society', *Studies in History*, 5(2): 159–75.
8. Raghava Iyengar, 1917, *Tolkāppiya Poruḻatikāra Araicci*, Madras.
9. P.T. Srinivasa Iyengar, 1929, *History of the Tamils*, Madras.

10. V.R. Ramachandra Dikshitar, 1936, *Studies in Tamil Literature and History*, Madras.
11. Xavier S. Thaninayakam, 1966, *Landscape and Poetry*, London.
12. K. Zvelebil, 1973, 'The Earliest Account of the Tamil Academies', *Indo-Iranian Journal*, 15(2): 109–35.
13. N. Subrahmanian, 1966, *Sangam Polity: The Administration and Social Life of the Sangam Tamils*, Bombay.
14. K. Sivathamby, 1974, 'Early South Indian Society and Economy', *Social Scientist*, vol. 29, pp. 20–37.
15. See Blanka Knotková-Capkova, 1999 'Some Remarks on Literary Analysis of the Symbolical Patterns in Ancient Tamil Poetry', in Jaroslav Vacek and Blanka Knotkova-Capkova (eds), *Flower, Nature, Semiotics: Kavya and Sangham. Journal of South Asia Women Studies*, 5(2). For a discussion of the symbolic meaning and problems of contradiction in the traditional interpretation, see A. Dubianski, 2002, 'The themes of *uḻiñjai* and *nocci* in classical Tamil poetry', in J. Vacek and Hana Preinhaelterová (eds), *Nature in Indian Literatures and Art*, Signeta E. Wilden seeks to examine the overall context of the symbolic code in the Tamil heroic literature and explain the complex nature of symbolic expression. See his 'Anthropomorphic nature: the symbolic code of *Akam* poetry'. J. Vacek probes into the symbolic meaning assigned to the *mullai* flower. See his 'Old Tamil literary formulae connected with *mullai* (attributive phrases)'. Also see his 2002, *Literary Clichés in Sangam: On the Syntagmatics and Symbolism of Neytal*', in *Archiv Orientální*, 70. Subsequently, he has edited studies in various aspects of the Tamil nature symbolism. See J. Vacek (ed.), 2003, *Nature as Symbolic Code in Old Tamil Love Poetry*', Prague.
16. For aspects of conceptualization, see Enninger *et al.*, 1984, 'Language ecology revisited: From language ecology to sign ecology', in Enninger and L.M. Haynes (eds), *Studies in Language Ecology*, Wiesbaden, pp. 29–50. Also Alf Hornborg, 1996, 'Ecology as semiotics: Outlines of a contextualist paradigm for human ecology', in P. Descola and G. Pálsson (eds), *Nature and Society: Anthropological Perspectives*, London, pp. 45–62.
17. See the concepts enunciated in I.G. Simmons, 1993, *Interpreting Nature: Cultural Constructions of the Environment*, London. Also Alf Hornborg, 1996, 'Ecology as semiotics: Outlines of a contextualist paradigm for human ecology', in Philippe Descola and Gisli Pálsson (eds), *Nature and Society: Anthropological Perspectives*, London, pp. 45–62.
18. Winfried Noth, 1994, 'Introduction', in W. Noth (ed.), *Origins of Semiosis*, Berlin, pp. 1–12.

SECTION II

Early Social Formations

4

Prehistoric Life in the Southern Western Ghats

Interpreting Rock-art*

Ever since the discovery of the first hoard of palaeolithic tools from Pallavaram in Madras as early as in 1863 by Robert Bruce Foote, archaeologists have been contributing to the knowledge about prehistoric India through discoveries and explorations of a number of Stone Age sites in different parts of India.[1] A few sites have yielded scientific dating according to which the available lower antiquity is about five lakh years. Kerala was put on the archaeological map of Indian prehistory only recently, thanks to the efforts of a few archaeologists who are specialists in Stone Age studies. Protected and insulated by the Western Ghats and the Arabian Sea, Kerala was seen as a land strip in isolation that was not inhabited by the Old Stone Age people. The long delay in the discovery of Old Stone Age relics in Kerala was due to the scarcity of investigations in the province by competent archaeologists, which was primarily due to the attitude about the discovery of Old Stone Age tools, taking it for granted that it was quite unlikely to find any, a mentality to a great extent contingent upon the often exaggerated geographical isolation thesis.[2] Isolation is a notion rooted in the consciousness of a sedentary life and therefore anachronistic in the context of the nomadic prehistoric people for whom the high ranges and seas seldom meant geographical barriers. It is a widely attested fact that the Old Stone Age peoples were on a never-ending search for habitats, searching all suitable geo-climatic

* Part of this chapter is a reproduction of, 1997, 'The Edakal Rock Engravings: Morphology and Meanings', *Studies in Humanities and Social Sciences*, 4(1): 43–60.

regions, making it more or less a rule that no part of the globe ideal for their existence had been left uninhabited by them.

Towards the middle of the nineteenth century, Todd had made a major discovery of a hoard of microliths at Chevayur, near the present-day city of Kozhikode (Calicut) in Kerala. Recently the late Stone Age tools and tool material in quartz have been discovered at Anjilora, close to Chevayur, and at Kuppakkolli in the Wayanad district. In fact, this discovery was enough to discard the geographical isolation hypothesis. However, the province had to wait until the archaeological explorations by Padmanabhan Thampi in 1973 and P. Rajendran in 1974, which brought to light the Mesolothic cave-art at Marayur in the Idukki district and Palaeolithic implements from Kanhirapuzha in the Palakkad district,[3] which disproved the hypothesis of Kerala's 'uninviting environment' and 'inaccessibility'.

PALAEOLITHIC CULTURE

The subsequent exploratory studies unveiled several archaeological evidences of both the Pleistocene and Holocene periods, that included Stone Age sites, both of the Palaeolithic and Mesolithic, from several places in the districts of Kannur, Waynad, Calicut, Malappuram, Palakkad, Kottayam, Kollam, and Thiruvananthapuram.[4] Paleolithic evidence as surface finds and in stratified context were discovered from places in Kanhirapuzha, Tenkara, and Mukkali in the Palakkad district; Kunnathubalu, Valluvasseri, Karimpulakkal, and Karalikkot in the Malappuram district; Kunnonni in the Kottayam district; and Kuvakkad and Abhayagiri in the Kollam district.[5] These sites are located in the basins of rivers such as Kanhirappuzha, Bhavani, Ponnani, Beypore, Meenachil, and Kallada. The Palaeolithic tools at Abhayagiri and Valuvasseri were obtained from the lateritic surfaces, while similar implements from Kanhirapuzha, Tenkara, Kunnathubalu, Karalikkot, Karimpulakkal, Mukkali, Pandikkad, and Kunnonni were collected from the gravel beds.

The Palaeolithic implements of Kerala are mostly made of the locally available river-worn quartz pebbles and stray gneiss pebbles and flakes. They are worked unifacially or bifacially. The Palaeolithic tools recovered from the sites in Kerala belong mainly to the chopper-scraper-flake tradition.[6] Tools mostly represented by chopper-scraper-flake assemblages made of quartz were collected from Valluvasseri, Karimpulakkal, and Kunnathubalu near Nilambur in the Beypore river basin in the Malappuram district; Tenkara and Kanhirapuzha near Palakkad in the Bharathapuzha basin and Mukkali in the Bhavani basin in the Palakkad district; Kunnonni in south

Poonjar in the Meenachil basin of the Kottayam district; and Abhayagiri in the Kollam district. Elsewhere in India, similar tools are made of quartzite, which is absent in Kerala. However, the quartz chopper-scraper-flakes of the region show morphological, typological, and technological affinities with some of the Lower Palaeolithic tools reported from various parts of India.[7] The recent discovery of a few hand axe types from Tenkara in the Palakkad district shows that the Kerala Palaeolithic industries have also an Acheulian element, a lower Palaeolithic design rarely seen on the west coast of India. In the west coast of India, except for a few sites in Saurashtra, Goa,[8] and Kerala, no other part in the region, especially south of Narmada, yielded any standardized tool-types such as hand-axes and cleavers.

The dating of the Palaeolithic culture of Kerala with any exactitude is a vexed issue because of the paucity of relics amenable to scientific dating. Only a tentative dating based on comparative archaeology is available now. The sites of Sri Lanka have been dated above 70,000 years old.[9] Keeping in view certain features common to the chopper-scraper-flake industries of Sri Lanka and Kerala, it might be reasonable to assign a comparable antiquity to the latter. The main components in Lower Palaeolithic Kerala were a variety of choppers, either flaked unifacially or bifacially. Unifacial choppers are generally made of flat-based raw material with flake-scars on the dorsal surface. Bifacial flaking was essential to get a sharp cutting edge of a spheroid pebble. Choppers generally have steep shallow flake-scars along the margin and the flakes are found detached from the original surface of the raw material. Only a minimum of flakes seem to have been removed to obtain the working edge on the tools.

Different types of scrapers, mostly made of flakes, come next to choppers. These flake implements are much smaller than the pebble tools and are fewer in number. Many of the implements retain cortex either on the dorsal or ventral surface near the proximal end. Most of the flake tools were removed from an unfaceted platform, and the bulb of percussion and the point of impact are well discernible. Some of these characteristics are closer to those of the Lower Palaeolithic culture.[10]

The people at that time were entirely dependent on the environment, which determined their mode of subsistence during this period. The Stone Age means of subsistence all over the world was big game hunting and gathering, but we do not have any concrete evidence for or against this to be specific about the situation in Kerala. However, the ecological conditions of Palaeolithic human existence largely remained the same in Kerala also, enabling us to assume the livelihood strategy was the same. There was no permanent settlement for the Palaeolithic peoples anywhere though they seem to have had inhabited suitable natural caves and rock-shelters for a long time. The occurrence of tools both in the gravel beds as well as lateritic zones with river-worn quartz pebbles suggests that their sphere of activities was wider. Living in natural rock-shelters on mountains of high altitude, they had obviously come down the river valleys to make pebble tools and roamed around hunting large animals in the grasslands, besides gathering food in the jungle. The strength of the population must have been extremely low though the extent of distribution seems to be relatively wider. However, there is still a great deal to know about their cultural practices.

MESOLITHIC CULTURE

Unlike in central and northern India, the coastal Mesolithic artefacts are made mostly of flakes with a smaller percentage of nodules, pebbles, and blades and they are not microlithic in morphology. The use of the locally available quartz raw material is quite evident in the case of tools discovered in many places in Kerala which date to the Lower Palaeolithic age and later periods. Different forms of quartz are seen in Kerala as boulders, cobbles, pebbles, gravels, and veins. They include both milky and transparent varieties with fine—and coarse-grained types. From the aspects of typology and morphology of the implements, it is clear that the Mesolithic peoples in Kerala were masters in working quartz, which was otherwise considered a poor raw material. Though to some extent weathering had affected the quartz raw material, people were capable enough to discard the weathered quartz and select the best. Irrespective of the varying qualities of quartz such as compactness, size, transparency, and weathering, the Mesolithic industries of Kerala are found typologically very rich. This further proves their mastery over the selection of the right kind of quartz for its fabrication into tools.

Mesolithic implements of Kerala are mostly made of flakes and the tool types mainly include bifacial points, blades, borers, baked knives, scrapers, discoids, and small choppers made of medium-sized pebbles. The absence of geometric types such as triangles and trapezes are conspicuous, while the presence of bilateral symmetric bifacial points is quite notable. Unifacial choppers made of small pebbles are peculiar to the Mesolithic tool types of Kerala. The overall assemblage of tools indicates that the industry was dominated by the flake element. However, the use of blade technology was not altogether absent as evident from the presence of fluted cores and blades. The varieties of scrapers made of flakes vouch for the richness of the industry.

Mesolithic culture in Kerala had its apex in the early Holocene age and it continued till 3000 BC.[11] Stone tools are the prime indicators of the technical skill of people. In the case of Kerala they could fabricate the most effective implements on quartz. Though the use of quartz during the Mesolithic period has been attested in various parts of south India, it forms only a smaller percentage compared to its extent in Kerala. The reason is obvious. Kerala had no alternative raw material while the other regions had different raw materials of the cryptocrystalline types. Among the tool types, bifacial points and small choppers are remarkable and they are not commonly seen in any other parts of India except Tamil Nadu. The backed blades, scrapers, and bifacial points vouch for their high level of technical skill in flaking quartz. The presence of smaller blades and fluted cores among other artefacts indicates the level of their blade technology. However, the extent of blade production was extremely marginal. The high percentage of flake artefacts probably shows that such tools were essential for subsisting in the local ecological systems of the times. Generally, the Stone Age industries of different regions owed the morphological and typological changes of tools to the nature of their environmental conditions. From a large number of Stone Age implements in Kerala, it is clear that the absence of quartzite or other cryptocrystalline raw materials did not hinder the early human habitation.

When this culture existed, there was a tremendous increase in the number of sites, probably indicating a rise in the population. These peoples had occupied more shelters and caves. It might also have been due to the splitting up of larger bands into small tribes and smaller clans. Hunting-gathering was the subsistence strategy of the Mesolithic peoples too, though there was a shift from hunting big game to smaller animals as well as birds. Naturally, there was a corresponding shift of the morphology of tools from the bigger types to the smaller ones. It appears that they had also started fishing. Apart from the variety of stone artefacts showing the nature of their material culture, the vestiges of their artistic activities have survived as petrographs and petroglyphs on the cave walls and rocks, shedding light on the non-material aspects of their culture.

Fishing in south Indian littoral tracts can be traced back to a hoary antiquity and the archeologists, the Allchins, have associated the south Indian sand dunes on the east coast to the south of Madras with the hunters or more probably, the fishermen.[12] The majority of the finished tools collected from the sites are made either of flakes or of chips of raw material and this is described as a microlithic industry. According to the Allchins, there is of course no reason no suppose that the dunes were only inhabited when the sea was at a higher level than what it is at present. They prove that there was a sheltered camping place within reach of the sea and of lagoons and estuaries suitable for fishing and rearing fowl. Fishing communities on the coast of India still live in situations of this kind, building their huts among sand dunes. As in the case of the Bombay sites, there seems little doubt that this was the industry of a Late Stone Age fishing community.

NEOLITHIC CULTURE

The disappearance of the great glaciers, and the consequent rise in temperature, brought early man out of the caves. The phenomenal changes in the environment along with various other factors led to the transformation of the long, protracted early Stone Age. Just as any other cultural transformation, the transformation of the Old Stone Age into the New was a slow process too, but fundamental in character. Therefore, the Neolithic or the New Stone Age in human history was far more than a mere Stone Age. Apart from the fact that the Neolithic peoples had used well-shaped and finely ground tools of smooth surfaces, they had invented agriculture, domesticated animals, manufactured earthen pots, fabricated cloths, and made use of fire for cooking. The polished celt or hand-axe is the tool type typical of the Neolithic peoples the world over, though the raw material differed from place to place. As the age that marked the transition from food gathering to food production, ushering in the first major social transformation, the Neolithic age is often conceived as a revolution. In many aspects of culture, the Neolithic stands out totally distinct and far advanced from other Stone Ages. The antiquity of the world Neolithic culture is about 12,000 years and its earliest Indian sites, over 5,000 years. In south India, the oldest known Neolithic site dates back to 4,000 years. There is no reliable dating in the light of evidence from the neighbouring regions, which seldom makes sense, for they vary glaringly from site to site. Moreover, no Neolithic habitation site has ever been identified anywhere in Kerala. Apart from a host of stray finds of hand-axes and a few rock-art depictions besides some scattered stratified indications, we have no reliable archaeological evidence to talk definitively about the nature of Neolithic culture in Kerala.

Philip Lake first discovered Neolithic axes from the foot of the Kannyakad hills in Kerala. Later, archaeologists Logan and Fawcett had collected a few quartz flakes, a fragment of a Neolithic celt, and a couple of beads from the Wynad area. Polished stone axes and beads that are typical of the Neolithic phase were reported from Kalpatta and Pulppalli in the Wynad district and the riverbeds of the Periyar in Aluva. Hand-axes were collected as stray finds from Thamarassery in 1975, Puthady in 1978, Parambikkulam in 1983, and Kundurmedu in 1986. Though very limited in number, the stray finds of the Neolithic hand-axe in Kerala show its distribution across all the three physiographical zones, the lowlands, midlands, and highlands. Most of this evidence comes from the surface, seemingly as objects carried away by people with little information about their provenance and precluding the possibility of knowing the stratified context. Neolithic axes were made either of gneiss or granite rock that was locally available.

Though the Neolithic hand-axes found in Kerala are very few in number, they represent the typology that is typical of the culture, despite differences in the raw material. This is a clear indication of the wider diffusion of the tool technology over an area of amazing extent testified by the discovery of stone axes, flakes, blades, and beads. Stone axes are well made through flaking, pecking, grinding, and polishing. Finished axes are symmetrical in shape and their working edge is well polished. Some of the axes bear use marks as striations at the convex working edge on the right angle. Some of the artistic representations on walls of the rock-shelters of Edakal, Ankode, and Marayur are probably products of the Neolithic culture.

The Neolithic artefacts discovered from Kerala show that the culture that obviously got diffused from the sites of the neighbouring states evolved here almost parallel to the development in other regions of south India. In spite of the dominance of the hand-axe among the tool types, certain features peculiar to the ecosystems had evolved here. Nevertheless, there is no way to reconstruct the culture exactly as it evolved out of the material processes of human adaptation to the ecological conditions of Kerala. The principal means of subsistence all over the world during the Neolithic Age was agriculture or stock-rearing as determined by the ecosystems. In south India, there is Neolithic evidence for both pastoral as well as agricultural means of subsistence under appropriate ecosystems. In Kerala it was presumably a combination of gathering and primitive cultivation, supplemental by hunting and fishing. However, stock-rearing was never a major subsistence strategy even in highland Kerala. which has a dearth of pastures. Extensive pastures in Kerala are confined to the high altitude mountain ranges of the Idukki district; this accounts for the indications of a pastoral base in the Neolithic stratum of paintings at Marayur.

The absence of habitation sites and excavated material keeps us ignorant of the ethnic, organizational, institutional, customary, and ritual aspects of the Neolithic material culture. However, in the light of the existing knowledge about the culture in the neighbouring regions, we assume that the earliest kin-based village settlements (*ūr*) in Kerala date back to the Neolithic times. Probably the earliest Proto-Dravidian-speaking communities of Kerala must have lived in these villages. It appears that the Neolithic phase of Kerala was very brief as it soon got exposed to the use of iron.

INTERPRETING PREHISTORIC ART

The significance if ancient rock-art as the most vital source of knowledge about the prehistoric culture of a region is enormous. Art represents the affective response of people to the objective conditions of their existence and hence signifies their material milieu of subsistence. Constituting the only surviving genre of objectification of prehistoric cultures, ancient rock-art provides the key to the mental world of contemporary peoples' imaginary relations, magic, witchcraft, and fantasies as well as their social milieu of ideas and institutions. Art as a mark of creativity distinguishes human beings from animals, more than anything else. It is a non-verbal language with unconscious meanings, but a medium that communicates with people of all ages. The precious treasure of prehistoric art therefore, gives an insight into prehistoric life. So scholars review the depictions of prehistoric times as a source of supreme importance that helps the reconstruction of the social software of prehistoric human existence. It helps us imagine the operational context of stone tools.

Studies in rock-art were begun in the later half of the nineteenth century in the wake of contemporary intellectual expansion into the varied aspects of human society and culture with specific foci. The pioneering study by Marcelino de Sauntuola at Altamira, Spain, opened prehistoric rock-art to the world of scholars, a new domain in 1879. India secured a legitimate place on the rock-art map of world prehistory in 1883 with the discoveries of the central and northern Indian rock-art sites by John Archebald Carlylle and John Cockburn. The discovery of prehistoric caves and their art was quite accidental, often during game hunting of British officials during the colonial period. F. Fawcett, the then superintendent of police of the erstwhile Malabar area, discovered a prehistoric rock-art site in Kerala as early as 1894. During a game-hunting trip to Wayanad, he happened to see a Neolithic celt recovered from the coffee estate of Colin Mackenzie, the first Surveyor General of British India and a philatelist in 1890. An enthusiast in prehistory, Fawcett went round exploring the Wayanad high ranges, which eventually led to the discovery of the Edakal rock-shelter. In spite of their artistic splendour and creative ingenuity, ancient rock-art had remained a relatively neglected subject of study for quite some time. However, as years passed, scholars in different parts of Europe, Asia, and Africa discovered more and more caves. The untiring efforts of many Western scholars such as Abbe Henri Breuil, Marie-Henriette Alimen, Pale Marie Grand, Paolo Graziosi, Magin Barenguer, Thomas Cole, James Mellaart, Andreas Lommel, Robert Sterling Clark, and others, resulted in prehistoric art being known widely as a subject of authority, authenticity, depth, and credibility. It was only in the last quarter of the present century that the Indian archaeologists were able to take big strides in the field of rock-art research. The study of prehistoric rock-art archaeology in India received scholarly attention through the sustained efforts of V.S. Wakankar, V.N. Misra, and Y. Mathpal.

All over the world the Mesolithic Age, the evolutionary intermediary stage between the Old and New Stone Ages, is noted for its richness of petrographs or rock paintings and petroglyphs or rock engravings. Kerala secured a place in the map of Mesolithic art only in 1973 with the discovery of the Marayur (Idukki) petrographs by Padmanabhan Thampi. Mesolithic peoples made paintings on the walls of open shelters or faces of rock cliffs in and around their habitation sites. Usually, the paintings are found on the cave walls and ceilings as well as in small hollow spaces or independent niches, formed by natural weathering. Generally these rock-shelters occur at considerable elevations and their art works at inaccessible heights on the rock walls, natural ceilings, and tightly packed passages. For all these there are examples in the rock-art sites of Kerala too. The main sites of prehistoric rock-art in Kerala are at Marayur, Chinnar, Edakal, and Tovari. In the Marayur rock-shelter, one set of depictions can be seen on the inner portion of the top ceiling and another on the top part of a hood stone. On the Edakal rock walls, there are petroglyphs on the topmost surfaces that are not easily accessible and in the Tovari rock-shelter there are petroglyphs on the natural ceilings of narrow and tiny passages.

Rock-art throughout the world has an amazing universal similarity in its contexts, basic style, and spacing irrespective of their geographical differences, be it Altamira (Spain), Lascaux (France), Valcamonica (Italy), Mirzapur (India), Marhouma (Sahara), Oran (Algeria), or Koodakkad (Marayur), yet depictions of no two sites are alike either. Rock-art and cave paintings have been recorded in the jungles of Sudan, Rhodesia (Zimbabwe), and other parts of Africa, including Egypt. Everywhere its themes included wild fauna on which the peoples' life depended for survival. The horse, deer, reindeer, bison, ibex, ostrich, woolly rhinoceros, and mammoths are the species most commonly depicted, but in some caves the depiction includes lions and bears as well. The depiction of fish, birds, and boats is generally rare among prehistoric representations, though at various places the ecosystem must have compelled them to take to fishing and bird hunting. Apart from the animal depictions, prehistoric peoples had depicted abstract signs with meanings that are unclear to us, in spite of the varied theories put forward by scholars to explain them as psycho-grams, magical symbols, and so on. Human figures became common in prehistoric depictions only at a later date, probably from the Iron Age onwards.

Studies have classified the development of Cave art into three phases: the primeval phase characterized by black outline drawings of wild fauna with thin monochrome fillings; the second phase noted for outlines filled in with two-colour modelling; and the third phase marked by polychrome paintings. In the first two phases, the pictures were depicted on projections and concavities of rock, taking advantage of natural light and shade. The third was the most impressive phase to which all world famous prehistoric paintings belong. The depictions of this phase show a high degree of naturalism and amazing impressionistic depth in rock painting, achieved in painting with the most basic materials, such as charcoal and vegetable colours, is amazing.

Dating of prehistoric rock-art is a hard task, for it could be an assortment of representations belonging to disparate periods ranging from prehistoric to historic. With additions as superimposed and interpolated, every rock-art site makes the petrographs bewildering for an archaeologist seeking to sort them out temporally. There are certain scientific techniques such as infra-red photography and spectrographic colour tests to date petrographs, but they are seldom found applicable to many a site. An assessment of the nature of the rocky terrain and the level of weathering over time might also help. So by and large, the methods of dating rely on the stratified context of the excavated objects and their scientific dating. The Palaeolithic as well as the Mesolithic rock-art assemblages throughout the world have a relative chronology depending upon their stone quality correlation and the nature of composition, theme, style, platination grades, and pigments of the paintings. Alimen, dealing with African rock-art, opined that though determination of the chronology of depictions with any degree of exactitude would be difficult, content analysis might sometimes provide clinching evidence. She dated African rock-art as mostly of the Neolithic and post-Neolithic periods on the basis of the contents in the depictions of group action human beings: for instance, the scenes of domestication that are obviously posterior to the European prehistoric petrographs, mostly in the Franco-Cantabrian region (that is to say, in south-central France and in the French Pyrenees) as well as in the Cantabrian mountains of northern Spain, with hunting scenes that belong to the Upper Paleolithic and Mesolithic periods. As it appears that the Aurignacio-Perigordian period was the most active phase of art production, the antiquity of the earliest work of art on rock may be traced back to about 18000 BC. There is a considerable gap of thousands of years, between the Franco-Cantabrian (around 12000 BC) and the Spanish Levante (ranging between 6000 to 2000 BC). But it is matter of controversy, whether or not the murals of prehistoric Catal Huyuk can be fitted into that interregnum. Asian petrographs, noted for their animal depictions, belong to Mesolithic times beginning in about 12000 BC.

We do not know to what extent the rock-art had developed in Kerala during the Holocene period, though its Mesolithic association is visible. The Mesolithic rock-art of Kerala must be of a much later date, say probably of around 4000 BC. There are Neolithic and Iron Age additions to the Mesolithic stratum by way of superimposition. The interpolations and superimpositions at all sites seem to have continued till the middle ages. The relative chronology of the Marayur cave art is from the Mesolithic through Neolithic to the early historic periods; the art of Edakal, Tovari, and Ankode is from the Neolithic to the Iron Age. Though art traditions are notoriously difficult to confine to chronological limits and cultural specificities, the rock-art tradition is generally linked with prehistoric times and the cultures of hunting, domestication, and cattle-keeping. The rock-art traditions from the Upper Palaeolithic, Mesolithic, Neolithic down to the Iron Age the world over have a huge time lag from continents to continents. In the Indian subcontinent the time lag is over many millennia. Their antiquity varies between about 20,000 and 500 years BP. However, until we get dating based on scientific techniques it would be safe to refrain from assertions through chronological imagination.

Rock Paintings of Marayur

There are three rock-shelters at the Anjanad valley in the high ranges of the Devikulam taluk, Idukki district: Koodakkad, Pallanad, Champakkad—also known as Ezhuthaḷa, meaning the cave of pictures—Āṭṭaḷa, and Purachi Aḷa. Aḷa means cave and the name Ezhuthaḷa denotes the cave of pictures. We do not know what the prefixes of the other two caves denote. Ezhuthupāṟa literally, rock of paintings is a common name of all the three sites. Geomorphologically, the Koodakkad shelter (77 05′E and 10 15′N) at an elevation of about 3,280 feet MSL is surrounded by tilted and fractured rock formations. The Pallanad shelter (77 05′E and 10 00′N) is at an elevation of about 5,500 feet MSL and the Champakkad shelter (78 00′E and 12 35′N) is at about 2,000 feet MSL. The petrographs at the Koodakkad site are depicted on a solitary, tall granite boulder with a wider concavity. All the paintings are within the concavity, which has given the rock the shape of a serpent hood towering to a height of 12 metres with a width of 10 metres and the paintings occupy roughly three-fourths of the stone and the concavity. The depictions are predominantly in red-ochre accompanied by grey, pinkish buff, saffron, and brownish yellow as in the case of rock-art sites elsewhere. The entire surface is covered by paintings depicting antelope, bull, elephants with and without mahouts, human figures with arms stretched apart, impressions of palm, certain other auspicious symbols and ritual dancers. Antelope, elephant riders, three human figures, and a prominent bull are the major depictions to be noted. The most significant of all is the picture of a tiger-like animal in the innermost layer of the superimposition.

Among the depictions in the stone concavity of the first shelter, the most prominent is a cattle group, a long-horned humped bull with three or more cows. The earliest layer visible in the whole complex is the depiction of cattle, which is partly superimposed by human figures. The hump, long horns, hind limbs, and genitals are clear in the case of the bull whose other parts are superimposed by the right hand of one of the human figures. The heads and frontal limbs of the cows are hidden beneath the largest human figure at the waist. Morphologically and stylistically, the bull with the resembles the bulls in the Neolithic and Iron Age petrographs of south India and Sri Lanka. The back of a horse appears between the right shoulder and head of a human figure. The cattle and horse seem to be in the same stratum, but the colour of the horse is pinkish brown, distinguished from the red-ochre and yellowish brown of the bull and cows. A horse, perhaps the most exquisitely depicted piece, whose whole body, except the tail, is superimposed by a huge human figure with wavy lines all over, is also suggestive of the Iron Age interpolation. An elephant with an armed rider in the periphery of the concavity is obviously an Iron Age addition. There are differences of opinion about the identification of figures in terms of cultural strata and their relative dating. S.P. Thampi ascribes the antelope, cattle, and horse to the Mesolithic period, roughly dating back to about 7000 BC, the human figures to the Chalcolithic time, of about 2000 BC, and the armed rider on the elephant to the early historic period, of about 300 BC. The absence of evidence precludes the possibility of postulating a Chalcolithic phase in Kerala. The wavy lines remind us of the ceramic decorative quite common in red slipped and russet coated ware of the Iron Age and this cultural association of the design could be taken as a clue to tentatively date the human figures. The depictions have been assumed to be of the time span of the Mesolithic–Neolithic–Iron Age sequence.

Unlike the first shelter, the petrographs in the Pallanad shelter are solely in white and on the inaccessible ceiling. The shelter looks like a giant lizard creeping with its mouth wide open. The depictions, probably the largest collection in the state, are about 400 in number, and are all in white pigment. The main portrayals are: human figures, elephants with and without riders, birds, acrobatics, combat scenes, magical symbols, geometrical designs like rectangles and triangles, a boat-like figure, lizards, other reptiles, trees, and a few orthographic signs as superimposed. Among these typical Mesolithic representations, the most prominent depiction is that of boats, which are probably suggestive of ancient marine or navigational activities. There are symbolic and ideographic representations too. Just as in the case of many other cave sites elsewhere in the country, the Marayur shelter has also yielded microlithic tools, reinforcing the Mesolithic affinity of the petrographs. Along with the surface collection of the microlithic tools, ground nodules of red ochre in hematite, which are quite common in prehistoric rock-art sites as the raw material for wall paintings, were discovered. Similarly bone pieces of animals and cattle, probably used as the painting sticks, were also discovered in the first cave.

The third shelter, big enough to accommodate about 50 people, is located at Champakkad, on a rock of sedimentary schist type, overlooking the Chinnar river. Area-wise, this rock-shelter is the largest of the three. The petrographs are on the sidewalls of the shelter whose inner surface is divided into two rooms full of fallen debris. The main depictions, all in small sizes from about 9 to 12 inches, are of human and animal figures in white lime-like pigment.

Red Ochre Paintings of the Chinnar Caves

A few more rock paintings have been identified recently on the walls of a few rock caves at the Alampatti hamlet in the Chinnar Wildlife Sanctuary near Munnar in the Devikulam taluk of Kerala. Alampatti is close to Marayur, a hill station with rock-art, already delineated above along with sites such as Āṭṭaḷa and Ezhuthaḷa bearing paintings studied since the 1970s.[13] Alampatti has been noted too, but only one rock cave with a red ochre line-drawing of sambar deer (*Cervus unicolor* sp.), was found in 2004. Five more caves with red ochre signs, primarily graffiti marks and handprints, have been explored recently. The Māṭattaḷa, Vāymala, and Jellimala caves are newly discovered sites. Other sites, such as Āṭṭaḷa and Ezhuthaḷa near Marayur, were reported by Thampi and subsequently studied by Mathpal.[14]

Māṭattaḷa is a complex of three natural rock-shelters located (N 10°18′43.4″; E 77°11′26.4″) at an elevation of 738.7 metres MSL, on the eastern slope of the Alampatti rock that lies in north–south orientation with Ālampaṭṭithōdu, a perennial stream on the west. The site was first explored by a local person, namely, K. Dhanushkoti in early 2004 and subsequently reported in the *Hindu* by P. Thampi. He and Sabi Varghese, Forest Ranger Officer, revisited the sites under the guidance of K. Dhanushkoti in December 2007 and January 2008. The first shelter in the complex is spherical in shape and measures five metres in length, with a floor of two metres width and walls of two-and-a-half metres in height. The red ochre line-drawing depicting two female sambar deer and the back of another occur in this shelter. At Mattala, two deer figures are displayed in profile, one behind the other. The deer heads look very graceful, with the neck, the ear, and the mouth depicted elegantly. The head of the deer on the rear is depicted above the deer in the front, covering almost half of it. The deer in the front seems to be squatting with folded rear legs and has a projected portion on the back as if it is about to give birth to a calf. Adjacent to this shelter are two more small shelters with red ochre line-drawings at two locations in the middle shelter, and at one spot on the last shelter, all small in size (ca. 63 cm × 46 cm × 84 cm). The middle shelter drawings appear to represent two honeycombs, a design repeated in the last shelter wall as well. There are red signs and graffiti marks in linear fashion smeared with red ochre at a few points. The surface of the Alampatti rock is full of small dolmens that number about 60, distributed in three clusters starting from the southernmost slope to the northernmost point at an elevation of 915 metres, where a large single dolmen exists. It is about 35 metres below on the eastern belly of the rock where the Matattala cave stands.

Vāymala (literally, mouth-like mountain or mountain with a mouth) is located at N 10°19′19.3″; E 77°11′56.9″ at an elevation of 878 metres MSL. It has three rock-shelters, one with a floor that is six metres long and two-and-a-half metres wide, and the slanting wall surface of uneven height varying between four and five metres. Some peculiar signs and graffiti marks in red ochre are found at two lower points (one metre above the floor level) on the wall. The adjacent shelters are on the northern side of the rock, which can be entered through a tiny passage although a visitor could easily lose balance from the cliff overlooking the deep valley below. The shelters contain red ochre designs and graffiti marks too.

Jellimala is located in N 10°18′35.2″ and E 77°11′29.3″ at an elevation of 779.2 metres, on the east of the Alampatti rock. It has two shelters, small in size, almost like box-holes, overlooking the valley. The first one is three metres long and one metre deep from the entry point, the floor two-and-a-half metres deep, and the wall two metres high. On the lower part of the wall, a peculiar red ochre design occurs with stray red marks at two points. The other is at an inaccessible point on the northern belly of the rock and the shelter looks like a bowl with a slanting orientation, measuring about two metres long and one metre wide floor at a depth of 0.60 metre with a one-and-a-half metre high wall. Red ochre signs and designs occur at two points.

These paintings may be prehistoric, but belong to different cultures from the Mesolithic to the Iron Age. The red ochre linear drawing of sambar deer at Matattala may be of the Mesolithic times if we go by the directness of appeal of the content and stylistic features. But in the absence of corroborative archaeological remains and scientific evidence in the form of data from chemical analysis and radiometric dating, identification of the culture and chronology remains a matter of conjecture. At the foot of the painted 'hood-rock' at Marayur, microlithic tools have been reported.[15] However, the paintings there are multilayered and belong to disparate phases down to the Iron Age. There is a superimposed human figure with wavy lines, graffiti very frequently met with in the Iron Age pottery at many places in south India and Sri Lanka. There are several dolmens in the surroundings. All along the surface of the Alampatti rock are about 200 dolmens. There are red ochre paintings at various dolmen sites of south India, but the dolmen sites of Kerala have not yielded them so far. Therefore, the probable relation of Chinnar red ochre drawings with the Iron Age culture cannot be ignored. However, the painting in red ochre is a striking point of anthropological significance in the primitive cultures.

It is well known that red ochre, made of silica, clay, and iron oxide, famous for its amazing permanence, occurs all over the world from prehistoric times, mainly as the colour of primeval emotion and a sign of blood symbolic of puberty and hence, fertility rites.[16] The significance of red is universal in all cultures for these reasons. Rock-art scholars, Emmanuel Anati and David Lewis-Williams, opine that prehistoric red ochre marks are indications of intense emotions and are suggestive of a primordial system of worldwide signs and meanings coming from *Homo sapien's* neurological processing.[17] Ochre was mixed with binders, such as vegetable juices, urine, animal fat, bone marrow, blood, or albumen from eggs, creating a red liquid similar in appearance and magnetic properties to blood. From the studies of the famous French prehistoric art specialist, Michel Lorblanchet, we understand that red ochre was mixed with blood as a binder and was sprayed either directly from the mouth or through hollow bones to the rock surface.[18] Viewed against the background of the scholarly studies on red ochre paintings the world over, the signs and drawings at the rock-art sites of Chinnar deserve a closer examination and scientific analyses.

Engravings at Ankode

Ankode, locally known as Pandavampara, the rock of the Pandavas, is located at an elevation of 1,000 feet, in the village of Perumkadavila (77E and 8N) of the Neyyattinkara taluk in the Thiruvananthapuram district. The site is about 96 cents (approximately an acre), quite congenial for early people to have set up their habitations here. Geomorphologically, it is a dyke type, with flattened stone alignments that underwent a fast weathering process. It is a weathered rock comparable to the rock of Tovari, with the entire surface easily amenable to deep engraving. This accounts for the deep engravings on the rock face. The tools were recovered from a depth of 15 centimetres. The Ankode portrayals are deeply engraved petroglyphs, like the works of art at the Tovari cave. The engravings are nearly 1.9 centimetres deep and about 1.5 centimetres wide and could have been executed by using a sharp stone flake like a Neolithic hand-axe, as in the case of the Edakal petroglyphs. However, there is no comparison between the works of art at Ankode and Edakal, for the former is too small in volume and diversity. Mesolithic tools were collected from the site in the stratified context.

The engravings comprised decorative floral designs at the entrance wall, and a few human figures, geometrical patterns, and sun symbols in the interior. The human figures are depicted in a hunting posture with bows and arrows. There is no correlative evidence at the site to reliably date the engravings. The debris is heavy, precluding the possibility of excavation. A fresh assessment of the petroglyphs is not feasible either, for they are completely chipped off.

Carvings of Tenmala Shelter

Tenmala in the Quilon district is another prehistoric rock-shelter with carvings. There are a few geometrical patterns like triangles, circles, and squares besides a flower motif. The circle has spoke-like marks in it, resembling a wheel. The entire rock surface is covered by incisions of parallel lines resembling those at Edakal. This rock-shelter has yielded Mesolithic implements in stratified context. The implements were found at 35 centimetres, deposited along the wood charcoal. This archaeological deposit has been dated through carbon 14 tests as 5210±110 years old.[19] In the light of the presence of Mesolithic artefacts within the rock-shelter as surface finds as well as below the surface, it is certain that the carvings on the exterior of the shelter rock were made by the Mesolithic people. This helps us assign the carbon 14 dating of the debris to the engravings too.

The Edakal Rock Engravings

The Edakal rock is on the crest of a hill known as Ambukuthimala in the Western Ghats, about 4,600 feet MSL and situated about 10 kilometres southwest of Sultan Battery in the Wynad district of Kerala. It is a prehistoric rock-shelter formed naturally out of a strange formation of three huge boulders, with one resting on the other two with the lower part jutting out in between and serving as the roof. Edakal literally means 'a stone in between'. The combination of the curves and protrusions of the boulders in the alignment is such that it virtually brings a two-storeyed cleft into existence. The lower storey can be entered through an opening of 5 × 4 feet into the interior measuring a length of about 18 feet, a width of 12 feet, and a height of 10 feet. A passage leads up to a small opening on the roof through which one climbs up to the next storey, with an entrance that is about 7 × 5 feet. Its interior is about 96 feet long, 22 feet wide, and 18 feet high. There is a big opening at the right-turn corner of the roof since the roofing boulder does not touch the facing wall, allowing enough light into the cave. The right and left walls of this upper cleft are replete with figures made in a mode that makes it difficult to classify them as engravings or carvings or etchings.

The site was identified way back in 1894 as a habitat of Neolithic people on the basis of the type of representations on the cave walls, that appeared to be engravings made of Neolithic celts.[20] Apart from the passing references to the Edakal cave by various authors on prehistory, there is no exhaustive archaeological study of the site. Strangely enough, it did not attract the attention of archaeologists, despite its representational richness and uniqueness, without any parallel anywhere in the world. There have been no serious and methodical interpretations of the archaeological context and meanings of the representations on the cave walls. The art-historiography of India could generate very little new knowledge about their styles and contents though scholars repeatedly emphasized the unique place of the site on the map of world prehistory. This historiographical desideratum justifies the attempt here to study the morphology and decipher the meanings of the representations on the cave gallery. However, a real access to the meanings needs a computerized database and appropriate software enabling global comparison of prehistoric pictographs.

Except for the discovery of a few Neolithic celts from the area around the site and the objectively verifiable fact that such engravings and etchings can be made of the celts, we have no direct clues to the archaeology of the figures under consideration. Actually a detailed plotting of the area needs to be done with points of archaeological finds, passages, and routes connecting highways, cult spots, and old and new settlements.

The Edakal cave site is on an ancient route connecting the high ranges of Mysore to the ports of Malabar, a route that was in continuous use during several historical periods. However, much of the historical importance of the site remains to be unravelled. We do not know what the site overlooks or hides, though it is easy to describe how accessible it had been in the past by looking at the present geography of the region. This would mean that much of what a student of history is looking for about the site remains inscrutably hidden.

Before one attributes interpretative meanings to the representations, it is essential to know the mode of objectification and the elements of object production, ensuring a heuristic control. It is in this context that the study of morphology becomes extremely important. At the outset, it is essential first to describe formally and structurally the representations on the cave walls by discovering their elements of production. The representations across the surfaces of the cave walls can be reduced to six basic elements of production: a canoe, cross, triangle, square, circle, and volute.[21]

The first element, the canoe like incision, seems to be the most elementary of all signs and the starting point of the representations in the gallery. In fact, it could be the initial sign of any engraved representation of prehistoric times, since it is the natural mark resulting from the process of grinding an axe or celt by rubbing it on the surface of a rock. The other signs such as the cross, triangle, and square are geometrical signs developed from the primary sign with which the prehistoric people were familiar in the context of tool-making. The circle and volute are tertiary signs resulting from mediating between the primary and secondary signs for the construction of figures.

The objects of the gallery text are on the two walls of the rocks shelter. On Wall 1 (left) the depiction consists of prominent human figures with headgear and other decorative objects, a human figure with an elaborate head-dress, an elephant, wild dogs, a peacock, plants and flowers, a human figure with a hand shaped like a jar, a human figure with a square head-dress, a wheeled cart, and a few geometrical signs. On Wall 2 (right) the representations comprise geometrical signs, male and female figures, a triangular sign representing a human figure, a human figure on a wheeled cart, and a human figure with conical sign attached.

As regards the *genre* of the art activity at Edakal, it is a straight-line geometric schema, which does not require any particular skill, except patience to carry on continuous grinding with the celt. This patience is developed as an imperative of the collective need. The linear geometric schema could be a development over the rigid style of combining primary signs into images. The images are not made through the linear representation of the physical features or anatomy of the object, but through a suggestive strategy of impressionistic marks that combine themselves with their shadows to make the images. It is, in fact, a strategy of representation by itself, enabling the making of images through a combination of incisions and their shadows, seemingly made in fire light rather than sunlight.

There are two distinct style of representation explicit in the Edakal rock-art gallery: one is the style adopting solely the primary sign and the other is the one adopting both primary, secondary, and mediating signs for the construction of figures. Similarly, there are two stages of evolution perceptible across the representations: one is the primary stage of a relatively simple representation through the ordering of independent signs. The next stage of evolution seems to be that of the mediating style, which has the advantage of avoiding disjunctions in image-making. In the representation of human figures, some are made solely of primary sign, others of primary and cross signs, and also figures made of primary, secondary, and mediating signs. The use of the triangle sign is dominant in the case of certain figures. In the assemblage of figures, there is a movement of both the style and strategy from simple to complex. As we move from the simple to the complex, the use of mediating signs increases and gradually the breaks and gaps between the constituent signs of figures vanish, indicating a continuous stylistic evolution. There are representations showing relatively earlier and later stages in terms of the evolution of style. The representations on Wall 1 show the primary style or strategy with no attempts at the mediation of signs, whereas the portrayals on Wall 2 are primarily of the secondary and mediating style or strategy.

It appears that in the construction of evolved figures, some new implements other than celt were used, probably an iron implement, as indicated by incisions that are relatively thinner and evenly deep. The evolved style of representing a human figure is associated with a wheeled cart. The wheels are spoked and different from the primordial ones made of planks, but the primary sign is used to outline the cart. These do not seem to be random images of a mutually exclusive nature, though several of them could have been added to from time to tome. There is an overall ordering principle upon which the assemblage of images signifies a determinate pattern of relationship, based on centrality versus marginality and projection versus recession of the objects of representation.

We know that looking at art can give the viewer a distinctive pleasure and that this response reflects an important feature of art as far as our society is concerned. Beyond what the representations appear lies what they meant to the society of their times. What is historically real about the affective response to art is our central concern, however elusive it is. All would agree that there is little that can be said with certainty about the historically real affective responses to a given artwork. Nonetheless, certain anthropological concepts and psychological theories of eminent scholars who have been grappling with the question of deciphering the historically specific meanings of art do help us say something about this elusive or mysterious aspect of ancient art.

The general anthropological assumption is that perceiving art as an object of gratification has little relevance to prehistoric representations since they were not consciously created artworks, but the structured outcome of a socially indispensable activity fulfilling certain significant purposes of life. They were part of a contemporary subsistence strategy and were not primarily the result of an aesthetic response. This is not to underscore their embedded artistic and creativity value. The argument is that for the prehistoric people it was not an activity for the sake of art. Anthropological studies on prehistoric art reiterate in one voice that the subject matter for the art of prehistoric people was related to important aspects of life, such as food, reproduction, combat, domination, or submission, Within this broad ideational unity, there are hermeneutic as well as methodological differences ranging from the functionalist approach of Abbe Breuil to the structuralist perspectives of Leroi-Gourhan, showing prehistoric art as part of the sympathetic hunting magic and the result of a determinate structuring. These ideas are central to the interpretation attempted here.

On Wall 1, the tall human figure portrayed on top, at the centre, could be the representation of a deity; the prominent human figure with head-gear looks like a chief; and the human figure portrayed in the projection facing the central figure seems to be a ritual dancer. Other human figures with a head-dress also seem to represent ritual dancers. The elephant, antelopes, wild dogs, peacock, plants, and flowers represent the forest, while the wheeled cart indicates the traffic of goods, probably in the context of the interaction between two different cultures in terms of ascriptive or customary exchanges.

It is not clear whether all these representations should be viewed as a single cultural production or as mutually autonomous ones. We could argue that the representations seem to have been added on in order to serve the purposes of a changing society within a broadly uniform culture. Art is practice, which once produced is reproduced, added on to, superimposed, re-appropriated, and reified to suit changing needs. Therefore, it becomes extremely difficult, if not impossible, to conclusively determine, whether or not the cluster of representations as a whole belonged to any single culture. However, if we take the whole representations as a single collection of codes of a changing culture, they do signify the various developmental manifestations of the culture. Across the variety of representations of independent objects, one can discern a binding code of a changing culture. Beyond the appearance of independent representations or figures, there is an interpretative realm of paradigmatic traces, which we discover through a comparison of figures. For example, above the human figures is a layer of ideas like the deity and laity mediated by ritual dancers, identifiable through a comparison of their forms.

The representations collectively signify a scene of ritual festivity of a tribe inhabiting the forest and subsisting on hunting and shifting cultivation. It could probably be the archaeo-anthropological context of the coexistence and interaction of the Neolithic and iron-smelting societies that is reflected in the structure of relations in the totality of representations. These are characterized by the presence of a simple style at the core and a relatively evolved one at the periphery. The representations at the core seem to be Neolithic and those in the periphery, Megalithic, providing a tentative dating of the gallery to the first millennium BC. However, the representations, despite their different points of origin, are organically woven into a single entity due to the unifying force of continuity embedded in the changing culture. In short, the representations seem to be symbolic of a new Stone Age society in transition. It is true that the representations in prehistoric art signify a realm of strange meaning intelligible only to the people of their times, but it is equally true that they signify a set of meanings which are intelligible only to us. We discover the meanings by analysing the social causes of the development of gratuitous complications and fantasy in the art works. However, there is the lurking danger about interpretations taking too much for granted in building semantic structures, often never to have anything to do with prehistoric reality. The contradictory dynamic of the relatively simple forms of tribal organization could probably be the generative source of strange decorative and contravening forms of duality in the representations of the Edakal rock-art. It has been observed that art works of gratuitous complications come into existence through a process of alienation and estrangement in society. In an unfallen social reality, there is no chance for the development of fantasy production in art because there is no contradictory dynamic that keeps the people perplexed. The existence of contradictions and the lack of their remedy at the social level, which generate confusion and disquiet in the people, lead to the creation of fantasy art. It is the projection of societal contradictions by a people that have the resolutions within them but are not able to objectively formulate them into the imaginary.

Such an explanatory framework helps us interpret the graphic decorative, such as huge head-dresses and contravening duality in the representations of Edakal as a fantasy production of a late Neolithic society perplexed at the changes in the wake of the introduction of iron by an alien society. It reminds us of a society passionately seeking to give symbolic expression to the resolution which it is unable to conceptualize at the social level. Alving Walfe has suggested that in Africa at least, the amount of fantasy art production by a people is roughly proportional to the extent to which they are divided by social cleavages.

Regarding how the gratuitous complications of art acted on contemporary society, many scholars like Douglas Fraser, Levi-Strauss, Payne Hatcher, Robert Paul, Lukacs, and Frederic Jameson have suggested that fantasy production as an imaginary resolution of contradictions helped maintain the cultural stability required for a developing society. Lukacs and Jameson viewed it as part of the containment strategy. Functionalists like Durkheim, Radcliffe Brown, and Talcott Parsons considered such manifestations of art as part of the solidarity maintaining mechanisms of a transitional society. However, what emerges on top of all in these theories is the symbolic objectification of an urge for social cohesiveness in a situation of flux.

Viewing the gratuitous complications of the Edakal rock-art in this perspective; we get the impression that the society behind it was facing the transitional crises and contradictions, which were insurmountable to the people, who found a purely imaginary resolution in the aesthetic realm through fantasy production. George Harley suggests that sometimes abnormal situations due to severe transient developments in the ecological system could also give rise to complexity in prehistoric art. The complexity appears as a psychic resolution of perplexing circumstances. We have no evidence for any such ecological crisis of the past that had affected the region. Gombrich observes that wherever Neolithic societies had come strongly under the influence of metal-using cultures, art had been significantly altered or modified.[22] This seems to be true of the rock-art under consideration, where the evolved linear representations, which are obviously modifications of the earlier style, resulted probably under the influence of the iron-using culture. It is important that down the hill there are several megaliths around the site surviving to our times as archaeological proof of the existence of the iron-using people.

There are certain symbols and exotic marks all along the representations which seem to have meanings and functions of their own, ranging from the explicit to the implicit and symbolic. Interestingly, all these graphic signs or symbols are found on the variety of megalithic pottery recovered from southern India and Sri Lanka. Moreover, the genre of art involved in the production of graphic signs is the straight-line geometric schema, which we have identified as an evolved stage of developmental complexity. The symbols may not always stand for a single meaning everywhere, but they do often signify one or the other among a cluster of closely related meanings in all cultures. This is particularly true in the case of libidinous symbols of genitals among the graphics of Edakal. They are shown explicitly as meaningful symbols by being attached to human figures. All the graphic signs do not seem to be symbols conveying specific meanings, but could be merely decorative, adding to the magical significance of the central images.

The Edakal archive of the Neolithic–Iron Age engravings stand out distinctly among the magnitude of prehistoric visual archives of paintings and graphic signs all over the world. It is the world's richest pictographic gallery of its kind. The images and signs jointly signify a strategy of combining deep incisions and their shadows in fire light, generating a three-dimensional visual effect.

Engravings at Tovari

The site generally known among local people as Ezhulthupara is on the slope of the Tovari hill, which is not far away from the famous rock-art site of Edakal in the same panchayat of Ambalavayal taluk. The engraved rock is a few metres below the summit of the hill. The site consists of three or four huge boulders with a massive rock slanting on them, forming a *pantal*. The engravings are found on the surface of the supporting rock on the left and the ceiling.

Tovari drawings consist mainly of geometrical figures like triangles, squares, and circles. One of the drawings is square, divided into eight parts. There are also triangles that are repeated more than once. On one of the supporting rocks, there is a stylized figure that resembles a bird with stretched wings. The Tovari art, as emerging from certain geometrical figures like the square, circle, and triangle in a specific combination, look like tools such as the hoe and arrow, a unique feature of this art. The importance of the figures lies in the fact that they imply economic and cultural ideas that throw much light on the primitive life in this area. A bone or stone tip fixed to a stick emerging from the square divided into eight seems to represent a hoe, a tool used in terrace cultivation by primitive people. The eco-climatic nature of the locality is suitable for such practices of primitive agriculture. On the ceiling rock there is a stylized arrow depicted with a circle. Similarly, on one of the supporting rocks an arrow is shown associated with a triangle. The tools and implements as well as the *mandala*-like geometrical figures encourage one to interpret them as figures of magical significance.

Stylistically. the Tovari figures fall roughly into two groups. Most of the figures are drawn with shallow and narrow lines. This indicates that they were drawn with smaller implements, probably stone blades of a smaller size. A few figures outlined in broad and deep strokes indicate the use of a bigger tool for engraving. The nature of lines clearly shows that they are drawn by rubbing on the surface of the rock with stone blades of different sizes.

The foregoing account presents some of the salient features of the prehistoric cultural heritage of Kerala, quite discernible in the art of the Palaeolithic, Mesolithic, and Neolithic periods. They show the prehistoric cultural continuity in the region. The technological development during these cultures appears remarkable, showing a separate identity. Dependence on the local environment, in fact, appears to be more prominent here. The prehistoric sites in Kerala do not show any concentration in any particular region, but are found all over the region in limited numbers. This again undoes any belief on large-scale migration from other regions through gaps in the Western Ghats. Above all, there is nothing substantial to show greater mobility of people between the adjacent regions. The material remains of various prehistoric cultures from Kerala point to the fact that the region had witnessed several technological innovations, developed by the people to cope with the local environment.

NOTES AND REFERENCES

1. R.B. Foote, 1916, *The Foote Collection of Indian Prehistoric and Protohistoric Antiquities: Notes on Their Ages and Distribution*, Madras.
2. See the discussion of the 'geographical model' conceiving 'attraction', 'relative isolation', and 'isolation' based on the evidence of archaeological sites, in B. Subba Rao, 1956, *The Personality of India: A Study in the Development of Material Culture in India and Pakistan*, Baroda.
3. S.P. Thampi, 1976, 'Marayur: A Key to the Pre-historic Archaeology of South Kerala', *Bulletin of the Deccan College Research Institute*, 35(3–4); P. Rajendran, 1977, 'Lower and Middle Stone Age Tools from Palghat District (Kerala)', *Current Science*, 44(4): 125–6.
4. P. Rajendran, 1989, 'Pre-historic Research in Kerala', *Current Science*, 56 (6): 266, Bangalore.
5. P. Rajendran, 1983, 'Palaeolithic Industries of North Kerala', *Bulletin of the Deccan College Research Institute*, 40: 145–64, Pune.
6. P. Rajendran, 1978, 'Flake-Scars and Stone-Strikes', *Bulletin of the Deccan College Research Institute*, 37(4): 124–7. Also see his 1983, 'The Coastal Mesolithic Industries of South India and Their Chronology', *Indo-Pacific Pre-history Association Bulletin*, 4: 18–31, Canberra.
7. Ibid. Also Rajendran, 'Pre-historic Research in Kerala'.
8. R. Korisettar, S. Mishra, S.N. Rajguru, V.D. Gogte, R.K. Ganjoo, T.R. Venkatesan, S.K. Tandon, B.L.K. Somayajulu, and V.S. Kale, 1989,

'Age of the Bori Volcanic Ash and Achulian Culture of the Kukdi Valley', *Bulletin of the Deccan College*, 49: 135–8, Pune, 1989.

9. A.K. Singhvi, S.U. Deraniyagala, and D. Singupta, 1986, 'Thermoluminiscence Dating and Quaternary Red Sand Beds: A Case Study of Coastal Dunes in Sri Lanka', *Earth and Planet Science Letter*, 80: 139–44.
10. See Rajendran, 'Pre-historic Research in Kerala'.
11. See Rajendran, 'The Coastal Mesolithic Industries of South India and Their Chronology'.
12. B. Allchin and R. Allchin, 1968, *The Birth of Indian Civilization*, London.
13. P. Thampi, 1998, 'Marayur: A Key to the Pre-historic Archaeology of South Kerala', *Bulletin of the Deccan College*, 35(3–4) and Y. Mathpal, 1998, *Rock Art in Kerala*, New Delhi.
14. Thampi, 'Marayur: A Key to the Pre-historic Archaeology of South Kerala', p. 135; Mathpal, *Rock Art in Kerala*, p. 20.
15. P. Thampi, contribution to the chapter on prehistoric art in Rajan Gurukkal and M.R. Raghava Varier, 1999, (eds) *Cultural History of Kerala*, vol. I, Department of Cultural Publications, Thiruvananthapuram.
16. R. Lawlor, 1990, *Sacred Geometry–Philosophy and Practice*, London; P.G. Bahn, 1998, *Cambridge Illustrated History of Prehistoric Art*, Cambridge.
17. E. Anati, *World Rock Art, The Primordial Language, Studi Camuni* V XII, 3 English Edition, 1994; D. Lewis-Williams, 2002, *The Mind in the Cave*, London.
18. M. Lorblanchet (ed.), 1988, *Rock Art in the Old World*, New Delhi; Bahn, *Cambridge Illustrated History of Prehistoric Art.*
19. Rajendran, 'Pre-historic Research in Kerala'.
20. F. Fawcett, 1901, 'Notes on the Rock Carvings in the Edakal Cave, Wynad', *Indian Antiquary*, 30: 209–21.
21. For details of interpretation, see Rajan Gurukkal, 1997, 'Edakal Rock Engravings: Morphology and Meaning', *Studies in Humanities and Social Sciences*, 4(1).
22. E.H. Gombrich 1956, *Art and Illusion*, Princeton.

5

Tribes, Forest, and Social Formation in Early South India*

Certain occasions sometimes enable us to look at old sources differently and gain new visibility quite worth the exercise. It is such a gratifying occasion to try and understand the place of tribes and forest in the early historic social formation of the Tamil macro region that is known in ancient Tamil heroic poems[1] as Tamilakam. The early historic time, often called pre-Pallavan, refers to the period from the closing centuries of the first millennium BC to about the AD fifth century. In this discussion, the term 'tribes' is intended to denote descent groups, while the term 'forest' is used in its generic sense, meaning untamed land covered by trees and shrubs as natural growth. Theoretically, a social formation refers to the interactive coexistence of two or more economies structured by the dominance of one. It is used here as an eminent conceptual framework for understanding the social history of any region where peoples of unevenly developed economies coexisted.

Any study of social formation at the outset necessitates knowledge about the material processes of human adaptation to the different ecosystems of the region and the social processes of appropriation. The identification of the peoples, their forms of subsistence/economies, technologies, kinds of labour and institutions of its realization, and patterns of the distribution of resources and power becomes the starting point for the study. Along with these it necessitates further knowledge about questions such as the nature of interaction among the various economies and the institutional

* This chapter is a reproduction of, 1995, 'Tribes, Forest and Social Formation', in B.B. Chaudhuri and A. Bandopadhyay (eds), *Tribes, Forest and Social Formation in India*, (Manohar: New Delhi), pp. 65–80.

or structural means evolved through the process, to identify the dominant economy and understand how it dominated the rest.

Our knowledge about the economic and socio-political processes of the space and time under review is almost entirely based on allusions in the Tamil heroic literature. This is not altogether accidental because the rise of the social formation under study synchronizes with the emergence of the Tamil heroic literary tradition. Other corroborative sources like *brāhmi* label inscriptions, foreign notices, and numismatic material, together with heroic compositions, push the social formation back to around the second century BC while Iron Age archaeology assigns its early phase to the beginning of the first millennium BC.[2] Generally historians accept the turn of the Christian era as its central period.

There were several groups of functionaries too such as *uḻavar* (wet-rice agriculturists), *toḻuvar* (cultivators of dryland called *punam* or *enal*), *taccar* (carpenters), *kollar* (smiths), *vanikar* (traders), and a few others as already discussed in Chapter 1. What emerges is an assemblage of coexistence and interaction of various tribes following the means of subsistence determined by the landscape ecosystems (*tiṇai*s) that they inhabited.

The findings of the past researchers help us conceptualize the above scenario in terms of coexistence and interaction of multiple economies, peoples, and the emergent power structure to characterize it as a social formation.[3] This is a social formation with hunting and gathering, fishing, agro-pastoralism, wet-rice agriculture, salt-manufacturing, crafts production, and exchange as the constituent economies, of course not as mutually exclusive, but overlapping status. The technology behind the economies was related to the multiple uses of iron. In all the economies, productive and distributive relations were based on kinship. The principal industries of the social formation were cattle-rearing, the cultivation of millet, ragi, and paddy, and a variety of crafts. Though paddy cultivation was the most superior industry of the times both in terms of productivity and technology, it was yet to articulate the conditions for its dominance.[4] Its production, linked as it was to kinship, was incompatible with development. The dominant economy of social formation was agro-pastoralism, which combined cattle-keeping with shifting cultivation as borne out by the preponderance of references to cattle raids and associated practices, rites, and rituals and the centrality of institutions such as gift-giving and redistribution besides the hegemony of heroic culture. Studies show that everything in the socio-cultural regime revolved round this economy and everything was disposed of so as to establish its hegemony over other economies.[5]

Organized under spontaneously evolved self-sustaining kinfolk units (*ūrs*) of production, the tribes maintained exchange relations (primarily of the goods for goods type) and shared cultural practices, which eventually led to the making of Tamilakam as a region of linguistic homogeneity. Exchange of goods and services hardly involved the concept of exchange-value/price and the peoples seem to have had no notion of interest/profit. It is true that both transmarine and inland traders from far away places like Rome and the Gangetic valley had entered into exchange relations with the region. Recent studies have shown that the long-distance exchanges were also based on the principle of use-value rather than exchange-value.[6] Though Roman currency was extensively used in the exchanges, it was only as a part of contemporary valuables rather than as a means of payment and measure of value. Roman money entered the transactions as goods of treasure that could be used for enhancing status and ranking, but not as a productive facilitator of labour.

An aspect to be significantly singled out in the context of the present topic of discussion is that the landscape ecotypes of the dominant economy were all within the forest ecosystem. The pastoral tracts (*mullai-tiṇai*) and tracts of shifting cultivation (*kuṛiñji-tiṇai*) that jointly constituted the larger terrain (*vanpulam*) of the economy were grassy hill-tops and vegetated slopes of the forests. The parched zone (*pālaittiṇai*) that extended in summer and dwindled during monsoon, and was inhabited by predatory clans called *maṛavar*, was also a part of the forest. In short, excepting the terrain of wet-rice agriculture, primarily confined to small pockets of fertile river planes (*menpulam*) and the littoral, most of contemporary human habitats were in the forest. Several allusions in the Tamil heroic poems show that contemporary human settlements and forests existed as subsumed by each other. The *aintiṇai* concept differentiating the terrain in terms of five eco-types (*tiṇais*) involves no rigid contrast between forest and non-forest. It is clear that peoples seldom conceived forestland (*kāṭu*) in contradistinction to human inhabited land (*nāṭu*), The kāṭu><nāṭu opposition as it existed in the landscape consciousness of the later agriculturists was not known to them.[7]

The poems clearly show that the political level of the social formation was characterized by tribal chiefdoms with a pattern of distribution of power varying from the simple to the complex along the small and big descent groups.[8] The *kuṭimākkal* or domestic segments of a descent group and their *ko-mān* or *perumakan* (chief) constituted the simplest structure that signified an organized settlement or *ūr* bound by kinship. The basic constituent in the structure was *kuṭi* or family. The heroic poems unveil before us an active scenario of coexistence and interaction of unevenly evolved chiefdoms of three types, that is, ūr, *Malai*, and Nāṭu headed by chiefs, that is, the *kiḻār, vēḷir*, and *vēntar* respectively. Most of the *vēḷir* and *kiḻār* were chieftains of the forest. One of the *vēntar*s, namely the *Cēras*, were chieftains of the forest too.

Several poems indicate that it was in the pastoral tracts (*mullai*) and hills (*kuṛiñji*) in the forest that the velir chieftains held sway over. The poems address them as hill chieftains (*malaiyaman*) heading the descent groups called *veṭar, iṭaiyar*, and *kuṛavar*. Venkatamalai, Kanṭīramalai, Kollimalai, Mutiramalai, Kutiramalai, Paṛampu-malai, Potiyilmalai, Pāyarmalai, Ēḻil-malai, and Nānjilmalai are the famous millet-rich hill chiefdoms celebrated in the poems (*Puṛanānūṛu* [*Pn.*] 143, 168). Ēḻilmalai was the most prominent hill chiefdom of Kerala and the lineage of Nannan, the hunter chief of *vēṭar* (*vēṭarkomān*) was related to that of the chiefs of Kanṭīramalaī. Another chiefdom closely linked to the southern end of Kerala was Potiyilmalai. A hill chief called Irunko-vēl, one of the traditional five *vēls*, is mentioned in a poem as *vēṭarkoman*, the chief of *vēṭar*, to have belonged to a long line of 49 generations of chiefs (*Pn.* 202, 201). The poems celebrate the Āy family as *kuṛavarperumakan*, the chief of *kuṛavar* in the hill called Potiyilmalai, rich in honey, jackfruit, elephants, and monkeys (*Pn.* 17–36). The Āy chief is addressed as *māvēl*, the big *vēl*, and mentioned as belonging to the *Aykuti* (the Āy family). The association of the term 'Āy' with *iṭaiyar* (pastoralists) and the claim of the later Āy chiefs to have belonged to the *vrishnikula* are referred to but as such there is no direct evidence to show that they were pastoral chiefs. Pāri, the chief of Paṛampumalai; Ōri, the chief of Kollimalai; Kāri who killed Ōri and became the chief of his hill, Eḻini, the chief of Kutiramalai and Pēkan, the chief of Vanmalai, Kumaṇan, and the chief of Mutiramalai are the most celebrated hunter chiefs of *vēṭar* or *kuṛavar* (*Pn.* 158). Sometimes the hill chiefs are called *vēṭṭuvar*. This would suggest that the term *vēl* derives from *vēt*, meaning hunter.

All these chiefs, unequal among themselves in their possession of resources, had to resort to plunder raids. Most of them seem to have maintained a predatory control over the agrarian zones in their proximity (*Pn.* 110, 168). The hill chiefs had plundered each other to accumulate resources for redistribution. Through the exchange of forest goods, some of the hill chiefs could have procured new resources like prestige goods. Irunko-vēl's hill is praised in a poem as a gold-yielding one (*Pn.* 202), obviously indicating the exchange of its resources like ivory, monkey, animal skin, sandalwood, and the like for gold coins from Rome. But how exactly the chiefs exchanged the forest goods and realized the returns is not clear. Nevertheless, the hills of certain chiefs had a relatively better potential of new resources, which is referred to in the poems with the term *yāṇar*. Parampumalai is called '*yāṇarara aviyan malai*', the hill with potential new resources (*Pn.* 16). It is evident that the resource potential varied from chief to chief and obviously some of them were comparatively more resourceful. For instance, the Āy chief is said to have possessed horses and chariots. His house was called *koil* and its surroundings as *nakar*. Pari is also mentioned to have possessed horses and chariots and Pittan Korran of Mutiramalai is called '*kaṭumān koṟṟan*', the possessor of horses. Horses were not common as possessions of chiefs and references to their gift-giving of horses and chariots seem to be a mere conventional mode of praise. Possession of rare goods always enriched the status and ranking of chiefs and in the case of the Āy, who is known after his family name, such a higher status is explicit. No other hill chief is known after his family, except perhaps the Cēras, who seem to have emerged from the level of hill chiefs.

The structure of the political level of the hill chiefs was essentially a simple one based on kinship. A chief is referred to in the poems as ko-mān (*ko-makan*) or *perumān* (*peru-makan*) of a given group of people as evidenced by *kuṟavarkomān* or *kuṟavar-perumakan*, and other such terms. Usually, a hill comprised several settlements (*ūr*) of the chief's people and a few others, the size of which varied depending on the extent of the hill and the form of subsistence. These others included the *kuṭis* of magico-religious and other functionaries like the *tuṭiyar* who made a kind of drum called *tuṭi*, and the *pāṇar* who composed *pāṭṭu* or songs (*Pn.* 269, 280, 285, 291). The range of redistributive relationship of a hill chief was limited, though a few bards from distant places also met him occasionally. Similarly, his predatory range was also small and could have managed only small-scale raids. With no relations transcending kinship involved in the form of production and resource circulation, the political power of this category of chiefship remained subsumed within the kinship system.

Like the *vēḷir* chiefs, the *kiḻār* chiefs were also hunter chiefs either of *vēṭar* or *kuṟavar* tribes. The poems mention them as the *ūr-kiḻān* or *ūr-mannar* who were generally chiefs of small settlements, mostly in *vanpulam*, the forest land (*Pn.* 177, 180, 181). The *ur-kiḻān* of a pristine type must have been a smaller variant of the *malai-kilavōn* or the hill chief. A poem praises the *kiḻāṉ* of Irntur, a settlement of vanpulam with marginal resources, depending primarily on plunder raids, as the enemy of hunger who would summon his blacksmith on seeing a hungry bard and order a new lance to go for a raid to appease the bard's hunger (*Pn.* 180). Certain *kiḻāṉ* are also mentioned as chiefs who held sway over agrarian tracts and were relatively more resourceful (*Pn.* 176, 376, 381, 388). However, they also had to maintain predatory control over other settlements to meet the redistributive needs. A few *kiḻār* seem to have functioned like bards of the well-to-do chiefs. Most of the *ūr-kilar* and ur-mannar were subordinates of bigger chiefs and were under the obligation of fighting for them.

Of the three *vēntar* types of chieftains represented by the chiefly lineages, that is, the Cēras, Cōḷas, and Pāṇḍyas, the Cēras are referred to in the poems as *kānaka-naṭān* (the chief of the forested *nāṭu*) or *malaiyan* (the chief of malai or hill), which is suggestive of their ecological region. A poet praising Cēramān Kōtai Mārpan, expresses confusion about how the chief should really be addressed (*Pn.* 49). The poet asks whether the chief could be called *nāṭan* as he had *marutam* lands, or *mān* as he had *kuṛiñji* lands, or *cērpan* as he had coastal tracts. This would suggest that the Cēra region was a mixture of diverse ecological zones with a predominance of hills and forests. The resource base of the Cēra was also, therefore, diverse though forest wealth was the main one. A poem incidentally refers to the hill products (*malaittāram*) and sea products (*kaṭ-arrāram*) of Cēran Cenkuṭṭuvan and the gold that reached ashore by boats (*Pn.* 343). The Pāṇḍya also had a mixed ecological region dominated by pastoral and coastal tracts. A Pāṇḍya chieftain calls himself the head of the land of numerous new resources, '*yāṇar maiyar komān*' (*Pn.* 71). The Cōḻa who is well known as '*kāviri kiḻavōn*' in the poems held sway over land in the Kaveri delta, rich in paddy and sugarcane (*Pn.* 61).

The poems address the *vēntar* as *kāvalar* (protector) of the *kuṭimākkal*, the settlers. *Pāṇḍya* Neṭunceḻiyan refers to his *kuṭimākkal* as '*en niḻal vāḻnar*', meaning those living under his shade. This would presuppose the exaction of something in return from the *kuṭimākkal* for the protection offered to them. In the case of the Cōḻa it is clear that the *vēntan* used to exact *puravu* (paddy) from the *kuṭimākkal* (*Pn.* 75). All the three *vēntar* are referred to in the poems with the term *iṛaivan*, which means he who exacts, which suggests that they had extorted what was feasible according to the resource potential of the region. However, it appears that even this kind of exaction had a predatory character. There is no evidence for any regular periodic exaction in fixed measure or quantity by any of these chieftains. So we may safely assume that the *vēntar* exacted resources through predatory operations and as prestations and voluntary offerings. Poems belonging to the *ceviyaṛivuṛu* and *porunmoḻikkānci tuṛai*s advise the chieftains how to keep the settlements productive and how to appropriate their surplus in a sustainable manner. A poem advises a vēntan not to behave like an elephant in the sugarcane field that destroys much more than what it eats. These are obviously exhortations by poets who have known the instituted modes of periodic exaction in developed kingdoms beyond Tamilakam.

That the *vēntar* category of chieftains also appropriated the resources through predatory means and voluntary offerings like prestations, shows that they were not far removed from the milieu of hill chieftains. There are indications in the poems of the expansion of these powers from their original *ūr* (*mutūr*) obviously through the process of subjugation (*Pn.* 54). The poet shows Cēraman Kuṭṭuvan Kōta, sitting as the *uṭaiyōr* (lord) of a *mutūr* in the place of its original chief, probably suggesting subjugation. The subjugation process seems to have involved three different methods: subordination with tributary obligations, expulsion, and marital alliances. There are many references in the poems to all these methods of enlarging the domain of the *vēntar*. Vaḻḻuvan, the chief of Nāñjilmalai, is mentioned in a poem as a Cēra subordinate with military obligations (*Pn.* 139). The chiefs of Pāyarmalai and Veṭṭāru were the other known Cēra subordinates. Similarly Nākan, the *kiḻavan* of Nalai, and Nampi Neṭunceḻiyan are mentioned as Pāṇḍya subordinates with military obligations (*Pn.* 179, 239). There are a few poems in praise of the chiefs, *ēnāti* Tirukkuṭṭuvan, *ēnāti* Tirukkiḻḻi, and ēnāti Tirukkaṇṇan as ēnāti of the Cōḻa (*Pn.* 167, 174, 394). Paṇṇaṇ, the *kiḻān* of Ciṛukuṭi and Aruvantai, the *kiḻān* of Ampar, were the Cōḻa subordinates with tributary and military obligations. Sometimes chiefs in the fringes were subordinated by two *vēntar* and naturally, this subordination fluctuated from one to the other (*Pn.* 380). In addition to such important subordinates, there were numerous minor chiefs called *cīrūr-mannar*, mostly maṛavar headmen of forest hamlets, who functioned as the military chiefs of the *vēntar*, particularly the Pāṇḍya and Cēra.

The returns from exchange relations must have enabled the *vēntar* to possess gold and other prestige items. As already noted, it is not clear how they were involved in the process of exchange. The poems show that the major activity of the *vēntar*, like the *veḻir*, was accumulation of resources and their redistribution, following the determinate pattern of social relationships. Plunder was indispensable for them also since their redistributive network was much more elaborate and complex than what they could have afforded with their actual resources. They had a large body of dependants such as their kinsmen (*kiḷaiñar*), scholarly bards (*pulavar*), warrior chiefs (*maṛavar*, *kiḷār*, and *mannar*), warrior men (*maravar*), bards (*pāṇar* and *porunar*), magico-religious functionaries, and others. The poetic flower symbolism, *veṭci* (cattle raid), *karantai* (cattle recovery), *vañji* (chieftain's raid), *kāñji* (chieftain's resistance to a raid), and *tumpai* (preparation for a raid) show how institutionalized and common the plunder was.

The structure of the *vēntar* level of political power was relatively more complex since its redistributive social relationship was elaborate. It involved some kind of a simple hierarchy from the *vēntar* to the *kuṭimākkal* with *kiḷar* or *mannar* intermediaries. The hierarchy cut across kinship and distanced the *vēntar* from the *kuṭimākkal*. But they did drink and dine with the *maṛavar* during *unṭāṭṭu*, the pre-raid or post-raid feasting at the residences of the *vēntar*. A complex redistributive political economy based on raids, precludes the formation of a structured polity with defined positions and functions.

There seems to be a lot of difference between the image that the poems try to secure for the *vēntar* and reality about them. We know that unlike the claims in the poems, the whole of Tamilakam did not belong to them and there were other tribute-receiving hill chiefs like Atiyamān who were almost nearer to the *vēntar* in status. A poem in praise of Neṭuman Añji warns all the chiefs of agrarian settlements to rush to him tributes (*tiṛai*) if they wished to keep their *ūr* with them (*Pn.* 97). Many of the hill chiefs were uncompromisingly opposed to the *vēntar*. Pāri of Paṛampumalai is one good example. He offered strong resistance to the *vēntar*, though he was subsequently defeated and killed. So the reality was that the *vēntar* were also chiefs, but of slightly higher category. The crucial difference was their relatively greater resource power, larger redistributive social relationship, and better sources of legitimation. They were surrounded by *brāhmaṇa pulavar* of the Vedic tradition and a few were well informed of the Śāstrāic and Purāṇic notions of kingship. But a predatory chieftain, whose status and power were linked up with the range of redistributive social network, could have hardly gone by Śāstrāic prescriptions. A poem by a scholarly bard reminds Pāṇḍya Nanmāran of the fact that '*aṛa neṛi mutaṟṟē aracin koṟṟam*' meaning greatness of royalty remained with the primacy of '*karma*' (*Pn.* 55). All songs in *Ceviyaṟivuṟutuṟai* contain ideas of this type, which sounded exotic in a milieu of plunder raids and redistribution. The *vēntar* drew upon heroism and gift-giving for ideological force. Bards were the main strength behind their name, fame, and legitimacy. They kept the image of the *vēntar* by roaming round the land with their songs in praise of the latter's exploits. The *pāṇaṟṟuppāṭai* category of poems itself exemplifies the instituted nature of such circuits.

Largely, the headship of clan ties, that is, the chiefly power or the source of authority to command collective labour from chieftains of higher levels could command their mercenaries (*viṭutoḻil*), who seem to have included potters and metal-workers. Probably the most subjected kind of labour they commanded must have been of captives. Possessing warrior power, they could probably command all kinds of specialized labour. There are references in the poems to warriors (*maṟavar*) offering paid protection to caravan troops of *umaṇaccāttu* or salt merchants (*Akanāṉūṟu* [*An.*] 39:10, 167:7, 245:6, and 291:15). In these poems, the means of payment is mentioned as *dravya* (wealth), the exact connotation of which is unclear.

The principal social mode of labour realization was familial or cooperative. A few crafts like metal-working and pottery that come under the category of skilled labour, must have been full-time hands of specialists and hence hereditary. Iron, the most extensively used metal, had a central place particularly as the base of weapons, the significance in a predatory society is explicit. Moreover, the practice of burying iron objects along with the dead had pushed a great deal of iron out of circulation, presupposing continuous iron-working as a full-time occupation of hereditary specialization. The production of earthen pots, a characteristically brittle artefact, was obviously a continuous full-time activity, for their use was extensive both for the living as well as the dead. The number of such full-time artisans and craftsfolk of hereditary occupations was relatively greater in the headquarters of bigger chieftains of the *veḷir* and *vēntar* levels. As the major redistributive pools of resources, the chiefly settlements could support more full-time crafts. Another function of a hereditary nature was that of warriors (*maṟavar*). Every settlement (*ūr*) needed full-time warriors since the main mode of political appropriation of resources was predatory. In association with the chiefly households, three other hereditary functionaries were the pāṇar (bards), *paṟaiyar* (who play a kind of raid drum called *paṟa*), and *tuṭiyar* (who play a small drum called *tuṭi*) were there.

The preceding discussions of the features of the economic and political levels of the social formation clearly indicate that they were predominantly characterized by the tribal polity and forest cultures. This is further endorsed by the various rites and rituals and instituted practices of the times. So do the various beliefs and customs, costumes and ornaments that characterized the regime of culture. Institutions for the chiefly celebration through group drinking and dining of warriors after and before cattle raids (*unṭaṭṭu*), the chieftains; public rice-feasts (*cōṟṟuviḻāvus*), and dances propitiating the battle goddess (*kuravaikkūttu*) by women are some of the examples, to mention only a few. The primacy of forest culture and the tribal way of life continued until the social formation got dissolved into a new one dominated by advanced wet-rice agriculture.

The dissolution of the tribes and forest social formation began to manifest itself in the form of a series of institutional and structural changes. Predatory marches of chiefs, their ravaging of settlements, redistribution of (*ūr*), and the consequent migration and immigration, were some of the ongoing events of the transforming effect on the social formation that was generating various contradictions within due to built-in factors like kin labour and redistribution. The most striking contradiction was the continued articulation of conditions totally uncongenial to the development of plough agriculture, which was the most potential form among contemporary forms of production. Predatory marches of chieftains, their destruction of agrarian settlements as part of the scorched-earth policy in raids, and the dominance of the ideology of war and booty redistribution provided an adverse circumstance for the development of agriculture. As we have already seen, redistribution exerted pressure on production, but failed to translate itself as a force generating intensified production since there was no scope for it within the kinship-based forms of production. Intensified labour mobilization for better production was beyond the working power of contemporary political apparatus that had little coercive ability. It was not possible for the social formation to persist for a long time in a set-up of complex redistribution, generating contradictions. Obviously the major bend in the process was that of the gradual dissolution of the social formation. The process involved the expansion of wet-rice fields, slow disintegration of tribes into domestic segments of hereditary arts and crafts, formation of agrarian villages as clusters of settlements (*cēris*), occupied by artisans, craftsmen, and tillers, that were owned and controlled by landed households. A corresponding manifestation was the receding of the forest from the mainstream world and the extension of the agrarian landscape as its contrast.

The seeds of the dissolution of the tribes and forest social formation can be discerned in the redistribution of resources, particularly in land beyond the social relationship of kinship, which had certain lasting consequences. It appears that at some point of time the institution of redistribution involved gifts of land, mainly to warrior chiefs. In the case of the warrior chiefs, the gift must have meant only transfer of predatory control rather than ownership. As scholarly *brāhmaṇas* were part of the redistributive social relationship, land seems to have been gifted to them too, though not extensively. Not being cultivators by themselves, *brāhmaṇas* had to get their land worked by others. This implied the making of a new system of relations in production, transcending the framework of kinship. We have a few references to prominent *brāhmaṇa* households. Kauṇiyan Viṇṇan Tāyan of Punjārrūr, is an example, but he appears in the poems as a householder with pastoral wealth rather than agrarian resources (*Pn.* 166). It is a fact that with their system of non-kin relations of labour the *brāhmaṇa* households witnessed the beginnings of social stratification.

What began taking shape in the *brāhmaṇa* households was crucial for the real beginnings of a hierarchy. The permanent workforce attached to the *brāhmaṇa* households had the greatest possibility of being conceived hierarchically because of the stratifying system of production relations and the brahmanical tradition of social differentiation. The notion of hierarchy was implicit in the system of production in which the relation between two objectively antagonistic classes was fundamental. The mid-first millennium AD was thus a turning point in terms of stratification and hierarchical ordering. The process took more than two centuries to characterize the social aggregate. During the fifth–sixth centuries the agrarian societies of Tamilakam were perceptibly becoming class-structured. This was directly related to the spread of plough agriculture and the corresponding new relations of production that meant social stratification based on entitlements to the nature of land-use. It was primarily a tripartite stratification of the people into landholders, leaseholders, and tillers. Since plough agriculture also meant specialization of a variety of arts and crafts, a further stratification of the people who were grouped along the line of occupations followed gradually. The nature of rights over land and the level of entitlement to the produce determined the strata of the people of different arts and crafts. Divided largely into the upper and lower strata the people were soon woven into a system of differentiation within each stratum. The social relations of the period resulted from an aggregate of these.

The social relations began to be further structured during the sixth–seventh centuries with the steady expansion of plough agriculture across the wetland. Expansion of agrarian settlements through the creation of *brahmadēyas* often involved the superimposition of the superior rights of the *brāhmaṇas* over the communal holdings and the clan families of the locality. It must have been an intricate process of transformation of primitive agriculture and clan settlements into advanced agriculture and farmer settlements, respectively. The main features of the process were differentiation, stratification, and political formation leading to the development of the state-system and authority structures. These were simultaneous developments taking place as supplementary and complimentary to one another, resulting from the growth of paddy economy. Such developments were in their turn ensuring the further growth of tire economy.

The relations of production in plough agriculture were expanding towards domination of the total society. This was a long institutional process involving the proliferation of occupational specialization and its ordering into a hierarchy.[9] The formation of agrarian localities was an ongoing process, and everywhere it accomplished a uniform structure of social relations. As agrarian expansion advanced, human settlements (*ūr*) originally bound by kinship got penetrated by the mechanisms of stratification. In short the transformation of non-*brāhmaṇa* villages into productive relations transcending kinship was a continuous process. The non-*brāhmaṇa* villages were called *velānvakai* in contemporary inscriptions. Such settlements began to be integrated as agrarian localities (*nāṭu*). This *nāṭu* was hence fundamentally different from the *nāṭu* that figures in the heroic poems. As agrarian localities of hierarchically structured social relations, the *nāṭus* subsequently acquired great political significance in the monarchical system. It represented a clear contrast to the forest.

The disintegration of clan-kin ties became almost total along the agrarian tracts as paddy cultivation expanded with the corresponding developments like social stratification and widening of the division of labour through specialization. In the process, the clan identity disappeared and *jāti* came in as the substitute, mostly by retaining the names of the clan. Several names like *pāṇa, paṛaya, vēṭṭuva, vela, kuṛava, maṛava,* and *paratava,* vouch for the retention of clan names for *jāti*. The first notable development towards the transformation of clans into *jātis* was specialization of labour. It was the practice of rewarding specialized labour with land-based entitlements that made specialization of labour hereditary. The reason was obviously the labourers' urge to perpetuate the entitlements. But how the labouring clans of hereditary specialization got absorbed into the *jāti* system cannot be explained easily. We know that the proliferation of hereditary occupations and their absorption into the *jāti* hierarchy were advancing side by side with the socio-spatial expansion of paddy-cultivation. Also we know that at a later period, new institutional agencies like the temple and service tenements were instrumental in crystallizing the *jāti* system. Further, the relation of the *jāti* system to brahmanism is taken for granted by all. But at the same time the actual social process of the making of the *jāti* system is largely unclear and still not understood.

The society became class-structured and the dissolution of tribal chiefdoms began anticipating formation of the state with the new agrarian system articulating its polity. The new political formation represented by the Simhavarman line of the Pallavas and the Kaṭunkon line of the Pāṇḍyas owed itself to the developing agrarian society whose expansion was linked to royal patronage. The Cōḷas of the Vijayālaya line at a later period represented the same kind of political authority engendered by the paddy-based economy. Though it is not clear whether the Cēras represented a comparable royal line of inheritance, the political authority represented by them too was engendered by the paddy economy. A perceptible institutional feature of agrarian expansion was the proliferation of *brahmadēya* villages throughout the fertile tracts of major river valleys in the region. This was an organized affair under royal initiative. A few copper plates, Velvikkuti plates for instance, speak about the restoration of the villages originally gifted to *brāhmaṇas* as *ēkabhōga* and subsequently lost through misappropriation by others. All such lost villages were later restored as *brahmadēyas* under the corporate control as the cases like the Velvikkuti vouch for. This shift from individual holding (ēkabhōga) to collective holding (corporate *brahmadēya*) is important in the context of the insecurity of the former. The proliferation of the latter meant the successful development of the new system of productive relations under a new institutional form and political patronage.[10]

With the expansion of the new relations of production and the spread of wet-rice agriculture that became characteristic to the period from sixth–seventh centuries, the social formation structured by the dominance of forest economies came to an end. In short, the disappearance of the social formation dominated by forest economies involved a series of transitions like those from kin-labour to non-kin labour, multiple functionaries to hereditary occupation groups, clans to castes, simple clannish settlements to structured agrarian villages, and chiefdom to monarchy.[11]

NOTES AND REFERENCES

1. 'Tamil Heroic Poems' as an expression refers to what is popularly known as the corpus of Sangam poems here. The corpus includes in its most archaic stratum some of the anthologies grouped under *Eṭṭuttokai* and *Pattuppaṭṭu*, roughly belonging to second century BC and AD third century. For a detailed analysis of the structure, diction, and context of the corpus, see K. Kailasapathy, 1968, *Tamil Heroic Poetry*, London.
2. Label inscriptions consist of the Tamil *brāhmi* labels belonging to about the third century BC to the AD fourth century. See I. Mahadevan, 1970, 'Corpus of Tamil Brahmi Inscriptions', in R. Nagaswamy (ed.), *Seminar on Inscriptions*, Madras. The foreign notices comprise mainly the Graeco-Roman writings. Archaeology of the Iron Age in south India is a well-studied topic. See Guru Raja Rao, 1972, *The Megalithic Culture of South India*, Mysore; L.S. Leshnik, 1974, *South Indian 'Megalithic' Burials: The Pandukal Complex*, Wiesbaden. Also A. Sundara, 1975, *The Early Chamber Tombs of South India*, Delhi. For studies in the cultural overlap and continuity between the periods of Megalithism and the early historic heroic society see K.R. Srinivasan, 1947, 'The Megalithic Burial and Cairn Fields of South India in the Light of Tamil Literature and Tradition', *Ancient India*, no. 2, pp. 9–16; R. Champakalakshmi, 1975–6, 'Archaeology and Tamil Literary Tradition', *Purātatva*, no. 8, pp. 110–22.
3. For details see Gurukkal, 'Forms of Production and Forces of Change', pp. 160–8.
4. This is argued at length in Gurukkal, 'Forms of Production and Forces of Change', pp. 168–75. For an analysis of the larger context, see Romila Thapar, 'Black Gold: South Asia and the Roman Maritime Trade', *South Asia*, n.s., 15(2): 1–28.
5. For a detailed consideration of the issue see Rajan Gurukkal, 'Forms of Production and Forces of Change...', pp. 162–75. Also his, 1998, 'Characterising Ancient Society: The Case of South India', Presidential Address, Indian History Congress, Ancient India Section, Patiala, pp. 24–5.
6. Ibid., pp. 21–3. For details of this process in the context of the transformations in Tamilakam see, Rajan Gurukkal, 'Forms of Production and Forces of Change...'.
7. See Rajan Gurukkal, 'Characterising Ancient Society: The Case of South India'.
8. This is considered at length in Rajan Gurukkal, 2002, 'Antecedents of State Formation in South India', in R. Champakalakshmi, K. Veluthat, and T.R. Venugopalan (eds), *State and Society in Pre-modern South India*, Trissur, pp. 39–45.
9. For a detailed consideration of the issue see Rajan Gurukkal, 1997, 'From Clan and Lineage to Hereditary Occupations and Caste in South India',

in Dev Nathan (ed.), *From Tribe to Caste*, Shimla, pp. 205–22. Also, his 'Characterising Ancient Society: The Case of South India'.

10. See Rajan Gurukkal, 'From Clan and Lineage to Hereditary Occupations...'.
11. Ibid., p. 220. Also see Rajan Gurukkal and Raghava Varier (eds), 1999, *Cultural History of Kerala*, vol. I, Trivandrum, pp. 257–63.

6

Forms of Production and Forces of Change in Ancient Tamil Society*

This chapter seeks to characterize the forms, features, and dynamics of the subsistence pattern of peoples in ancient Tamilakam, which covered roughly the whole of the deep south of peninsular India, from the northern banks of the river Kaveri to Kanyakumari, the southernmost tip. Ancient here means the time span between circa third century BC to AD third century. The choice of the area and the period is determined by the sources available for the study, which fall into five different categories: (a) archaeological, or relics of Iron Age burials and habitats; (b) epigraphical, a host of labels in Tamil Brāhmi characters; (c) numismatic, a few hoards of pre-Roman and Roman coins; (d) classical accounts by Graeco-Roman geographers and navigators; and (e) ancient Tamil literary anthologies. Using these varied sources, scholars, mainly specialists in archaeology, epigraphy, numismatics, and literature, have generated a lot of knowledge about the past. These scholars set the precedent of labelling peoples and cultures with the names of source categories that yielded knowledge about them. For instance, archaeologists conceived Iron Age megalithic people/culture; epigraphists, heterodox following/culture; numismatists, long-distance trading people/Indo-Roman transmarine culture; and literary scholars, Sangam Age heroic people/culture. The present study seeks to transcend this approach of source-category-based identification of peoples and cultures by postulating a landscape and people/material culture approach, according to which the varied source categories converge with their overlapping peoples, cultures, and chronology.

---

* This chapter is a revised version of, 1989, 'Forms of Production and Forces of Change in Ancient Tamil Society', *Studies in History*, Vol. 2, n.s., pp. 159–75.

Iron Age relics cover a larger area, probably the whole of peninsular India, and a longer period, probably the whole of the first millennium BC. In the region under review, they represent the most widespread strands of an ancient culture type.[1] The dawn of history in the region is marked by the diffusion of this culture. Burial monuments and grave goods dominate Iron Age relics. Iron objects of a wide variety, different types of black and red ware (BRW), other pottery types, and beads, constitute the major items among grave goods.[2] Among the iron artefacts, spears, swords, tangled daggers, wedge-shaped blades, barbed arrowheads, and horse fittings are notable.[3] A large number of knives, tripods, and bell-like objects, lamps, a few hoes, shovels, spades, and ploughshares were also collected.[4] Bronze and copper objects were also seen, though not commonly.[5] Generally, hunting tools were more numerous than grave goods (see Fig. 6.1). Of

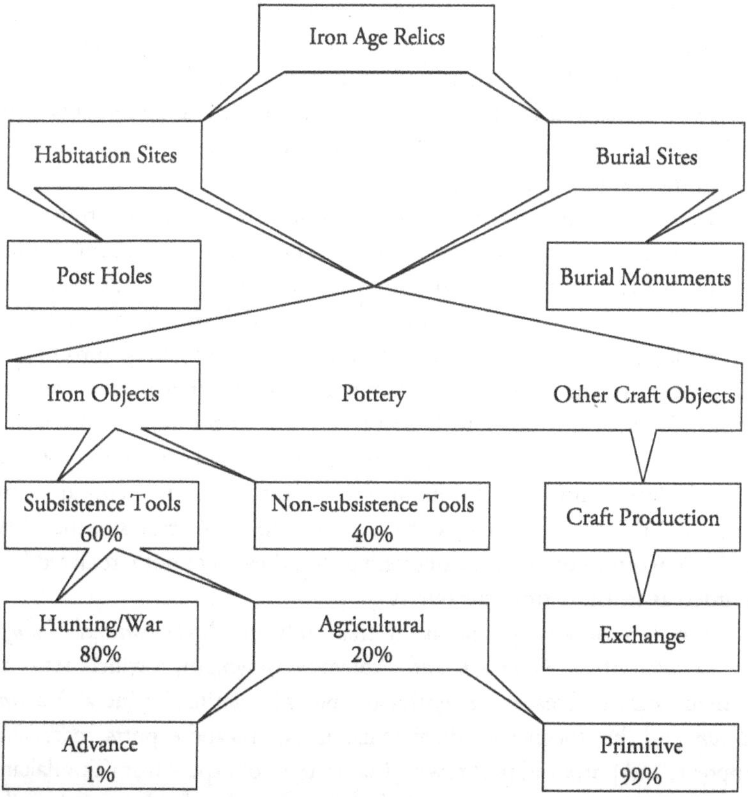

Figure 6.1 Iron age archaeological data profile

the marginal number of agrarian tools, the majority are of the primitive type. Post-holes at the habitation sites, horse fittings, and war implements indicate a relatively non-sedentary life of warrior communities, who seemed to have been ironsmiths also.[6] Iron was a part of all contemporary forms of subsistence and diverse social groups could resort to each of these forms.

The Tamil *brāhmi* labels mostly contain personal and occupational names of donors who endowed the Buddhist and Jain monks with stone beds in natural caverns.[7] Out of the fifteen cavern sites with labels of the third to the first centuries BC, ten are on the routes of the third to first centuries BC, while another ten are on the routes from Madurai to its neighbouring towns with a dense distribution in the north-east, on the routes to Tiruchirapalli. The labels refer to specialist merchants such as *pon-vāṇikan* (gold merchant), *aṛuvai vāṇikan* (textile merchant), *koḻu-vāṇikan* (ploughshare merchant), *uppu vāṇikan* (salt merchant), and *pānita vāṇikan* (toddy merchant).[8] Specialist craftsmen like pon-kolavan (goldsmith) also figure in a label.[9] The distribution of the cavern sites shows a network of merchant routes and the presence of certain agricultural settlements. The evidence suggests an economy based on rudimentary specialization in crafts-production and exchange.

The numismatic evidence consists of several hoards of punch-marked and Roman coins recovered from various places such as Pollachi, Karur, Vellalur, Kalayamuttur, Madurai, Coimbatore, Yesvantpur, and Pudukkottai in Tamil Nadu and Eyyal, Kottayam, Valluvalli, and Puthenchira in Kerala.[10] The punch-marked coins belonged to the pre-Mauryan kingdoms of the Gangetic valley and Roman coins from the reigns of Augustus (first century BC) to Constantinus (AD fourth century). Most of the Roman silver and gold coins in the hoards belong to the reigns of emperors and empresses from the first century BC to the AD second century. Coins appear to be fresh from the mint and many of them have loops or apertures so that they could be worn as ornaments, suggesting that they were not circulated but hoarded as treasure, from the outset.

The classical writings relevant to this study are Pliny's *Natural History*, the *Periplus Maris Erythraei*, and Ptolemy's *Geography*,[11] which refer to contemporary overseas trade centres and ports in peninsular India. *Natural History* and *Periplus* give us a detailed list of imports and exports, marts and emporia, and ports and port towns. Major items of export from Tamilakam were aromatics, pepper, ginger, cardamom, cloves, and other spices; wild fauna, animal skins, ivory; timber like teak and sandal; cotton fabrics;

precious stones; and pearls and gems.[12] Gold and silver coins were the main items of import.[13]

The ancient Tamil anthologies, popularly known as Sangam literature, consist of *Tolkāppiyam* (a work on grammar), *Eṭṭuttokai* (the eight anthologies), *Pattupāṭṭu* (the ten idylls), and *Patinenkīḻkaaṇakku* (the eighteen didactical texts). It is now well known that the chronology of these collections is not uniform and they are not contemporaneous with *Sangam* which collected, classified, and redacted the poems.[14] There is a time lag of three or four centuries between the composition of the poems and their collection. Further, each anthology has four chronological strata: those of the actual text, the commentary, the invocatory stanzas, and the colophons.[15] Of the whole corpus of this literature, the *Eṭṭuttokai* collection, excluding *Kalittokai* and *Paripāṭal* is considered to be the most archaic, belonging to about the third century BC to the AD third century. Some of the idylls of the *Pattupāṭṭu* collection are also of a nearer antiquity.[16] The present study relies on these relatively archaic ones. As source material, this literature poses certain other problems, besides that of their confused chronology. One problem is that it consists of heroic poems, their limitations in understanding contemporary society being obvious. Another is that the literature broadly belongs to the tradition of oral compositions, characterized by formulaic diction, stock phrases, highly stylized expression, and the administration of symbols of unconscious meaning.[17] So the use of this literature as source material has to be preceded by a series of difficult exercises starting from the basic syntagmatic analysis of morphology to the complex paradigmatic, psycho-analytical, and semiological analyses for grasping the principles of versification and the genuine meaning of the poems.[18] Though one cannot go by the apparent contents of the poems, their overall institutional and ideational contexts, which are not far removed from reality, can be depended upon.

Scholars have been using the foregoing data for historical studies of ancient south India with an inordinate emphasis on the political aspects,[19] though some did try to focus on the social aspect too.[20] But this made no difference since the perspective has been the same. There been scarce attempts at examining the socio-economic processes instead of viewing the social, economic, political, and religious mutually exclusive facets. An integrated utilization of the source categories in an anthropological perspective is yet to gain currency in the historiography of south India; the practice of identifying culture types behind the sources categories or naming the cultures after source-types persists, particularly among specialists.

Archaeologists speak about the Iron Age culture or/and Megalithic culture; epigraphists about heterodox religious groups; numismatists and specialists on classical accounts about a civilization of maritime commerce; and specialists on ancient Tamil literature about the Sangam society. These specialists sometimes borrow from certain other categories of sources also when discussing the culture-type behind the category of their specialization. But all of them conveniently forget the fact that these different categories of sources point to one phase or the other of the same social formation. The historiographic justification of the present discussion is that it tries to integrate the variety of sources in order to understand the contemporary socio-economic processes.

The main exercise here is the integration of clues from the sources in which the use of clues from the anthologies is central. We propose to use the clues drawn from poems ascribed to the period between the third century BC and the third century AD. But there is no precise dating of each poem to enable organization of the clues in a chronological order. This does not mean that there is nothing to indicate the gradients in the long span of about six centuries and the corresponding socio-economic changes. Clues are identified as relatively earlier or later on the basis of a general ideological notion of social evolution.

As we have already seen in the previous chapters most relevant aspect of the anthologies is their concept of *tiṇai* according to which Tamilakam consisted of five tiṇais or physiographical divisions—*kuṟiñji* (hilly backwoods), *pālai* (parched zone), *mullai* (pastoral tract), *marutam* (wetland), and *neital* (littoral).[21] It is not mechanical compartmentalization of nature into five segments. While dividing nature into five discontinuous segments, the whole was conceived as a continuum too.[22] Where exactly a tiṇai begins and where it ends cannot be demarcated since each one merges with the other. Whatever be its semiological implications as a poetic concept of oral literature, the existing geographical setting of the region proves it a reflection of reality.[23]

The poems involve the description of the mode of human adaptation in each *tiṇai* and the various social groups there: the *kanavar, kuṟavar*, and *vēṭar* were the inhabitants of the *kuṟiñji-tiṇai* and hunting and gathering their form of subsistence (see Fig. 6.2).[24] Similarly, in the *palai-tiṇai*, the inhabitants were *kaḷavar, eyinar*, and *maṟavar* living by plunder and cattle lifting.[25] In the *mullai-tiṇai* they were *āyar* and *iṭaiyar* subsisting on the shifting agriculture and animal husbandry.[26] *Uḻvara* and *toḻuvar* were the inhabitants of the *marutam-tiṇai* and plough agriculture their form of subsistence.[27] In the *neital-tiṇai* they were *paratavar, valayar*, and *mīnavar* dependent on fishing and salt extraction.[28]

We do not see all these people now, but certain groups have survived to our times as anthropological relics. For instance, there is no tribe called *kuṛavar* now, but *vēṭar* and *kuṛavar*. Similarly *āyar* and *iṭaiyar* need not necessarily be two different tribes, but synonyms of one and the same pastoral tribe as evidenced by later inscriptions.[29] The name *eyinar* does not exist today, but *maṛavar* and *kallar* do. It appears in the poems that *maṛavar* and *eyinar* were synonyms for each other, if not of the *kallar*.[30] Neither uḻvara nor *toḻuvar* survives today. The current term for agriculturists is *veḷḷāḷar*.[31] It appears that *valayar* and *mīnavar* were synonyms of *paratavar* whose name still exists. There is no anthropolotical evidence for *umaṇar* who were the salt merchants associated with the *neital-tiṇai*.

Eliminating the synonyms, the use of which is essential in versification based on metrical prescriptions, we get a total of eight social groups: *kuṛavar, vēṭar, iṭaiyar, kaḷḷar, uḻvara, paratavar*, and *umaṇar* as the main inhabitants of the five tiṇais. A group called panar, who were wandering bards, are associated with all the tinais in the poems,[32] making a mixed appearance. Groups such as *paṛaiyar, tuṭiyar, vēṭṭuvar*, and *kaṭampar* figured probably in the *kuṛiñji-palai* or *mullai–palai* blending zones. Both *kuṛiñji* and *mullai* had cultivable slopes at their merging zones which enabled *vēṭar* and *kuṛavar* to take to shifting cultivation. Poem 159 of *Puṛanānūṛu* (*Pn.*) has a reference to the *vēṭar* of *Kollimalai* carrying on slash-and-burn agriculture. *Pn.* 231 refers to *kuravar* of *Kollainilam* doing slash-and-burn operations, probably for cultivation. *Naṛṛiṇai* (*Nar.*) 266 and 289 refer to shifting cultivation by the *āyar* or *iṭaiyar* of the *mullai*.

Similarly, people in the *mullai–marutam* blending zones seem to have practised spinning and weaving and those in the *neital–marutam* blending zones, pot-making. Metal smelting seems to have been important in both the zones: *Pn.* 125 refers to a woman engaged in spinning, *Nar.* 353 also shows spinning as an activity of the women folk; *Pn.* 170 and 312 and *Akanānūṛu* (*An.*) 96 refer to people smelting iron and the devices they used. The poems follow a further grouping of the *tiṇai*s on the basis of the nature of production, according to which the plough agriculture zone (*marutam)* was called *menpulam* and the rest, excluding neital, were collectively called *vanpulam.*[33] In short, they were the zones of advanced agriculture and primitive agriculture, respectively. *Menpulam* produced paddy and sugarcane as the main crops and *vanpulam* grew pulses and dryland grains.[34]

A closer understanding of the poetic specifications of the tiṇais leads us to the identification of contemporary forms of production. Leaving the primitive forms of subsistence such as hunting and gathering besides their extended forms, such as fishing and plundering, there were four other forms of material production: animal husbandry, shifting agriculture, petty-commodity production, and plough agriculture. There are signifiers of all these forms of production in the archaeology of Iron Age relics though we do not know the chronological stratum of each one's origin. The ploughshare, which is rarely represented among the grave goods, seems to have appeared only at a late phase.[35] If we can take the *koḻuvāṇikan* of the cave-label for a ploughshare merchant, we can say that the antiquity of the iron-tipped plough, at least in the Vaigai valley, is certainly not less than the second century BC.[36] The use of the plough during the days of ancient Tamil *mēḻi* and *nāñjil* are the two most commonly used terms in the poems for plough and *er* for ploughshare.[37] The term *er* referred to the act of ploughing, *uḻavu* and,therefore, the terms *ērōr* and *uḻavar* were used for the ploughmen.[38] It is clear from the poems that the plough was drawn by a pair of bullocks (*erutu*) or buffaloes (*erumai*) which were harnessed with a crossbar (*nukam*) on their necks.[39]

Of the four forms of production, plough agriculture was obviously the superior one in terms of technology and productivity. But this superior form was confined to small pockets of menpulam which was surrounded by large tracts of vanpulam. Poems give us enough evidence, direct and indirect, to believe that a large majority of the population took to stock-rearing and shifting cultivation.[40]

Most of the crafts production seems to have persisted as part of animal husbandry and primitive agriculture. Some of them, particularly metal-working and pot-making, must have required full-time specialists as indicated by references to *pon-kolavan* (goldsmith), *kolavan* (blacksmith), and *kuyavan* or *kalancei-kōvan* (potter) in the poems.[41] Iron-working must have been quite significant as the society of the period was characterized by warrior hegemony. Clues in archaeology to numerous burials containing iron artifacts and the references to them in the poems would lead us to infer that a large quantity of iron goods were going out of circulation, thus adding to the significance of continuous iron-working.[42] However, unlike agriculture, iron smelting did not require so many workers (see Fig. 6.2).

The basis of production relations was kinship, signified by *iḷaiyarum mutiyarum kiḷaiyuṭan tuvaṛi*, which is a stock expression in the poems

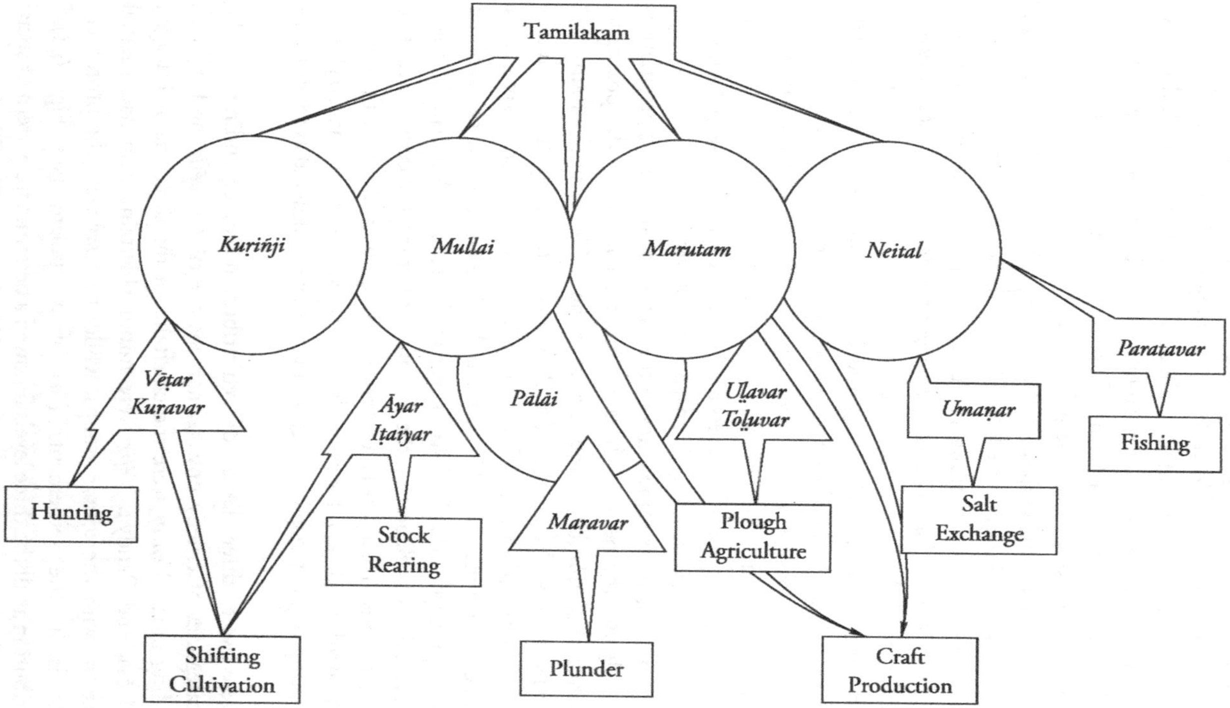

Figure 6.2 Ecological zones, people, and forms of subsistence

referring to the labour process in any tiṇai. *Iḷaiyar* means youngsters, *mutiyar* means elders, and *kiḷai* means agnatic kin.[43] The term *kiḷai* stands as the Tamil counterpart of *jnāti*. Even in plough agriculture, kinship was central to the organization of the labour process and it precluded any system of evolved social division of labour. But it did not entirely preclude the development of specialist forms of production such as metal-working, pot-making, weaving, and salt manufacturing.[44]

This was also the case with specialist exchanges. We hear about specialist merchants both in the cave labels and Tamil anthologies, However, these specialists appear to be nothing more than functionaries in a complex system of cooperation based on the network of social relations of kinship.[45] It is well known that the surplus potential of kinship-based production would be very limited.[46] However, the level of productivity in plough agriculture, despite its kinship base, would be much higher compared to other forms of subsistence. We have enough evidences in the poems to show that surplus in menpulam was large enough to sustain a variety of non-productive but socially necessary functionaries such as preceptors, bards, dancers, magicians, physicians, and astrologers.

The poems give us some clues to the modes of surplus appropriation prevalent during the period. There are many references in the poems to the practice of accumulating the harvest at the residence of chieftains and to its redistribution by them.[47] *Pn.* 353 speaks of paddy heaped like a hill in the courtyard of a chieftain. *Pn.* 376 praises the paddy stock of a chieftain called Oyman. *Pn.* 391 refers to the skyscraper paddy heaps of the *kiḻān* of Poṟaiyāṟṟūr and *Pn.* 396 to that of Eḻiniātān of Veṭṭāru. All these poems are eulogies celebrating the munificence of the respective chieftains who redistributed their stocks of paddy among their kinsmen (*kiḷaiñar*), scholarly bards (*pulavar*), lesser bards (pānar), warrior men (maṟavar), and the various groups of magico-religious people who wandered as mendicants (*iravar*).

There were three levels of redistribution corresponding to the three categories of chiefly powers, namely, the *vēntar*, *vēḷir*, and *kiḻār* in descending order. *Vēntar* were the chieftains of the three major lineages: Cēra, Cōḻa, and Pāṇḍya. *Vēḷir* were minor chieftains who had marital connections with the *vēntar* groups, while the *kiḻār* were the prominent households in the settlements (*ūr*) of menpulam (see Fig. 6.3).[48] Redistribution at all the three levels followed a determinate pattern of social relationships which involved the basis of kinship as well as interpersonal relationships beyond kinship. The institution of gift (*koṭai*) was an integral

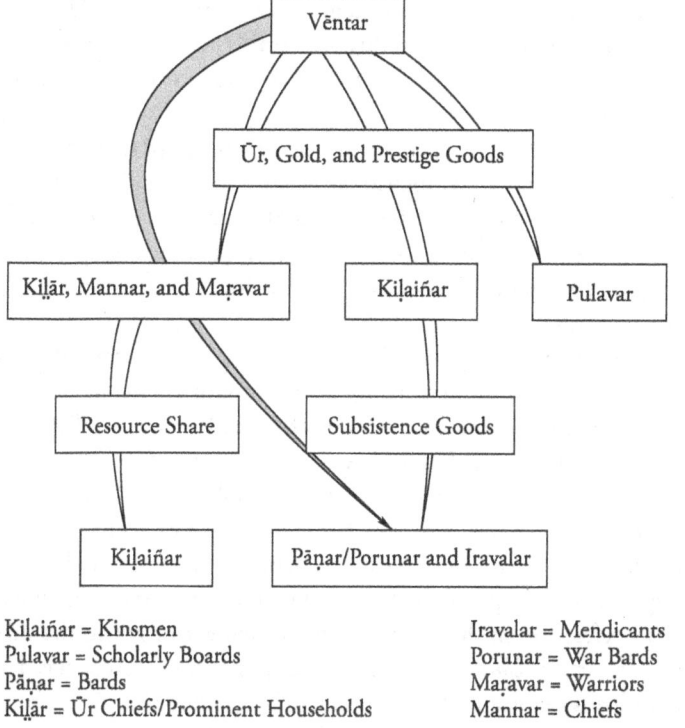

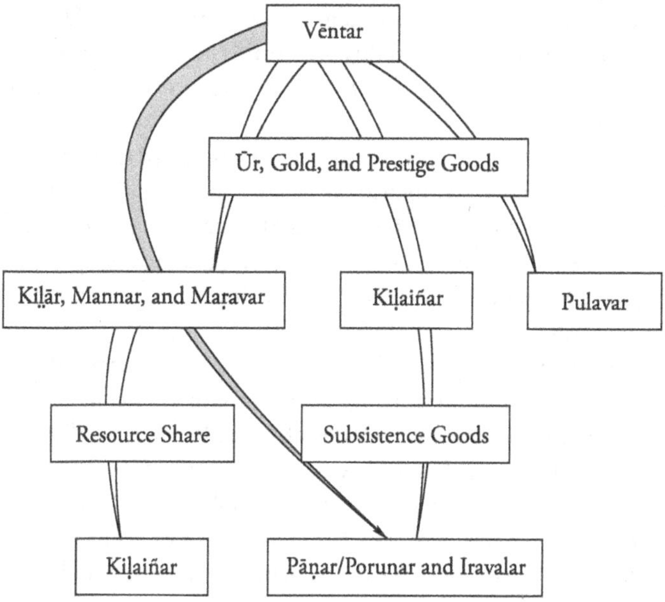

Kiḷaiñar = Kinsmen
Pulavar = Scholarly Boards
Pāṇar = Bards
Kiḻār = Ūr Chiefs/Prominent Households
Iravalar = Mendicants
Porunar = War Bards
Maṟavar = Warriors
Mannar = Chiefs

Figure 6.3 Iron age archaeological data profile

part of contemporary redistribution.[49] Gifts marked a development in the primeval kinsmen-centred redistribution since entitlement to gifts was extended beyond the clan or kin network.

In the routine kind of redistribution at the *vēntar* and *vēḷir* levels, cattle and grain constituted the major items. Pulavar and pāṇar claim to have received gifts of elephants, golden lotuses, chariots, gems, muslin, and land. These claims are the conventional motifs used in poems for glorifying the munificence of the patron heroes. However, it is not unlikely that pulavar, particularly *brāhmaṇas*, received gifts of such prestige items, but a *pāṇa* in most cases seems to have received only subsistence goods. Gifts at the level of *kiḻar* were confined to a meal, or a bowl of millet, maize, or rice, or some old clothes. The military valour of a chieftain was celebrated with as much glory as his munificence. Plunder was the institutional means to extract resources from the centres beyond the network of redistributive social relationships for every chieftain, and appear to be fundamental to the maintenance of the contemporary redistributive system. *Pn.* 180 presents a *kiḻar* in a state drained of all resources calling to his blacksmith for a new lance to set out on a raid in order to satisfy a hungry bard. Though the *vēntar* and *vēḷir* groups were much more resourceful, plunder was indispensable for them too, since insufficiency haunted them at all levels. All of them raided each other. The poetic flower symbolism associated with the different kinds of raids such as *veṭci* (cattle raid), *karantai* (cattle recovery), *vañji* (a chieftain's raid), *kañji* (defence against a chieftain's raid), and *tumpai* (preparations for resisting the enemies), shows exactly how institutionalized and common a plunder raid was.[50]

The redistribution system did not prelude other forms of resource circulation, even specialized exchanges. One form that is frequently referred to in the poems is the exchange of goods for goods (*noṭuttal*). People from their *tiṇai*s reached menpulam and exchanged their goods for paddy at fixed points of exchange (*āvaṇam* and *angāṭi*).[51] People from *kuṛiñji* had ivory, honey, wild meat, animal skins, and bamboo-rice for exchange, while those from *mullai* had dairy products, millet, maize, horse-gram, and forage for exchange. The coastal people had mainly fish and salt for exchange and there are many references in the poems to the movement of salt to the interior in bullock-carts.[52] *Umaṇar* who were specialists in salt exchange, had to cart their loads to distant places through difficult and inhospitable terrains, which is why they moved as caravan troupes which are referred to in the poems as *umaṇaccāttu*.[53] There are references in certain poems of the *Akam* collection to the caravan troupes of *umaṇar* taking the help of *maṛavar* (warriors) for security at required points.[54] The exchange of craft goods was carried on by specialists. However, all these exchanges were fundamentally of the same use-value form. There is no evidence for transactions based on exchange value even in the case of specialist goods.[55] Poems refer to a kind of loan of commodities (*kuṛittumāretirpai* or *kuṛiyetirpai*) which was to be paid back in the same kind and quantity.[56] This was, in fact, part of the reciprocity of goods and informal gift exchange through which a lot of resources circulated among neighbours within a settlement.[57] The concept of profit or interest appears to be anachronistic in the context of contemporary exchanges.[58]

Much has been said about south India's maritime trade during this period. Actually, there is no clear evidence of the people of contemporary Tamilakam organizing maritime trade or external long distance trade.[59] The nature of internal exchanges helps us presume that this lack of evidence was not altogether accidental. The evidence is only for the arrival of foreign merchants and shipping of the required goods in their own vessels. To Tamil society, it meant only an extension of its barter system of exchange, and probably the only difference was that the goods were exchanged for prestige objects, gold and silver coins being predominant. In a redistributive society of presentations and gifts, where no idea of price and profit prevailed, coins could have seldom functioned as money, but only as a category of valuables.[60] The survival of coins as hoards fresh from the mint and with apertures or loops on many, suggests that they were preserved as treasure and often used as ornaments. It is true that there were craft products such as gems, pearls, and muslin, but they were obviously not enough for the emergence of real trade mechanisms in Tamilakam.[61] However, the internal forms of exchange indicate a fairly developed network of economic interaction within Tamilakam, reinforced by an overarching culture.[62]

What emerges is a social formation based on the combination of four forms of production structured by the dominance of a complex of redistributive social relationships. The combination as a system had been generating a series of contradictions through the process of its functioning. Of all the contradictions, the outstanding one was the continued articulation of conditions totally unfavourable to the development of plough agriculture. Predatory marches of chieftains, their destruction of agricultural settlements and crops, and the dominance of the ideology of war and booty redistribution were adverse to the growth of agriculture. *Malapula vañjitturai* songs in *Pn.* are full of allusions to the destruction of settlements (*cēri*) and cultivated fields (*kaḻani*). Setting fire to crops and settlements was common and was called *eriparanteṭuttal.*[63] Pāṇḍaran Kaṇṇanār in *Pn.* 16 praises Cōḻan Perunar Kiḻḻi's burning of his enemy's marutam tracts which knew no forests other than those of sugarcane. Kārikkaṇṇanar in *Pn.* 57 mentions Pandyan Nanmarān's burning of enemy crops. Neṭṭmaiyar sings about Pandyan Mutukuṭumi's destruction of agricultural fields by riding his horses in raids. Kallāṭanār Pandyan Neṭunceḻiyan's looting of crops and destruction of what was left over in enemy fields. The cultivators were not warriors by themselves and their helplessness in times of raids is portrayed in some poems: Kurumkōḻiyur's *kiḻār* in *Pn.* 20 says that the cultivators knew no weapon other than plough and no bow other than the rainbow.

The songs of *Porunmoḻikkāñji tuṛai, Ceviyaṛivūṛutuṛai,* and *Mutumoḻikkāñji tuṛai* in *Pn.* stress the indispensability of peace and protection for the growth of agriculture, albeit without any effect on the routine of war and plunder. Plunder raids being fundamental to the maintenance of the contemporary redistributive economy, all major ideas and institutions pertained to their legitimation. Marital rejoicing in the form of *kuravai-kūttu* (field dance) and *unṭāṭṭu* (group drinking and dining of warrior men with their chieftain) figure prominently in the poems as the chief amusement of the chieftains, *maṛavar*, *porunar*, and other allied groups.[64] Several *tuṛai*s of *Pn.* are explicit in their idealization of raids and raiders. *Mutinmullai tuṛai* songs speak of the marava wife's bursting into tears of joy at the sight of her husband returning with multiple wounds on his chest. *Kuṭinilaiyuraittal tuṛai*, *Ēṛāṇmullai tuṛai*, and *Vallāṇmullai tuṛai* songs idealize the tradition and lineage of the warrior chiefs. *Centuṛaippāṭān-pāṭṭu* and *Vañjituṛaippatanpāṭṭu Patirruppaṭṭu* (*Prp.*) glorify the warriors' might and mien. It is true that all these are conventional war poems and one cannot make generalizations on the social situation on their basis. But once we identify them as signifiers of a plunder-based redistributive social system, the dominance of the warrior culture becomes natural to it. Such a set-up could hardly have helped agrarian development. This predicament would mean that plough agriculture, though superior in terms of productivity, was yet to become dominant through the articulation of its conditions of expansion. The conditions characterized by predatory political control and collective appropriation of the resources were rooted in the material milieu of primitive agriculture and animal husbandry, resulting in the disharmony with plough agriculture. The material premises of this disharmony contained the forces that subsequently led to the dissolution of the social formation.

The most striking manifestation of the forces of change is tied up with the consequences of resource redistribution. As resources included land, its redistribution was important. Warrior leaders and *brāhmaṇa*s were the major recipients of land through the process of redistribution. We have some clear evidence in the poems to show that warrior headmen aimed at gaining productive settlements (*ūr*) as a reward for their services in *vēntar* level raids.[65] *Pn.* 297 describes a warrior headman disclosing to a fellow headman that he would not receive a small, gram-growing settlement (*cīrūr*) as reward but only *marutam*. It is clear that such rewards gave rise to individual holdings against communal holdings. In the case of warrior headmen, this must have led to the development of privileged groups who branched off from their clans. When land was given to *brāhmaṇas* the consequences were more crucial for *brāhmaṇas* who were not agriculturists by themselves, but had to get their land cultivated by others. This gave rise to a new system of relations in production, transcending the framework of kinship ties upon which the relations of contemporary agriculture were based. The novelty of the system was that it was a relation between two objectively antagonistic classes—the non-cultivating landowner and his tillers. The poems refer to several *brāhmaṇa* households which, in this context, have to be understood as representing a new production unit that could transcend the limitation of kinship base. The *brāhmaṇa* land as an independent unit of production required working families attached to it for ensuring permanency of labour. So naturally, several families of clansmen must have become tied up with *brāhmaṇa* households with specific functions. It is reasonable to presume that the crystallization of functionally specific families into castes had its beginnings in these households. The proliferation, albeit little by little, of *brāhmaṇa* households was an ongoing process throughout the days of the anthologies. With the brahmanical institutions and ideas at the organizational level, plough agriculture in the *brāhmaṇa* households was able to secure the conditions of its development. But elsewhere it remained locked in kinship ties with the inherent disabilities or expansion.

In short, the combined systematic existence of the four forms of production had been persistently giving rise to forces of its own dissolution. It was not possible for the combination to continue for a long period with a system of complex redistribution that could hardly raise the low labour productivity and facilitate economic reproduction. Predatory marches, migrations, disintegration of kinship, and above all, the increasing number of *brāhmaṇa* households were steadily accentuating the process of dissolution. The set-up anticipated a total crisis and the final breakdown of the system.

NOTES AND REFERENCES

1. The different strands are studies in B. Narasimaiah, 1964–5, 'Exploration in Districts North Arcot and Salem', in *Indian Archaeology: A Review (IAR)*. Also the exploration reports on Shimoga (*IAR*, 1964–5) and Dharmapuri (*IAR*, 1967–8). L.S. Leshnik, 1974, *The South Indian Megalithic Burials: The Pandukal Complex*, Wiesbaden; A. Sundara, 1975, *Early Chamber Tombs of South India*, Delhi; B. Narasimaiah, 1980, *Neolithic and Megalithic Culture in Tamilnadu*, New Delhi.
2. Ibid. Also N.R. Banerjee, 1965, *The Iron Age in India*, Delhi; B.K. Gururaja Rao, 1972, *Megalithic Culture in South India*, Mysore; T. Balakrishnan Nair, 1977, *The Problem of Dravidian Origins: A Linguistic, Anthropological and Archaeological Approach*, Madras.
3. B.K. Gururaja Rao, *Megalithic Culture in South India*, pp. 265–6.
4. Ibid., pp. 298–9. T. Balakrishnan Nair, pp. 166–72.

5. Ibid., pp. 188–93. Also Gururaja Rao, *Megalithic Culture in South India*, p. 269.
6. It has been argued that the Megalithic people knew the techniques of irrigated agriculture and led a sedentary life. R.E.M. Wheeler, 1941, 'Brahmagiri and Chandravalli Excavations', *Ancient India (AI)* no. 4, pp. 181–308. Also Gururaja Rao, pp. 298–306. While this is not unlikely in a later phase of this culture, we have no clear evidence for the early phase.
7. T.V. Mahalingam, 1974, *Early South Indian Palaeography*, reprint, Madras, pp. 201–14; I. Mahadevan, 1966, 'Corpus of the Tamil Brahmi Inscriptions', *Seminar on Inscriptions*, Madras, pp. 57–63. Also his *Tamil Brahmi Inscriptions*, Madras, 1970.
8. I. Mahadevan, 'Corpus of the Tamil Brahmi Inscriptions', nos 1–14.
9. Ibid. See the label of Alakarmalai that mentions a pon-kolavan of Madurai.
10. W. Elliot, 1886, *Coins of Southern India*, Trubner; R. Sewell, 1904, 'Roman Coins Found in India', *Journal of the Royal Asiatic Society*, pp. 40–8. Also his *List of Antiquities*, vol. I. Spots are given in K.V.S. Aiyer, 1917, *Historical Sketches of the Dekhan*, vol. I, Madras, pp. 86–7. The Roman coins recovered from Kerala are discussed in P.L. Gupta, 1965, *The Early Coins from Kerala*, Trivandrum. See also Sashibhushan 1987, 'Roman Coins from Kerala', *Malayalam Literary Survey*, Trichur, pp. 75–80.
11. W.H. Schoff, 1912, *The Periplus of the Erythraean Sea*, New York; J.W. McCrindle, 1975, *Ancient India as Described in Classical Literature*, reprint, Westminster. See also his *Ancient India as Described by Ptolemy*. R.C. Majumdar (ed.), 1960, *Classical Accounts of India*, Calcutta; K.A. Nilakanta Sastri, 1939, *Foreign Notices of South India*, Madras.
12. Ibid. Also McCrindle, 1974, *The Commerce and Navigation of the Erythreaean Sea*, London, pp. 28–9.
13. Ibid.
14. K. Kailasapathy, 1968, *Tamil Heroic Poetry*, London, p. 3. For a discussion on the chronology of the poems, see K.A. Nilakanta Sastri, 1973, *The Sangam Age: Its Cults and Culture*, Madras; M.G.S. Narayana, 1977, *Reinterpretations in South Indian History*, Trivandrum, pp. 83–4.
15. Kailasapathy, *Tamil Heroic Poetry*, p. 3.
16. Ibid., p. 4.
17. For the characteristic features of oral compositions, see C.M. Bowra, 1966, *Heroic Poetry*, London and R. Finnegan, 1977, *Oral Poetry*, Cambridge. Aspects of symbols and unconscious meaning are discussed in A. Dundes, 1975, 'The Study of Folklore in Literature and Culture: Identification and Interpretation', in A Dundes *Analytic Essays in Folklore*, The Hague, pp. 28–34, and William P. Murphy, 1978, 'Oral Literature', *Annual Review of Anthropology*, vol. 7, pp. 113–36.
18. For the details of syntagmatic structural analysis, see F. Saussure, 1959, *Course in General Linguistics*, New York and R. Jacobson, 1956, *Fundamentals of Language*, The Hague. See also V. Propp, 1979, *Morphology of the Folktale*,

New York. For aspects of paradigmatic structural analysis, see Levi Strauss, 1963, *Structural Anthropology*, London.

19. Kanakasabhai Pillai 1904, *The Tamils 1800 Years Ago*, Madras; S. Krishnaswami Iyengar, 1918, *Beginnings of South Indian History*. Madras; P.T. Srinivasa Iyengar, 1929, History *of the Tamils*, Madras; N.S. Subrahmanian, 1966, *Sangam Polity*, New Delhi.
20. K.K. Pillai, 1975, *A Social History of the Tamils*, Madras; S. Singaravelu, 1966, *Social Life of the Tamils: Classical Period*, Kuala Lumpur. There is no difference in their perspective although the theme is social. The studies of K. Kailasapathy, J.A. Marr, and G.L. Hart indicate a departure from the traditional approach. But a real departure is seen in K. Sivathamby, 1966, 'An Analysis of the Anthropological Significance of the Economic Activities and Conduct Code Ascribed to Mullai- *tinai*', *Proceedings of the First International Conference Seminar on Tamil Studies* (PFICS), vol. I, Kuala Lumpur, pp. 320–31. See also his 'Early South Indian Society and Economy: The Tinai Concept', *Social Scientist*, vol. 29, 1974, pp. 20–37.
21. See *Poruḷatikāram*, 5 (Porul.) of *Tolkāppiyam, Iḷampūraṇam*, Madras, 1965, p. 5 and Nāccinārkiṉṉiyam, Tirumalai, 1948, 1948, p. 5. To Tolkappiyar it was nothing more than a mere poetic concept. His commentators of *Parul*, Iḷampūraṇar and Nāccinārkiṉṉiyar, interpreted the concept as pertaining to the 'general theme or content' and 'behaviour', respectively. The commentators, far removed from the period of the poems, had no grasp of the original implications of the concept or of the anthropological context of its origins. Historians have offered various interpretations. Some have discerned a pattern of social evolution in the fivefold division and debated the actual order of the five tiṇais, see P.T. Srinivasa Iyengar, *History of the Tamils*, p. 14; V.R.R. Dikshitar, 1936, *Studies in Tamil Literature and History*, Madras, p. 178. Xavier S. Thaninayakam, 1966, *Landscape and Poetry*, London, p. 39; K. Zvelabil, 1963, 'Tamil Poetry 2000 Years Ago', *Tamil Culture*, vol. X, p. 16. It signified the pattern of human evolution in world history to N. Subrahmanian. See *Sangam Polity*, p. 49. Sivathamby agrees fundamentally with the unilinear evolutionist concept but he rightly stressed the fact that the *tiṇais* were contemporary physical reality, K. Sivathamby, 'An Analysis of the Anthropological Significance of the Economic Activities and Conduct Code Ascribed to Mullai-*tiṇai*', p. 26. He has given evidences from *Āṟṟuppaṭai*, II, 143–202 and *Perumpāṇārruppaṭai*, II. 46–392.
22. The concept of *tiṇaimayakkam* has to be interpreted to this effect.
23. The *Āṟṟuppaṭai*, literature provides interesting evidences as cited in K. Sivathamby, 'An Analysis of the Anthropological Significance of the Economic Activities ...', pp. 25–6.
24. *Pn.*, 159, 168, 231; *Nari.*, 266, 289, *An.*, 65.
25. *An.*, 7:14; 63:17; 257:12; 276:4; 69: 273; 306; *Pn.*, 454.
26. *Pn.*, 132:8; 390:1.

27. *An.*, 3:8; 37:2; 41:6; 211:5; 314:4; 346:5; 366:8; *Nar.*, 60:2; 97:9; 315:4; 331:1; 340:7; *Pn.*, 13:11; 65:4; 109:3; 209:2; 230:13; 289:3; 384:8; 395:1; *Prp.*, 90:41.
28. *Pn.*, 52; 378.
29. *South Indian Inscriptions,* vol. XIV, *Paripatal.*
30. *Pn.*, 351; 6.
31. Vellalar is late term. *Nāṇmanikaṭikai,* 55:1; *Paripāṭal, 20:63.*
32. *An., passim; Pn., passim.*
33. *Prp.*, 75:8; *Perumpāṇārrupaṭai, 206. Pn.*, 395.
34. *Pn.*, 28,61, 140, 318, 328, 335, 371, 395, 399. *An.*, 12, 32, 62, 68, 73, 82, 118, 132, 188, 192, 288, 303. *Ainkuṛunūṛu (Aink.),* 263, 283, 288, 289, 296, *Kuṛuntokai (kur.)* 54, 291, 357, 360, 369, *Nar.*, 13, 60, 102, 108, 128, 180, 194, 209, 259, 336, 344, 386, 389.
35. There is no convincingly dated Iron Age site that has yielded a ploughshare. A few porthole cists of Wynad are reported to have contained ploughshares but the dates are yet to be determined. M.R. Raghava Varier, 1988, 'Report on Kuppakkolli Exploration', unpublished report, Calicut University. For a discussion on the origins of plough agriculture in south India, see T. Balakrishnan Nari, *The Problem of Dravidian Origins*, pp. 165–76.
36. *Koḷuvāṇikan* figures in a label of Aḷakarmalai. I. Mahadevan translates the term as ironmonger. See his 'Corpus of the Tamil Brahmi Inscriptions', no. 9.
37. *Pn.*, 33:4; 375:6; *An.*, 42:5; 141:5; 224:4; 350:6. The imagery in *Ērkaḷuruvakamtuṛai* songs in *Pn.* illustrates the contemporary art of ploughing.
38. *Cirupanāṛruppaṭai, 233.*
39. See reference under 37 above. Also *An.*, 56:3; 91:15.
40. See the *Veṭci-tiṇai* songs in *Pn.* Also *Aink.*, 263:1; 283:2; 288:4; 289:2; 296:1; *Kurum.*, 54:2; 72:4; 291:1; 357:5; 360:5; *Nar.*, 119:1; 102:9; 108:1; 128:7; 194:9; 209:4; 259:10; 336:2; 344:2; 386:3; 389:6; *Pn.*, 28:9; *An.*, 12:6; 32:1; 73:14; 82:13; 118:12; 132:1; 188:10; 192:8; 288:5.
41. *Nar.*, 200:4; 293:2; 394:3; *An.*, 72:6; 202:5; 224:2; *Pn.*, 21:7; 36:6; 170:15; 180:12; 312:3; *Kuṛum.*, 27, 138, 145, 217, 240, 373.
42. K.R. Srinivasan, 1947, 'The Megalithic Burial and Cairn Fields of South India in the Light of Tamil Literature and Tradition', *AI*, no. 2, pp. 9–16. See also Champakalakshmi, 1975–6, 'Archaeology and Tamil Literary Tradition', *Purātatva*, no. 8, pp. 110–22.
43. *An.*, 161, 164, 182, 188, 216, 248, 269, 328.
44. See the relevant concepts formulated in the context of ancient social formations in B. Hindess and P.Q. Hirst, 1979, *Pre-Capitalist Modes of Production*, London, pp. 51–69. For a non-Marxian analysis of the problem of specialist forms in tribal societies, see E.M. Brumfiel and T.K. Earle (eds), 1987, *Specialisation, Exchange and Complex Societies*, London.

45. Studies on similar situations elsewhere provide us insights. See the discussion in Hindess and Hirst, *Pre-Capitalist Modes of Production* pp. 73–8; C. Meillassoux, 1972, 'From Reproduction to Production', *Economy and Society*, vol. I no. 1, E. Terray, 1972, *Marxism and Primitive Societies*, New York, pp. 96–104.
46. See C. Meillassoux, 1973, 'The Social Organisation of the Peasantry: Economic Basis of Kinship', *Journal of Peasant Studies (JPS)*, 1(1): 81–7.
47. The concept of redistribution refers to the centralization of goods or rights over goods and their subsequent reallocation. K. Polanyi, 1959, 'The Economy as Instituted Process', in Polanyi *et al.* (eds), *Trade and Market in the Early Empires*, Glencoe, pp. 243–51. In this context the concepts depended upon are more from Hindess and Hirst, *Pre-Capitalist Modes of Production*, pp. 450–9.
48. Some *ki̤ḻārs* were poets of the pulavar category. See *Pn.*, 177, 178, 261, 281, 293, 300, 301, 304, 308, 313, 318, 322, 323, 324, 335, 338, 342. Some of the *ki̤ḻārs* were sung by the poets also. *Pn.*, 177, 179, 180, 181, 381, 384, 385, 388, 391. For a comparison, see the insightful portrayal of *gahapati* in Romila Thapar, 1984, *From Lineage to Stage*, New Delhi, pp. 36–42.
49. The background concepts of the observations here are drawn from M. Mauss, 1954, *The Gift*, London. Romila Thapar, 1978, 'Dāna and Dakshiṇa as Forms of Exchange', in *Ancient Indian Social History*, New Delhi, pp. 105–21; C.A. Gregory, 1982, *Gifts and Commodities*, London.
50. Following *Tolkāppiyam* most of the scholars took veṭci for one of the five stages or situations of war. Its implication as actual cattle lifting was first brought to light in M.G.S. Narayanan, 1977, 'The Cattle Raiders of the Sangam Age', *Proceedings of the Indian History Congress*, Bhuvaneswar, pp. 70–82.
51. *Nar.* 142, 303, 331, 372, 388; *Aink.* 47, 48, 111, 195; *An.* 10, 60, 65; *Pn.*, 33, 102, 289, 327, 370. There is a detailed discussion on exchange relations of the *neital-tiṇai* in M.R. Raghava Varier, 1988, 'Economic Activities of the *Neital Tinai*', unpublished paper, Calicut University.
52. *Pn.*, 3, 102, 289, 327, 370, 370; *An.*, 37; *Nair.* 125:9; 198:9; 315:4; *prp.* 27:13. See also M.R. Raghava Varier, 'Economic Activities of the Neital Tinai'. There are interesting similarities in the nature of the organization of salt exchange elsewhere. See A.P. Andrews, 1983, *Maya Salt Production and Trade*, Tuscon; J. Muller, 'Mississippian Specialization and Salt', *American Antiquity*, 49(3), 'Salt, Chert and Shell: Mississippian Exchange and Economy', in E.M. Brumfiel and T.K. Erle (eds) *Specialisation, Exchange*, pp. 10–21.
53. *Cattu* is *sartha. An.* 39:10; 167:7; 291:15.
54. M.R. Raghava Varier, 'Economic Activities of the *Neital Tinai*'.
55. For the concepts, see C. Meillassoux (ed.), 1971, *The Development of Indigenous Trade and Markets in West Africa*, London, pp. 67–9; R. Mac Adams,

'Anthropological Perspectives on Ancient Trade', *Current Anthropology*, 15, pp. 239–58; M. Sahlins, 1968, 'On the Sociology of Primitive Exchange', in M. Banton (ed.), *The Relevance of Models for Social Anthropology*, London, pp. 139–42.

56. *Pn.* 333:12.
57. When the gift is returned, the quantity would always be higher. See the discussion in C.A. Gregory, *Gifts and Commodities*, pp. 41–9.
58. Generally, exchanges in a society of strong kinship would hardly be profit-oreinted. M. Sahlins, 'On the Sociology of Primitive Exchange'.
59. Reacting to the charge that the people of Tamilakam were not active in foreign trade, the following are cited as evidence in *Pn.* Kunhan Pillai, 1970, *Annatte Keralam*, Kottayam, pp. 52–3; *Prp.* 2:6; *Pn.* 66, 126; *An.* 152; *Kur.* 240 are the references cited. *Prp.* 2:6 refers to ships sailing for acquiring gold. *Pn.* 66 addresses Kārikala Cōḻa as born in the lineage of the one who controlled the wind and set the ships on the vast ocean for sail. *Pn.* 126 refers to the inability of others to enter the western sea where the Cēra led his gold-giving ship. *An.* 152 mentions the ships of Tittan Veḷiyan bringing gold. *Kur.* 240 is no evidence for what it has been adduced to. It contains only an imagery of a sinking ship that looked like a mountain. Pliny's reference to an Indian ship carried off to the German coast by wind is also given as evidence. Recent excavations on the Red Sea coast has brought to light pottery grafitti in Tamil *brāhmi* characters, probably the two names, Cātan and Kaṇan. This could be another piece of evidence if we take them to be names of two traders from Tamilakam.
60. See the discussion in K. Polanyi, 1957, *The Great Transformation: The Political and Economic Origin of Our Time*, Boston, pp. 55 ff; S. Ratnagar, 1981, *Encounters: The Westerly Trade of Harappa Civilization*, Delhi, pp. 231 ff; the introduction in C. Renfrew and S. Shennen (eds), 1982, *Ranking, Resource and Exchange: Aspects of the Archaeology of Early European Society*, Cambridge.
61. See the concepts regarding the socio-economic and political prerequisites of real trade in K. Polanyi, 1975, *The Great Transformation*, the introduction of L. Karlosky and J. Sabloff (eds), *Ancient Civilization and Trade*, Albuquerque, S. Ratnagar, *Encounters*, p. 231.
62. The Tamil language and the Tamil *brāhmi* script which were two major integrating factors evidence the formation of the unevenly evolved economies into a system. People of diverse economic formations communicated with one another and entered into transactional relations as has already been shown.
63. See songs of *vañji-tiṇai* in *Pn.*
64. *Pn.* 257, 258, 262, 269, 297, 24, 129, 371, 396.
65. For a detailed examination of such references in *Pn.* See M.G.S. Narayanan, 1982, 'Warrior Settlements of the Sangam Age', *PIHC*, pp. 102–9.

7

Early Iron Age Economy

Problems of Agrarian Expansion in Tamilakam*

Archaeology shows that Tamilakam had emerged more or less as a single culture-zone by the first millennium BC, with the diffusion of iron-using people of the black-and-red ware tradition.[1] Though excavated Iron Age settlements are very few in peninsular India, Iron Age burial relics, often in the thin debris of a relatively uniform date, are quite widespread.[2] Language, perhaps the archaic Tamil, must have come into being as an important factor of the broad cultural unification during this period. But behind this cultural homogeneity was the isolated existence of uneven material cultures as a historical reality. There seems to have developed no major integration of these unevenly developed people for organized production, though iron technology was widely known then. For a very long period, the idea of the Neolithic–Chalcolithic digging stick survived in the form of thrust-hoes made of iron, indicating some sort of stagnancy.[3] Even when the ploughshare began to be used, it was confined to very few localities of wetland. Archaeological knowledge of the ancient agriculture of south India is primarily based on the finds in Adichanellur, which give us some idea about the thrust and draw-hoes and the actual ploughshares of circa 1000 BC.[4] The ancient Tamil works, generally ascribed to the first two or three centuries of the Christian era, depict the same technology of agriculture, which obviously illustrates the alleged snail's pace progress of the Iron Age.[5] In the light of evidence in the ancient Tamil anthologies, an attempt is made in this chapter to offer an explanation for the remarkably slow process of agrarian expansion in

---

* This chapter is a reproduced version of, 1981, 'Aspects of Early Iron Age Economy: Problems of Agrarian expansion in Tamilakam', Indian History Congress Proceedings, (Delhi).

the Iron Age at its organizational and institutional levels and also how this expansion was ultimately achieved.

The chief source for the present study is the *Eṭṭuttokai* collection excepting *Kalittokai* and *Paripāṭal*, which may be comparatively late.[6] Whatever be their drawbacks as literary compositions based on oral poetry with stock-expressions and stereotypes, the richness of ancient Tamil anthologies in historical details can never be exaggerated.[7] In spite of editions, classifications, and compilations which have put the ancient Tamil works in a big chronological mesh, they serve as invaluable sources of early south Indian life. The most archaic stratum in this literature has definitely much to do with the early Iron Age, and one cannot say that this stratum is absolutely beyond reconstruction. However, such a task is not within the scope of this paper. The focus here is on the material matrix of life and activity reflected in the anthologies, which has not received much attention from the historians.[8]

Whether or not the concept of *aintiṇai* was a mere poetic convention is not a question that one need dwell on, since the existing physiographic features of Tamilakam can very well substantiate the fivefold division of man-nature situations in its historical and anthropological context. There is not much meaning in discerning social evolution in the concept since all situations as marks of uneven development coexisted simultaneously.[9] The thoughts regarding the actual order of the five *tiṇai*s as provided for in the literature are also therefore meaningless.[10] How the *kuṟiñji, pālai, mullai, marutam,* and *neital* divisions of nature suited the poetic delineation of human behaviour pattern do not arise here. To us the classification of land and nature involved in the concept alone matters. We only take note of the poets' references to the life and activity in each situation of physiographic importance. It gives a clear picture of five types of terrain (*aintiṇai*), peoples and their means of subsistence or economies as already noted in the first chapter. These diverse economies were obviously due to the physiographic differences and the people in each situation constituted a segment. This shows a broad as well as horizontal segmentation of people separated by the physiographic peculiarities and the economic possibilities of each situation. But this was never rigid as situations in nature were often co-mingled and overlapping. Both *kuṟiñji*, and *mullai* had cultivable slopes, *punam* or *ēnal* which enabled the *vēṭar* to take to shifting agriculture as the *kuṟavar*. In a song of Perumeittiranar about Kumanan, we find a reference to the *vēṭar* of the Kollimalai doing slash-and-burn agriculture (*Puṟanāṉūṟu*, 159, hereafter *Pn.*).

In one of the oft-quoted *Pn.* songs, we have the four chief clans—*tuṭiyar, pāṇar, paṛaiyar*, and *kaṭampar*, each clan with a magico-religious musical instrument, referred to incidentally (*Pn.*, 335), as the people of *vanpulam*. These clans are referred to in the anthologies as dependents, playing some magico-ritual roles, but not in the context of farming. Being inhabited such clans of diverse ways, *vanpulam* was a region of wild food economy, cattle keeping, and subsistence farming. On the other hand, the material basis of *menpulam* was advanced plough agriculture. Anthologies refer to *uḻavar* or *toḻuvar* as the tillers of *menpulam*.[11] They knew the technique of harnessing the bullocks (*erutu*) at their necks with a cross-bar (*nukam*) to a ploughshare (*mēḻi* or *nāñjil*), obviously iron-tipped, for furrowing.[12] Buffaloes (*erumai*) were also used for ploughing.[13] Tank irrigation (*āyam*) and minor dam (*ciṛai*) irrigation are mentioned in the anthologies.[14] They ensured the availability of water for agriculture in the required plots of land through the sluices from tanks or through the diversions of harnessed streams. Animal power was widely utilized for various agrarian jobs such as threshing and pounding.

However, we do not know much about the exact relations of production in the *menpulam*, though it appears that the division of labour was somewhat structured there. It is not quite clear whether the society was economically differentiated and relations stratified. Land was collectively owned and controlled by communities whose heads as ruling chiefs embodied the community's power to transact, as poetic allusions to their gifts of property to scholars (*pulavar*, including *brāhmaṇas*), the warriors and bards (*pāṇas*) would have us believe. The *brāhmaṇas* were called *uyarntōr*, the high-born and the rest as *iḻiśinar*, the low-born.[15] It appears that the tillers produced and the craftsmen worked for the landowning chieftains, the *pulavār* and the warrior chiefs, but not on the basis of any stratified relations of appropriation. The land in vanpulam was also owned by the chieftains and their bards and warrior-chiefs. From *Pn.*, 49 we understand that the owner of land in *vanpulam* was called *nāṭan*, the owner of the land in *menpulam* was called *ūran*, and the owner of the *neital*, *cērpan*.

Reciprocity was the mode of exchange, though paddy and salt at times served as the leading commodities in the field of exchange, with a relative inter-commodity exchange. Profit-oriented exchanges are not referred to in the anthologies in the context of rural transactions. However, *kaṭam* or *kaṭan*, meaning debt, is mentioned in them.[16] The loan of a fixed commodity to be paid back in the same kind and quantity, called *kuṛittumāretirppai* or *kuṛiyetirppai*, was in vogue.[17] *Āvaṇam* or *ankāṭi* were the main organized points of exchange where standard weights and measures were in use and *paṭṭaṇam* or the coastal towns were the centres of long-distance trade. Certain weights of gold known as *kāṇam* and *kaḻañju* were used as media of exchange in the *paṭṭaṇam*, perhaps in certain higher transactions too. The exchange points in the hinterland were far removed from the formal centres of exchange, such as paṭṭaṇams. It is clear from certain poems in *Pn.* that there was no convenient or safe infrastructure in the hinterland. *Pn.*, 102, refers to *umaṇar*'s bullock carts loaded with salt moving through undulated and marshy routes and to *umaṇar* retrieving the wheels of their carts from the mire by filling ruts with dry sand. In *Pn.*, 3, a poet clearly illustrates how scarce human settlements in Pāṇḍyan territory were. He says that extensive areas of dry land full of fierce *maṛavar* had to be crossed to reach the Pāṇḍyan fort. Kārikiḻar, the headman of a settlement and a bardic poet, while praising Muṭukutumi says that the *Pāṇḍyan* fort was surrounded by *menpulam* tracts (*Pn.*, 6). This shows that *menpulam* was often encircled by large inhospitable zones of *vanpulam*.

Poverty of the chieftains or the landowners of *vanpulam* is clear from certain *Pn.* songs. Kapilar, a *brāhmaṇa* poet (*puḷavar*) singing like a bard, eugolized his patron chief the chief of the Paṛampu hill, by recounting the four kinds of yields from the hill, which were bamboo-rice, jackfruits, creeper roots, and honey. In fact, there is no notion of poverty or the scarcity of resources in the description by the poet. Instead, it is the wealth peculiar to the landscape that the poet seeks to characterize. Nevertheless, the term poverty makes sense in a comparative appreciation of the economies of the hill and the valley, which were primarily the hunting/gathering economy of the hill and the agrarian economy of the valley respectively. It is the relative scarcity or near absence of agricultural products especially, rice, which puts the large hill tracts (*vanpulam*) in contra-distinction to the economy of the valley rich in millet and paddy. We get an interesting instance in *Pn.*, 180, of an impoverished chieftain of *vanpulam* calling his blacksmith and asking him to prepare a sharp spear for plunder-raids when his dependents approach him for help. In *Pn.*, 127, 327, 328, 329, 330, and 331–3, we have clear references to the poverty of the chieftains and landowners of the non-agrarian regions. Instances of giving away even the small quantity of millet reserved for sowing, a stock expression of poets for extolling the munificence of chieftains, interestingly occur only in poems praising the chieftains of *vanpulam*. The chieftains who held sway over menpulam were affluent. Their large paddy farms and huge stock of paddy are referred to in the anthologies. Kārikkaṇṇanār in *Pn.*, 353 speaks of a chieftain's hill-like paddy heaps; Nannākanar in *Pn.*, 376 speaks of Oyman's paddy fields and the harvest heaped at his court, while Kallaṭānār in *Pn.*, 391 refers to Poṟāiyaṟṟūkiḻāṉ's skyscraper paddy heaps. Maturai Nakkīranār praises the large crop fields of Tittan in *Pn.*, 392. Mānkuṭi Kiḻār in *Pn.*, 396 refers to Veṭṭārreḻiniyātan's paddy fields and paddy heaps. All these abundant crops are mentioned to have been lavished as gifts to bards.

The institution of gift-giving was immanent in the contemporary economic setting since the majority of people who lived at the subsistence level had to depend on the gift-givers as *iravar*. Certain songs in *Pn.* show that the lesser bards (*pāṇar*) sang in praise of chieftains who gave all kinds for food and clothing. *Pn.*, 376, 382, 398, and 400 are some of the examples which illustrate the acute poverty of the lesser bards. *Pn.*, 392 and 393 show how badly clothed a *pāṇar* was. Marutan Iḷanākanār in *Pn.*, 139 refers to the miserable condition of the *viṟali*, the womenfolk of the *pāṇar*, who had to live as labourers who carried head-loads. It appears that these poor bards wandered about the courts of chieftains and the houses of village headmen, singing praises and playing their musical instrument, the *yāl*. But the scholarly bards (*pulavar*) sang in praise of the chieftains for land and gold and such rich bards were depended upon by the poor. The whole economy was thus based on the institution of gift-giving, which in its process involved mutual plunders, a necessary component of the instituted form of resource redistribution.[18]

Plunder-raids being fundamental to the maintenance of contemporary economy, all ideas and institutions in the broad superstructure helped the plunder-based redistribution function effectively. This chapter cannot include a total survey of all the beliefs and institutions of the people in question, but only those that had a direct bearing on the contemporary economy alone. The beliefs such as 'cattle raid begets the chieftain'; martyrs join damsels in heaven; plunder as a traditional inspiration of the *maṟavar*; martial bravery of the sons as a passionate aspiration of mothers; cowardice as ignominious, and the like, glorify raids and involvement in plunders. Their totems, musical instruments, ritual dances, and songs were all magical and symbolic, capable of stimulating active involvement in cattle raids.[19] Their ethics (*aṟam*) justified raids and plunders. How institutionalized the battle was is clear from the descriptions of *veṭci* (cattle raid), *karantai* (cattle recovering battle), *vañji* (chieftain's attack of a territory), *kāñji* (defending battle), and *tümpai* (getting ready for battle) in *Pn.* Martial rejoicing was the chief amusement as we find in customs like *vākai* (the enthusiastic killing of enemies with clamour), *unṭāṭṭu* (social dining and drinking before and after wars), *peruñcōṟṟuviḻāvu* (grand feast), and *ciṟucōṟṟuviḻāvu* (small rice feast). Some of the poetic conventions in *Pn.* clearly demonstrate their idealization of war and war leaders. *Uvakaikkaluḻci tuṟai* songs in *Pn.* poeticize a wife's bursting into tears in happiness at the sight of her husband with many wounds by the sword. *Mūtinmullai tuṟai* songs in *Pn.* idealize the womenfolk of the *maṟavar* as brave as their warrior husbands. *Kuṭinilaiyuraittal tuṟai*, *ēranmullai tuṟai*, and *vallanmullai tuṟai* songs in *Pn.* are all examples of idealizing the tradition and family lineages of the warrior-chiefs. In short, the ethos of war dominated and moulded contemporary socio-political ideals and institutions of the early Iron age.

Destruction of cultivated fields (*kaḻani* or *paḻanam*) and settlements was an inevitable part of war. *Malapuḻavañji tuṟai* songs in *Pn.* describe how land was plundered and settlements destroyed in wars. *Eriparanteṭuttal*, setting fire to crop-fields and settlements, was the sequel to every clash between chieftains. Certain songs in *Pn.*, show how detrimental the scorched-earth policy of wars was to agriculture. In a song of Neṭṭimaiyār, the destruction of crop-fields by the stamping of rough-ridden horses harnessed to the war chariot of Pāṇḍyan Muṭukunumi is described (*Pn.*, 15). Pāṇṭaran Kaṇṇanār while praising Cōḻan Perunar Kiḷḷi, refers to his burning of the enemy's marutam tracts which knew no forest other than that of sugarcane (*Pn.*, 16). Kārikkaṇṇanār while praising Pandyan Nanmarān incidentally refers to the destruction of crop-fields by fire as a common atrocity of war (*Pn.*, 57). In a song of Kallāṭanār in praise of Pāṇḍyan Neṭuñjeḻiyan, there is a reference to the destruction of land to no use after plundering all that could be plundered from it (*Pn.*, 23). It is significant to note that at times possession of *marutam* land was also aimed at while executing plundering raids. In *Pn.*, 297 one poet has described a warrior chief telling his fellow warrior-chiefs assembled for an *unṭāṭṭu* before an ensuing *veṭci*, that he would not accept the arid gram-growing areas as reward for fighting, but only paddy-growing *marutam*. Often the landed people had to support their chieftains in wars. A song of Perumkunrur Kiḻār in *Pn.*, while praising a landowner says that his land suffers in war and prospers in peace (*Pn.*, 318). In addition to the chieftain-led raids there were incessant attacks from the non-agrarian tracts by the *maṟavar* or *eyinar*.

It appears that the peasants were neither warriors by themselves, nor were they offered sufficient protection by their chieftains. The warrior-power of the chieftains was often not enough to defend against the onslaughts. The chieftains mobilized warriors, arousing tribal loyalty through *unṭāṭṭu* and *cōṟṟuviḻāvu*, during which the bards sang to strengthen the loyalty to the chieftain. With words of honour, chieftains gave drinks with their own hands to the warrior-chiefs, intensifying the bond and loyalty. The warriors took a pledge of loyalty (*netumoḻi puṇarttal*) on the occasion of *uṇṭāṭṭu*. Most of the *veṭci* and *karantai* songs in *Pn.*, throw light on these matters. It is clear that the organization of warriors was only at its tribal stage, with no territorial bond or bureaucratic contract. The body of warriors was an ad hoc one, raised on demand and never stationary. Its purpose was the conduct of cattle and plunder raids, and not the permanent defence of any particular territory. This made the peasants vulnerable to attacks of all kinds. The passiveness and helplessness of the peasants is incidentally described in a poem of Kuṟumkōḻiyūr Kiḻār, who says that the peasants knew no weapon other than the plough. They knew no bow other than the rainbow (*Pn.*, 20).

Some of the poems in *Pn.* show an awareness of the danger of raids in the context of agriculture. Songs of *ceviyaṟivūṟutuṟai* in *Pn.* exhort the chieftains to maintain peace. *Pn.*, 18 makes it clear that the growth of agriculture was the basis of the chieftains' strength and fame. *Pn.*, 35 advises the chieftain to say that paddy is the basis of his strength and further warns him to lend no ear to intrigues which lead to war. The poem stresses the need for the protection of the peasants and the undeniable significance of agriculture in the prosperity of the land. He was influencing some poets to make use of agrarian imagery even for describing battles. The poetic ideals of *ērkaḷuruvakamtuṟai* in *Pn.* provide us with these examples. In a song of Paranar on Cēran Velkeḻu Kuṭṭuvan, there is a beautiful description of a battlefield in an agrarian setting (*Pn.*, 369). Kāllaṭanār, while praising Netunceḻiyan's martial adventures, uses agrarian imagery to describe a raid (*Pn.*, 371). Similar examples can be found in a song of Avāiyar (*Pn.*, 392) and in *Pn.*, 370 and 373. However, the ideology of peace, which had relevance to the agrarian regions, could not dominate since the general material milieu nurtured war as an economic necessity.

It was amidst these adversities that the people of menpulam had to carry on production, which is why advanced farming remained absolutely confined to small pockets of wet land in the valleys of the Kaveri, Vaigai, Tamraparni, and Periyar without any remarkable progress till the seventh to eighth centuries. It has been argued elsewhere that the technology of the iron ploughshare was known to the people of Tamilakam as early as against 1000 BC itself. We have seen that it did not make any major advance during the first two or three centuries of the Christian era. In the light of ancient Tamil works it could be argued that the advanced production centres, *menpulam*, were surrounded by large non-agrarian regions, *vanpulam*, of uneven economies of the subsistence level. Evidences in the anthologies would have us believe that until an organized agrarian set-up emerged under the initiative of a managerial group from outside, the production field of Tamilakam was caught up in an equilibrium trap. Knowledge of technology alone does not lead to the expansion of advanced production. The availability of the required ecology and terrain also by themselves do not suffice. It is again incorrect to argue in the lines of Boserup that population pressure makes it inevitable.[20] The expansion of advanced fanning requires a managerial group, capable of organizing peasants either through coercion or a situation created by the false consciousness of loyalty to a fanatical extent, which amounts to coercion in disguise. It was with the arrival of this coercion in disguise that the agrarian scene of Tamilakam began to wrench itself out of the trammels of conflicting interior economic modes. *brāhmaṇas* with their special status and ritual primacy took the lead in the task of making organizational and institutional changes in the menpulam agrarian set-up, through a new ideology of loyalty.

Brāhmaṇas had begun to possess wetlands during the days of the theologies themselves. *Patirruppaṭṭu* mentions the gift of a village called Okantur, which was famous for a fine variety of paddy, to *brāhmaṇas* by the Cēra ruler Celvakaṭunko Vāḻiyatan.[21] Kūmaṭṭar Kaṇṇanār, a *brāhmaṇa* bard, is mentioned as the receiver of a gift of some five hundred villages from his patron.[22] Perumkunrur Kiḻār refers to the numerous villages gifted to Kapilar, another *brāhmaṇa* bard.[23] Āvūr Mūlan Kiḻār's song in *Pn.* praises a landowner called Kauṇiyan Viṇṇan Tāyan (*Pn.*, 166). But large-scale control of land by the *brāhmaṇa*, as corporate bodies of *brahmadēyas*, was definitely a feature of the Pallava–Cōḻa periods. Considering the special position enjoyed by the *brāhmaṇas* in contemporary society, one may not be wrong in assuming that their lands must have been comparatively free from the havoc of plundering wars. It is quite reasonable to argue that the *brāhmaṇas* had a better grip of the peasants under them, who stood for peace, morals, and devotion which were lacking in Tamilakam during the pre-Pallava period.[24]

The major problem that hindered the advancement of peasant-economy during the major part of the pre-Pallava period was the absence of an effective managerial power which could harness agricultural labour and the required skills. The chieftains who squandered manpower in plundering wars were not in the material matrix of the advanced peasant economy to use coercion for better production. Those landowners, who lived as managers of advanced farming, were incapable of making a stable organization of peasants. It is against this background of the absence of managerial groups capable of using coercion for better production that one has to view the emergence of the *brāhmaṇas* as corporate bodies capable of large-scale peasant integration. The peasant-backed *brāhmaṇa* landowners could easily establish themselves as the nuclei of the new monarchy manifested through the ascendancy of the Pallavas, Pandyas, Cēras, and Cōḻas in due course. It is clear that the material basis of the Pallava-Cōḻa warrior power was the *brāhmaṇa*-controlled peasant economy. But once warrior power could give sufficient protection to the peasants, it became easier for *brāhmaṇas* to venture on large-scale colonization of agrarian land. Royal grants of agrarian villages now brought more and more *brāhmaṇas* to the far south, studding the whole wetland with brahmadēya villages. Thus from long protracted stagnancy the agrarian region, with its acquired managerial force, spread widely by the seventh to eighth centuries.

NOTES AND REFERENCES

1. Bridget Allchin and Raymond Allchin, 1968, *The Birth of Indian Civilization: India and Pakistan Before 500 BC*, Baltimore, p. 232.
2. Arikamedu, J.M. Casal, *Feuilles ce Uikrampatnam*, Paris, 1919. Kunnattur, *Indian Archaeology: A Review* (hereafter *IAR*), 1954–5, 1955–6, 1956–7, Tirukkampuliyur, *IAR, 1961–2*, and Alagarai, *IAR 1963–4*, are the chief Iron Age sites. Iron Age burial relics are found all over the south. Cf. Allchin, *The Birth of Indian Civilization*, p. 231.
3. To quote Allchin: 'Certainly the excavated settlements do not give much indication of any major change in the way of life accompanying the arrival of iron. One is left with a feeling of a remarkable conservatism among the population of South India throughout the period.' Allchin, *The Birth of Indian Civilization*, p. 232.
4. Balakrishnan Nair, 1977, 'Adichanallur and the Antiquity of Iron in South India', in *The Problem of Dravidian Origins: A Linguistic, Archaeological and Anthropological Approach*, p. 166–9, Madras.
5. The title 'Sangam' commonly used to denote ancient Tamil works is deliberately avoided, since it is a misnomer. Some Western scholars have substituted the term *classical* for it. George L. Hart III, 1976, 'Ancient Tamil Literature: Its Scholarly Past and Future', in Burton Stein (ed.), *Essays on South India*, New Delhi, pp. 40–60. Also, Burton Stein, 1980, *Peasant State and Society in Medieval South India*, New York, p. 64–5. But the term *classical* is even more misleading. It is used in the context of Hellenic Greece or Mauryan India, but cannot be used for ancient south India as the level of culture bears no comparison with that of the former. For an explanation

regarding the unintelligibility of the title 'Sangam', see K. Kailasapathy, *Tamil Heroic Poetry*, 1968, New Delhi, pp. 2–3.

6. George L. Hart III has referred to his 'Related Cultural and Literary Elements in Ancient Tamil and Indo-Aryan', PhD thesis, Harvard University, in the article above, note. 5, in Stein (ed.), *Essays on South India*, as the source discussing the chronology of ancient Tamil works, see Hart, 'Ancient Tamil Literature: Its Scholarly Past and Future', p. 60, note 1.
7. Hart III, 'Ancient Tamil Literature: Its Scholarly Past and Future'. Also Hart III, 1975, *The Poems of Ancient Tamils: Their Milieu and Their Sanskrit Counterparts*, Berkeley.
8. An outline of the economy of the people in ancient Tamilakam is given in K. Siva Thampy, 1974, 'Early South Indian Society and Economy: The *Tiṇai* Concept', *Social Scientist*, 29 December.
9. A discussion regarding the concept of evolution involved in the concept of *tinai* is given in N. Subrahmanian, 1966, *Sangam Polity*, Madras, p. 249.
10. On the problem of the order of the five tiṇais there is a discussion in Subrahmanian, *Sangam Polity*, p. 249.
11. For *uḻavar* see *Akanāṉūṟu* 30:8, 37:2, 41:6, 211:5, 266:17, 314:4, 346:5, 366:8; *Naṟṟiṇai* 60:2, 97:9, 315:4, 331:1, 340:7; *Padirruppaṭṭu* 90:41; and *Puṟanāṉūṟu* 13:11, 65:4, 109:3, 230:13, 289:3, 384:8, 395:1. For *toḻuvar*, *Puṟanāṉūṟu* 24:1, 209:2.
12. See *Akanāṉūṟu* 244:4, 350:6; *Puranāṉūṟu* 103:1, 179:9, for the idea of the crossbar. The term *mēḻi* occurs in *Puranāṉūṟu* 388:11 and *nañjil* occurs in ibid. 19:11, 20:11, 40:1, 56:4, 138:8; and in *Akanāṉūṟu* 42:5, 141:5; *Padirruppattu* 119:17, 115; 1, 6:2, 58:17. The term *ulupadai* is also used to mean plough share, *Puranāṉūṟu* 35:25.
13. *Akanāṉūṟu* 56:3, 91:15, see N. Subrahmanian, 1966, *Pre-Pallavan Tamavan Tamil Index, Index of Historical Material in Pre-Pallavan Tamil Literature*, Madras, pp. 162–3.
14. The term *āyam* is referred to in *Akanāṉūṟu* 62:1, 68:2, and the term *sirai*, ibid. 76:11, 200:9, 208:19, 346:9.
15. See *Puṟanāṉūṟu* 82:3, 170:5, 287:2, 289:10.
16. Ibid. 327:7.
17. Ibid. 333:11.
18. For details of the concept of redistribution see Karl Polanyi *et al.* (eds), 1957, 'The Economy as Instituted Process', *Trade and Market in Early Empires*, Free Press: Glencoe, pp. 243–57. In the context of ancient Tamilakam the concept is used in Richard S. Kennedy, 1976, 'King in Early South India: A Chieftain and Emperor', *Indian Historical Review*, p. 3.
19. George L. Hart III has referred to the magical element in their musical instruments which were infected with the sacred called *ananku*; see his article in Stein (ed.), 'Ancient Tamil Literature: Its Scholarly Past and Future', p. 44.

20. Ester Boserup, 1965, *Conditions of Agricultural Growth: The Economics of Agrarian Change under Population Pressures*, Chicago.
21. The reference is in the *Patikam* 9 of die seventh *pattu* in *Patiṟṟuppattu*. So it might be later. See Kailasapathy, *Tamil Heroic Poetry*, pp. 222–4, for a discussion regarding land and references to it in the anthologies.
22. The second unit of ten poems, *Patiṟṟuppattu*. This is also a *Patikam* version. See note 21 above.
23. *Patiṟṟuppattu, Patikam* 9; Perūnkunrur Kiḻar confirms the tradition that Kapilar was given numerous villages as a gift by one of his patrons, Ilamceral Irumpoṟai.
24. Burton Stein accepts the tradition of the *Kaḷabhra* invasion as an interregnum which toppled the three ruling families—Cēra, Cōḻa, Pāṇḍya, for some time. Stein, 'Ancient Tamil Literature: Its Scholarly Past and Future', pp. 7–9. To him, the Kalabhra invasion was the culmination of the non-peasant attacks on the peasants, and he views it in a dichotomy of the urban Jains and the hinterland *brāhmaṇas*. See cf. Stein, 'Ancient Tamil Literature: Its Scholarly Past and Future', pp. 78–9. A detailed discussion on this point is made by him in John F. Richards (ed.), *Kingship and Authority in South Asia, All the Kings Mana: Perspective on Kingship in Medieval South India*.

    Stein has formulated a concept of *brāhmaṇa*–peasant alliance, which was voluntary and peaceful, in order to explain the nature of agrarian integration in early medieval south India. He says that the alliance became strong because of its symbiotic character. See Stein, 'Ancient Tamil Literature: Its Scholarly Past and Future', pp. 82–4.

8

Writing, Literacy, and Social Formations in the Tamil South*

Picturing the state of literacy in a historical society can hardly be of neutral value today, for we take it for granted that higher literacy rates signify greater social development. Despite the controversies among scholars, the positive effects of literacy are now more or less matters of tacit recognition.[1] To try and asses the extent of literacy and the corresponding social progress has been central to most studies on literacy in history.

The present study, however, does not envisage such a project. Not only is it impossible to adequately assess the extent of literacy in early south India, but the presupposed correlation between literacy and social development is also unacceptable as valid *a priori* reasoning.[2] A debate on the determining role of literacy is not within the scope of this chapter, which seeks to focus on the determinants of the spread of literacy in a given spatio-temporal context. In short, this is not a study of the effects of literacy, but an enquiry into the reverse. It is necessary to define at the outset what literacy means in the context because its modern assumptions have little relevance to the past. The 'illiteracy' one discovers in pre-colonial periods results from a reading within the colonial definition of literacy. So we use the term here, in all its inherent ambiguity, to mean people's functional association with written texts, an aspect quite fluid and relative, varying in terms of skill and competence across society.

This discussion is an attempt to grasp the dynamic behind the gradual expansion in the uses of writing in the Tamil-speaking area during the period of two social formations which we identify as pastoral-agricultural

* This chapter is a revised version of, 1996, 'Writing and Its Uses in the Ancient Tamil Country', *Studies in History*, 12(1): 67–81.

and plough-agricultural, respectively.[3] The earliest societies demarcating a compact area of linguistic and cultural homogeneity roughly date back to the mid-first millennium BC but their pastoral-agricultural phase is better known from the closing centuries of that millennium up to the AD fourth century. The succeeding social formation of plough agriculture emerging around the fourth century became a well-articulated system by the seventh–eighth centuries and continued to ramify subsequently. We have chosen to locate the beginnings of the pervasive dynamic of early literacy and indicate the ongoing trend.

Writing was known in the region as early as the third century BC, as evidenced by the Tamil *brāhmi* label inscriptions. It is now well established that Tamil *brāhmi* developed out of the *brāhmi* script as a local adaptation. That the knowledge of the *brāhmi* script reached the Tamil region in the wake of the Jain and Buddhist expansion, trade movements and the rise of the Mauryan empire is equally well established. To pursue the origins of *brāhmi* (its arrival from the Semitic world is generally accepted) is beyond the scope of this chapter. In general, it came into use in the Gangetic region in a period of characteristic productive forces, social relations, surplus, trade, and state systems. The situation in the Tamil south, where the script spread, was different and no simple diffusionist perspective will work in this case since the causal preconditions of the spread are of fundamental significance. Knowledge of writing cannot be transplanted irrespective of the level of socio-economic development, so even when the question is one of adaptation of a script invented elsewhere, the study of the socio-economic context of the concerned region becomes crucial.

The Tamil *brāhmi* inscriptions are few in number and too brief (mere labels) to relate to the question of contemporary social uses of writing. *Poṛittininaṭṭanarekal* and *peyartarappeyartanṭukal* seem to mean burial stones with the names of the dead inscribed upon them.[4] The term *eḻuttu*, now made out to invariably mean writing, was used in old Tamil to mean painting, which in ancient times was a form of writing. An eleventh century commentary on *Yāpparunkalam*, explaining the concluding *sūtra*, refers to *uruveḻuttu* (pictograph) as the first of the four varieties of writings.[5] It seems that the allusions in the poems to eḻuttu by and large mean the practice of *uruveḻuttu*, which has archaeological corroboration at megalithic sites.[6] The few instances that really refer to *taniyeḻuttu* (alphabetical writing) in connection with the practice of planting burial stones seem to suggest the symbolic dimension of the social use of writing because we do not see much chance of the direct utility of writing in the locality.

The poems indicate that memorial stones were planted on the wayside in the parched zone interspersed across the hilly backwoods and pastoral tracts. That was the zone of cattle raids, thronged by gangs of warriors escorting caravan troops (*cāttu*). The people who traversed these inhospitable tracts were obviously merchants, chieftains, and warriors, the majority being salt merchants (*umaṇar*) carting their merchandise to the interior. We do not find knowledge of writing essential for these merchants since the mode of exchange was value-based barter (*noṭuttal*) and the clientele more or less of the same linguistic culture. The volume of internal exchange was also relatively very small. In a system of exchange where the notion of exchange value, price, and profit was not mediated by money, detailed accounting through writing would be unnecessary. The bulk of internal exchange in the Tamil region during the period was based on barter, reciprocity, and redistribution.[7] The merchants and their goods that moved along the same routes, networking the fixed points of exchange and contacting the same personages, hardly needed the use of writing for communication. However, it is reasonable to assume that traders had access to writing and that the inscribed monuments communicated to them, if only symbolically.

As evident from the poems, the burial stones with labels commemorated warrior chieftains and warrior headmen. The immediate followers of these people were warriors (*maṛavar*) engaged with them as full-time fighters. The writing on burial stones would by itself have made no sense to them except for what it symbolized in a heroic society. The situation of their headmen and chieftains could scarcely have been far different. The bigger chieftains could have had access to the symbolic use of writing for the sake of honour, status, and ranking. The Jambai inscription testifies to Atikaman's use of writing for its symbolic significance. But this is a rare instance and the general absence of inscriptions is seemingly not altogether accidental because the day-to-day functioning, legitimacy, and authority of the chieftains' power did not have to depend upon writing. The reproduction and perpetuation of their power, based on predatory control, prestations, redistribution, and gifts, operated in a cultural milieu where communication was through morality, not literacy.

The next set of people who could have been the target of the hero-stone inscriptions were the wandering bards (*pāṇar*) and other mendicants (*iravalar*). But the bards who were based in the tradition of oral transmission of information had no professional need to learn the art of writing. so the inscriptions could have communicated to them what they symbolically meant in the society of heroic culture. This also seems to be the case of the scholarly bards (*pulavar*) who followed the bardic techniques of oral transmission practised by the *pāṇar*. Similarly, it goes without saying that the art of writing was irrelevant to mendicants and minstrels.

The Tamil heroic texts were bardic compositions versified through the techniques of oral literature, as evidenced by their formulaic diction, stock phrases, stylized expressions, stereotypes, and symbolic representation of unconscious meaning.[8] The status of the bardic compositions in the contemporary culture is explicit in the practice of pulavar (*brāhmaṇa* poets) pretending to be pāṇar. The genre of bardic poems set the diction in society for organizing thought and recognizing truth. For forms of knowledge in the society to be legitimate and authentic, they had to be framed within the structure of bardic poems. Even the *Kīḻkkaṇakku* texts, mostly composed towards the closing phases of the social formation, testify to this.[9] This was the 'hegemonic' status of the bardic mode of representing knowledge. There is corroborative evidence for the knowledge of writing in the Tamil heroic poems, dating back roughly to the run of the Christian era. This evidence hardly tells us anything about the extent of the uses that people made of writing during the period. Much more detailed examination of the evidence is required to ascertain the relevance and instrumentality of writing in the context of the socio-economic processes. What writing meant and how it worked in early societies needs to be ascertained first by situating the evidence of writing in context.

The social formation in question is perhaps best represented semiotically in the *tiṇai* concept of the Tamil heroic poetics, the details of which have been given in earlier chapters. As already explained elsewhere it was a combination of unevenly evolved forms of subsistence pursued by clan-based descent groups dispersed into domestic segments (*kuṭi*) in their respective settlements (*ūr*). Every ūr was a self-sustaining system of independent production units (*kuṭis*) based on the familial labour of the respective clan members (*kuṭimākkal*). Each kin group had its headman (*kiḻār*) at whose instance the resources of the ūr were pooled and redistributed. This basic chiefdom structure under different ecosystems and productive forces acquired varying degrees of complexity (in terms of the nature and extent of the redistributive social relationships).

The first main evidence of writing, as already stated, is a set of label inscriptions sparsely distributed in the districts of Tirunelveli, Ramanathapuram, Tiruchirappalli, Coimbatore, North Arcot, and Chingleput with a concentration in the district of Madurai. Out of the fifteen sites of label inscriptions, ten are on the routes from Madurai to neighbouring towns on the way to Tiruchirappalli, with a dense distribution in the northeast. The labels are palaeographically assigned to the period between the third and first centuries BC. These are votive inscriptions recording the names and occupational identities of donors and specific endowments of facilities, like a stone bed or a seat in one cave or another, for Jain, Buddhist, or Ājívika monks. The sites are associated with the heterodox religious sects that reached the region presumably in the wake of the influx of merchants and the development of trade routes during the Mauryan period. Scholars have been arguing about the monumental status of the sites in order to establish their Buddhist or Jain identity. The time, mode, and range of the Jain, Buddhist, and Ājívika penetration into the south are controversial. The question of the identity of the authors of the label inscriptions has often been confused with issues regarding the spread of heterodox sects in the region. Though the question of the social base of these sects is not insignificant here, our immediate concern is the people behind the inscriptions.

The people mentioned in the inscriptions were mostly specialist merchants as evident from the occupations mentioned: *pānitavāṇikan* (toddy merchant), *koḻuvāṇikan* (iron ploughshare merchant), *ponvāṇikan* (gold merchant), *koḻuvāṇikan* (ploughshare merchant), *aṛuvaivāṇikan* (textile merchant), and *uppuvāṇikan* (salt merchant).[10] There are others like *ponkolavan* (goldsmith) and *vaṇṇakkan* (specialist in gems) who were also part of the community of specialized exchanges.[11] They were local people, as names like Āṭan, Neṭumāḷan, Ula Cēntan, Neṭṭi, Kīran Koṟṟan, and Tēvan Cāttan indicate, and also as clearly shown by the place-name prefixes such as Mattirai (Madurai) in certain cases. One of the labels of Āriṭṭappatti refers to the *nikamattōr* (members of a corporation), obviously itinerant merchants, of a place called Vellarai. A non-merchant category that figures in a few labels is *kaṇaka* or *kaṇiyān* (*gaṇaka*, the astrologer) who seems to be one among the many *upāsaka*s of the heterodox sects, probably an admirer of the Ājívikas, who were famous as fortune-tellers. A label of Pugalur mentions llamkatunko of the lineage of the chiefs of the Cēras. These specializations have to be viewed as a structured outcome of contemporary long-distance trade dependent on the economic activities, surplus, material demand, and socio-political processes in northern India. Engaged in full-time exchange and attached to big marketing centres like Madurai or Kaveripattinam, these specialists constituted a very small section, but were yet to sever all local clan ties and emerge as a caste. They were different from ordinary folk at any rate and perhaps could be compared with clan headmen.

Strictly speaking, the question of whether these people were followers of the heterodox religions or not hardly makes sense since it is anachronistic to assume that people other than monks were part of these sects. The inscriptions themselves reveal the social identity of these people as merchants, chieftains, or craftsmen, never monks. However, their veneration of monks and belief in the ethical merit of charity are explicit in the endowment. The impact of monks on the contemporary society of the period was minimal and primarily normative since their relationship to it was that of mendicants. Moreover, the monks signified a parallel society, precluding the question of their absorption into local society.

The act of inscribing the names and social identity of donors was certainly mundane, not ethical or religious. It had something to do with status and ranking. Who were the literate people addressed by the inscriptions, who could confer honour and status upon the donors? We are not sure whether all the people who figure in the labels could have read and understood the inscriptions all by themselves. Anyhow, the question of who the literates were, leads us to the question of the language used in these inscriptions, which according to recent advances in research was old Tamil.[12] The use of this language by the merchants and monks is a matter generally agreed upon. But the language, which is considerably different from the old Tamil of the heroic poems, does not appear to be the language of all the people of the Tamil region. The language of the heroic poems has often been considered quite scholarly and highbrow, a view that makes little sense in the case of oral compositions.

The label inscriptions seem to have addressed themselves mainly to itinerant merchants, monks, and predatory chieftains who had cross-cultural contacts, a set of wider social relations, and mobility. All of them, irrespective of whether they could themselves read and write, had functional accessibility to writing for either direct or symbolic communication. Itinerant merchants whose profession necessitated some permanent means for storing memory and a stable information service must have been able to use writing for direct communication. However, even this seems to have been full of short-forms and symbols as the inscribed pots from places like Arikamedu, Alagarai, Karur, Korkai, and Poluvampatti indicate. They are primarily personal names. Inscribing personal names on pots, explicitly an individualizing cultural practice could hardly have been part of the folk life of collective existence. So the potsherd labels, as such, cannot be taken as proof of literacy among potters. The number of inscribed potsherds at centres of craftwork and marketing, such as Arikamedu, Alagarai, Karur, Korkai, and Poluvampatti suggest their association with merchants and guilds rather than with potters. There could have been literate potters as well as merchants in such centres. Similar mercantile or guild connections cannot be ruled out even in the case of the apparently non-urban sites such as Alagarai or Poluvampatti. However, it is difficult to assume that these potsherds belonged to ordinary folk.[13]

In the absence of direct evidence in the sources as to who really learned the art of writing, we approach the question by probing into its relevance, which may have been direct and extensive if we assume that those who wrote had continued in their caverns the tradition of framing and reproducing the canonical texts. However, writing was symbolic to most of the people who had a functional accessibility to it. Inscriptions must have made sense to them not in terms of letters, but as a cluster of visible signs of various qualities such as dedication, religious merit, honour, status, power, and authority depending upon what their concern was.

The skill of actually writing for oneself was in all probability confined to a small minority like monks and merchants. However, the social accessibility to its symbolic use was certainly much wider. One should examine the evidence for the use of writing in this context, such as allusions to *eḻuttuṭai nāṭukal*, generally translated as inscribed menhirs commemorating dead heroes in the Tamil heroic poems.[14] In the light of these allusions, scholars have assumed the practice to have been quite extensive in the age of heroic poems. The discovery of the Chengam hero-stones with inscriptions, although of a later period, has strengthened the assumption which, by extension, suggests a wider use of writing. However, this assumption does not bear close scrutiny because the poetic allusions are not always to writing, but to painting. However, in two or three instances the expression of *peyār* implies that communication by word of mouth was common and the use of writing in the period was correspondingly marginal.

Production, exchange, social appropriation, political control, and cultural practices notwithstanding, the differences in the degrees of complexity indicate that writing had a very marginal role. This is comprehensible given the material processes of contemporary social existence. It was by and large a system based on individual means of production and collective appropriation through complex redistributive relationships. In the biggest chiefdoms represented by the *mūvēntar* (Cēra, Cōḻa, and Pāṇḍya), a differential allocation of roles, functions, and status did occur in the process of redistribution and exchange of gifts beyond clan ties. Such individual differences in terms of material possessions, status, and ranking within the relatively flexible social stratification into the high-born (*uyarntōr*) and low-born (*iḻipiṟappāḷar*) were sustained by oral traditions. The warrior headmen often received control over *marutam* tracts (seemingly the right of exaction) as the chieftain's reward for their service in predatory campaigns. For the preservation of such rights or privileges also, the oral traditions reproduced and perpetuated by bards were quite sufficient.

A *brāhmaṇa* household, representing a totally different site in terms of productive relations, implied certain privileges on the means of production. A *brāhmaṇa* household constrained to subsist on agriculture necessitated some permanent arrangement for the supply of labour on the land. This required the privilege of expropriating the familiar labour of the neighbouring clansmen and proprietary control of land. In a set up of communal holding and kin labour, the productive relations of the *brāhmaṇa* households did signify a fundamental difference that eventually signalled the dissolution of the social formation. As an aggregate of conflicting economies, they were incapable of surviving for a longer period with their low labour productivity and shrinking potential of economic reproduction[15]. The new, expanded system of redistribution generated certain new rights and privileges, and apparently, for quite some time these rights and privileges were sustained through oral traditions.

However, at some point written records seem to have become essential for legitimizing new rights and privileges that were entirely strange to the traditional system. The earliest major document so far known is the set of two large inscriptions, of about AD 500, on a rock at Pulānkuṟichi in the Tiruppattur taluk of the Ramanathapuram district.[16] These inscriptions register land grants by a warrior chief and a royal order regarding the priests and cultivators of three temples. The kinds of land rights and royal stipulations seen in the records were totally strange in the sense that they were almost entirely unknown to the heroic texts. They indicate the presence of a new social formation structured by the dominance of relations in plough agriculture. We do not know much about the presages of this relatively well-articulated system of productive relations structured into a hierarchy of landholders, leaseholders, and tillers in the descending order. The inscriptions lay bare the presence of a political power regulating the conditions essential for the working of the new productive relations. They further reveal the socioeconomic context of the uses of writing. In order to understand the implications of writing as documentation of power, as validating new rights and imposing their acceptance, it is necessary to have a closer look at the contents of the inscriptions.

The first is land grants, probably to a temple under the control of *brāhmaṇa* landholders in the status of the village headmen (*ūr-kiḻār*). The donor is said to have purchased some strips of land scattered in a few *brāhmaṇa* villages and endowed them with the right of cultivation (*kārāṇmai*) and superior right (*miyāṭci*). The record places the cultivators and other people under the control of the *brāhmaṇa* landholders and under the protection of the watch and ward of the locality (*nāṭukāppār* and *puṟamkāppar*). What is signified here is a moment in the historical process of the expansion of the *brāhmaṇa* land control around the villages headed by them. That they were ur-kilar is an indicator of the development of old *brāhmaṇa* households into full-fledged agrarian settlements probably through the institution of *ēkabhōga brahmadēya*. The process certainly involved the acquisition of new rights over both land and labour, the establishment of which required the backing of political authority as evidenced by the inscriptions. The first inscription prescribes rights over resources, including labour, and the repressive apparatus punitive clause, which was a heavy fine in case of violation. Similarly, the second power legitimizing and validating changes it imposed on the traditional structure of land control and productive relations is also present.

This would help us suggest that the use of writing implicating a relatively wide society was linked to the emergence of a class with superior rights over land and the formation of state power. The rights and privileges of this class with its substantial political base and increasing resource control, were essentially new. They were rights arbitrarily superimposed on the conventional set up by the political power effecting a transformation in productive functions, responsibilities, and ties. They were too non-local, disparate, and diverse to be absorbed as part of local tradition or to be sustained by the social memory. The use of writing becomes essential in such a situation to record specifications stipulated beyond the purview of conventions and traditions. Against these stipulations, enhancing control over the means of production and imposing contradictory relations of appropriation, some kind of resistance was likely, making coercion indispensable. That a political authority capable of enforcing the social acceptance of the new pattern of resource control and appropriation makes its presence felt in the inscriptions is thus logical. Writing is, therefore, symbolic of the repressive dimension of political power in the case of inscriptions bearing orders to be obeyed.

The large majority of the people addressed by these inscriptional orders would never have read them for themselves. What they had possibly known was only an oral version of the inscriptional message. To them the inscriptions were, perhaps, symbolic of the power that dominated them. We do not know how exactly they were told about the contents of the inscriptions. Some of the copper plates of a slightly later period inform us that the oral orders of a king (*tirumukam*) were issued as *aria-ōlai* (a palm-leaf copy of the text of proclamation) before being inscribed permanently. The contents of royal orders must have been pronounced publicly in the concerned area as royal proclamations. However, for the people who shared the political power, these inscriptions were documents validating their claims. It was their material need to read and understand them because they regulated their rights and privileges.

The privileges always required documents of authority to validate and preserve them. It appears that such documents were initially in the form of proclamations inscribed boldly on rock, presumably to demonstrate the rupture they make with the conventional through their non-conventional messages. They must have acted as monumental signs of non-traditional impositions commanding public attention. It is true that copper plates precede rock inscriptions in the Tamil country (as evidenced by the Udayendiram plates of Nandivarman I, the famous Pallava king).[17] But such early copper plates register privileges of exemptions relevant to the relations between the donees and the state, rather than those between themselves and the people. The first copper plate charter seriously implicating the people is recorded in the Pallankovil plates of Simhavarman III (the famous Pallava King), of about AD 550.[18] Normally, a charter granting rights and privileges affecting the people in a locality where the act was totally unknown would be promulgated as a public announcement demanding obedience. Once such orders became common and were accommodated into the local traditions, the charters must have been issued as official documents to be retained in personal custody as deeds rather than public announcements. Most of the characters were initially palm-leaf documents which, for permanency, were converted into copper plates subsequently. The making of copper plates as permanent deeds of granted rights and privileges soon became a regular feature.

What was decisively at the fundamental level of the creation of new rights and privileges was the internal dynamic of the new social relationships of plough agriculture. A system of unequal entitlements and hierarchy was slowly encompassing society. The relations of domination had started articulating the juridico-political space that eventually led to the making of the state power and promulgation of rules ensuring the conditions of agrarian expansion. The institution of royal land grants indicates the decisive intervention of the economic in the political for the expansion and legitimacy of both and along with the proliferation of the brahmadēya and *dēvadana* villages, a monarchical state power was also in the making. Here was a complex historical process of the formation of new institutions, groups, and relations through a variety of material transactions generating a new pattern of resource control and appropriation.

The material transactions represented by land grants involving exemptions, privileges, and rights acquired a phenomenal dimension during the three or four centuries that marked the emergence of the Pallavas of the Simhavarman III line, the Pāṇḍyas of the Kaṭunkon line, and the Cōḷas of the Vijayalaya line. Founding hundreds of *brahmadēyas* and dēvadanas throughout the length and breadth of the region, the kings of these dynasties issued numerous copper plate charters of which a considerable number have survived. They issued charters of land grants to the heterodox religious institutions too, particularly the Jain temples and monasteries, as evidenced by the copper plates registering the *paḷḷiccantam* endowments.

The copper plate charters denote the birth of a document-based polity whose day-to-day functioning, legitimacy, and authority depend heavily on the use of writing. Elaborate eulogies (*praśatis*) and genealogical accounts that formed a considerable portion of the copper plate charters show the role of written records in the making of the *cakravartin* model of kingship. As the kingship, based on military power and ties with chieftains and landlords, stabilized through the administration of land dues (*puravuvari tiṇaikkaḷam*), the role of written documents became crucial. The maintenance of land-records and dues-registers was inevitable for the administration of tolls, agrarian dues, and other taxes. A state system based primarily on the periodic exaction of agrarian surplus, the south Indian monarchy had to maintain a variety of offices for book-keeping and accounting. In short, the use of writing became essential in a fundamental way for conducting the royal government. The terms *ōlai* and *pottakam*, the palm-leaf and its organized bundle respectively, appearing in the copper plates and monolithic inscriptions signify the archival basis of the royal office. There are several royal offices of olai and pottakam such as *ōlai-nayākam*, *paṭṭōlai*, *varippottakanāyakam*, *varippottakakkaṇakku*, and *puravuvarippottakam* mentioned in the inscriptions of the period.

The use of writing was important not only for keeping records but also for issuing receipts of remittances. Normally, such documents of contemporary relevance rarely survive beyond their time. So the volume of palm-leaf records with royal insignia, issued as receipts, and other documents of temporary value could have been many times the quantity that has come down to us. An interesting panel in the Thanjavur frescoes belonging to the Cōḻa period portrays a seated figure (Siva in the guise of an old man) waving palm leaves before a group of servile people).[19] This is a telling illustration of the power of documents in contemporary society. Landholders, particularly *brāhmaṇas*, seemed compelled to secure royal charters granting superior rights over productive land. The instances of *brāhmaṇas* obtaining copper plate charters for lost or encroached villages, recalled in certain royal charters of the Pāṇḍyas, are worth mentioning. The realm of transactions being increasingly governed by the legitimacy and validity of written deeds, a document-conscious approach steadily grew among landed people over the few centuries of agrarian expansion.

Agrarian expansion, which was an ongoing process during the period, went on augmenting the domain of unequal rights and privileges. Correspondingly, the use of written documents was also increasing. The volume of written documents the society generated during a period of three or four centuries was amazingly large. Writing acquired an unprecedented dynamic to spread across the region as a symbol of power, legitimacy, authenticity, and truth.

Unlike the *brahmadēyas* that generated written documents at the time of their charter, the *dēvadānas* went on generating written deeds at the temples that were perhaps the most significant sites of contemporary material transactions. The temples themselves became landed magnates with enormous resource control. As the institutional agency of both the *brāhmaṇa* and non-*brāhmaṇa* landholders, agrarian management and surplus appropriation, the temple was pivotal to the socio-economic life of the time. Most of the temples were great repositories of gold and other precious objects, the transactions of which, involving the sale or mortgage or purchase of land, necessitated the execution of a variety of deeds. The temples pooled and redistributed all kinds of resources that reached them by way of endowments.[20] The redistribution of the land endowments involved assignment of rights over land and regulation of entitlements to the beneficiaries. In the process, the temples became archives of copper plate charters and monolithic records dealing with endowments, material transactions, regulations of the management of their property, conduct of temple rituals, administration of functionaries, and stipulations of punitive measures. There are orders by the kings and chieftains (*srīkāriyam* or *tirumukam*), decisions by the *sabha* (*karumam* or *kaccam* or *vyavastha*) and resolutions by the *vāriyams*, recorded in the temples. The temple records constitute a good index to the extent of the uses the landed people made of writing.

We do not know whether all the landed people like the *brahmadēya-kiḻavar* and *nāṭṭār* had learnt how to read and write. But it is certain that they made use of writing for communication, which is explicit in their document mentality.[21] The kings, chieftains, their service personages, big merchants, and scholars in the various branches of contemporary knowledge must have secured, in varying degrees, the skill to read and write because it was the functional necessity in their social domain.

This does not mean that writing completely replaced oral expression as a mode of organizing knowledge for communication. The use of writing was only as an extension of orality at this stage.[22] It would not be possible to postulate any autonomy for literacy as separated from orality for the period. Oral traditions were still valid and the society often perpetuated written documents through oral versions. Most of the documents were party or mainly records of orally transmitted knowledge. The genealogical *praśastis* in the copper plates were entirely drawn from oral traditions. In the Velvikkuṭi plates there is a clear instance of the reigning Pāṇḍya king seeking local tradition for the validation of an ancestral claim put forward by a donee on the gift village.[23] This would suggest that oral traditions were still a source of validation. Though bards and bardic activities had ceased to dominate the regime of knowledge and the channel of cultural communication, the significance of oral traditions continued. The popular texts of the time were all orally composed and not written down for many years. All the hagiographic works were oral compositions based mostly on oral traditions.

To conclude, the central argument of this chapter is that the social widening of the uses of literacy in early south India was a consequence of the fundamental changes in production relations. Another contention is that the relative shift of social emphasis from orality to literacy was necessitated by the emergence of non-traditional rights and privileges that required written document for validation. Diversified rights, privileges, and powers not known to the conventional oral traditions necessitated written documents for their validation. The emergence of land as the principal object of labour, the superimposition of superior rights on the conventional, gradation of entitlements into a hierarchy, formation of temple-centred agrarian corporations, proliferation of temples and temple-centred transactions of goods and services, consolidation of a state power based on agrarian economy, and differential allocation of status and ranking based on land rights led to the making of a document-minded society. The expansion of material processes, ramification of social relations, alienation of conventional rights, and superimposition of superior privileges strengthened the pervasive dynamic of the use of writing. Incidentally, it has also been argued that the social pervasiveness of writing did not preclude the continuation of oral traditions in society. What writing could contain was only an extremely small portion of the enormously vast compendium of oral traditions. However, writing was almost an integral part of oral concepts and traditions.

NOTES AND REFERENCES

1. There have been controversies about the social effects of literacy. A well-known thesis is that literacy was responsible for the development of rational thought, historiography, individuality, and democracy. See J. Goody and I. Watt, 1968, 'The Consequences of Literacy', in J. Goody (ed.), *Literacy in Traditional Societies*, Cambridge, pp. 27–68. Also, W. Ong, 1982, *Orality and Literacy*, London. For a criticism of Goody and Watt, see J. Halverson, 1992, 'Goody and the Implosion of the Literacy Thesis', *Man*, New Series, 27(2): 301–38. The controversies pertain to whether one particular effect is historically borne out or not. However, they all agree with regard to the positive nature of the effects. H.J. Graff, 1981, *Literacy and Social Development in the West*, Cambridge.
2. The ambiguity of the term is discussed by Rosalind Thomas, 1989, *Oral Tradition and Written Record in Classical Athens*, Cambridge, pp. 16–22.
3. The concept of social formation used here has been explained in the Introduction to this volume. It is meant to represent the socio-economic aggregate of a period intelligibly, as a system combining different forms of production structured by the domination of the relations specific to one particular form. See discussions in Barry M. Hindess and Paul Q. Hirst, 1979, *Pre-Capitalist Modes of Production*, London, p. 51. Plough agriculture figures in the context as a technical expression for higher productivity, new kinds of social relationships, and the beginnings of surplus accumulation. It is the novelty of the relationships implying a new mode of social realization of labour that is underlined here as the basis of surplus.
4. *Puṛanāṉūṛu*, 260; 25–6: 263; 5–6; 33–4.
5. See the discussion in T.V. Mahalingam, 1967, *Early South Indian Palaeography*, p. 126. *Paripāṭal*, vol. 19, p. 53; *Kuṛuntokai*, 89.

6. See K. Rajan, 1986, 'Megalithic Culture of North Arcot Region', *Oātatva*, vol. 22, pp. 35–47. Also his, 1992, 'Memorial Stones in Tamil Nadu', in N.C. Ghosh and B.V. Nayak (eds), *New Trends in Indian Art and Archaeology*, Goa, pp. 251–90.
7. Though large quantities of punch-marked and Roman coins have been recovered from various places in the region, there is no proof for their use in local transactions. They formed part of social valuables and treasure, but hardly money. Rajan Gurukkal, 1986, 'Forms of Production and Forces of Change in Ancient Tamil Society', *Studies in History*, 5(2): 162. Recent reports refer to the discovery of numerous coins allegedly of the *vēntar* chiefs. These coins are not adequately studied as yet to know whether they had functioned as money at all. Anyhow, the forms of exchange that one is able to reconstruct from the literature preclude the use of coins as money. For the nature and context of Roman trade, see Romila Thapar, 1992, 'Black Gold: South Asia and the Roman Maritime Trade', *South Asia*, 15(2): 1–27.
8. For the characteristic features of oral compositions, see C.M. Bowra, 1966, *Herioc Poetry*, London; R. Finnegan, 1977, *Oral Poetry*, Cambridge; A Dundes, 1975, *Analytical Essays in Folklore*, New York, pp. 28–9; W.H. Murphy, 1978, 'Oral Literature', *Annual Review of Anthropology*, vol. 7, pp. 113–36.
9. Even works like *Tirikaṭukam, Ēlāti*, and *Ciṛupañcamūlam*, which deal with the knowledge of treatment and health care, follow the heroic diction.
10. I. Mahadevan, 1970, 'Tamil Brahmi Inscriptions', Madras, pp. 2–3.
11. Ibid.
12. Ibid.
13. For a counter-argument, see I. Mahadevan, 1995, 'From Orality to Literary: The Case of the Tamil Society', Seminar on Literacy and Communication in Indian Tradition, Jawaharlal Nehru University, March 1993, *Studies in History*, fol. 11:2, pp. 173–88, New Delhi, March.
14. For the correlation between the poetic references and the archaeological relics, see R. Champakalakshmi, 1972, 'Archaeology and Tamil Literary Tradition', *Purātatva*, vol. 8.
15. Gurukkal, 'Forms of Production', pp. 159–75.
16. R. Nagaswamy, 1981, 'An Outstanding Epigraphical Discovery in Tamil Nadu', Proceedings of the Fifth International Conference on Tamil Studies, vol. 1, Section 2, Madurai, pp. 67–71. Also, Natana Kasinathan, 1983, 'Pulānkuṛichi Inscription: A Re-look', *Tolliyal Karuttaranaku*, Madras, pp. 157–68. For an updated text of the inscriptions, see Y. Subbarayalu and M.R. Raghvan Varier, 1991, 'Pulānkuṛichi Kalvettukkal', *Āvaṇam*, 1(2): 57–69. Also Y. Subbarayalu, 1993, 'A Note on the Socio-economic Milieu of the Pulānkuṛichi Rock Inscriptions', unpublished paper, Tamil University.
17. T.V. Mahalingam (ed.), 1988, *Inscriptions of the Pallavas*, Delhi, pp. 58–61.

18. Ibid., pp. 89–93. This seems to be the first inscription mentioning eviction of the original settlers. The grant was of the *kuṭinīkki*, depriving the original cultivators of their rights. Hence the serious social implication.
19. See R. Champakalakshmi, 1973, 'New Light on the Cola frescoes of Tanjore', *Journal of Indian History*, Golden Jubilee Volume, pp. 349–59.
20. For the economic activities of the south Indian temple, see Burton Stein, 1960, 'Economic Functions of a Medieval South Indian Temple', *Journal of Asian Studies*, 19(2): 163–76; George W. Spencer, 1968, 'Temple, Money-lending and Livestock Redistribution in Early Tanjore', *Indian Economic and Social History Review*, 5(3): 277–92; A. Appadurai and C.A. Breckenridge, 1976, 'The South Indian Hindu Temple: Authority, Honour and Redistribution', *Contributions to Indian Sociology*, New Series, 10(2): 187–211.
21. For a discussion of the growth of the document mentality, see M.T Clanchy, 1979, *From Memory to Written Record*, London, pp. 202–3. The author talks about the middle ages of Europe and the mixed use of oral and written texts. Also in J. Goody, 1986, *The Logic of Writing and the Organisation of Society*, London.
22. See the discussion of a similar situation in medieval England in Clanchy, *Memory to Written Record*, pp. 20–6. Also the discussion on the coexistence and complementarity of orality and literacy in Rosalind Thomas, 1989, *Oral Tradition and Written Record in Classical Athens*, Cambridge, pp. 28–32.
23. See the Velvikkuti plates: *Panḍyar Ceppēṭukal Pattu*, Madras, 1967, pp. 19–32. The relevant expressions in the plates are *nāṭṭānin paḷamai* and *nāṭṭāṟṟan paḷamai*, The intended meaning seems to be the *paḷamai* (tradition) of the *nāṭṭār* (*nāṭṭār = tam paḷamai*). The term *nāṭṭār* means the non-*brāhmaṇa* landholders whose conformity to and participation in the act were ensured when a brahmadēya grant was made. They constituted the dependable subjects.

9

Towards a New Discourse

Discursive Processes in Early South India*

In south Indian historiography, religion is the central focus of ideological history, the object of the study being conceived as a completed entity rather than as an ongoing process. Ideology, though predominantly manifest in religion, is never exclusively confined to it. As a leavening substratum, it pervades every intellectual and cultural practice of a society. Religion-centred analysis of ideology not only fails to capture this leavening substratum, but also loses sight of its historical context of social totality. The most useful framework that transcends these limitations is the social formation paradigm, in which a society is perceived as a system resulting from the coexistence and interaction of diverse forms of subsistence.[1] This provides the conceptual prerequisite for the present attempt to understand the discursive processes of society in early south India.[2] In south Indian historiography, discourse analysis is a relatively new exercise both in terms of the perception of ideological phenomena and analysis of their historical context. The attempt here is to view the breakdown of a discourse and the emergence of another in the wake of the deliverance of a new social formation from the pre-existing one. To be specific, the attempt is to discuss the dissolution of the heroic discourse and the emergence of *bhakti*, in terms of how one episteme is supplanted by another.

Early south India, as used here, represents almost a millennium from about the third century BC, as the sources indicate. Spatially it comprises

---

* This chapter is a reproduced version of the article with the same title from, 1996, R. Champakalakshmi and S. Gopal (eds), *Tradition, Dissent and Ideology: Essays in Honour of Romila Thapar*, (Oxford University Press: New Delhi), pp. 313–34.

the landmass between the hills of Venkatam and the tip of Kanyakumari. The temporal extent subsumes the long duration of the emergence and dissolution of a social formation. The regional specificity, as expressed in the term Tamilakam, rests on historically contingent factors such as the linguistic identity and cultural homogeneity of its inhabitants.

The social formation in question was agropastoral, characterized by redistributive economy, predatory polity, and heroic culture, the details of which have been considered at length earlier. Redistribution did not preclude other formal means of circulating the resources. The early forms of exchange, as ascriptive and customary practices, date back to the late Stone Age. Formal exchange became more extensive in the Iron Age, the closing phase of which overlaps with the period of the Tamil heroic poems. The punch-marked coins that reached from the Gangetic region, the names of specialist merchants seen in the Tamil *brāhmi* label inscriptions, the Roman coins brought by the long-distance traders, and the writings by the Graeco-Roman geographers provide evidence of mercantile circulation of resources.[3] We start getting coins of the *vēntar* chiefdoms and pottery graffiti shedding more light on the extent of local participation in organized exchanges. However, the overall nature of contemporary internal exchanges, as depicted in the heroic poems, was by and large that of reciprocity based on use-value. The influx of gold and silver as coins and bullion that characterized the period thus provides insufficient proof to argue for the existence of a monetized economy. The coins and bullion seem to have functioned as part of valuables rather than as money.[4] What emerges is the picture of a social formation dependent on multiple forms of economies, kin-based relations of production, redistributive system of social appropriation, and predatory political control.

As chiefdom-level societies of prestations, gifts, and redistribution maintained through the politics of frequent raids for plunder, the production and circulation of heroic discourse was central to their cultural practices. The Tamil heroic poems that are amazingly extensive vouch for this. These were primarily bardic compositions embodying knowledge based on the discursive practices of the heroic society. The bardic form of communication and dissemination of knowledge dominated the prevalent culture of redistributive economy and discursive social relationships. The social conditions of the realization of the familial labour of the *kuṭis* that were interlocked through the clan ties of the *ūr*, were obviously discursive. This would suggest that the role of discourse in the relations of production was decisive.

The discursive processes of a society are best represented in its literature, which is a domain of innovative expressions linked to the power-knowledge praxis. In this context, the Tamil heroic poems derive enormous importance as a collection of socially symbolic texts. Projecting chieftains and warriors as heroes and glorifying their might, mien, and munificence, the poems legitimize raids for plunder, capture of booty, redistribution, and gift-giving. Articulated under the structural imposition of the social formation and facilitating the reproduction of redistributive social relationships, the form and content of the heroic poems were discursive.

Besides their baffling problem of chronology, the ancient Tamil texts pose a variety of other problems for historians attempting to derive evidence from them. Following the diction of heroic compositions, they use formulaic expressions, stock phrases, and symbols representing underlying meaning, preventing us from taking them literally. The task of decoding the real meaning of the texts thus involves arduous exercises, ranging from syntagmatic analysis of morphology to paradigmatic, psycho-analytical and semiological analyses.[5] The absence of precise chronology or symbolism is not a serious impediment since the focus here is essentially on what is discursively significant in the poems, and this scarcely requires the specific date of each poem to be established. What I attempt to chart is the discursive internality of literature and its relation to the social formation.

The discursive constituents, as clusters of semantic signs of the heroic poems, are encapsulated in a series of poetic codes in the Tamil heroic poetry. What is fundamental to the Tamil heroic poetics is the dual concept of *tiṇai* and *tuṟai*, denoting the situation and context respectively, for the presentation of specific moods in the poems.[6] The concept of tiṇai has a wider connotation in the sense that it articulates the reality about the man–nature situation of the times. Beyond this apparent reality, it has a realm of interpretive meaning that transcends its formal structure and function. Similarly, the concept of *tuṟai*, which denotes the thematic context of the poems, has a regime of interpretive meaning hidden beneath its apparent meaning and formal function as defined in the poetics. Both tiṇai and tuṟai bear a series of enunciative codes within their form that help us delve into their semantic world of signs and paradigms.

There are about nine enunciating codes in the poetics, around the concept of tiṇai, as listed here: (a) *tumpaittiṇai*, versifying the situation of warriors getting ready for a raid; (b) *vañjittiṇai*, of warriors arriving to raid the enemy's territory; (c) *kāñjittiṇai*, of defending against a raid; (d) *noccittiṇai* of warriors guarding the wall; (e) *veṭcittiṇai*, of raiding cattle; (f) *karantaittiṇai*, of raids for recovering the cattle; (g) *vākaittiṇai*, of devastation and martial rejoicing after killing enemies in a raid; (h) *uḻiññaittiṇai*, of warriors returning after a raid; and (i) *pāṭāntiṇai*, of the situation of a bard singing about the hero's fame, might, mien, and munificence. Among these, all except the last are based on flower symbolism according to which the flowers such as *tūmpai, vañji, kāñji, nocci, veṭci, karantai, vākai*, and *uḻiññai* represent the respective situations. In the poetics these constituted distinct thematic situations, but in the hermeneutics with which we are concerned, they constitute the diverse codes of a single discourse. There are about 35 enunciating codes around the concept of *tuṛai*, which may be grouped here into five clusters of closely related meanings:

1. *Tuṛais* extolling individual heroism, for instance, *tānainilai*, versifying the kind of heroism exalted both by the fighters and the fought; *nallicai vañji*, the context of a hero's march with an intrinsic potential of devastation; *aḻilāṭṭu*, the context of a hero destroying the enemies with a spear pulled out from his own chest; *piḷḷaippeyarcci*, the courage of a hero ignoring evil omens; *makaṭpārkānji*, a hero's courage to deny his daughter even to a *vēntar* seeking to marry her; and *erumaimaṛam*, the context of a hero fighting the enemies single-handedly.
2. *Tuṛais* extolling the family tradition and heritage of heroes, for instance, *ēṛāṇmullai*, versifying the context of praising the family tradition of a hero; *kuṭinilaiyuraittal*, of praising the heroic tradition of a warrior family; *mūṭal vañji*, of praising a warrior's ancestral tradition of heroic exploits; *vallāṇmullai*, of praising the place and family of a hero; and *mūtinmullai*, of praising the warrior families by depicting even their womenfolk as innately courageous.
3. *Tuṛais* extolling the virtues of raids for plunder, for instance, *malapuḻavañji*, versifying the context of raid and devastation of settlements; *koṛṛavaḷḷai*, of expressing grief at the plight of the devastated as an indirect way of praising the might of the hero; *ceṛumalaital*, of praising a hero shedding horror through his cattle raid; and *vāṇmankalam*, of praising the power of a hero's sword.
4. *Tuṛais* extolling the collective passion of the communities for raid, for instance, *unṭāṭṭu*, versifying the context of collective drinking and dining by the warriors before setting out for a

raid; *peruñcōṟṟunilai*, of the rice feast offered to the warriors; *talaittōṟṟam*, of collective rejoicing at the news of a hero bringing cattle as booty; *uvakaikkalūḻcci*, of a wife shedding tears of joy at the sight of her husband's chest covered with wounds.

5. *Tuṟais* extolling the act of gift-giving, for instance, *iyanmoḻivāḻttu*, versifying the context of praising the boundary of a chief; *pāṇāṟṟuppaṭai*, of a bard directing another to a chief by praising his generosity; *viṟali-yāṟṟuppaṭai*, of a *viṟaḷi* (female bard) persuading another to go to a chief by singing his bounty; *pulavarāṟṟuppaṭai*, of a poet praising a chieftain's bounty in order to secure a specific gift.

All these distinct enunciating codes of poetics are signifiers of the same discursive formation. They signify the discursive formation behind the dominant mode of organizing and recognizing contemporary thought and action. Beyond their functional meaning as distinct classificatory elements of poetics, they project the message of the primacy of the values and passions of a heroic society. They signify the various intrinsic notions of a society based on raids for plunder and redistribution of booty. It is quite natural that the enunciating categories of heroic poetics do so.

This would suggest that generalizations about the hegemonic status of the heroic discourse made solely on the basis of clues from heroic poetics need not invariably be true since we cannot expect the heroic poems to represent all aspects of the society. The heroic compositions do, however, also contain allusions to the non-martial aspects of life. Indeed, several anthologies among the corpus of heroic narratives are entirely devoted to non-martial, non-heroic themes, though their diction clearly exhibits the link with the heroic literature. Even the compositions that are exclusively about martial exploits do maintain a resonance of the other dimensions of contemporary society. What is brought to bear in all compositions is, however, the hegemony of the heroic discourse. It is quite unlikely to be otherwise in a society of plunder-based redistributive economy.

All institutional forms and cultural practices of the period vouch for the hegemony of the heroic discourse. The institution of *vaṭakkiruttal*, which was a ritual of self-immolation by a hero wounded on his back, fasting and seated in penance facing the north, is one example. To be wounded on the back was ignominious for a warrior who always cherished death by wounds to his chest. Cultural practices such as *uṇṭāṭṭu*, the collective drinking and dining of the warriors; *tuṇankai-kūttu*, a dance performed by female bards, and *kuravai-kūttu*, a dance by the womenfolk of the warriors, are direct manifestations of the heroic discourse. The nature of deities and modes of worship in the various *tiṇai*s is another pointer to the hegemony of the heroic discourse. *Cēyōn* or *Murukan* of the *kuṛiñji*, hero stones of the *pālai*, *Māyōn* of the *mullai*, *Vēntan* of the *marutam*, and *Varuṇa* of the *neital* are the deities or objects of worship prescribed in the poetics.[7] The cult of heroism was central to the worship of all these deities despite their distinct functional meanings in relation to the economic processes of the respective *tiṇai*. Thus we see Cēyōn as a deified hunter hero, Māyōn as the deified cowherd hero, all exhibiting, though in varying degrees, the effects of the heroic discourse. However, an agriculturist not being a warrior by himself, the deity of the farming communities, *Vēntan*, the rain god, was not given a context to incarnate as a hero. Though often taken as the counterpart of Indra, the warrior image of the Vedic deity is absent in *Vēntan*. It is significant that he is largely celebrated in later works such as *Paripāṭal*, *Cilappatikāram*, and *Maṇimēkalai*. However, the system of worship among the agriculturists too had to function within the broad social unity of shared cultural practice.

This does not mean that there was no dissenting voice within the overarching hegemony of heroic discourse. The discursive content of contemporary cultural practices, institutional structures, and political operations could never have been univocal since the social formation was an ensemble of different economies with contradictory interests. The coexistence of antagonistic voices with the hegemonic is attested to by the enunciating codes in poetics. They are grouped into three categories of discursive prescriptions:

1. The category of the *tuṛai* codes stressing the importance of peace and security as exemplified by *ceviyaṛivūṛu*, versifying the context of offering advice to chieftains regarding the maintenance of peace, order, and security in society.
2. The category of the *tuṛai* codes stressing the importance of asceticism and the other-worldly life as exemplified by *porunmoḻikkāñji*, versifying the context of advising a chieftain about what gives strength in this and the other worlds; and *peruñkānji*, the context of appraising a chieftain about the transient nature of the worldly life
3. The category of the *tuṛai* codes stressing the importance of *brāhmaṇa*s and the Vedic, Śāstrāic, and Purāṇic discourses as

> exemplified by *pārppanavākai*, versifying the context of praising *brāhmaṇas* and brahmanical rituals; *mutumoḻikkānji*, of conversing on *dharma, artha,* and *kāma*; and *manaiyaṛam*, of distinguishing between the ascetic and family life.

These are obviously discursive signs transmitting values and passions antagonistic to what was hegemonic in the social formation. Emphasis on values of peace, spirituality, and order was antagonistic to the discursive milieu of raids for plunder and redistribution of booty. Some of the poems of these *tuṛais* advise the chieftains to offer protection to agriculturists from the raids and to hold themselves aloof from the instigators of raids. They exhort the chieftains to refrain from predatory campaigns that lead to the destruction of agricultural settlements. This is a reflection of the voice of dissent against the heroic discourse which was reproducing the conditions of its perpetuation through various institutions and practices.

The coexistence of the antagonistic voices with the hegemonic was rooted in the contradictory dynamic of the social formation. The contradictions were being generated through the process of the coexistence of conflicting forms of production and their collective functioning as a system. The plight of plough agriculture, as enmeshed in the institutional structures and strategies of primitive agriculture and pastoralism, shows perhaps the most glaring of all the contradictions. The institutions, ideas, and other forms of culture generated and maintained by the society of cattle-breeders and primitive agriculture were altogether inimical to the growth of plough agriculture. The former was the dominant form of production despite the fact that the latter was superior in terms of both technology and productivity. The political practices and institutional forms were the result of articulations at the economy of agro-pastoralism.[8] The instituted practices like raids for plunder, gifts, redistribution, and bardic compositions, dominated the social life of the period. Predatory marches of chieftains and their destruction of agriculture and agrarian settlements were extremely detrimental to the development of plough agriculture. Burning of crops and settlements referred to in the poems as *eriparanteṭuttal* was routine in all kinds of raids.[9] As discussed earlier, there is an echo of the helpless voice of agriculturists in certain poems that characterize them as defenceless people. In *Puṛanāṉūṛu* (*Pn.*) 23, Kallāṭanār gives a representative instance of agrarian settlements devastated by a raid. Pāṇṭaran Kaṇṇanār alludes in *Pn.*, 16 to the burning of agricultural fields which knew no forest other than fields of sugarcane.

Neṭṭimaiyār describes in *Pn.*, 15 another instance of burning fields of crops as part of the atrocities of a raid. The raids of predatory chieftains that swept through the agrarian tracts caused far wider destruction of grain than was exacted.

Being stereotypical and formulaic, these poetic allusions are hardly historical as regards social life per se. They are only conventional poetic motifs. However, these conventional motifs should be historicized in the sense that they signify the collective reality of contemporary society, albeit not in terms of their apparent meanings. The cry for the protection of agriculturists and the exhortations for abstaining from raids and encouraging peace emerge as a voice of dissent from this collective reality.

At the same time, however, the importance of plough agriculture was also a matter of social recognition. Its overall significance and primacy is reflected in the poems. The poetics has a specific enunciating code under the *tuṟai* concept, namely *ērkaḷuruvakam*, dealing with constructs based on imagery from the labour processes of plough agriculture. All poems belonging to this *tuṟai* draw upon a hero's fight in a language of metaphors relating to the activities of plough agriculture, equating him with an agriculturist, his weapon with the plough, fighting ground with the agricultural field, fighting with the act of ploughing, and so on.[10] This would suggest that though the significance of plough agriculture was tacitly recognized in the social rhetoric, the contradiction involved in the reproduction of institutional forms and cultural practices impeding the growth of agriculture was not realized. There is nothing unnatural about this since the dominant form of production was agro-pastoralism, which generated and perpetuated the politics of plunder as fundamental to the maintenance of the complex system of redistributive social relationships.

Elsewhere it has been argued that plough agriculture was the dominant economic form during the period, but this conclusion on the basis of heroic poems could be misleading.[11] The argument makes no sense since, theoretically, a society with such an enormous volume of heroic compositions could only have been a system structured by the dominance of the heroic discourse. The antagonistic voices that we have identified from the enunciating codes of heroic poetics themselves are clear indicators of the subordinate status of agriculturists in comparison to that of the warriors. Moreover, the overarching political structure of the period is strong evidence of the domination of the redistributive economy in which sedentary agriculture was struggling to secure its conditions of development.

The contradictions at the economic level were being regenerated continuously through the coexistence and interaction of the conflicting forms of production. An outstanding consequence of the economic process of resource redistribution in the discursively realized pattern of social relationships, was intensification of the contradictions. Raids involved capture of an *ūr* (settlement) and its redistribution among warrior chiefs, which would mean imposition of predatory rights of alien chiefs over descent groups.[12] Though not in the form of actual land grants, *brāhmaṇas* as scholarly bards and Vedic priests, seem to have been given gifts of ūr, obviously as a part of the redistribution system. Such gifts must have given rise to individual holdings against communal holdings. In the case of gifts of *ūr*, probably the right of exaction to warrior chiefs beyond the clan kinship must have given rise to the formation of chieftains' lineages branched off from clans. But the gifts of ūr to *brāhmaṇas* would mean formation of their households involving far-reaching changes in terms of relations of production, because it was much more than the superimposition of an alien right of exaction. The *brāhmaṇas* being a non-cultivating group by themselves had to depend upon the familial labour of neighbouring clans for the cultivation of their land. This meant making some permanent arrangement for the supply of labour in the *brāhmaṇa* households, obviously a system transcending kinship. The *brāhmaṇa*'s land with his household thus emerged as an independent unit of production with working clansmen families attached to it. The centre of *brāhmaṇa* households is referred to in the poems as *pārppanaccēri*, which in the present context signifies the alternative system of agrarian relations counterposed to what was dominant. The development of the alternative system was itself a process aggravating systemic contradictions.

The *brāhmaṇa* household as a nexus of new relations reverberated with the anticipatory traits of a new discourse through the Vedic, Śāstrāic, and Purāṇic texts. They inevitably emitted the values and norms of *brāhmaṇa* households as the antagonistic voice struggling to be heard in the heroic society. Discursive formations broadly akin to the brahmanical ones in terms of their antagonism to the heroic discourse were gradually beginning to appear also with the spread of the heterodox religions. Though there is no reason to assume that the Jains and Buddhists were concerned about the values of agrarian society, their interest in social peace can indeed be assumed. The Jains and Buddhists had always been in favour of the communities engaged in exchanges whose operations required peace and order as an essential prerequisite. This circumvents the discursive needs of agriculturists and the social groups engaged in exchange of goods. It must be remembered here that the new discursive formation that was yet to secure dominance in the social formation of the Tamil south had already become the dominant discourse in the Deccan and further north, even before the close of the first millennium BC. In the Deccan, the society contemporaneous with the Tamil heroic society was structured enough to constitute a full-blown state apparatus while the latter was weltering in the presages of state formation.[13] The concept of a king, kingdom, and kingly authority does exist at the level of the rhetoric of heroic Tamil poetry as a bardic implantation for the glorification of the status of chiefdoms. Ideas on periodic exactions, patronage of agriculturists, and intensification of production as opposed to predatory campaigns, do reach the ears of chieftains, but fall flat as dissonant impulses within a pre-state society.

Similarly, the brahmanical discourse of social differentiation and stratification does seek to express itself through the changing conditions around the brahmanical households themselves. But stratification was primarily confined to the binary between the high-born (*uyarntōr*) and low-born (*iḻipiṟappāḷar*), primarily differentiating the *brāhmaṇas* and patrons from the clan. Though the beginnings of caste system can be made out as implicit within the social nexus of *brāhmaṇa* households, the larger society remained casteless.[14] At the same time it was not entirely classless either, albeit without an objectively identifiable level of class domination. As the contradictions immanent in the social formation and the voices of the heroic discourse would indicate, the process of class differentiation was continuing and the strategies of domination were in the making. An impending crisis was implicit in the contradictory dynamic of the social formation that could hardly sustain itself for long with its low labour productivity and limited scope of economic reproduction.[15]

There is however no direct evidence for a total crisis leading to the dissolution of the Tamil heroic society. A disjunction is explicit in the sources, both archaeological and literary, which in terms of their existing chronology and historical context would have us believe that the principal chiefdoms went into oblivion by the close of the AD third century. None of the heroic poems sing the exploits of a chieftain belonging to the period after the third century nor can the historians clearly identify any chieftain of the well-known chiefdoms reigning during that period. The heroic compositions of typical bardic diction too seem to have been discontinued by this time. There is a corresponding discontinuity also of the institution of raids and booty redistribution. This is synchronized by a marked decline in the post-third century layers of the major archaeological sites. The sites with Buddhist association, however, provide evidence for continued development.[16] Historians have associated the period with the inroads by the predatory *Kaḷabhras* who belonged to the uplands of Karnataka.[17] They seem to have swept through the domains of the Tamil chieftains and caused their eclipse. However, the *Kaḷabhra* episode can hardly be so fundamental as to usher in major changes and the disappearance of the chiefdoms calls for an alternative explanation that can account for the substantial socio-political changes.

What is to be considered fundamental here is the contradictory dynamic of the social formation that matured over the years and culminated in a rupture. It is not unlikely that the predatory marches of the *Kaḷabhras* accentuated the culmination process which seemingly had evil effects on the *brāhmaṇas* whose hardships of that time have been recorded as the Kali age in a few copper plates of the eighth and ninth centuries.[18]

The historical process of the maturing of the contradictory dynamic and the consequent dissolution of the social formation can only be understood as a theoretical construct and not as empirical reality, for the characteristic frailties of the sources seldom bear directly upon what is investigated. The question therefore of direct evidence in matters concerning the transformation of Tamil heroic society into a new system of relations and values does not arise, a search for indirect clues being the only way to reach an understanding of what went on. The most valid clues are those suggesting the discontinuity of ideas and institutions typical of the heroic society. The discontinuity explicit in the existing chronological understanding of the heroic poems need not be accidental. Both the present state of knowledge about the poems and the absence of evidence for the continuation of the chiefdoms indicate the ever-intensifying contradictory dynamic immanent in the heroic society of prestations, gifts, and redistribution, making systemic dissolution inevitable. This would at once confirm the alleged discontinuity and account for the absence of evidence, which is not altogether accidental.

A much greater and more substantive factor that stresses discontinuity is the presence of a new class of literature and inscriptions datable to about a century later, which were radically different from the heroic compositions and the cave labels. Their objects, contexts, and strategies bear no comparison with those of the heroic texts and cave labels.

The *Kīḻkkaṇakku* texts belonging to the AD fourth to fifth centuries constituted the new class of literature significantly separated from the diction of the heroic tradition, although without moving away from the domain of oral compositions.[19] Most of these texts are didactic, specializing in the social ethic and personal conduct. Even in others which are not avowedly ethical, there is a stress on the importance of peace, loyalty, and social morality. The existence of a body of literature emphasizing such values presupposes a situation desperately in need of them. They all seemingly address themselves to a society of transitional complexities ranging from a general disorder to specific problems of new relations and values replacing the old. The texts are not directly concerned with the ethical task of highlighting the social imperative to establish order in the collective life that is incidental to their central thematic concerns. But as discursive impulses generated under the influence of social processes, their ethical postulates are more important in the context of discourse analysis. They constitute the running thread across the texts that draw upon diverse themes. In certain cases, the didactic elements are explicit and direct, while in others they are implicit and succinct. Those that are explicit and direct are in the form of exhortations for obedience, hard work and loyalty in the society.[20] All those that are implicit and succinct exude the values of the agrarian society organized into relations transcending kinship. In sum, the new class of literature seems to take the form of statements of a new discursive formation transcending the semantic regime of the heroic discourse.

The other category of a radically different source indicating the breakdown of the heroic discourse is a set of two rock inscriptions in Tamil *brāhmi* characters of the AD fifth to sixth centuries.[21] The date of one inscription is given in the beginning as the 192nd year of an unspecified era. The inscription refers to a certain King Cēntan Kūṟṟan, who is not mentioned in any of the known royal genealogies. He could probably be the father of Kūṟṟap-Perum Cēntan of *Mutoḷḷāyiram*, a work not far removed from the period. Unlike the earlier label inscriptions, they document a land transaction for the creation of an agrarian settlement under the *brāhmaṇa*s and set down the rights, privileges, and obligations of landholders, leaseholders, and actual tillers. The records represent the transactional relations of an asymmetrically structured society composed of diverse categories of people grouped on the basis of their rights over land. This is a social structure almost entirely alien to the heroic society. The records registering the orders of the ruling powers voice an echo of a political authority that bears no comparison with that of predatory chiefdoms. One might feel sceptical about the assumption of the alleged discontinuity as it is grounded on the availability of certain new types of sources whose data are different. But, as has already been pointed out, the availability of new types of sources only at a relatively later date is not accidental because they represent a social formation that is altogether new. A document like the Pulānkuṛichi rock inscription registering a land transaction and land rights is anachronistic to the heroic period, which was characterized by co-operative farming and collective appropriation. Though gift-giving played a very crucial role in the maintenance of the status, ranking, and authority of chieftains, it did not seem to have developed into the institution of land grants during the heroic period.

It is true that the colophons of the heroic anthologies do refer to land grants to bards, particularly the *brāhmaṇa* bards who also officiated at Vedic rituals.[22] But there is a time lag of three or four centuries between the poems and their colophons, which accounts for their presence.[23] Landholding by the *brāhmaṇas* as distinguished from communal holding was known to the heroic society, but it was, as has already been noted, the beginnings and rights over land were yet to be evolved through the emergence of intermediaries. The *brāhmaṇa* households of the heroic period were in fact anticipatory constituents of the evolving social system that manifested itself with its institutional structures by the time of the Pulankurichchi records. Despite the linkage in terms of the mode of production, the earlier *brāhmaṇa* households and the subsequently structured brahmanical society were two different entities, the former as part of the social formation dominated by primitive agriculture and animal husbandry and the latter dominated by irrigated agriculture. What appears therefore as disjunction between the old and new sources is the distance of the evolutionary process between two social formations.

Treating the *Kīḻkkaṇakku* texts as a new class of literature representing the discontinuity of heroic society can be controversial since their existence as a single corpus owes to their compilation and not to their origin. There is no uniformity of theme nor chronology for these texts which are classified as *Kīḻkkaṇakku* on arbitrary criteria adopted by the compilers. In addition to their thematic diversity, the texts had different religious affiliations through their brahmanical, Jain, and Buddhist authors. Above all, what is important is the thread of social ethics running through the diversity of their themes and religious affiliation. Even if no uniform chronology for them exists, they all fall within a comprehensive period during which their appearance amounts to a spate of didactical compositions. It is this spate of ethical texts during the fourth to fifth centuries that makes the assumption of discontinuity reasonable. The intellectual construct of one social formation dissolving into another, accounts for the crowding of works on social ethics during a specific span of time. It is not the potential of a discursive breakthrough in their ethical postulates that enables these texts to represent the discontinuity of heroic tradition, but their potential for domination.

The discursive content of the *Kīḻkkaṇakku* texts had its rudimentary beginnings in the heroic society itself, as we have shown while discussing the enunciating codes of certain tuṛais like *Ceviyaṛivūṛu*, *Porunmoḻikkāñji*, *Mutumoḻikkāñji*, *Pārppanavākai*, and *Manaiyaram*, stressing the values of peace, order and security of social life. These enunciating codes emitting antagonistic impulses have to be viewed as anticipatory constituents of the discursive formation taking shape in the *Kīḻkkaṇakku* texts. Despite this linkage, there is a distance of two social formations between them. One was part of the dissonant voice counterposed to the heroic discourse of the ancient social formation where it lacked the potential for domination. The other represented the initial statements of the emerging hegemonic discourse with the potential for domination.

What is reflected in the ethical postulates of the *Kīḻkkaṇakku* texts and the transactions of the Pulānkuṛichi records is the developmental process of a newborn social formation structured by the dominance of agrarian relations. It was a long process, witnessing the development of a complex system of hierarchical social relations of production and distribution out of the essentially simple system of production relations evolved in the earlier *brāhmaṇa* households. In the background were the waning trails of the dissolving heroic society, concomitant with a dialectical process of discursive transformation that was also taking place. What was the voice of dissent in the heroic society subsequently becomes a new discourse and the voice of dominance in the agrarian society. Here the contours of the new discourse are not complete and final since they were augmented further through the process of subjectification within the new social formation. Just as the social relations were yet to acquire greater complexity, the discursive domain was also very much in the making.

The social relations began to be further structured during the sixth and seventh centuries with the steady expansion of plough agriculture across the wetland. A perceptible feature of agrarian expansion was the proliferation of *brahmadēya* villages throughout the fertile tracts of the major river valleys in the region. It was a complex process of differentiation, stratification, and political formation, leading to the development of a state system and authority structures. Discursive development was inextricably woven into the process and the formation of institutions was part of it. The new political formation represented by the Simhavarman line of the Pallavas and the Kaṭunkon line of the Pāṇḍyas owed itself to the developing agrarian society whose expansion was linked to royal patronage.[24] Expansion of agrarian settlements through the creation of *brahmadēyas* often involved the superimposition of the superior rights of the *brāhmaṇas* over the communal holdings and the clan families of the locality. It must have been an intricate process of transformation of primitive agriculture and clan settlements into advanced agriculture and farmer settlements, respectively.

Discourse played the crucial role, probably as the coercive instrument in transforming and organizing people for the labour processes of wetland agriculture. The ethical didactics of the *Kīḻkkaṇakku* works, stemming from the discursive elements of Vedic, Purāṇic, and Śāstrāic texts, provided the foundation for social organization. It was an extremely intense process of reification that filled the discursive domain, offering prescriptions, explanation, meaning, and legitimacy to the variety of rights, ranks, positions, privileges, entitlements, and obligations binding the hierarchical social relationships. The most potent discursive instrument that stabilized the relations of production was caste, accommodating in its fold a variety of economically stratified functionaries of hereditary trades. As agrarian expansion advanced, human settlements originally bound by kinship got integrated as agrarian localities (*nāḍu*) which subsequently acquired great political significance in the monarchical system.[25] The role of caste in the integration of the agrarian society whose mechanisms of appropriation were based on extra-economic coercion, was extremely crucial. In sum, the realm of ideology became enormously complicated through reification and discourse production catered to the changing functional requirements of the expanding agrarian society.

The formation of agrarian localities was an ongoing process, and everywhere it accomplished a uniform structure of social relations irrespective of whether they were *brāhmaṇa* settlements (*brahmadēya-kiḻavar*) or *veḷḷān-vakai* settlements (ūr). The social structure was a hierarchy with landholders (*brahmadēya-kiḻavar* in the case of *brahmadēyas* and *Ūrār/ naṭṭar* in the case of veḷḷān-vakai settlements) at the apex and the large number of leaseholders (*kārāḷar*) who were mostly artisans and craftsmen, in the middle, placed over the primary producers (*aṭiyāḷar*) who were at the bottom. Almost parallel to the leaseholders there were many who held small strips of land as hereditary holdings (*kuṭi*) which were also tilled by the primary producers. The circulation of the produce in given shares thus took a structured path through all these categories enjoying differing levels of entitlement. The most benefited were the landholders who were ensured goods and services by the settlers in their land while the most exploited were the primary producers. As part of the social mechanisms of ensuring goods and services to the landholders through the notion of obligation, all artisans and craftsmen were subjected to immobility. The conditions of subjection together with the objective reality of the producers being stripped off their produce constituted the major contradiction in the system. Perpetuating relations of domination through the reproduction of the contradictory dynamic, the discursive regime became distinct by the breakdown of the heroic discourse and the emergence of the alternative.

The most powerful discourse born out of the contradictory dynamic that began to develop during the sixth to seventh centuries was *bhakti*. As a new religious sensibility, it gradually made its appearance in the invocatory stanzas of the heroic anthologies before being institutionalized through the *Āḷvār* and *Nāyanār* hymns.[26] The *Paripāṭal*, one of the collections under *Eṭṭuttokai* introduces the concept of *bhakti*, placing it at the beginning of the new discourse, that is, the *bhakti* of the *Āḷvār*/*Nāyanār* hymns.[27] However, the historical context of *bhakti* as a discourse whose genealogy goes far back in time, was the expansion of structured agrarian society of contradictory relations. There it mirrored the way the subjected and exploited lived, the relation between themselves and the objective conditions of their existence. It glossed over the material reality of the conditions of domination by inventing other-worldly explanations for the social contradictions. The discourse provided a psychological basis for social acceptance of the explanation of the plight of the pressed in the agrarian society. The psychological basis took the form of a cult of complete surrender at the feet of gods as the final refuge acting as an illusory solace to the miserable. It gained momentum as a cult of personal gods housed in temples that grew up as the nerve centre of agrarian settlements more or less as a sequel to the expansion of agriculture. The hymns of the *Āḷvārs* and *Nāyanārs* were composed in praise of these personal gods of temples whose distribution and sacred geography corresponded to the course of agrarian expansion.[28] With the manifestation of the bhakti discourse as a temple-based movement in the seventh and eighth centuries, the formation of the dominant ideology of the agrarian society was complete. Within the mystifying discourse of *bhakti*, voices of dissent against the hegemonic were not precluded. Since it was a social formation of contradictory relations involving the tension of subjection and exploitation, voices of protest were inevitable.[29] The hegemonic discourse was so imposing that the elements of protest and dissent could be articulated only through its discursive practices that neutralized them through the strategy of containment.[30] A detailed analysis of the process is not within the scope of this essay, which stresses the emergence of the voice of dissent in a social system of contradictory relations. To conclude, what is perceptible about the discursive processes across the two social formations in early south India are: the breakdown of the heroic discourse along with the redistributive social relationships enchained by it; the dissemination of the Vedic, Purāṇic, and Śāstrāic prescriptions as the dissonant impulses; enlargement of the dissonant impulses into the ethical postulates of didactic texts; reification and discourse production within the hegemonic framework in response to the expanding agrarian relations of domination; emergence of bhakti as the mitigating force within the social contradictions of subjection and exploitation; and their convergence into a new discourse.

NOTES AND REFERENCES

1. The concept of social formation is developed in Nicos Poulantzas, 1980, *State Power Socialisms*, London. For ideas about the mode of production as a combination of several forms of subsistence, see Emmanuel Terray, 1972, *Marxism and Primitive Societies*, London. Also M. Godelier, 1977, *Perspectives of Marxist Anthropology*, London, pp. 33–6; Barry Hindes and Paul Hirst, 1975, *Pre-capitalist Modes of Production*, London, pp. 45–9. The overall perspective here is that of the structuralist reading of the mode of production paradigm.
2. The concept is borrowed from Michel Foucault, 1972, *Archaeology of Knowledge*, New York, but used here within the framework of the materialistic theory of history, the central instrument of analysis for the study. Discourse means power–knowledge combine acting decisively on its subject, the people. The concept is adopted here, notwithstanding the 'radical' uses to which the post-structuralists have put it. Structuralist Marxists from Althusser to Poulantzas have drawn this crucial distinction between the 'dominant' instance and 'determinant' instance in any mode of production. For them the 'economic' is both dominant and determinant only under capitalism, while in pre-capitalist forms, non-economic instances may be dominant. This opens up the space for using insights derived from discourse analysis.
3. The labels refer to specialist merchants such as *ponvāṇikan* (gold merchant), *koḻuvāṇikan* (ploughshare merchant or ironmonger), *aṟuvaivāṇikan* (textile merchant), *uppuvāṇikan* (salt merchant), and *pānitavāṇikan* (beverage merchant probably dealing with toddy). See the interpretations

in I. Mahadevan, 1970, *Tamil Brahmi Inscriptions*, Madras. See for the details of Graeco-Roman writings, W.H. Schoff, 1912, *The Periplus of the Erythraean Sea*, New York; J.W. McCrindle, 1975, *Ancient India as Described in Classical Literature*, reprint, Westminster; K.A. Nilakantha Sastri, 1939, *Foreign Notices of South India*, Madras. For details about the numismatic evidence, see W. Elliot, 1886, *Coins of Southern India*, Trubner; H. Mattingly, 1960, *Roman Coins*, reprint, London. Details of places and their coin hoards are given in K.V.S. Aiyar, 1917, *Historical Sketches of the Dekhan*, vol. 1, Madras, pp. 86–7. Also see P.L. Gupta, 1965, *The Early Coins from Kerala*, Trivandrum, p. 65.

4. In a society of kin-base' redistribution and of gifts and presentations, profit-oriented exchange would be unlikely. See M. Sahlins, 1968, 'On the Sociology of Primitive Exchange', in M. Banton (ed.), *The Relevance of Models for Social Anthropology*, London, pp. 139–43. Also, Kathleen MacAdams, 'Anthropological Perspectives on Ancient Trade', *Current Anthropology*, no. 15, pp. 239–58. Another point is that in such a society money does not make any sense. Money enters its exchange systems as a valuable and forms part of the treasure. See the relevant concepts in C. Meillassoux (ed.), 1971, *The Development of Indigenous Trade and Markets in West Africa*, London, pp. 67–9. K. Kailasapathy, 1968, *Tamil Heroic Poetry*, London, pp. 3–4.
5. For the details of syntagmatic analysis, see F. Saussure, 1959, *Course in General Linguistics*, New York. Also see the demonstration of the method of syntagmatic structural analysis in V. Propp, 1979, *Morphology of the Folktale*, New York. For the method and concepts of paradigmatic structural analysis, see Claude Levi-Strauss, 1963, *Structural Anthropology*, London. Aspects of symbols and unconscious meaning analysed in psychoanalytical studies are discussed in Alan Dundes, 1975, 'The Study of Folklore in Literature and Culture: Identification and Interpretation', in Alan Dundes, *Analytic Essays in Folklore*, The Hague.
6. See discussions in Kamil Zvelebil, 1973, *The Smile of Murugan*, Leiden, pp. 9–22; Kailasapathy, *Tamil Heroic Poetry*, pp. 16–19.
7. For details of the concept of deities in each *tiṇai*, see N. Subrahmanian, 1966, *Sangam Polity*, Bombay, pp. 352–3. Also see R. Champakalakshmi, 1972, 'Vaishnava Concepts in Early Tamil Nadu', *Journal of Indian History*, LXX(III).
8. The political practices point to a chiefdom-level society. Institutions and ideas such as plunder raid, redistribution, and heroic poems signify the economic milieu of agro-pastoralism. The conceptual scenario invoked here is that of the processes of the political evolution of early society as discussed in Hindes and Hirst, *Pre-Capitalist Modes of Production*, pp. 26–8. See the characterization of pre-state societies in Claessen and Skalnik (eds), 1978, *The Early State*, The Hague. Also Romila Thapar, 1984, *From Lineage to State*, New Delhi, pp. 24–5.

9. See the songs of *Vañjittiṇai* in *Puṟanāṉūṟu.*
10. See *Ērkaḷuruvakamtuṟai* songs in *Puṟanāṉūṟu.*
11. There are studies characterizing the society in an entirely different way. For instance, a well-developed civilization has been attributed to the society in question in V. Kanakasabhai, 1904, *Tamils Eighteen Hundred Years Ago*, Madras. Indeed, almost every nationalist historian of south India conceived the society more or less in the same way. The perspective also recurs in certain modern works. N. Subrahmanian, *Sangam Polity*; Singaravelu, 1966, *Social Life of the Tamils*, Kuala Lumpur.
12. Such evidence is examined at length in M.G.S. Narayanan, 1982, 'Warrior Settlements in the Sangam Age', *Proceedings of the Indian History Congress*, pp. 102–9.
13. The processes of state formation in south India are examined in Seneviratne, Forthcoming, 'Pre-State to State Societies: Transformations in the Political Ecology of South India with Specific Reference to Tamil Nadu', in R. Champakalakshmi (ed.), *State in Pre-Colonial South India*. Also Rajan Gurukkal, 'Social Formation and Political Processes in Early Tamilakam'.
14. Scholars have sought to argue that four castes existed in Tamilakam that were different from the castes under the *varṇa* order. See N. Subrahmanian, *Sangam Polity*, pp. 255–60. But this argument is not sustained by evidence. What is often considered is a poem in *Puṟanāṉūṟu* (335) that mentions the four *kuṭis* of the settlement. The poem obviously talks only about the particular village. Moreover, the term kuṭi acquired the meaning of caste only later.
15. Following the studies on complex redistributive societies, one can conceptualize the internal economic dynamic of the early historic Tamil society. The contradictory dynamic as an ever-mounting problem of complex redistributive societies is discussed in Terray, *Marxism and Primitive Societies*, pp. 53–4. Also Godelier, *Perspectives of Marxist Anthropology*, pp. 81–3. A conceptual generalization about the problem of low labour productivity and limited prospects for economic reproduction as features immanent in the redistributive society is given in Hindes and Hirst, *Pre-Capitalist Modes of Production*, pp. 42–4.
16. *Indian Archaeology: A Review*, 1964–5 and 1970–1.
17. Almost all historians of south India who had to discuss the early history have referred to the *Kaḷabhras*, and many have attempted to identify them. The generally accepted view is that they were a marauding tribe from the uplands of Karnataka. For a specialized study on the period, see M. Arunachalam, 1979, *The Kalabhras in the Pandya Country and Their Impact on the Life and Letters There*, Madras University.
18. The Velvikkuti plates of the *Pāṇḍyas* provide us with direct allusions to the period of the *Kaḷabhras* as equal to that of the Kali, but it is a relatively later record referring to the earlier period. As a recurring motif the *Kaḷabhra*-Kali

terms of evil social experiences appear in a few other copper plates belonging to the *Calukyas* and *Cōḷas*.

19. There are 18 texts in *Kīḻkkaṇakku* literature. Most of them deal with ethical postulates. The *Tirukkuṛal* may be the most popular.
20. *Tirukkuṛal*, verses 731–4.
21. See the particulars of the inscription in R. Nagaswamy, 1981, 'An Outstanding Epigraphical Discovery in Tamil Nadu', *Proceedings of the Fifth International Conference Seminar on Tamil Studies*, Madurai. Also, Y. Subbarayalu, 1993, 'A Note on the Socio-economic Milieu of the Pulankurichi Rock Inscription', *Āvaṇam-3*.
22. N. Subrahmanian, *Sangam Polity*, pp. 275–6; Kailasapathy, *Tamil Heroic Poetry*, p. 4.
23. K. Kailasapathy, *Tamil Heroic Poetry*, p. 4.
24. These kings represented the *cakravartin* mode of consecrated monarchy. See the discussions in B. Stein, 1977, 'All the Kings' Mana: Perspectives on Kingship in Medieval South India', in J.F. Richards (ed.), *Kingship and Authority in South Asia*, Wisconsin.
25. The process has been discussed in the light of inscriptions in Y. Subbarayalu, 1977, 'The Place of Or in the Economic and Social History of Early Tamil Nadu', Madras. Also his *Political Geography of the Cōḷa Country*, Madras, 1973. The evolution of ūr/kuṭi into nāḍu as implicit in certain place names figuring in the early Pāṇḍya inscriptions is discussed in Rajan Gurukkal, 1984, 'The Agrarian System and Socio-Political Conditions in the Early Pāṇḍya Period, AD 600–1000', PhD dissertation, Jawaharlal Nehru University, pp. 105–08. The place-names with *ūr-kūṟṟam, kuṭi-nāḍu*, and *ūr-nāḍu* as suffixes exemplify the process.
26. See the detailed study on the problem in M.G.S., Narayanan and V. Kesavan, 1980, 'Bhakti Movement in South India', in S.C. Malik (ed.), *Dissent, Protest and Reform in Indian Civilization*, revised edition, Shimla.
27. See the discussion in Zvelebil, *The Smile of Murugan*, pp. 23–4.
28. Veluthat Kesavan, 1979, 'The Temple Base of the Bhakti Movement', *The Proceedings of the Indian History Congress*, Delhi.
29. How the elements of dissent were absorbed as part of bhakti, is discussed in Narayanan and Kesavan, 'Bhakti Movement in South India'.
30. The concept of the strategy of containment is developed in G. Lukacs, 1971, *History and Class Consciousness*, Berlin. For an elaboration of the concept by postulating ideology in terms of the strategy of containment, whether intellectual or formal, see Fredrick Jameson, 1983, *The Political Unconscious*, pp. 53–4. For an insightful demonstration of the historical process in which one may discern the operation of the mechanisms of containment, see Romila Thapar, 1978, 'Renunciation: The Making of a Counter Culture', in her *Ancient Indian Social History*, New Delhi. Also her, 1979, 'Dissent and Protest in Early Indian Tradition', *Studies in History*, 1(2).

Section III

Social Transformations

10

Social Formation from the Ancient to Early Medieval*

Social formation, defined as an articulated combination of several unevenly developed forms of subsistence structured by the dominance of one among them, is perhaps the best paradigm for representing the human affairs and social processes of a region of cultural homogeneity and economic heterogeneity. The Tamil south (Tamilakam), inclusive of Kerala, over a millennium between circa 500 BC and circa AD 500 is such a typical spacio-temporal entity for us to represent through the social formation paradigm. Integrating clues from the various sources such as archaeological relics of iron, epigraphs, ancient coins, Graeco-Roman writings, and Tamil heroic poems we discover that contemporary forms of subsistence were hunting or gathering, herding cum shifting cultivation, plough agriculture, and crafts production. Adapted to different ecosystems, these forms of subsistence were obviously unequal in terms of productive forces and productivity of labour. The social formation was the aggregate of coexistence and interaction of these forms of subsistence structured by the dominance of agro-pastoralism. It seems to have dissolved itself into a new social formation during the sixth–seventh centuries. The present chapter seeks to discuss the features, processes, and dynamics of the ancient social formation and its transformation into a new one, commonly identified as early medieval.[1] Studying how the ancient social system dissolved itself into Indian feudalism, the historians did discuss the nature of the pre-existing system albeit without conceptualizing its transition, for their focus has been primarily on the taxonomy of the given social formation and categorization of a social formation comparable on the basis of

---

* This chapter is a modified version of the, 1998, Sectional Presidential Address, (Indian History Congress: New Delhi).

external manifestations in the form of institutions, relations, practices, and structures. This resulted in the attainment of greater clarity in the exposition of the social formation but also set in a serious ode of production debates about the categorization of feudalism. The debate led to a remarkable historiographical growth in the characterization of the processes and dynamic of the dissolution of the social formation that preceded the one that had been categorized as feudal.[2] The structural features, relations, institutions, and the contradictory dynamic of the social formation that preceded were construed by D.D. Kosambi in the perspective enabled by the theory of mode of production but notwithstanding the problem of deviation incompatible with Marxism. Researches of R.S. Sharma and Romila Thapar have brought forth enormous details about the institutional, structural, and processual characteristics of ancient society, the former through materialistic conceptualization in terms of particular social formations and the latter through social theoretical analysis, of textual as well as archaeological data.[3]

In the case of South Indian historiography, there is a fairly good body of literature providing primary knowledge about archaeology and text-based history of ancient period although not as much commendable as what exists for the subsequent periods. However, conceptualization of ancient society is at low ebb. There have been some attempts at conceptual characterization of ancient societies in the Tamil South as we have already discussed at length in the first chapter. Attempts at conceptualization of ancient human life and culture of the region have succeeded to a certain extent not only in the characterization of institutional and structural features in the light of the perspective of social formation but also in the identification of the embedded contradictory dynamic or prime movers in the historical processes as construed in the light of the theory of mode of production.[4] The attempts have been basically a land-and-peoples approach in which the landscape ecosystem and the interactive coexistence of multiple peoples with their uneven technologies of material appropriation received centrality in the interpretation of the concept of *aintiṇai* of ancient Tamil poetics. The details of the five *tiṇai*s and their respective means of subsistence have been discussed in the preceding chapters at length. What is relevant here by way of recapitulation is the overall nature and contradictory dynamic of the social formation as a combination of several unevenly developed forms, forces, and relations of production structured by the dominance of the agro-pastoral economy, polity, and culture. Despite the differing strategies of subsistence from eco-type to eco-type, kinship was central to the division of labour, the primacy of which precluded the possibility of social stratification of any perceptible kind. A unit of production that was in contrast to the kin-based production units of the clan settlements, was that of the *brāhmaṇa* households that represented a system of productive relations devoid of kinship. The social formation remained the same all over the Tamil macro region that included Kerala also. The relatively well inhabited zones of Iron Age Kerala were predominantly of the *kuṛiñji* ecosystem that corresponded to the red soil ranges and plains. Next in importance was obviously the *neital* ecosystem, thanks to the extensive littoral and backwaters. As regards the other micro ecosystems, the *mullai* was virtually absent, the *pālai* very rare, and *marutam* confined exclusively to the few pockets of highland fields and elevated alluvial plains. The major forms of subsistence in the region must have been hunting or gathering, shifting cultivation, crafts production and dryland agriculture of the semi-forested red soil midlands. As in the Tamil macro region, the social formation in the red soil plains of Kerala too was a system of multiple forms of subsistence structured by the dominance of dryland agriculture. Her semi-forested red soil tracts, as elsewhere in the Tamil macro region, were peopled by descent groups dispersed as *kuṭis* clustered into self-sustaining *ūrs* conducted under their headmen. However, there is a lot of ecological difference between the agro-climatic zones of Kerala and those of the rest of the Tamil macro region in terms of seasons, rainfall, permeability, landscape, and soil structure. The most striking difference about the wet-rice landscape ecosystem is the excess of water in the case of Kerala and its scarcity in regions elsewhere. This would suggest differences in the nature of cultivation followed and labour processes required at the two places. In the wetlands of the former the management of the excess water has been the central problem whereas in those of the latter, irrigation.

Each descent group had its headman called *kiḻār* who pooled and redistributed the resources of the *ūr*. This elementary structure of chiefdom acquired varying degrees of complexity depending upon the numeric strength as well as the nature and extent of redistributive social relationships. This, in turn, depended upon the ecosystems and productive relations within them. There were three categories of chieftains in the ascending order, namely *kiḻār*, *vēḷir*, and *vēntar*, the redistributive social relationships of which involved a corresponding increase in complexity. This order was naturally the order of the resource strength as well. However, the chiefly levels from *kiḻār* to *vēntar* were not structured into a single system of formal hierarchy of power distribution with a running thread of political control. They were theoretically independent from one another though the incessant predatory marches of the more powerful demanded their allegiance.

Commanding the resources of numerous settlements within a region through predatory control and subjugation, sometimes extending over the domains of the *vēḷir* and the three *vēntar* lineages, the *Cēras*, *Cōḻas*, and *Pāṇḍyas*, had emerged as well-established ruling powers without clan ties. The resource potential of the *vēntar*-level chieftains was obviously very high. Exchange relations with Rome must have enabled them to secure gold, silver, horses, and other prestigious objects as the poems would have us believe. They are praised in the poems as 'chieftains of new wealth' (*yāṇarmeyyar-kōman*) or as 'chieftains of wealth from sea and hills' (*katarrāramum-malaittāramum*). Some of the *vēḷir* chiefs are also eulogized as custodians of 'new wealth'. However, the range of domination by the *vēntar* was naturally extensive and redistributive social relationships elaborate and complex.

Plunder was the principal means of exacting the resources and was beyond the control of clan ties for all categories of chieftains. Predatory campaigns and booty redistribution as the central means of resource-sharing were fundamental to the maintenance of the chiefly status. Prestations and predatory exactions were the usual modes of chiefly appropriation of resources, and gifts and redistribution their instituted channels of social sharing. Even for the highest chiefly lineages collective appropriation through the institution of redistribution was the common practice, though they received prestations from their own people and exacted tributes (*tiṟai*) from the enemies. The *vēntar* level chieftains were patrons of Vedic rituals and assumed titles of status and legitimacy relating to their patronage. A Pāṇḍya chieftain, Muṭukutumi, was qualified as *palyāgaśālai-mutukuṭumi-peruvaḻuti* and a Cōḻa chieftain as *rājasūyamvēṭṭa perunārkkiḷḷi*. They were able to attract many *brāhmaṇa* bards (*pulavar*) who gave them exposure to the Vedic, Śāstrāic, and Purāṇic sources of legitimization. This shows a totally different ritual as well as a material status far superior to that of other categories of chieftains in the region. It is true that the *brāhmaṇa* bards eulogized a few *vēḷir* chiefs also.

At the *kiḻār* level, the settlement of the descent group determined the domain and at higher levels transcending such settlements, there was some concrete geographical sense often expressed in the form of specific landmarks especially hills, like Potiyil-malai or Ēli-malai or Paṟampu-malai, as the seat of the chieftains. At the *vēntar* level there was some sense of territory, but without any concrete notion of boundary. The boundary waned and enlarged in tune with predatory marches and retreats. Following perhaps the Mauryan model, some of the poems have referred to them as 'the beloved of god' as evidenced by the titles attributed to a Cēra chieftain: *imayavar-ampan* and *vānavavarampan*, the Tamil forms of *dēvānāmpriya*. Poems do glorify the *vēntar* as great rulers and historians on early south India, mostly calling them kings symbolic of state power. However, evidence shows that the social formation of ancient and early historic south India was not class structured and its polity was not based on state power. Instead, it was chiefdom-level polity of a pre-state situation.

The Nature of Exchange and Its Impact

In addition to the early forms of ascriptive and customary exchange practices, formal exchange seems to have become more extensive towards the closing phase of the Iron Age, which overlaps with the period of the Tamil heroic poems. The punch-marked coins from the Gangetic region, the names of the specialist merchants seen in the Tamil *brāhmi* label inscriptions, evidence of an organized merchant body (*nikamam*), the Roman coins brought by the long-distance traders, and the writings by the Graeco-Roman geographers provide evidence of a mercantile circulation of resources. There were several tributary channels to the pan-Indian exchange routes diverging from *Praṭistān* to the different parts of the Tamil macro region. The Kerala region was also well connected to the network through ports like Muciṛi and Tonṭi, as well as inland markets. The volume of goods exchanged from the coasts of both the west and east across the sea and land was amazingly high.[5]

However, the overall nature of contemporary internal exchanges, as depicted in the heroic poems, was largely that of reciprocity based on use-value. It was primarily a system of goods-for-goods exchange (*nēr-kol*) based on haggling (*noṭuttal*) that involved no notion of exchange-value, price, and profit.[6] This does not preclude the existence of route communication and formal points of exchange. The network of exchange was fairly large and people of different ecosystems with diverse resources entered into frequent transactions. There were fixed points of exchange such as *āvaṇam*/*ankāṭi* (market) as well as occasional markets like *nāḷangāṭi* (day market) and *antik-kaṭai* (evening shop). Poems refer to a kind of commodity loan (*kuṛittumāretirpai* or *kuṛiyetirpai*) to be returned in the same kind and quantity that precludes the notion of interest.[7] Even the exchange of specialist goods was primarily based on the notion of use-value.

This necessitates a rethinking about the nature of south India's exchange relations with the Roman world. The loose generalizations apart, it is a fact that there is no clear evidence of ancient Tamils organizing trade with Rome. The nature of internal exchange shows that the lack of evidence is not altogether accidental. The evidence is for the coming of the foreign traders, particularly the Greeks and Arabs, in their vessels for shipping goods. It was hardly trade for the Tamil society, for trade would mean a profit-oriented exchange, using the medium of money. The mere presence of coins is not enough to confirm a monetized society. There should be evidence for the use of money both as a means of payment and measure of value, which sources hardly vouch for in the case of ancient Tamil society. On the contrary, there are plenty of indications in the sources to believe that the society was largely non-monetized, and that the Roman coins functioned as part of social valuables and not as money.[8] The survival of coins as hoards fresh from the mint and with apertures or loops on many, suggests that they were preserved as treasure and often used as ornaments. This does not rule out the possibility of the use of coins as the medium in higher transactions and as a gift item, enhancing status and ranking.

The exchanges and incessant interaction among the self-sustaining entities with one another, accomplished a common horizon of shared cultural practices facilitated by the Tamil language. Exchange involved circulation of ideas, which meant dissemination of knowledge systems and worldviews. Long-distance exchange relations did carry forces of production and strategies of subsistence from one place to another, modifying and transforming the pre-existing ones to conform to the ecosystems and social relations. To a great extent, the dissemination of the brahmanical, Jain, and Buddhist knowledge systems and worldviews did determine the nature of institutional transformation in the late Iron Age south India. The *brāhmaṇa* presence in the Kerala region around the closing centuries of the first millennium BC is attested by the allusions in the ancient Tamil poems. It is important to note that most of the traditional *brāhmaṇa* settlements of Kerala have megaliths or urn burial complexes close to them, suggesting their rise adjacent to the pre-existing human settlements. There is hardly any direct evidence of an equally ancient Jain and Buddhist presence in the region, though it is reasonable to assume their ideas to have spread at least to those areas accessible through exchange routes. The impact of the Mauryan state was a very significant factor. The descent groups even of Kerala find mention in the Ashokan edicts. Scholarly bards, particularly the pulavars from the north, accustomed to the administrative tradition of the Maurya and Satavahana reigns, carried ideas of state power, periodic exaction, and bureaucracy right to the ears of the *vēntar*-level chieftains. However, as major institutions like state never come up as a transplant, the chiefdom-level polity, in spite of being exposed to both *brāhmaṇa* and heterodox religious ideologies, remained the same until the dissolution of the social formation. The net result of these internal and external influences was presumably the further development of the social milieu of clans segmenting into lineages and lineages fissioning into domestic groups subsisting on multiple forms of economies with kin-based relations of production, redistributive system of social appropriation, and predatory political control.

Labour Expropriation and Stratification

The level of technology around the turn of the Christian era was marked by metal-smelting, weaving, glass-making, stone-cutting, pottery, and other crafts mentioned in indigenous literary sources and foreign notices. Archaeology correlates metal-works, the glass industry, weaving, pearl fisheries, stone-cutting, and pottery. Metal-working included the alloy metallurgy of bronze casting. Except for small brick constructions, elaborate burial caves, and rock-cut chambers, no monumental buildings are testified by the relics though they vouch for a fairly good knowledge in architecture. The few habitation sites excavated could reveal only dwellings of the hutment type. Stone-cut benches and cots in the big burial caves shed light on the kind of furniture in use, obviously not in huts, but in more affluent households. The big burials must have been of prominent descent headmen and chiefs who could have commanded the collective labour of the clan. The wide variety of utensils, implements, lamps, and other artefacts suggests the existence of specialized craftspeople. How the people worked and who controlled each craft under what social conditions constitute the most crucial aspects for us to characterize the social formation, but that we would never know precisely. However, the fragments found on various sites help us conceptualize the overall set up conjecturally.

As already noted in the previous chapters, the principal mode of appropriation extended from the kin-based production relations was reciprocity and redistribution involving agnatic relationships, clan-ties, intra-clan/inter-clan marital relations, and a variety of functional relations and dependence across clan-kin connections. The redistributive relationships had acquired a greater complexity in the realms of functional obligations and patronage transcending kin/clan ties, in the nucleus or headquarters of the chiefdoms of the highest order. The nature of resources that circulated through reciprocity and redistribution is an indicator that helps us imagine the level of stratification that was likely in contemporary society. It is true that to a certain extent redistributed valuables included gems and gold as well, which suggests the plausibility of the rise of a privileged group with some kind of distinct status and ranking, constituted by the recipients of such rare valuables. They were mostly scholarly bards and chieftains whose identity as a different stratum never appears in contemporary sources. The scholarly bards hailed mainly from the *brāhmaṇas*. The big merchants, involved in long distance exchange, the monks and *brāhmaṇas* were certainly different from the ordinary folk. However, this does not seem to have become conspicuous as a class. As already noted in the previous chapters, the social division was confined to the binary between *uyarntōr* (the high-born) who comprised *brāhmaṇas* and *iḻipiṟappāḷar* (the low-born), comprising even chieftains. Similarly, the differentiation in terms of objective conditions of life was confined to the binary between *puravalar* (redistributors) and *iravalar* (redistributees/dependents), suggestive of a situation choice rather than a social structural consequence of appropriation. It is evident that the division was too flexible to be taken indicative of real social stratification. Lack of indications to the existence of intermediary positions confirms the fluidity of contemporary society.

Material Contradictions

The contradictions at the economic level were being generated continuously through the material processes of coexistence and interaction of the conflicting forms of subsistence. The seminal factor to be focused here is the level of concord between the technology of the economy of highest productivity and the dominant social relations of the time. As already discussed, the economy most significant in terms of technology and productivity was wet-rice agriculture, but the dominant social relations were of kin/clan ties. There is no concord between the technology of plough and kin-based division of labour. This is suggestive of the predicament of incompatibility between forces and relations of production heading for retardation of a potential technology in the fetters of inelastic social relations. The details of contradictions emanating from the dominant socio-political and cultural practices of the period, which were utterly unsuitable for the development of plough agriculture have already been discussed in a previous chapter.

A point to be recapitulated here is the limiting influence of kin–labour resulting in low labour productivity persisting on as an inherent draw back of contemporary social formation. An economy with its productivity sticky downward was another fundamental but unavoidable problem.[9] Thus it was not possible for the socio-economic aggregate to continue as a system for a longer period with its low labour productivity and ever falling potential of economic reproduction. The incompatibility between relations of production based on kin-labour and plough-based forces of production that demanded a larger set up of productive relations involving non-kin labour was the fundamental aspect of the contradictory dynamic. The potential of plough technology, could be developed and realized only with various institutions of labour mobilization, structures of domination, stratified social relations, hierarchical control and forced appropriation. These aspects were to be historically evolved as yet and the social formation lost in the fetters of relations and structures incapable of generating them, was heading for an inevitable breakdown.

Pointers to a Crisis

There is, however, no direct evidence for a total crisis leading to the dissolution of the social formation that characterized the whole of Tamilakam. Nevertheless, a disjunction is explicit in the sources, both archaeological and literary, which in terms of their existing chronology and historical context would have us believe that the principal chiefdoms had ceased to exist with the close of the AD third century. None of the heroic poems sings the exploits of a chieftain belonging to the period after the third century nor can the historians clearly identify any chieftain of the well-known chiefdoms reigning during the period prior to it. The heroic compositions of typical bardic diction too seem to have been discontinued by this time. There was a corresponding discontinuity of the institution of raids and booty redistribution, synchronized by a marked decline in the post-third century layers of the major archaeological sites.[10] It is true that the Indo-Roman transmarine contacts continued even after the third century but not in the same magnitude of the period anterior to it. The ports and trade enclaves in Tamilakam seem to have been deserted as the excavation at Aricamedu in the past and the findings of archaeological operation of two seasons at *Pattanam*, have testified. This is not to say that the ports owed their decline to regional historical processes such as the crisis of redistributive economy and the politics of plunder. This is also not to argue that none of the centres of long distance exchange survived. The sites with Buddhist association, however, provide evidence for continued development. Nevertheless, there is a marked discontinuity about various features that had once distinguished the period. The three major ruling lineages and their chiefdoms in the Tamil South show up a perceptible gap of about two centuries between the subsequent manifestations in their economy, polity, and culture.

Historians have associated this period of discontinuity with the inroads by the predatory *Kaḷabhras* who belonged to the uplands of Karnataka.[11] They are said to have swept through the domains of the Tamil chieftains and caused their eclipse. This has led to the construction of an interregnum labelled after the *Kaḷabhras*. Actually the *Kaḷabhra* episode is based on a weak evidence, but that is enough for the construct of an invasion. It hardly explains anything, for a predatory march would not be enough to usher in major socio-economic and political changes. An invasion thesis might do for explaining the disappearance of the chiefdoms, but that was not the only development. There were a series of radical transformations at the fundamental level causing discontinuity. The construct of invasion is a weaker explanation of the discontinuity. The negation of discontinuity through the gradualist hypothesis is mere truism and hence the weakest. That any social change is gradual neither makes change unreal and nor its explanation unnecessary. Explanation through conceptualization of the emerging new properties and their interconnections is the way for the production of new knowledge. Conceptual explanation is enabled not by the empirically given facts and pre-existing evidence. Instead, they are theoretically produced through fresh cognitive encounters with the source material.

A fresh look at the old sources has yielded new clues. The incidental allusions in a few copper plates of the eighth–ninth centuries to the age-old tradition of the *brāhmaṇas* about an evil period of hardships that they were doomed to face, is an example.[12] The allusions show that the situation was chaotic enough for the *brāhmaṇas* to have represented the period in the metaphor of the Kali Age. However, there is no reason to believe that the *brāhmaṇas* all over the south were affected by the Kaḷabhra attack. Kerala, for instance, had been affected by no such onslaughts from the part of the non-*brāhmaṇas*. Unlike places elsewhere in the Tamil macro region, where the *brāhmaṇas* had at times non-*brāhmaṇa* threats to their gift villages, the Kerala sub-region had no rivals to the *brāhmaṇas* who owed the land enjoyed by them to none other than Bhargava Parasurama, the sixth incarnation of Lord Vishnu. However, the problem of socio-economic and political discontinuity remained the same as elsewhere, providing ground for a conjuncture of a fundamental crisis inherent to the economy that characterized the whole region.

Conceptual Explanation

The conceptual explanation of the socio-economic and political discontinuity hinges on the material processes within the social formation. As already noted, the processes were characterized by the accretion of internal contradictions leading the social formation to an inevitable breakdown. This long historical process of the maturing of the contradictions immanent in the system and the consequent dissolution of the social formation can be understood only as a theoretical construct. It is not to be conceived nor tested empirically, for the characteristic frailties of the sources seldom bear directly upon the investigator. The question, therefore, of direct evidence of the transition of the Tamil society from heroic social formation to a new social formation, does not arise. One could only search for indirect clues. Those suggesting the discontinuity of ideas, institutions, and structures typical of the heroic society are our most valid clues. The discontinuity explicit in the existing chronological understanding of the heroic poems need not be accidental. Both the present state of knowledge about the poems and the absence of evidence for the continuation of the chiefdoms go well with the ever intensifying contradictions immanent in the heroic society of prestations, gifts, and redistribution, making systemic dissolution inevitable. This would at once confirm the alleged discontinuity and account for the absence of evidence, which is not altogether accidental.

New Sources and Clues to the Post-heroic Society

A much greater and more substantive factor that stresses discontinuity is the presence of a new class of literature and inscriptions datable to about a century later and radically different from the heroic compositions and the cave labels. Their objects, contexts, and strategies bear no comparison with those of the heroic texts and cave labels. It is the *Kīḻkakkaṇakku* texts belonging to the AD fourth–fifth centuries that constituted a new class of literature significantly separated from the diction of the heroic tradition, albeit without moving away from the domain of oral compositions.[13] Most of these texts are didactic, specializing in the social ethic and personal conduct. Even in others which are not avowedly ethical, there is a stress on the importance of peace, loyalty, and social morality. The existence of a body of literature emphasizing such values presupposes a situation desperately in need of them. They all seemingly address a society of transitional complexities, ranging from a general disorder to specific problems of new relations and values replacing the old.[14] The texts are not directly concerned with the ethical task of highlighting the social imperative to establish an order in collective life that is incidental to their central thematic concerns.

The other category of a radically different source indicating the breakdown of the heroic ideology is a set of two rock inscriptions in Tamil *brāhmi* characters of the AD fifth–sixth centuries.[15]

One might feel sceptical about the assumption of the alleged discontinuity as it is grounded on the availability of certain new types of sources whose data are different. But, as has already been pointed out, the availability of new types of sources only at a relatively later date is not accidental in the sense that they represent a social formation that is altogether new. A document like the Pulānkuṛichi rock inscription registering a land transaction and land rights is anachronistic to the Tamil heroic period that was characterized by cooperative farming and collective appropriation. Though gift-giving played a very important role in the maintenance of the status, ranking, and authority of chieftains, it did not seem to have developed into the institution of land grants during the heroic period. The records introduce two terms, *miyātci* and *kārāṇmai*, indicative of control over the means of production and entitlement to a share of crop respectively, the former vested with the *brāhmaṇa* households and the latter with the non-*brāhmaṇa* settlers (*kuṭis*). They provide indications of several *brāhmaṇa* settlements (*mangalam*) having come into existence by the time through royal land grants, as evidenced by the term *pirammatāyam*. The founding of *pirammatāyam*, which a century later acquired greater frequency, as evidenced by a number of copper plates registering *brahmadēya* grants, involved superimposition of the *miyātci* rights over the settlers of the land and transformation of the settlers into *kārāḷar*. What is significant about the new process was the allocation of a new position called *kārāṇmai* to the *kuṭi* with implications of their alienation from the control of means of production.

It is true that the colophons of the heroic anthologies do refer to land grants to bards, particularly the *brāhmaṇa* bards who also officiated at Vedic rituals. But there is a time lag of three or four centuries between the poems and their colophons, which accounts for their presence. Landholding by the *brāhmaṇas* as distinguished from the communal holding was known to the heroic society, but it was, as already been noted, the beginnings and rights over land were yet to be evolved through the emergence of intermediaries. The *brāhmaṇa* households of the heroic period were in fact anticipatory constituents of the evolving social system that manifested itself with its institutional structures by the time of the Pulānkuṛichi records. Despite the linkage in terms of mode of production, the earlier *brāhmaṇa* households and the subsequently structured brahmanical society were two different entities, the former as part of the social formation dominated by primitive agriculture and animal husbandry and the latter dominated by irrigated agriculture. What appears therefore as disjunction between the old and new sources is the distance of the evolutionary process between two social formations.

Towards a Stratified Society

The social relations began to be further structured during the sixth–seventh centuries with the steady expansion of rice agriculture across the wetland. The development of relations in plough agriculture towards domination of the total society was a long process of the proliferation of occupational specializations and their ordering into a hierarchy. What began taking shape in the *brāhmaṇa* households was much more crucial for the real beginnings of a hierarchy. The permanent workforce attached to the *brāhmaṇa* households had the greatest possibility of being conceived hierarchically because of the stratifying system of production relations and the brahmanical tradition of social differentiation. The notion of hierarchy was implicit in the system of production in which the relation between two objectively antagonistic classes was fundamental. The mid-first millennium AD was thus a turning point in terms of stratification and hierarchical ordering, which took more than two centuries to characterize the social aggregate. It is with the sixth century that we see the new agrarian system articulating its political control as manifested in the new monarchies. The proliferation of hereditary occupations and their absorption into the *jāti* hierarchy were ongoing processes through new institutional agencies of which the temple ranked the foremost. Other institutional formations like service tenements both in the domains of the temple and the king, crystallized hereditary occupations into *jāti* hierarchy.

Jāti Hierarchy

As regards the brahmanical tradition of social differentiation, with the experience of social stratification as a part of the history of brahmanism and its theoretical abstractions into *varṇa* and *sankīrṇa jāti* as central to its legacy, there is no need of any explanation. It is only natural that the *brāhmaṇas* of contemporary south India, who inherited the Vedic, Śāstrāic, and Purāṇic scholarship, had the traditional perception and appreciation of their society. They could have conceived the society of functionally specific families attached to their households only in terms of the hierarchy of occupations and social status implicit in the Śāstrāic explanations about *jātis*.

The brahmanical perception and appreciation of social groups would, however, just not be enough for the society to become hierarchically structured in the idiom of *jāti*. Even the existence of preconditions such as hereditary occupations, asymmetrical social relations, and differential allocations of positions would not help us deduce from them the prevalence of the *jāti* hierarchy. It was the dominant position of the *brāhmaṇas* that was crucial in the operation of the *jāti* hierarchy. The tacitly recognized ritual supremacy, resource potential, social control, political influence, and cultural skills provided the *brāhmaṇas* with the best conditions of domination. They symbolized the collective norms and took precedence over the ruling powers. Their hegemony over the communication channels and ideological structures of legitimization had made them a determinant force of political authority by the sixth century. On top of all, their status as custodians of higher wisdom about the universe, practical knowledge about the cycles of seasons and their calendrical measurements enabling prediction of natural changes had added to the charisma of the *brāhmaṇas*. It was this enormous potential of social control coupled with the growing control of means of production which, subsuming all differential categories and groups in due course, encompassed the total society.

This is not to suggest that brahmanization of social stratification was a conscious project of the *brāhmaṇas*. It was a historically and culturally contingent effect rather than the result of a conspiratorial scheming, though articulations of *brāhmaṇas* as a group of spatio-temporally and culturally significant community were causally linked to the process. The *brāhmaṇas* do not seem to have manipulated the political space for ordering the differential relations of production into the hierarchy of *jātis*. The notion of the pure self and the impure other, which originally constituted the basis of *jāti*, was tribal and a part of the horizontal social division of the primeval kind. The formation of *jātis* along with the domestic groups of hereditary occupations was also not brahmanical. In fact, even in northern India, the proliferation of *jātis* owed to the socio-economic processes and not to brahmanism which only explained the phenomenon through the Śāstrāic idiom. What seems to be causally linked to the *brāhmaṇas* is the imposition of their notion of purity and pollution as fundamental and of themselves as the central point of reference for determining the relative status of each *jāti*. In short, what is brahmanical is not *jāti* but the notion of hierarchy. Hierarchy as such, however, is not merely a notional construct of brahmanism but is derived from the objective conditions related to the forces and relations of production. And it had the specific historical context of operation at the juncture of an agrarian technology and social strategy of labour realization necessitating institutional devices for stabilizing hierarchical stratification.

How brahmanism succeeded in providing the institutional devices has to be examined in the context of the culturally and historically contingent conditions of social domination which we have briefly indicated earlier. The emergence of brahmanism as the major world view generating knowledge about the *Dakṣiṇāpatha*, its peoples and cultures, spreading a new pattern of thinking and transforming the local modes of social existence constituted the historical context. The argument is that the success of brahmanical domination and the establishment of *jāti* hierarchy were discursively realized goals. *Jāti* hierarchy was, in short, the effect of the brahmanical form of social representation which became hegemonic around the mid-AD first millennium, a temporal juncture that witnessed the expansion of a technology of production and social strategies of labour realization, leading to the proliferation of hereditary occupations.

A perceptible feature of agrarian expansion was the proliferation of *brahmadēya* villages throughout the fertile tracts of major river valleys in the region. It was a complex process of differentiation, stratification, and political formation leading to the development of a state system and authority structures. The new political formation represented by the Simhavarman line of the Pallavas and the Kaṭunkon line of the Pāṇḍyas owed itself to the developing agrarian society whose expansion was linked to royal patronage. Expansion of agrarian settlements through the creation of brahmadēyas often involved the superimposition of the superior rights of the *brāhmaṇa*s over the communal holdings and the clan families of the locality. It must have been an intricate process of transformation of primitive agriculture and clan settlements into advanced agriculture and farmer settlements, respectively.

As agrarian expansion advanced, human settlements (*ūr*) originally bound by kinship got integrated as agrarian localities (*nāṭu*) which subsequently acquired great political significance in the monarchical system. The role of caste in the integration of the agrarian society whose mechanisms of appropriation were based on extra-economic coercion, was extremely crucial. The formation of agrarian localities was an ongoing process, and everywhere it accomplished a uniform structure of social relations irrespective of whether they were *brāhmaṇa* settlements (*brahmadēyas*) or *vēlān vakai* settlements (*ūr*). The social structure was a hierarchy with landholders (*brahmadēya-kiḻavar* in the case of *brahmadēyas* and *ūrār/naṭṭar* in the case of *vēlān vakai* settlements) at the apex and the large number of leaseholders (*kārāḷar*) who were mainly artisans and craftsmen, in the middle, placed over the primary producers (*aṭiyāḷar*) who were at the bottom. Almost parallel to the leaseholders, there were many who held small strips of land as hereditary holdings (*kāṇi*) which were also tilled by primary producers. The circulation of the produce in given shares thus took a structured path through all these categories enjoying different levels of entitlement. The most benefited were the landholders who were ensured goods and services by the settlers in their land while the most exploited were the primary producers. As part of the social mechanisms of ensuring goods and services to the landholders through the notion of obligation, all artisans and craftsmen were subjected to immobility. The conditions of subjection together with the objective reality of the producers being stripped off their produce constituted the major contradiction in the system.

In terms of the material processes and socio-political structure there was no difference about what evolved in Kerala during the period. It was the antecedents that were remarkably different. The absence of royal land grant tradition is perhaps the most striking among them. As already pointed out, *brāhmaṇa* households existed adjacent to clan settlements, as independent production units as early as the closing centuries before Christ. They sprang up on their own as sparsely distributed households along the red soil fringes of the alluvial ecosystem, using clan labour in the neighbourhood. How they spread to the wetland ecosystem and converged into temple-centred corporate settlements when, are conjectures. One has to visualize here the overall economic processes of the Tamil macro region that generated contradictions within the social formation. The transformation of individual *brāhmaṇa* households into corporations was the result of the economic processes. As the processes that led to the dissolution of the chiefdom level social formation of the descent groups were the same as those in the places elsewhere in the Tamilakam, and as the alternative to it was to evolve from the production relations of the *brāhmaṇa* households, the emerged social formation in Kerala was more or less the same. What was crucial about the new formation was its binary basis between landholding and landlessness which eventually got mediated by intermediaries to form a complex structure. Specialized division of labour, its crystallization into hereditary occupations and their non-economic coercive modes of social realization were the main characteristics.

NOTES AND REFERENCES

1. Historians have discussed this as a transition from pre-feudal to feudal. D.D. Kosambi discusses the trends towards feudalism after studying the vestiges of pre-class and class societies. See D.D. Kosambi, 1975, *An Introduction to the Study of Indian History*, Bombay, (reprint), pp. 295–8, and 1975, *Culture and Civilization in Ancient India*, New Delhi, (reprint), pp. 166–9. R.S. Sharma discusses the origins and the first phase as distinguished from the classical period. See his 1965, *Indian Feudalism: c. 300–1200*, University of Calcutta. How the medieval period stands out distinctly in socio-economic terms is the concern in the discussion of transition. The focus is on the beginnings of feudalism, for the context of discussion relates to the search for a better rationale for periodization. Niharranjan Ray, 1968, 'The Medieval Factor in Indian History', Presidential Address, Indian History Congress (IHC), Patiala. R.S. Sharma, 1974, 'Problem of Transition from Ancient to Medieval in Indian History', *Indian Historical Review* (*IHR*). 1(1): 1–9. Also R.N. Nandi, 'Client, Ritual and Conflict in the Early Brahmanical Order, *IHR*, 6(1–2): 64–118. There is an able exposition of related conceptual issues in D.N. Jha, 1979, 'Early Indian Feudalism: A Historiographical Critique', Presidential Address, IHC, Waltair. The debate on Indian feudalism took a conceptual turn in Harbans Mukhia, 1979, 'Was There Feudalism in India?', Presidential Address, IHC, Waltair. Also in *Journal of Peasant Studies*, 8(3): 273–310. See a comprehensive response to the debate on the issues in R.S. Sharma, 1984, 'How Feudal was Indian Feudalism?', *Social Scientist*, no. 124, pp. 16–23.
2. The debate attracted scholarly attention to the historical process of transition from the ancient to the feudal. B.N.S. Yadava, 1978–9, 'The Kali Age and the Social Transition', *IHR*, 5(1, 2). There is a serious conceptual consideration of the presages of the feudal society in R.S. Sharma, 1982, 'The Kali Age: A Period of Social Crisis', in S.N. Mukherji (ed.), *History and Thought: Essays in Honour of A.L. Basham*, Calcutta.
3. R.S. Sharma, 1983, *Material Culture and Social Formations in Ancient India*, Delhi; Romila Thapar, 1984, *From Lineage to State: Social Formations in the Mid-First Millennium* BC *in the Ganga Valley*, New Delhi.
4. See the discussion in Rajan Gurukkal, 1998, 'Characterising Ancient Society: The Case of South India', Presidential Address, Ancient India Section, *IHC*, 59th Session, Patiala, pp. 8–14.

5. See the Graeco-Roman writings: W.H. Schoff, 1912, *The Periplus of the Erythraean Sea*, New York. McCrindle, 1975, *Ancient India as Described in Classical Literature*, Westminister, reprint.
6. In a redistributive society of gifts and prestations, a profit-oriented exchange is unlikely. See Marshall Sahlins, 1968, 'On the Sociology of Primitive Exchange', in M. Banton (ed.), *The Relevance of Models for Social Anthropology*, London. Also Kathleen MacAdams, 1998, 'Anthropological Perspectives on Ancient Trade', *Current Anthropology*, no. 15, pp. 239–58.
7. *Puṟanāṉūṟu*, 333:12.
8. It is natural that in such a society money hardly functions as a measure of value or a means of payment, but as a part of intangible social values. See the discussion in Rajan Gurukkal, 'Forms of Production and Forces of Change in Ancient Tamil Society', pp. 171–3. The relevant concepts are formulated in C. Meillassoux (ed.), 1971, *The Development of Indigenous Trade and Markets in West Africa*, London, pp. 67–9. For the nature and context of Roman Trade, see Romila Thapar, 1992, 'Black Gold: South Asia and the Roman Maritime Trade', *South Asia*, 15(2): 1–72.
9. The inevitable accretion of internal contradictions as a part of the economic processes of complex redistributive societies is conceptualized in E. Terray, 1972, *Marxism and Primitive Societies* (trans. Mary Klopper), New York, pp. 96–101. Also M. Godelier, 1977, *Perspectives in Marxist Anthropology*, Translated by Robert Brain, Cambridge, pp. 81–5. A conceptual generalization about the low productivity of labour based on kinship and the sticky downward nature of economic reproductivity is highlighted in B.M. Hindess and P.Q. Hirst, 1975, *Pre-capitalist Modes of Production*, London, pp. 42–6. See the relevant concepts about the limitations of redistributive economy discussed in C. Meillassoux, 1972, 'From Reproduction to Production', *Economy and Society*, 1(1). Also see his discussions on the economic implications of kin-labour in 1973, 'The Social Organization of the Peasantry: Economic Basis of Kinship', *Journal of Peasant Studies*, 1(1): 80–6.
10. It is true that certain centres showed continuity. See T.V. Mahalingam, 1970, *Report on the Excavations in the Kaveri Valley*, Madras University. Also *Indian Archaeology: A Review* (1964–5). For empirical data on the post-third century decline reflected along the archaeological sites, see R.S. Sharma, 1987, *Urban Decay in India*, New Delhi.
11. P.T. Srinivasa Aiyangar was probably the first to recognize the *Kaḷabhra* factor as an interregnum, p. 537. Also see K.A. Nilakanta Sastri, 1975, *The Cōḻas*, Madras University, reprint, pp. 101–2. He assumes the Cōḻa rule to have been put an end by the *Kaḷabhras*, as in the cases of the Pallavas and Pāṇḍyas. The references in a few copper plates of the Pallavas and Pāṇḍyas, and the writings of Buddhadatta, are taken as evidences by these historians for the assumption. A.P. Buddhadatta (ed.) *Buddhadatta's Manuals*, part I (1915) and part II (1928) of the Pali Text Society. Buddhadattas

Abhidhammāvatāra, at its end, refers to the prosperous Kaveri town and *Vinayaviniccaya* composed by him on the bank of the river Kaveri refers to Accutavikkānta of the *Kaḷabhrakula* ruling the earth at that time. *The Tamil Nāvalar Caritai* (vv. 154–7) records the literary tradition that the Cēra, Cōḻa, and Pāṇḍya rulers were kept in confinement by Accuta. See Nilakanta Sastri, *The Cōḻas*, p. 102.

12. See the Velvikkuṭi copper plates. The plates give us a direct reference to the reign of the *Kaḷabhras* as equal to that of the evil age of the *Kali*.
13. The *Kīḻkkaṇakku* texts are in a cluster of eighteen, obviously grouped at a later date as in the case of the Tamil heroic poems that were redacted and grouped into anthologies. Most of them deal with ethical postulates. *Tirukkuṟal* is perhaps the most popular text among them. Texts like *Ēlāti* and C*iṟūpancamulam* deal with herbal medicine.
14. For instance, see *Tirukkural*, verses: 731–137.
15. See the particulars of the two inscriptions in R. Nagaswamy, 1981, 'An Outstanding Epigraphical Discovery in Tamilnadu', *Proceedings of the Fifth International Conference Seminar on Tamil Studies*, Madurai. Also Y. Subbarayalu, 1993, 'A Note on the Socio-economic Milieu of the Pulankuricchi Rock Inscription', *Āvaṇam*, 3.

11

Historical Antecedents of the State Formation in the Deep South*

Historians have assumed that the pre-Pallavan Cēras, Cōḻas, and Pāṇḍyas celebrated in the Tamil heroic poems[1] were dynasties of kings. An inescapable contingent of the historiography of the Tamil south, this assumption has remained central to attempts at characterizing the pre-Pallavan polity. Its discussion of polity in the historiography hardly involved any focus on structure, process, and dynamic, precluding the possibility of conceptualizing the formation of the state, which is not external. Inevitably *sui generis*, the state gets neither diffused nor transplanted, turning the notion of secondary state formation to a misnomer.[2] Theoretically, the state is possible only in a stratified society, the non-stratified form of which presupposes a pre-state situation.[3] The history of pre-state societies unveils antecedents of the state formation.[4] In the historical process, the state appeared as kingdoms and empires created by class-structured societies, encouraging us to equate the state in history with dynastic rule or monarchy.[5] This chapter seeks to study features of the polity, its structure, process, and dynamic with a view to understanding the historical antecedents of the formation of the state.

Our knowledge about the pre-Pallavan polity of Tamilakam (the region between Venkaṭadri and Kanyakumari) is almost entirely based on the Tamil heroic literature. Literary compositions, Tamil *brāhmi* label inscriptions, and foreign notices indicate that the features, structures, processes, and dynamic of contemporary polity were that of chiefdoms.[6] The archaeology of these processes takes us back in time to the centuries

---

* This chapter is a revised version of, 2002, 'Antecedents of the State Formation in South India', in R. Champakalakshmi *et al.*, (eds), *State and Society in Pre-modern South India*, (Current Books: Thrissur), pp. 39–59.

of expansion of the Iron Age descent communities.[7] It is not possible to trace these archaic processes in the absence of exhaustive archaeological studies. A later phase of the process, assignable to the period between the closing centuries of the first millennium BC and the first quarter of the first millennium ADC, is signified in the label inscriptions, Graeco-Roman accounts, and heroic poems. The temporal span of archaeological relics overlaps the period. It is evident from the heroic poems that they were composed after the headmen of descent communities had grown into chiefs who possessed political power that had evolved from them. There are different levels of chiefly status represented in the poems that contain clues to the pattern of distribution of power, from the simple to the complex, along the small and big descent communities. The heroic poems unveil an active scenario of co-existence and interaction of these unevenly evolved chiefly systems that can be broadly classified into three: the *kiḻār, vēḷir,* and *vēntar.*

Kiḻār is the primary category of chiefship figuring in the poems as the *ūr-kiḻār* or ūr-*mannar* who were generally lowland chiefs of small settlements, mostly in *vanpulam,* the dryland zone (*Puṟanāṉūṟu* [*Pn.*] 177, 180, 181). A poem praises the *kiḻār* of Irntūr, a settlement of *vanpulam* with marginal resources, depending primarily on plunder raids, as the enemy of hunger who would summon his blacksmith on seeing a hungry bard and order a new lance to arm him for a raid to appease the bard's hunger (*Pn.* 180). The *kiḻār* chiefs were hunter chiefs either of the *vēṭar* or *kuṟavar* descent communities. Certain *kiḻār* chiefs also held sway over agrarian tracts and turned out to be more resourceful (*Pn.* 176, 376, 381–8). However, they had to maintain predatory control over other settlements to meet the redistributive needs. A few *kiḻār* seem to have functioned like bards of the bigger category of chiefs. Most of the *ūr-kiḻār* had to participate in the predatory campaigns of the bigger chiefs and fight for them. Some of them were designated as *ēnāti* which is a corrupt form of *sēnapāti* of the highest category of chiefs (*vēntar*). The *ūr-kiḻār* of a pristine type must have been a smaller variant of the *malai-kiḻavōn* or the hill chief, represented by the *vēḷir.*

The level of power represented by the *vēḷir* seems to be the most archaic and lineage-conscious. A hill chief called Irunko-*vēḷ,* one of the traditional five *vēḷs* is mentioned in a poem as *vēṭarkōmān,* the chief of *vēṭar,* who belonged to a long line of 49 generations of chiefs (*Pn.* 202, 201). The poems show that the *vēḷir* chieftains held sway over the forested hills of the *kuriñji* and the *mullai* tracts of pastoral forest hills. They were hill chieftains heading the descent communities called *vēṭar*, *iṭaiyar*, and *kuṛavar*. Venkaṭamalai, Kanṭīramalai, Kollimalai, Mutiramalai, Kutiramalai, Paṛmpumalai, Potiyilmalai, Pāyarmalai, Ēḻilmalai, and Nāñjilmalai are the famous millet-rich hill chiefdoms celebrated in the poems (*Pn.* 143, 168). Ēḻilmalai was the most prominent hill chiefdom of Kerala and the lineage of Nannan, the hunter chief of *vēṭar* (*vēṭarkoman*) was related to that of the chiefs of Kanṭīramalai. Another chiefdom closely linked to the southern end of Kerala was Potiyilmalai. Pāri, the chief of Paṛampumalai; ori, the chief of Kollimalai, Kāri who killed ori and became the chief of his hill, Eḻini, the chief of Kutirmalai and Pēkan, the chief of Vanmalai, and Kumaṇan, the chief of Mutiramalai are the most celebrated hunter chiefs of the *vētar* or *kuṛavar* communities (*Pn.* 158). Sometimes the hill chiefs are called *vēṭṭuvar*. This would suggest that the term *vēḷ* derives from *vēt*, meaning hunter. However, all the *vēḷir* were not hill chiefs. For instance, *ēḻini* the chief of Veṭṭāṟu, was a *vēḷ* in control of agrarian lowland.

All these chiefs had to resort to plunder raids too. Most of them seem to have maintained a predatory control over the agrarian zones in their proximity (*Pn.* 110, 168) and had plundered to accumulate resources for redistribution. Through the exchange of forest goods, some hill chiefs seem to have procured new resources like gold coins, precious stones, and horses, the main prestige goods of the times. Irunko-*vēḷs* hill is praised in a poem as gold-yielding (*Pn.* 202), obviously meaning the exchange of its resources like ivory, monkeys, animal skins, and sandalwood for gold coins from Rome. Nevertheless, how exactly the chiefs exchanged the forest goods and realized the returns is not clear. Nevertheless, the hills in the possession of certain chiefs had a relatively better potential for new resources, which is referred to in the poems as *yāṇar*. Parampumalai is called '*yāṇaṛara aviyan malai*', the hill with the potential of new resources (*Pn.* 116). It is evident that the resource potential varied from chief to chief. For instance, the *Āy* chief is said to have possessed horses and chariots; his house was called *kōil* and its surroundings *nakar*. It is also mentioned that Pari possessed horses and chariots. *Pittan koṛṛan* of Mutiramalai is called '*kaṭumān koṛṛan*', the possessor of horses, but since these chiefs did not usually possess horses, references to their giving these animals and chariots as gifts seem to be a mere conventional mode of praise. Possession of rare goods has always enriched the status and ranking of chiefs and in the case of *Āy*, who is known by his family name, such a higher status is explicit. No other hill chief is known after his family, except perhaps the Cēras, who seem to have emerged from the level of hill chiefs.

The range of redistributive relationship of a hill chief was limited, though a few bards from distant places also met him occasionally. Similarly his predatory range was small, enabling only small-scale raids. With no relations transcending kinship in the system of production and circulation, the political power of this category of chief-ship remained subsumed within the kinship system.

The next category of political power is that of the *vēntar* represented by the three major chiefly lineages, the Cēras, Pāṇḍyas, and Cōḻas. These three are referred to in the poems as *mūvēntar* or *mūvar*. The poems show that they had their core areas in Karūr, Madurai, and Uṟaiyur, respectively and the peripheral strategic points at Muciṟi, Kōrkai, and Puhār, respectively. The Cēras held sway over the *kuṟiñji* dominated zones of the Western Ghats towards sea, the Pāṇḍyas, the *mullai*, *pālai*, *neital* dominated zones in the south central region of Tamilakam, and the Cēras, the *marutam* dominated Kāvēri region. There was no notion of precisely demarcated territory and apart from references to core areas of each, the poems give us no clues to the actual spheres of each one's control. The control was transmitted through subordinate chiefs towards the periphery where it waned and constantly fluctuated.

The Cēras are referred to in the poems as kānaka-naṭan (the chief of the forested *nāṭu*) or *malaiyan* (the chief of *malai* or hill) which is suggestive of their ecological region. A poet praising *Cēraman Kōtai Mārpan*, expresses confusion about how the chief should really be addressed (*Pn.* 49). The poet asks whether the chief could be called *naṭan* as he had marutam lands or *ūran* as he had kurinji lands, or *cērpan* as he had coastal tracts. This would suggest that the Cēra region, their resource base, was a mixture of diverse ecological zones with the predominance of hills and forests, with forest wealth as the main resource. A poem incidentally refers to the hill products (*malaittārm*) and sea products (*katarrāram*) of Cēran Cenkuṭṭuvan and the gold that reached ashore by boats (*Pn.* 343). The Pāṇḍyas also had a mixed ecological region dominated by pastoral and coastal tracts. A Pāṇḍyan chieftain calls himself the head of the land of numerous new resources, *yaṇar maiyar kōmān* (*Pn.* 71). The Cōḻa who is well known as *kāviri kiḻavōn* in the poems, had his land in the Kaveri delta, rich in paddy and sugarcane (*Pn.* 61).

How did the *vēntar* category of chieftains appropriate the resources is the most pertinent question here. Their core areas were not bigger than an *ūr* and the surrounding areas were held by numerous other chiefs. It is implicit that their incipient mechanism of appropriation was predatory too. There are indications in the poems to the expansion of the predatory control beyond their original *ūr* (*mūtūr*) obviously through the process of subjugation (*Pn.* 54). The poet shows Cēramān Kuṭṭuvan Kōta, sitting as the *uṭaiyōr* (lord) of a mūtūr in the place of its original chief, probably suggesting subjugation. The subjugation process seems to have involved three different methods: subordination with tributary obligations, expulsion, and marital alliance. There are many references in the poems to all these methods of enlarging the domain of the *vēntar*. Vaḷḷuvan, the chief of Nāñjilmalai, is mentioned in a poem as a Cēra subordinate with military obligations (*Pn.* 139). The chiefs of Pāyarmalai and Veṭṭāṟu were the other known Cēra subordinates. Similarly Nākan, the *kiḻavan* of Nalai and Nampi Neṭunceḻiyan are mentioned as Pāṇḍya subordinates with military obligations (*Pn.* 179, 1239). There are a few poems in praise of the chiefs, Tirukuṭṭuvan, Tirukkiḷḷi, and Tirukkaṇṇan as *ēnāti* of the Cōḻa (*Pn.* 167, 174, 394). Paṇṇan, the *kiḻān* of Ciṟukuṭi and Aruvantai, the *kiḻān* of Ampar were the Cōḻa subordinates with tributary and military obligations; sometimes chiefs in the fringes were subordinated by two *vēntar* and naturally, this subordination fluctuated from one to the other (*Pn.* 380). In addition to such important subordinates, there were numerous minor chiefs called *cīṟūru-mannar*, mostly, *maṟava* headmen, who functioned as the warrior chiefs of the *vēntar*, particularly the Pāṇḍya and Cēra. Most of these small chiefs were made *ūr-mannar* by the *vēntar* in lieu of their service (*vitūtoḻil*) in the latter's subjugation campaign. The participation in such campaigns enabled the *maṟava* headmen to receive predatory control over *ūrs* as their reward (*Pn.* 285, 287). Several poems are in praise of such warrior-chiefs who were ready to rush to their *vēntar* in times of emergency and die fighting for him.

It appears that in the expanded area, control was maintained by stationing the kinsmen of the *vēntar* at different points for collateral management of resources as necessitated by the limitations of contemporary transport and communication facilities. The poems show that the people in the subjugated areas could remain fearless only by submitting a share of their resources to the *vēntar* in the form of *tiṟai* or *koḷ* (tributes) in kind (*Pn.* 51, 387), *Cēramān Celvakaṭunko* being one of the recipients of tiṟai (*Pn.* 387). However, it appears that every time the *vēntar* raided the settlements to exact *tiṟai*, for there was strong resistance from many a chieftain.

The poems address *vēntar* as *kavalar* (protector) of the *kuṭimākkal*, the settlers. Pāṇḍya Neṭunceḻiyan refers to his *kuṭimākkal* as '*en niḻāl vaḻnar*', meaning those living under his shade. This would presuppose the exaction of some goods in return from the *kuṭimākkal* for the protection offered to them. In the case of the Cōḷa, it is clear that the *vēntar* used to exact *puravu* (paddy) from the kuṭimākkal (*Pn.* 75). All the three *vēntar* are referred to in the poems with the term *iṟaivan*, meaning 'he who exacts'. This would suggest that they had exacted from the people what was feasible according to the resource potential of the predatory character. There is no evidence for any regular or periodic exaction in fixed measure or quantity by any of these chieftains. So we may safely assume that the *vēntar* exacted resources through predatory operations and voluntary offerings. Poems belonging to the *ceviyaṟivūṟu* and *porunmoḻikāñcittuṟai* mostly sung by the *pulavar*, advise the chieftains about how to keep the settlements productive and how to appropriate their surplus in a sustainable manner like a bee that sucks honey from the flower. A poem advises a *vēntar* not to behave like an elephant in the sugarcane field that destroys much more than what it eats. These are exhortations by poets from the north (*vaṭamar*) who have known the instituted modes of periodic exaction in developed kingdoms north of Tamilakam.

The returns from exchange relations must have enabled the *vēntar* to possess gold and other prestige items. As already noted, it is not clear how they were involved in the process of exchange. The poems show that the major activity of the *vēntar*, like the *vēḷir*, was accumulation of resources and their redistribution, following the determinate pattern of community relationships. Plunder was indispensable for them too since their redistributive network was much more elaborate and complex than what they could have afforded with their actual resources. They had a large body of dependents such as their kinsmen (*kiḷaiñar*), scholarly bards (*pulavar*), warrior chiefs (*maṟavar, kiḻar*, and *mannar*), warriors (*maṟavar*), bards (*pāṇar* and *poruṇar*), and magico-religious functionaries. The poetic flower symbolism of *veṭci* (cattle raid), *karantai* (cattle recovery), *vañji* (chieftain's raid), *kāñji* (chieftain's resistance of a raid), and *tumpai* (preparation for raid) show how institutionalized and common the plunder was. There is no evidence for the *vēntar* maintaining a ready troop of warriors like a standing army. A poem refers to the *maṟavar* of Cōḷa Nalankiḷḷi as *paṭaimākkal*, meaning fighters (*Pn.* 25). There is no evidence for a systematically organized militia under the *vēntar* though the term *ēnāti* (*sēnāpati*) occurs in connection with the titles of a few headmen, as noted earlier. However, the chieftains had only a set of people belonging to the fighter clan with kinship ties who could be mobilized instantaneously by the beating of a battle drum.

The need for frequent redistribution and the strain of raids should have acted as a compulsion on the *vēntar* to intensify production in their own land, but this is not indicated by the source. The well-known tradition of Karikala Cōḷa causing the anicut built on the Kaveri is indeed an indication of the chieftains' initiative in irrigation. There are pieces of advice here and there in the poems exhorting the chieftains to show more care and attention to agriculture, but ideas glorifying plunder and redistribution push them to insignificance.

The structure of the *vēntar* level of political power was relatively more complex since its redistributive social relationship was elaborate. It involved some kind of a simple hierarchy from *vēntar* to the *kuṭimākkal,* with *kiḻar* or *mannar* intermediaries. The hierarchy cut across kinship and distanced the *vēntar* from kuṭimākkal. But they did drink and dine with the maṛavar during unṭaṭṭu, the pre-raid or post-raid feasting at the residence of the *vēntar*. A complex redistributive political economy based on raids precludes the formation of a structured polity with defined positions and functions: the only institutions of some political character mentioned in the poems is *avaiyam* (*sabha*) which seems to have functioned as an assisting body of *vēntar*. The members of this body seem to have been mainly the warrior chiefs and the pulavar (the scholarly bards). However, the ideas of an instituted process of polity were quite well known albeit without any correspondence to reality. For instance, the *mūvēntar* were conceived by the poets as the three crowned kings of ancient Tamilakam.

The Cēras are the only line of chieftains bestowed with a collection of eulogizing songs, *Patiṟṟuppattu,* solely dedicated to them. The prominence of the Cēra lineage is clear from the songs as well as the separate collection[8]. It is said that originally there were ten units of ten songs, dedicated to ten Cēra chieftains, but the first and last units of ten are lost.[9] The surviving eighty songs (eight units of tens), dedicated to eight Cēras in the anthology, contain invaluable clues to the structure of political power, nature of authority, and sources of legitimacy. Many of the features attributed to the Cēras are applicable to the other *vēntar* also, but that they are specifically assigned to the Cēra lineage is important. A notable fact about the Cēra *vēntar* is that they are invariably praised as performers of *vēḷvi* (Vedic sacrifices), though they are also described as devotees of *Koṟṟavai,* the war goddness, and Murukan. The poems equate the Cēras with the Vedic gods such as Surya, Agni, Marut, the *Pancabhūta*s, the constellations, and the *navagraha*s (*Prp*. II.5). The equation reminds us of the *lōkapāla* theory of the *itihāsa-purāṇa* tradition. Poets eulogize the Cēras as wearing garlands made of seven crowns (*Patiṟṟuppattu* [*Prp.*] II.6, V.5). A poem says that just as a mother fosters her child, Ko-perumcēral Irupoṟai protects his *kuṭimākkl* (*Pn.* 5). This reminds us of the Asokan concept of parental relations between the king and his subjects (Separate Edict 2). However, the mother-metaphor is very important in the context of the kinship-basis of contemporary polity. Could it be indicative of a mother-centred system of inheritance? All these attributes of the Cēras are indicative of a high degree of influence of the Vedic brahmanic as well as the Buddhist culture.

The claim of identity with the brahmanic tradition becomes valid in a cultural milieu of the dominant ideology which was introduced to Tamilakam, probably even before the emergence of the *vēntar* level chiefdoms. It is futile to go by the poetic expressions and descriptions in *Patiṟṟuppattu* to characterize the nature of the political authority of the Cēras. What one can see in the anthology is the gradual ideological constitution of the political power drawing heavily from Vedic itihāsic-Purāṇic-Śāstrāic brahmanism. In many songs, the Cēras are described as the overlord of all monarchs in the land between the Himalayas and Kanyakumari. Such a notion of over-lordship was alien to contemporary socio-economic and political alignment. The image of the emperor attributed to the Cēras in poetic embellishments has little to do with the actual institutional character of power and authority. There are references in the poems to the Cēras possessing an army of the classical four fold division, conquering many rulers and subjecting them to a subordinate level. There was no notion of a *de facto* ruler or any concept of territory, but a tacitly recognized chief of predatory power and an overall general perception of the landscape as demarcated by the eastern hill and the western sea. They are poetic stereotypes for praising the *vēntar* and not expressions of reality.

The poems hold the authority of the *mūvēntar* over Tamilakam as a matter of tacit recognition. It is maintained in the poems that the whole of Tamilakam belonged to them. Their authority is characterized in terms of Śāstrāic–Purāṇic notions and status legitimized by comparing and associating them with epic characters. A poem claims that Cēraman Perumcōṟṟutiyan conquered the land of the Pāṇḍavas and hosted a feast for both the Pāṇḍavas and Kauravas after the Bhārata war (*Pn.* 2). All the *vēntar* are mentioned to have incised their emblems on the Himalayas and hoisted flags on its peaks. Each one of them is said to have ruled the land surrounded by the Himalayas and the seas. A poem eulogizes Pāṇḍya Māran Vaḻuti as ferocious enough to frighten the north Indian kings (*Pn.* 52). Several are such examples of high-sounding claims which seek to legitimize the status of the *vēntar*. The poems try to attribute all the epic, Purāṇic regalia to them. Even some of the hill chiefs are eulogized by attributing Śāstrāic royalty to them. It is significant to note that the Mauryan emperor Asoka referred to them not as individual rulers, but as clans of kindred descendants in his edicts as expressions like *Satiyaputo* and *Keralaputo* suggest. So it is not difficult to recognize the image of the *vēntar* as a poetic rendering of reality in Śāstrāic–Purāṇic notations.

There seems to be a lot of difference between the image that the poets try to secure for the *vēntar* and the reality about what they were. We know that the whole of Tamilakam did not belong to them and there were other tribute-receiving chiefs like Atiyamān, who were almost nearer to the *vēntar* in status. A poem in praise of Neṭumān Anji warns all the chiefs of agrarian settlements to rush to him with tiṛai if they wished to retain their ūrs with them (*Pn.* 97). Many of the hill chiefs were uncompromisingly opposed to the *vēntar*. Pāri of Paṛampumalai is one good example. He offered strong resistance to the *vēntar*, though he was subsequently defeated and killed. So the reality was that *vēntar* were also chiefs, but the crucial difference was their relatively greater resource power, larger redistributive intercommunity relationship, and better sources of legitimization. They were surrounded by *brāhmaṇa pulavar* of the Vedic tradition and a few were well informed of the Śāstrāic–Purāṇic notions of kingship. But a predatory chieftain, whose status and power were linked with the range of the redistributive community network, could have hardly gone by Śāstrāic prescriptions. A poem by a scholarly bard reminds Pāṇḍya Nanmāran of the fact that '*aṛaneṛi mutaṛṛe aracin koṛṛam*' meaning 'greatness of royalty' remained with the primacy of '*dharma*' (*Pn.* 55). All songs in *Ceviyaṛivūṛu* tuṛai contain ideas of this type, which sounded exotic in a milieu of plunder raids and redistribution. The *vēntar* drew upon heroism and gift-giving for ideological force. Bards were the main strength behind their name, fame, and legitimacy. They kept the image of the *vēntar* by roaming round the land with their songs in praise of the latter's exploits. The *Pānāṛṛuppaṭai* category of poems itself exemplifies the instituted nature of such circuits.

Now we may try an abstraction of the broad trends in the political process. Before we identify the forces of change in the process and understand their direction, the structure of the process has to be made a little clearer. The basic constituent in the structure was *kuṭi* or family. A particular *kuṭimākkal* or a host of families of one particular group and their *kōmān* or *perumakan* (chief) constituted the simplest structure that signified an organized settlement or *ūr* bound by kinship. This could spontaneously evolve as a *naṭu* through the process of the segmentary expansion of one and the same *kuṭimākkal* as exemplified by the hill chiefdoms. A collection of kinship-based *ūrs* of a variety of *kuṭimākkal* integrated under a chief as his nāṭu signifies the subsequent structure of complex relations transcending kinship, as exemplified by the lowland chiefdoms. Within such *nāṭu* units, the structure of the *ūr* also involved complex relations when an alien chief and his *kuṭi* were superimposed on it. In short, the disintegration of the kinship base of the *ūr* was the crux of the process of change in the total structure.

We have already noted that the central character of the contemporary political process was linked up with predatory operations and booty redistribution. Predatory marches of chiefs, their ravaging of settlements, arbitrary redistribution of the ūr, and the consequent migration and subsequent immigration were the characteristic features of the period under review. The formation of dispersed settlements in the place of nuclear units of kinship groups was a major consequence of these events. The redistribution of resources, particularly land beyond the social relationship of kinship, also had certain crucial consequences. It appears that at some point in time the institution of redistribution involved gifts of land, mainly to warrior chiefs. In the case of the warrior chiefs, the gift must have meant only transfer of predatory control rather than ownership. As scholarly *brāhmaṇas* were part of the redistributive social relationship, land seems to have been gifted to them too, though not extensively. Not being cultivators, *brāhmaṇas* had to get their land worked by others. This implied the making of a new system of relations in production, transcending the framework of kinship. We have a few references to prominent *brāhmaṇa* households. Kauṇiyan Viṇṇan Tāyan of Pūṇjaṟṟūr is an example, but he appears in the poems as a householder with pastoral wealth rather than agrarian resources (*Pn.* 166).

The characterization of the political structure of a complex of unevenly evolved chiefdoms that are actively interrelated is extremely difficult as it defies labelling or categorization based on known models. In the sense that the state means a centralized political authority of due sanction and legitimization within a defined territory, with a regular taxation system and a standing army and bureaucracy, this is not the political structure of a state system. It is not the structure of an easily explicable pre-state either. The various levels in the set-up signify different stages of pre-state developments. Further, there is an overlap of these stages at all levels, adding to its complexity. At the *vēntar* level authority, some features of the state are found interspersed with predominantly non-state features. Similarly, at the level of hill chiefs or forest chiefs, there are no features of state at all. Historians have generally taken the *vēntar* as a monarch. Proceeding on this old assumption, a recent study has sought to equate the political structure of the *vēntar* level to that of a state system.[10]

In fact, there is no evidence for the emergence of even the preliminary infrastructure of a near-state in the *vēntar* level polity. It does not appear to be accidental since there was no possibility of any near-state infrastructure in the low level of economy that characterized the period, despite the fact that their resource potential was growing. Overseas exchanges did enrich their status and ranking through the acquisition of prestige goods and through their redistribution, but that could hardly have led to the basic transformation of the political level. The chieftains were actively interested in promoting overseas exchange traffic. The measures taken by some Cēras to prevent the pirates on the western coast and the 'arrangements of lights' made on the shore as indicators of the coastline for the ships at night, show how the chiefdom-level polity responded to contemporary overseas exchange needs. But it was beyond the capacity of the chieftains' infrastructure to extend such services to a wider range. A large number of songs in the anthologies refer to the hazardous nature of the long journey of merchants and caravans through forests and arid planes where no facilities of life or protection from wayside robbers were available (*Pn.* 60, 116, 310, 313; *Akanāṉūṟu* [*An.*] 190). This probably points to the nature of the political formations that precluded the instituted arrangements for protecting and maintaining trade and trade routes. A comparison of this system with that of the early empire and also the subsequent kingdoms in northern India and the Deccan, with their explicit interest in the organizational and institutional aspects of long-distance trade, would suffice to show the difference.

As already noted, the principal social mode of labour realization was familial and co-operative. However, at least a few, like metal-working and pottery, which come under the category of skilled labour, must have been full-time trades of specialists and hence hereditary. As the most extensively used metal, iron had a central place among metals as the base of weapons whose significance in a society of predatory operations is explicit. Moreover, the practice of burying iron objects along with the dead had pushed a great deal of iron out of circulation, presupposing continuous iron-working as a full-time occupation of hereditary specialization. The production of earthen pots, a characteristically brittle artefact, was obviously a continuous full-time activity, for their use was extensive both for the living as well as the dead. Moreover, the fabric, polish, glazing, slips, paintings, texture, and decorative designs of pottery suggest that it was a full-time technology of specialized expertise.

The number of such full-time artisans and craftsmen of hereditary occupations was relatively more in the headquarters of bigger chieftains of the *vēlir* and *vēntar* levels. As the major redistributive pools of resources, the chieftains' settlements could support more full-time crafts. Another full-time function of a hereditary nature was that of the warriors. Every settlement (*ūr*) needed full-time warriors since the main mode of political appropriation of resources was predatory. In association with the chiefly households, there were three other full-time hereditary functionaries: the *pāṇar* (bards), *paṟaiyar* (who play a kind of raid drum called *paṟa*), and *tuṭiyar* (who play a small drum called *tuṭi*).

The tendencies towards social stratification were much more evident in the headquarters of the Cēras, Cōḻas, and Pāṇḍyas. In the ports and ruling headquarters, several hereditary craftsmen and specialized functionaries drawn from the hinterland worked and perhaps got organized into corporate bodies (*nikamam*). In the ports like Kōrkai, Muciṟi, and Toṇḍi, there seem to have existed artisan and craftsfolk settlements (*cēris*) of hereditary occupations. Probably both the ruling authority and organized merchant groups must have used the labour of a class of servile people under conditions of coercion and relations of labour transcending kinship. Poems refer to captives working in pearl fisheries. There was a slow emergence of hereditary occupations in the *vēntar* level chiefly settlements with a greater proportion in coastal towns, marketing centres, and ruling headquarters. In the process of predatory operations and redistribution, some kind of differential allocation of new position, status, roles, and prestige within the complex redistributive relationships was natural. The trend of differential allocation of positions and roles at the instance of the highest chiefly authority anticipated the formation of a hierarchy. However, the poems do not contain pointers to a clearly stratified society.[11] Social differentiation was confined to the binary between *uyarntōr* (the highborn) that comprised *brāhmaṇas* and *iḻipiṟappāḷar* (the lowborn), the people. That the second category comprised all people suggests a very flexible kind of social division, and lack of indications to the existence of intermediary positions confirms the fluidity. Similarly the differentiation in terms of the objective conditions of life was also confined to the binary between *puravalar* (redistributors) and *iravalar* (redistributes/dependents).

The process of redistribution and differential allocation involved the generation of a series of contradictions within the social formation. Much more crucial were contradictions immanent in the working of the social formation itself, the most striking being the continued articulation of conditions totally uncongenial to the development of plough agriculture, which was the most potential form among contemporary forms of production. Predatory marches of chieftains, their destruction of agrarian settlements as part of the scorched-earth policy in raids, and the dominance of the heroic ideology of raids and booty redistribution provided an adverse circumstance for the development of agriculture.[12] As we have already seen, redistribution exerted pressure on production, but failed to translate itself as a motor of intensified production since there was no scope for it within the kinship-based forms of production. Intensified labour mobilization for better production was beyond the working power of contemporary political apparatus that had little coercive ability. The major trend in the process was that of the gradual dissolution of the social formation due to the development incompatibility between plough technology and relations of kin labour.[13]

The process of the emergence of the new social formation was characterized by the expansion of plough agriculture into suitable agro-climatic landscapes through the institution of royal land grants to *brāhmaṇas*. It involved the development of the technology of irrigation and social organization of labour, both under the over patronage and covert influence of the emerging political power. This was a mutually supplementing homologous process of development of the agrarian economy and its polity, the former developing under royal support and the latter under agricultural surplus. Thus began to emerge a new authority structure through the interconnected process of simultaneity of economy and polity from AD sixth century, as exemplified by the Pallava of the Simhavarman line, Pāṇḍyas of the Kaṭunkon line, and subsequently Cōḻas of the Vijayālaya line. The paddy-based economy articulated a comparable political structure in Kerala too as illustrated by the new Cēras, despite the difference in their system of dynastic inheritance. All of them except the Cēras were founders of *brahmadēya*s and hence brahmanised and legitimised as dynasties of purāṇic genealogies. The Cēras were legitimized too but not through eulogies (*meikirtis*) in land grant charters of *brahmadēyas*, the creation of which involved superimposition of the superior rights of the brahmans over communal holdings of the locality and transformation of clan settlements into occupation groups of hereditary specialization. The main features of the process were differentiation, stratification, and political formation leading to the development of the state-system and authority structure.

The ideology played a crucial role as the coercive instrument in transforming and organizing people for the labour processes of wetland agriculture. The ethical didactics of the *Kīḻkkaṇakku* works, stemming from the ideological elements of Vedic, Purāṇic, and Śāstrāic texts, provided the foundation for social organization.[14] It was an extremely intense process of reification that filled the ideological domain, offering prescriptions, explanation, meaning, and legitimacy to the variety of rights, ranks, positions, privileges, entitlements, and obligations binding the hierarchical social relationships. The most potent ideological and institutional instrument that stabilized the relations of production was caste. It accommodated into its fold a range of economically stratified functionaries of hereditary trades.

The role of caste in the integration of the agrarian society, whose mechanisms of appropriation depended on extra-economic coercion, was extremely crucial. We do not know exactly how caste as an institution evolved in Tamilakam. It is reasonable to assume that the crystallization of functionally specific families into *jātis* had its beginnings in the *brāhmaṇa* households. However, this had not acquired institutional form in the early years though the disintegration of kinship ties was a natural consequence in the clan settlements linked to *brāhmaṇa* households. The disintegration of clan-kin ties became almost widespread along the agrarian tracts as paddy cultivation expanded with corresponding developments, such as social stratification and widening of the division of labour through specialization. In the process the clan identity disappeared and *jāti* came in as the substitute, mostly by retaining the names of the clan. Several terms like *pāna*, *paṛaya*, *vēttuva*, *vēṭa*, *kuṛavar*, *maṛavar*, and *paratavar* vouch for the retention of clan names for *jāti*.

The first notable development towards the transformation of clans into *jātis* was the specialization of labour. It was the practice of rewarding specialized labour with land-based entitlements that made specialization of labour hereditary. The reason was obviously the labourers' urge to perpetuate the entitlements. But how the labouring clans of hereditary specialization got absorbed into the *jāti* system cannot be explained easily. We know that the proliferation of hereditary occupations and their absorption into the *jāti* hierarchy were advancing side by side with the socio-spatial expansion of paddy cultivation. We also know that at a later period, new institutional agencies like the temple and service tenements were instrumental in crystallizing the *jāti* system. Further, the relation of the *jāti* system to brahmanism is taken for granted by all. But at the same time the actual social process of the making of the *jāti* system is largely unclear.

The brahmanical tradition of social differentiation needs no description, for the Śāstrāic abstractions of *varṇa* and *sankīrṇa jāti* are quite well known. *Brāhmaṇas* all over the subcontinent had inherited this perception of social stratification as a common legacy. It is only natural that the *brāhmaṇas* of contemporary south India, who inherited the Vedic, Śāstrāic, and Purāṇic scholarship, had the traditional perception and appreciation of their society. They could have conceived the society of functionally specific families attached to their households only in terms of the hierarchy of occupations and social status implicit in the Śāstrāic explanations about *jātis*. The brahmanical perception and appreciation of social groups would, however, just not be enough for the society to become hierarchically structured in the idiom of *jāti*. Even the existence of preconditions such as hereditary occupations, asymmetrical social relations, and differential allocations of positions would not help us deduce developments in the prevalence of the *jāti* hierarchy.

It was the dominant position of the *brāhmaṇas* that was crucial in the operation of the *jāti* hierarchy. The tacitly recognized ritual supremacy, knowledge systems, resource potential, social control, political influence, and cultural skills provided the *brāhmaṇas* with the best conditions of domination. They symbolized the collective norms and took precedence over the ruling powers. Their hegemony over the communication channels and ideological structures of legitimization had made them a determinant force of political authority by the sixth century. On top of it all, their status as custodians of higher wisdom about the universe, practical knowledge about the cycles of seasons, and their calendrical measurements enabling prediction of natural changes had added to their ritual charisma. It was this enormous potential of cultural resources coupled with the extensive control of means of production that enabled the *brāhmaṇas* to wield social dominance. Subsuming all differential categories and groups in due course, they encompassed the total society.

The brahmanization of social stratification was a historically and culturally contingent effect rather than the result of any conscious conspiratorial scheming. However, the articulations of *brāhmaṇas* as a spatio-temporally and culturally dominant community were casually linked to the process. The net effect was ordering the differential relations of production into the hierarchy of *jātis*. The notion of the pure 'self' and the impure 'other' that originally constituted the basis of *jāti* was tribal and a part of the horizontal social division of the primeval kind. The formation of *jātis* along the domestic groups of hereditary occupations was also not brahmanical. In fact, even the Gangetic region owed the proliferation of *jātis* to the socio-economic processes and not to brahmanism, which only explained the phenomenon of social stratification through the Śāstrāic idiom. What seems to be causally linked to the *brāhmaṇas* is the imposition of their notion of purity and pollution as fundamental and of themselves as the central point of reference for determining the relative status of each *jāti*. In short, what is brahmanical is not *jāti*, but the notion of hierarchy.

Hierarchy as such, however, is not merely a notional construct of brahmanism and was derived from the objective conditions related to the forces and relations of production. Further, it had the specific historical context of operation at the juncture of an agrarian technology and social strategy of labour realization, necessitating institutional devices for stabilizing hierarchical stratification. How brahmanism succeeded in providing the institutional devices has to be examined in the context of the culturally and historically contingent conditions of social domination. The emergence of brahmanism as the major worldview generating knowledge about the Daksiṇapātha, its peoples and cultures, spreading a new pattern of thinking and transforming the local modes of social existence, constituted the historical context. The argument is that the success of brahmanical domination and the establishment of the *jāti* hierarchy were the ideologically realized goals. *jāti* hierarchy was, in short, the effect of the brahmanical form of social representation that became hegemonic around the AD sixth-seventh centuries. This was the temporal juncture that witnessed the expansion of a technology of production and social strategies of labour realization, leading to the proliferation of hereditary occupations.

To sum up, the central argument of this chapter is that a closer examination of the socio-economic processes and the corresponding pattern of distribution of power shows that contemporary society was largely non-stratified and, therefore, the postulation of the state an anachronism. The political process evident in the principal source material is that of predatory operations and booty redistribution by chiefly lineages. There is no evidence for the emergence of even the preliminary infrastructure of a near state at the *vēntar* level polity. It is further argued that the absence of evidence for the existence of features such as a social hierarchy, territory, standing army, bureaucracy, and periodic exaction is not accidental. It does not appear to be accidental since there was no possibility of any near state infrastructure in the low level of economy that characterized the period, despite the fact that their resource potential was growing. Their authority was determined by the range of redistributive social relationships sustained through predatory accumulation of resources. With the expansion of the new relations of production and the spread of wet-rice agriculture that became characteristic in the sixth and seventh centuries, the society became class-structured and the birth of the state plausible. The birth of a new political structure, different from that of the chiefdom, was a major simultaneous process with the development and expansion of wet-rice agriculture.[15] Its antecedents involved the transition from kin-labour to non-kin labour, multiple functionaries to hereditary occupation groups, clans to castes, simple clannish settlements to structured agrarian villages, and chiefdom to monarchy.

NOTES AND REFERENCES

1. Tamil heroic literature refers to what is popularly known as the corpus of *Sangam* literature. The corpus includes in its most archaic stratum some of the anthologies grouped under *Eṭṭuttokai* (The Eight Anthologies) and *Pattuppāṭṭu* (The Ten Idylls) roughly belonging to the second century BC and AD third century. U.V. Swamynatha Iyer has edited and published the texts of idylls and anthologies belonging to the Tamil heroic tradition, during 1955–7. Also see Kailasapathy, 1968, *Tamil Heroic Poetry*, London; George L. Hart, 1979, *Poets of the Tamil Anthologies: Ancient Poems of Love and War*, Princeton.
2. See the discussion in E.R. Service, 1982, *Formation of the State*, London, pp. 66–71.
3. Karl Marx was the first to theorize clearly the historical context of the origins of the state. Marx's theory is examined and probed deeply in L. Krader, 1968, *Formation of the State*, London.
4. The theoretical issues about the state are considered in several articles in H.J.M. Claessen and P. Skalnik (eds), 1978, *The Early State*, The Hague. Also see the discussion of the conceptual preliminaries in R. Thapar, 1984, *From Lineage to State*, New Delhi, pp. 3–7.
5. See Krader, *Formation of the State*, p. 37; also Service, *Formation of the State*, p. 63; and the relevant discussions in C. Drekmeier, 1962, *Kingship and Community in Early India*, Bombay.
6. Label inscriptions consist of the Tamil *brāhmi* labels belonging to c. third century BC to AD fourth century. For texts of and detailed comments on the inscriptions see, I. Mahadevan, *Tamil Epigraphy from the Earliest Times to 6th Century* AD, 2003, pp. 60–5.
7. The foreign notices comprise mainly the Graeco-Roman writings. See K.A. Nilakanta Sastri, 1972, *Foreign Notices of South India, From Megasthenes to Ma Huan*, Madras, reprint.

8. A separate anthology of hundred poems grouped as units of ten, each of which dedicated to a ruler, is a unique thing about the *Cēras*.
9. It is said that originally there were ten units of ten poems (10×10) each dedicated the ten *Cēra* chieftains. The first unit of ten poems and the last unit of ten poems (the first ten and the last ten) are not available, for they are lost.
10. For a study of Iron Age in the Tamil south, see Guru Raja Rao, 1972, *The Megalithic Culture of South India*, Mysore: Prasaranga; L.S. Leshnik, 1974, *South Indian 'Megalithic' Burials: The Pandukal Complex*, Wiesbaden. Also A. Sundara, 1975, *The Early Chamber Tombs of South India*, Delhi.
11. For a different perception, see Richard S. Kennedy, 1976, 'The King in Early South India as Chieftain and the Emperor', *Indian Historical Review*, 3(1): 1–15. An alternate view is developed in Sudarsan Senevaratne, 1990, 'The Pre-state Societies to State Societies: Transformations in the Political Ecology of South India with Special Reference to Tamil Nadu', unpublished seminar paper, Jawaharlal Nehru University.
12. See details given in Rajan Gurukkal, 1987, 'Problems of Agrarian Expansion in Early Iron Age', in B.D. Chattopadhyaya (ed.), *Essays in Ancient Indian Economic History*, Delhi, pp. 56–7.
13. For a detailed consideration of the issue, see Rajan Gurukkal, 1997, 'From Clan and Lineage to Hereditary Occupations and Caste in South India', in Dev Nathan (ed.), *From Tribe to Caste*, Shimla, pp. 205–22.
14. Rajan Gurukkal, 1998, 'Characterising Ancient Society: The Case of South India', Presidential Address, Indian History Congress, Ancient India Section, Patiala, p. 23.
15. Ibid., pp. 25–6.

12

Aspects of Great Transformation in Ancient Kerala*

The chapter seeks to have a closer look at the processes of social change in ancient Kerala, most of which formed part of the Tamil Macro Region (*Tamilakam*) in the larger archaeological context of the spread of iron using, Dravidian speaking descent groups, roughly dating back to first millennium BC.[1] We have already discussed in detail the descent groups and their unevenly evolved economies that resulted from human adaptation to different ecosystems of the landscape, with the help of clues in various sources particularly the Tamil heroic poems, which point to the scenario of the interaction and coexistence of these economies accomplishing a social formation structured by the dominance of agro-pastoralism, towards the closing centuries of first millennium BC.[2] We have also observed the manifestation of features like complex redistribution generating differentiation, the limiting influence of dominance of agro-pastoral economy, predatory politics and plunder raids on paddy culture, and the incompatibility between kin-labour and plough technology, as intensified over a few centuries, heading for a series of transitions around mid-first millennium of the Christian Era (CE): the transition from kin labour to non-kin labour; from millet to paddy; from clan and kin ties to hereditary occupation groups and caste; from chiefdom to monarchy and; from heterodox religious ideology to *āgamic* brahmanism.[3]

Kerala, a landscape integral to the social formation underwent the same historical processes of transformation to a great extent. Nevertheless,

* This chapter is a partly reproduced version of the chapter with the same title in, 1999, Rajan Gurukkal and Raghava Varier (eds), *Cultural History of Kerala*, Vol. I, Department of Cultural Productions, Government of Kerala, Thiruvananthapuram.

it stands out distinct in terms of human ecological processes in the wake of the dissolution of the social formation, adding a major ecological feature to the transitions. These were transformations of radical and fundamental nature bringing forth a higher phase of productive forces with totally new relations, groups, institutions, structures, and practices deserving the prefix great, with little or no implications of the Polanyian sense.[4] The chapter seeks to examine aspects of the transformations that aggregately led to a total breakdown of the social formation and the making of a new one.

THE TRANSFORMATION SCENARIO

The material and socio-political processes of the transformation scenario were common to all the regions of the Tamil macro region. It was perhaps the historical antecedents of Kerala, which were remarkably different. The absence of the tradition of royal land grant is the most striking among them. *Brāhmaṇa* households sprang up on their own, sparsely along the red soil fringes of the alluvial ecosystem in the region by the closing centuries before Christ. They came up as independent production units using clan labour in the neighbourhood and belonging to the agro-pastoral social formation that was heading for a crisis due to a series of inherent contradictions such as incompatibility between the plough technology and kin-based relations of production leading to low labour productivity and ever falling scope of economic reproduction.[5] We have already described earlier the nature of evidence in the sources, the veracity of indirect clues to the crisis, the possibility of a reinterpretation of the Kaḷabhra invasion as predatory marches involving loss of landed property and migrations, and the brahmanical charters equating the epoch as the Kali Age, the implications of which in the context of a major crisis of production.

The central feature of the transformation scenario was the absence of conditions favourable to the maximisation of the development potential of plough technology that was caught up in the fetters of clan-kin ties of a non-stratified society. The productivity of plough agriculture was widely recognized by the turn of the CE. However, its effective application in the wet-rice eco-zone was impeded by the relations of production based on kin-labour, the elasticity of which was at its best in its expanded and complex form realised through the incorporation of affinal relatives. The expansion of plough could be wider through the accustomed alternative namely, the cooperative labour across families, which at any rate would not facilitate the adoption of the technology beyond the wet-rice eco-zone, due to the inherent incapability of that mode of labour mobilization to ensure permanent supply of labour. A variety of other reasons such as the dominance of agro-pastoral means of subsistence, community's preference to millet, absence of appropriate irrigation techniques, lack of technical know-how among the people, and hence insufficient labour and so on.

FROM KIN LABOUR TO NON-KIN LABOUR

As already noted earlier the transformation of the kinship basis of productive relations was indispensable since even the institution of cooperative labour had no capability to provide the required stability of the supply of specialized labour. Some forms of labour mobilization transcending kinship were to evolve and get institutionalized. Inevitably it could only be through the transformation of kin labour into non-kin labour. Plough agriculture with its potential of expansion was exerting pressure on relations based on kinship, which were stressed to be as much elastic as possible, for its operation necessitated a complex division of labour involving specialization of arts and crafts. Specialized labour in different arts and crafts would not be possible without transcending kinship. Therefore, disintegration of kin-labour was a natural process under the specific situation of incompatibility between the productive forces and relations.

A *brāhmaṇa* household as a self sustaining unit of production, owning and controlling some land, presupposed involvement of non-kin labour, however informal it might be, since it necessitated external labour support, be it the economy of cattle keeping or cultivation or both. The household economy of *brāhmaṇas*, therefore, meant a system of productive relations transcending kinship with some kind of arrangement for the supply of labour. The *brāhmaṇa* households in Kerala were of a migrant population pursuing the tradition of Vedic rituals and the function of preceptors. In short the *brāhmaṇas* were either Vedic priests officiating sacrifices or scholarly bards engaged in the composition of heroic poems. As full time priests and preceptors, they spent their time at the site of rituals and the courts of chieftains. Therefore, their land was to be cultivated and cattle grazed by some of the members of the nearby clan families. This naturally evolved ties of dependence outside kinship must have become a permanent arrangement of the *brāhmaṇa* household economy in due course. Subsequently when the household economy got transformed into village economy it was probably this arrangement with the clans' families for labour force that got augmented, systematized, and institutionalized, as the proximity between *brāhmaṇa* villages and Iron Age archaeological sites would have us assume.

It is reasonable to assume that in Kerala some of the ancient *brāhmaṇa* households had appeared in the wet-rice ecosystem pockets in the Western Ghats where clan labour was available. The reason for this assumption is the absence of technology for the productive use of wetlands in the plains. There is no archaeological evidence as to associate the early Iron Age people with wet-rice agriculture in the plains of Kerala. At the same time there is archaeological evidence like the occurrence of iron ploughshare among the mortuary goods of Megaliths at a few places in the Western Ghats to vouch for cultivation in the wet-rice ecosystem of highlands. The sites excavated at Kuppakkolli in the Wayanad District that have yielded ploughshare are worth mentioning here both for the wet-rice eco-type and clannish inhabitants.[6] So the earliest paddy fields of Kerala were probably in the high ranges and the elevated alluvial beds in the plains rather than along the low lying wetlands. Such areas have been identified at several points along the Western Ghats. Some of them are now within forests where fields with paddy as wild growth have survived as an organic relic of the past culture. In such areas often the remnants of brahmanical temples though of a relatively later period are also found. Tellikkal Vayal within the Parampikkulam Reserve is a good example of an archaic paddy field with the remains of the temple.

It is significant to note that most of the traditional *brāhmaṇa* settlements of Kerala have Iron Age burial complexes in their vicinity. It is explicit that there was some correspondence between the early *brāhmaṇa* settlements and the Iron Age sites.[7] The indications from places elsewhere in Tamilakam also tend to suggest that *brāhmaṇa* households had emerged as independent units of production with working clannish families linked to them. They had existed in clusters well representing a new mode of appropriation of labour as well as surplus and signifying an alternative system counterpoised to what was dominant.[8] Anyway, one of the major processes in the social formation was the emergence of non-kin labour in the agrarian sector through the interaction between *brāhmaṇa* households and the neighbouring clannish folk.

Whatever was the form of realization of the clan labour in the initial phase, the fundamental aspect of the subsequent system was a tenurial tie between the tilling clansmen and the non-tilling *brāhmaṇa* households as two objectively antagonistic classes. This was a system of stratified relations of production based on a variety of specialized non-kin labour force. Even the prototype of the system in the *brāhmaṇa* household economy was a contrast to contemporary agro-pastoral clan settlements. The growth of *brāhmaṇa* households, an ongoing phenomenon, incessantly led to the continuous disintegration of the system of productive relations based on kin labour with a corresponding emergence of a non-kin workforce of tillers, specialized artisans and craftsmen.

THE HUMAN ECOLOGICAL TRANSFORMATION

The process of institutional transformation of the mode of labour realization depends on the extent of the labour process involved in the development and expansion of plough agriculture. The volume of labour and its diversity in their turn depend upon the ecological conditions of the landscape, which in the case of Kerala were unique. There have been a lot of ecological differences between the agro-climatic zones of Kerala and those of the rest of Tamilakam in terms of seasons, rainfall, landscape, soil structure, permeability, retention, resilience, and so on. It is necessary to imagine the nature, feature, and dynamic of the landscape ecosystem during the mid-first millennium CE in the light of environmental history. Extensive forests, large catchments, numerous micro watersheds, many natural aquatic networks of rivers and streams mostly flowing towards the west and well drenched aquifers constituting wet plains, vast stretches of water logged/saturated depressions, thickly vegetated large marshes and isolated swamps surrounded by undulating lateritic mid-terrains merging with hillocks and low lying fluvio-marine land forms had made the landscape of Kerala a major ecological distinction at that time. The most striking difference about the wet-rice landscape ecosystem was the excess of water in contrast to its scarcity in most other parts of the Tamil macro region. Naturally technology and the labour processes in the two agro-climatic zones would be substantially different from each other in the context of the expansion of plough agriculture.

Expansion of plough agriculture from the small wetland pockets growing paddy and sugarcane in the forests of the Western Ghats to the inhospitable eco-tracts of lateritic hill slopes and undulating midland terrains of millets, was extremely difficult wanting irrigation facility and labour. Expansion into the water logged/saturated areas was all the more difficult wanting both technology and labour. Though the technology of wet-rice agriculture was already known, its extension to the vast low-lying wet-plains, heavily vegetated, marshy and waterlogged, and not easily amenable to reclamation, was almost impossible, for the mobilization of enormous volume of hard labour indispensable for turning the landscape into paddy fields was far beyond the capability of clannish households and their chieftains. It was a major long-term massive endeavour of human ecological transformation of traumatic dimension necessitating a competent class with leadership and coercive social control, a fairly evolved technology of water management, knowledge of seasons and practices of paddy culture, and appropriate institutional, structural, and ideological means of large-scale social mobilization, division and realization of labour.

The Tamil heroic poems are perhaps the only reliable source for us to assume *brāhmaṇa* households to have existed in ancient Kerala. It is certain that the number of the *brāhmaṇa* households was obviously very small in those times and that they must have been within the domains of hunter chieftains, small and big. In the plains they must have concentrated in areas of wet-rice landscape ecotypes adjacent to the red soil terraces and between the forested hill tracts and waterlogged low-lands. The expansion of paddy cultivation beyond these small patches was not easy under the socio-political set up of the heroic age, as we have already discussed. It was not possible for the period to expand plough agriculture to low-lands that were marshy and waterlogged, because the absence of royal land-grants to *brāhmaṇas* in Kerala and the claim of the brahmanical origin legend assigning to Parasurama's axe the credit of reclaiming 160 *kaṭam* (an old time measure) of land that lay between Gokarnam and Kanyakumari, are clear indications of the direct acquisition of the arable land of Kerala by the *brāhmaṇas* without being obligated to anybody. It appears that the culturally contingent brahmanical authority, ritual charisma, legitimacy, social command, structures of control, institutional devices, the various systems of knowledge and technologies of management succeeded in coercing the massive labour of the clans for the conversion of the wet-landscape ecosystem of Kerala into paddy fields. Indeed it must have been a long process of two or three centuries and involving the series of simultaneous transitions that we have already discussed. This model of labour mobilization and coercion must have been replicated by the ruling class also as the royal holdings indicate. How they spread to the wetland ecosystem and converged into temple centred corporate settlements when, are conjectures. The transformation of individual *brāhmaṇa* households into corporations was the result of the economic processes. As the processes that led to the dissolution of the chiefdom level social formation of the descent groups were the same as those in the places elsewhere in the Tamilakam, and as the alternative to it was to evolve from the production relations of the *brāhmaṇa* households, the emerged social formation in Kerala was more or less the same. What was crucial about the new formation was its binary basis between landholding and landlessness which eventually got mediated by intermediaries to form a complex structure. Specialized division of labour, its crystallization into hereditary occupations and their non-economic coercive modes of social realization were the main characteristics.

FROM CLANS TO HEREDITARY OCCUPATION GROUPS AND CASTE

The processes of human ecological transformation of the low-lying landscape into paddy-fields were homologous to the formation of a diversified workforce of hereditary specialization, which was indeed a gradual institutional manifestation of practices engendered by the rise and concentration of *brāhmaṇa* households into corporate settlements. The processes might have started by the mid-first millennium CE and continued for over a couple of centuries effecting transformation of clansmen families into permanent workforce attached to the emerging paddy-fields. The transformation must have certainly involved physical coercion, for it meant subjection of clansmen into servitude that was a prerequisite for ensuring permanency of hard labour. Probably ideological coercion might have become sufficient only later when it was feasible, thanks to the social ordering of diversified labour through hereditary specialization and institutionalization under the system of caste and caste-based occupational obligation. Nevertheless, at the inception it must have been a process of capture and forceful subjection to servitude with most features of slavery, in the case of the constitution of the category of primary producers/full-time tillers called the *pulayar* whose counterpart, *malapulayar* (the pulayar of the hills) still exist in the forests.

The various artisans and craftsmen such as metal workers, weavers, gem-cutters, and potters existed among clans, of course with certain level of flexibility, and hence their transformation into hereditary occupation groups was the result of a natural process of their integration with the new agrarian settlements. The emergence of a class of intermediaries between the primary producers and the *brāhmaṇa* landholders was a concomitant phenomenon. As the *brāhmaṇa* settlements and their land control increased, the intermediaries and hereditary occupation groups including the primary producers also naturally enlarged. Soon the new system of relations of production characterized by the full-time tillers of servitude and intermediary peasantry with hereditary occupational specialization must have enabled some kind of reorganization of labour in the chiefly holdings of clan kin ties too. Nevertheless, the stratification and hierarchical ordering might have taken two or three centuries more to characterize the social aggregate. It appears that social relations in the wet-rice areas had become structured and institutionalized during the sixth–seventh centuries with the steady expansion of the making of paddy-fields.[9]

It is reasonable to presume that social stratification began in the settlements of *brāhmaṇa* households, obviously as a result of the differentiated economy represented by plough agriculture and its division and specialization of labour transcending clan kin ties. The transformation of the hereditary occupation groups of clan ties into castes and the establishment of a hierarchy also started there. The concept of caste or *jāti* was not brahmanical though the notion of *varṇa* was, and hence the permanent workforce attached to the settlements of *brāhmaṇa* households certainly had the possibility of being conceived as *sudra-varṇa*. The notion of hierarchy was implicit in the system of production in which the relation between two objectively antagonistic classes was fundamental. It was implicit in the brahmanical social ordering too. *Jāti* is a matter of distinction based on the belief of purity and pollution, which each *jāti* held to make it pure as distinguished from the polluting other. However, as it is in the brahmanical texts the *jāti* phenomenon is theorized, the brahmanical perception of the stratified system of production relations headed by the *brāhmaṇas* would certainly be based on the brahmanical tradition of social differentiation.

The development of relations in plough agriculture involving the proliferation of occupational specialization and emergence of hereditary occupation groups was a faster process, the transformation of each occupation group into an endogamous caste and its ordering into a hierarchy took more time. Even in the turn of the second millennium CE, the manifestation of the *jāti* society was not complete. The emergence of hereditary occupations, asymmetrical social relations and differential allocations of positions was not enough for the prevalence of the *jāti* hierarchy as the dominant feature of contemporary society. The process required other institutional formations like rise and spread of service tenements, the institutional emergence of the temple and the transformation of the chieftain into the king, for crystallization of hereditary occupation groups into endogamous *jāti* hierarchy.[10] The mode of brahmanical perception and appreciation of differentiated hereditary social groups of occupational identity was yet to be dominant enough for the society to construe social hierarchy as structured in the idiom of *jāti*. It was indeed advancing through better land control, uncritically accepted ritual supremacy, and socio-political influence. The historically contingent hegemony of the *brāhmaṇas* over the cultural channels of social communication and ideological structures of legitimization was fast making them a decisive force of political authority in the region by the eighth–ninth centuries. The status of the *brāhmaṇas* as the custodians of the Vedic, Śāstrāic, epic, and Purāṇic ideas, the higher wisdom about life, the various systems of knowledge about the universe, practical know-how about the cycles of seasons and their calendrical measurements enabling prediction of natural changes, and the like, added to their charisma. This expanding socio-political influence and growing control of means of production, supplementary and complimentary to each other, were what made their worldview to be acceptable to the social aggregate.

FROM CHIEFDOM TO MONARCHY

Transformation of the chiefdom into monarchy was the political manifestation of the process of development and expansion of plough agriculture into more localities sufficient to change the structure of chiefly power relations. This was a gradual process of the transformation of the pre-existing ideas, institutions, relations, and structures of political control dominated by predatory practices, gifts, and prestations. The chiefdoms were of three types as already described elsewhere and they varied between the small and big ones with some kind of acceptance of the superiority of the biggest but without any running thread of political control other than predatory threats. The shift was more or less in the form of integration of the smallest ones, *ūr*s into larger agrarian localities called *nādu* by the biggest chief of the region through the support of the local chieftain. This transformation process presupposes a homologous connection between the expansion of the agrarian economy and increase of political power of the Cēra *vēntan*. Economic growth enhanced political power, which in its turn ensured further economic growth through protection and patronage. This mutuality between the economy and polity was the motor of the transition from chiefdom to monarchy, a new political structure different from that of the former.[11] The Cēra *vēntan* thus becomes the king, as the survival of the name of the biggest chiefly lineage, Cēra, suggests.

The expansion of plough agriculture involving acquisition of new rights over both land and labour, required the backing of political authority. Instances recalled in the brahmanical records in the Tamil region show that in the absence of strong political authority, the *brāhmaṇa* households at certain places had faced onslaughts as already mentioned previously.

Nevertheless, the situation of Kerala was different because the *brāhmaṇas* never owed the founding of their villages in Kerala to any king. Their tradition attributes the emergence of their settlements throughout the fertile tracts of major river valleys in the region to none other than Parasurama, the sixth incarnation of lord Vishnu, as noted earlier. In Kerala, therefore, monarchy was a direct creation by the *brāhmaṇa* landlords not so much for overcoming the resistance against superimposition of superior rights of the *brāhmaṇas* over the communal holdings and the clan families of the locality, but to prevent discords among the *brāhmaṇa* landlords themselves.

FROM HETERODOX IDEOLOGY TO BRAHMANISM

The ideological aspects of Tamilakam, which Kerala also shared were a mixture of all sorts of cults and rituals from animism to worship of anthropomorphic deities overwhelmed by the cult of the dead. The cult of heroism was central to the social formation, for the dominant economy with plunder and booty redistribution involving raids and counter raids for lifting or recovering cattle at the mercy of the death of several fighters required the cult as a resuscitating passion. It was necessary for the society to believe that the dead were heroes received by damsels in the heaven and that their souls lived with the fighters as the source of inspiration and courage.

At the same time, the ethical postulates of the Jain, Buddhist, and Ajivika orders had been in circulation, thanks to the monks, merchants, and bards of the time. There were Jain and Buddhist monks among the pulavar category of singers and they had influential contacts with their chieftains who had considered them their preceptors. Several monks of the Jain, Buddhist, and Ājívika orders seem to have taken shelters in the cavern at different parts of the Tamil region and the chieftains of their times must have visited them. There is epigraphic evidence at Pugalur for a Cēra chieftain's (Atan Cel Irumpoṛai) association with a cavern as its donor. Generally the songs of the *tuṛais* such as *Porunmoli* and *Ceviyaṛivūṛu* contain heterodox values and ethical postulates. The heterodox religions especially Jainism and Buddhism who had brought the art of writing and the tradition of literacy to the Tamil South were responsible to a great extent for the entire major socio-economic and intellectual changes of Tamilakam during the period. Writing seems to have spread extensively through merchants, monks, and probably the chieftains as the tradition of label inscription would have us believe. There are a couple of label inscriptions in the Kerala part of the Tamilakam too. The Jain and Buddhist monks taken to learning the language of the region, had in turn helped the development of Tamil and its enrichment with specialized knowledge and intellectual traditions. The archaic stratum of the ideological superstructure of the ancient social formation was full of ideas drawn from the Jain, Buddhist, and Ājívika perception of life. The influence of the Buddhist ideology was remarkable. In this sense, it is reasonable to argue that the most vital core of contemporary culture and civilization in Tamilakam was made up of the values of heterodox religions.

Along with heterodox ideas, brahmanical concepts are also seen in the Tamil heroic poems. In the initial phase the structure of political power, sources of legitimacy and nature of authority of chiefdoms were influenced by the heterodox values. The poems show the growing significance of Vedic Brahmanism too. The political ideology of the chiefdoms seems to have borrowed heavily from the Vedic, itihasic, Purāṇic, Śāstrāic brahmanism. Some of the pulavar singers like Kapilar and Paranar were *brāhmaṇa* priests officiating Vedic sacrifices. Some of them have praised the Cēra chieftains as the patrons of *vēḷvi* (Vedic sacrifices) and equated them with the Vedic gods such as *Surya*, *Agni*, *Marut*, the *Pancabhūtas*, the constellations and the *navagrahas*. The equation reminds us of the *lokapala* theory of the *itihasa-purana* tradition (*Prp*. II.5). However, the nature and extent of brahmanical influence upon monarchy were markedly different and fundamental. The new sources contain indications of a different social formation in the making. The land relations and ideology of *brāhmaṇas* were central to the new social formation though the heterodox religions did continue to co-exist. There is a trajectory of the shift of dominance from the heterodox ideology through the Vedic brahmanical to the temple-based *bhakti* that became best expressed subsequently in the compositions of the Saivite and Vaisnavite hymnists called the *Nāyanārs* and *Ālvārs*.

CONCLUSION

The chapter seeks to argue that the social formation of ancient Tamilakam characterized by the interactive co-existence of multiple economies dominated by the agro-pastoral economy was true of Kerala too, because a major part of it in the past was integral to the Tamil macro region. The social formation underwent a radical transformation with its contradictory structure dissolving itself into a production crisis due to the maturing of the ever-intensifying incompatibilities between the kin-labour-based productive relations and plough-technology-based forces of production. The kin-labour and its limiting effect led to a steady decline of productivity and finally to a serious production crisis and the inevitable dissolution of the social formation. The dissolution process comprised a series of interconnected transitions of simultaneity—the transitions of the economy, division of labour, social relations, political structure, and religious ideology. The processes of transitions such as the one from kin-labour to non-kin-labour, from clan to hereditary occupations and caste, from chiefdoms to monarchy, and from heterodox ideology to Brahmanism, are summarized in the chapter. All these jointly signified the dissolution of the agro-pastoral social formation of redistributive economy based on kin labour into a new one dominated by wet-rice agriculture based on hereditary occupation groups and castes. The Kerala region witnessed an additional transformation—a major human ecological transformation. This was a traumatic and fundamental transformation of the low-lying wetland ecosystem through the slow but steady process of the making of paddy fields out of the water-logged and water saturated natural landscape. Presumably a massive but diffuse task of labour mobilization probably involving capture and forceful physical subjection of many to servitude akin to slavery, it required several structural, institutional, and ideological means of coercion, besides the relevant knowledge system and technology of social management enabled by the brahmanical hegemony.

NOTES AND REFERENCES

1. See V.C. Haimendorf, 1982, *The Tribes of India*, Los Angeles, CA, pp. 41–2; V.C. Haimendorf, 1953, 'New Aspects of the Dravidian Problem', *TC*, 2(2); F.R. Allchin, 1963, *Neolithic Cattle-Keepers of South India*. Cambridge, pp. 62–4. For archaeological details specific to the region see, T. Balakrishnan Nair, 1977, *The Problem of Dravidian Origins: A Linguistic, Anthropological and Archaeological Approach*, Madras, pp. 30–6. For a study of Iron Age in the Tamil South, see, Guru Raja Rao, 1972, *The Megalithic Culture of South India*, Mysore; L.S. Leshnik, 1974, *South Indian 'Megalithic' Burials: The Pandukal Complex*. Wiesbaden; A. Sundara, 1975, *The Early Chamber Tombs of South India*, Delhi.
2. For details see, Rajan Gurukkal, 1989, 'Forms of Production and Forces of Change in Ancient Tamil Society', *Studies in History: New Series*, 5(2): 159–75.
3. For details see, Rajan Gurukkal, 1998, 'Characterising Ancient Society: The Case of South India', Presidential Address, Indian History Congress, Ancient India Section, Patiala, pp. 24–5.
4. For details of the concept see, Karl Polanyi, 1957, *The Great Transformation: Political and Economic Origins of Our Time*, Boston.

5. For the relevant concepts see, Claude Meillassoux, 1972, 'From Reproduction to Production', in *Economy and Society*, 1(1): 93–105; Claude Meillassoux, 1973, 'The Social Organisation of the Peasantry: Economic Basis of Kinship', *Journal of Peasant Studies*, 1(1): 81–90.
6. Unpublished report on the excavation by Y. Subbarayalu and M.R. Raghava Varier, Calicut, 1997.
7. Several sites like Peruncellur or modern Talipparampa, one of the earliest *brāhmaṇa* settlements in northern Kerala, is noted for Iron Age relics in and around it. Payyannur to the west of Peruncellur and Tiruvadur to the northeast are examples. It is certain that the burial complexes predated the *brāhmaṇa* settlements as consolidated entities. However, the mention of Chellur in an *Ākam* poem by a singer called Mamulanar of about second century BC, as an age old seat of Vedic ritual, points to the possible existence of *brāhmaṇa* households in some centres.
8. A cluster of *brāhmaṇa* households is referred to in the poems as *pārppanac-ceri*. With the tilling clans and non-tilling *brāhmaṇas* each of these *ceris* represented a nexus of new relations of production transcending kinship.
9. *Kīḻkkaṇakku* texts belonging to the AD fourth– fifth centuries that constituted a new class of literature significantly separated from the diction of the heroic tradition. The other category of a radically different source indicating the breakdown of the heroic social formation is a set of two rock inscriptions in Tamil *brāhmi* characters of the AD fifth–sixth centuries. Pulankurichchi Rock inscriptions register the orders of a political authority that bears no comparison with that of predatory chieftains. They provide indications of several *brāhmaṇa* settlements (*mangalam*) having come into existence by the time through royal land-grants, as evidenced by the term *pirammatāya*. The founding of *pirammatāyam*, which a century later acquired greater frequency, as evidenced by a number of copper plates registering *brahmadēya* grants, involved superimposition of the *miyāṭci* rights over the settlers of the land and transformation of the settlers into *kārāḷar*. What is significant about the new process was the allocation of a new position called *kārāṇmai* to the *kuṭi* with implications of their alienation from the control of means of production. For details see, Rajan Gurukkal, 'Characterising Ancient Society'.
10. For a detailed consideration of the issue see Rajan Gurukkal, 1997, 'From Clan and Lineage to Hereditary Occupations and Caste in South India', in Dev Nathan (ed.), *From Tribe to Caste*, Shimla, pp. 205–22.
11. For details of this process in the context of the transformations in Tamilakam as antecedents to the formation of the state in Kerala, see Rajan Gurukkal and Raghava Varier (eds), 1999, *Cultural History of Kerala*, Trivandrum, pp. 257–63.

13

From Clan and Lineage to Hereditary Occupations and Caste*

The transition from 'tribe to class' used to be a universal paradigm for discussing social change in the perspectives of a Marxist evolutionary scheme.[1] Now there is an increasing realization of the fact that a simplistic evolutionary generalization cannot explain the institutional formation, role, dynamics, and foundations of caste, which is why the paradigm of transition from 'tribe to caste' is being discussed here. This however, cannot preclude the relevance of class dynamics in the context, though nobody can ignore the autonomy of caste dynamics.[2] What is required is the study of complex institutional processes involved in the transition from a largely unstratified simple society to a highly stratified complex one. Barring the centrality of caste, which is common to the subcontinent, the process by and large seems to be historically contingent and region-specific. In view of this, this chapter attempts to capture the historical processes of non-complex societies in south India that acquired different modes of stratification, both vertical and temporal. A study of non-complex societies in the region is constrained to anchor on the early historic period in the absence of more archaic sources.

The dawn of early historic India is marked by the widespread distribution of iron-using people belonging to different stands of the Black and Red Ware (BRW) tradition, probably giving a linguistic and cultural homogeneity to the region by about the mid-first millennium BC.[3] But these societies were hardly homogeneous in terms of their economic situation, which, in spite of the technology of iron, represented varying strategies of subsistence

* This chapter is a reproduced version of, 1993–4, 'From Clan and Lineage to Hereditary Occupations and Caste in South India', *Indian Historical Review*, XXII(1–2): 22–33.

such as hunting, gathering, herding, and shifting cultivation adapted under different ecological conditions.[4] There were considerable variations in the productivity of labour even in the same economy under different ecological conditions and social processes. However, these differences were not enough to extricate any of them from the status of non-complex societies.[5]

Transcending their socio-economic variations, these self-sustaining entities coexisted and interacted with one another, accomplishing a common horizon of shared cultural practices, apart from the internal dynamic as part of the historical process of the subcontinent determining the nature of institutional transformations. The external dynamic was constituted by the brahmanical, Jain, and Buddhist intrusion, trade contacts, and the impact of the Mauryan state.[6] It was a long process, resulting in a social milieu of class segmention into lineages that festooned into domestic groups subsisting on one economy or the other.

The overall socio-economic scenario of the region in the Christian era is perhaps best represented in the *tiṇai* concept of the Tamil heroic poetics, which comprehends Tamilakam (the land between the hills of Venkatam and the tip of Kanyakumari) as consisting of five micro eco-zones: ***kuṛiñji*** (hilly backwoods), ***pālai*** (parched areas), ***mullai*** (pastoral tracts), ***marutam*** (wetland), and ***neital*** (the littoral).[7] It is not a mechanical compartmentalization of the natural landscape into five segments; the whole was conceived as a continuum with no point of beginning or end, interspersed with the the relative dominance of one or the other of the tiṇais. The concept of eco-zones includes the people and their modes of subsistence in the respective ecotypes. Accordingly, the ***vēṭar*** and ***kuṛavar*** (hunters and shifting cultivators) inhabited the ***kuṛiñji***; the ***maṛavar*** (warriors) the ***pālai***; the ***iṭaiyar*** (pastoralists) the ***mullai***; the ***uḻavar*** (ploughmen) subsisted on the ***marutam***; and the ***paratavar*** (fishing community) settled along the ***neital***. In areas where ***tiṇais*** merged, the social groups as well as the form of subsistence made a mixed appearance. The poetic specifications about the eco-zones and the modes of human adaptation to them help us identify contemporary forms of production in different landscape ecosystems of the Tamilakam of those times and the archaeological relics of the Iron Age which overlap the period of the poems corroborate the identification.[8]

As discussed, the poetics have a further physiographic classification of the land into the ***vanpulam*** (all the ***tiṇais***, except ***marutam***) and the ***menpulam***, which differentiates the large tracts of lesser productivity from those of better quality. These concepts of physiographic division and classification are not just poetic prescriptions to build imaginary relations: they are representations of reality carried forward to poetics. What we deduce from them is some idea about the historically existing micro eco-zones and their respective economies such as hunting, herding, shifting agriculture, crafts production, and wetland cultivation. The use of the plough during the period is well attested by the allusions in heroic poems.[9] Of all the forms of production, plough agriculture was obviously the superior one in terms of technology and productivity. But it was more or less confined to river banks and other wetland tracts surrounded by extensive dry zones of stock rearing and shifting cultivation. Most of the crafts seem to have been attached to pastoral agriculture.

The peoples of the micro eco-zones, irrespective of their forms of production, were clan-based descent groups dispersed into domestic segments (*kuṭis*) around each one's clan settlement (*ūr*). Each *kuṭi* was an independent production unit belonging to the *ūr* led by a headman (*kiḻār*) whose authority resided on clan ties.[10] The *kiḻār* as the embodiment of the clan, commanded the resources of the *ūr* to which the respective clansmen (*kuṭimākkal*) had access through the institution of redistribution.[11] Each clan had its own *ūr* and *kiḻār*, as is borne out by the poems. The principal clans referred to as *kuṭimākkal* were *vēṭar*/*vēṭṭuvar*, *kuṟavar*, *āyar*, *maṟavar*, *uḻavar*, and *paratavar* who had their own specific settlements and headmen along the respective eco-zones bound by kinship. The headmen are referred tom in the poems as *kō-makan*/*perumakan* (the hero son) of the respective clans, indicating the centrality of kinship, which was the basis of production relations. Despite the differing strategies of subsistence from ecotype to ecotype, kinship was central to the division of labour. In all forms of production, the *kuṭi* functioned as the repository of familial labour generated by the young (*iḷaiyar*) and the old (*mutiyar*) among the agnatic kin.[12] The primacy of kin labour precluded the possibility of social stratification or division of an evolved type.

This is not to suggest that kinship-based production units of a uniform nature existed all over the region in a pure form, as has often been construed. There were differences. What can be discerned is an array of variants representing different stages of transformation, the relative status of which is intelligible only against a defined category. The degrees of differences apart, the societies were structured by the dominance of kinship. It is relevant here to characterize the levels of differences in order to see what tended to erode the centrality of kin labour in which pattern of subsistence. This requires us to try and understand the nature of accessibility of each economy to an appropriation of contemporary technology, social conditions of labour realization, and productivity of labour.

The level of technology around the turn of the Christian era is marked by metal-smelting, weaving, glass-making, stone-cutting, pottery, and other crafts mentioned in indigenous literary sources and foreign notices. There are archaeological correlations for metal works, glass industry, brick construction, weaving, pearl fisheries, stone-cutting, and pottery.[13] Except for huge dolmens and rock-cut chamber tombs, no monumental buildings seem to have existed, as testified by the relics. How the people worked and who controlled each craft under what social conditions constitute the most crucial aspects, which we would never be able to precisely know about. But the fragments that have been found help us formulate ideas about the broad features of the overall social milieu of the archaeological relics.

The most significant of such fragments is found in the heroic poems. There are references to the womenfolk of the pastoral tracts engaged in weaving, which suggest that the craft was practised by the *kuṭi*-based relations of kin labour.[14] Metal-working and pot-making were different. As the most widely used metal, iron had a central place among metals as the base of weapons; its significance in a society based on plunder, booty capture, and redistribution is irrefutable. Moreover, the practice of burying iron goods along with the dead must have pushed large quantities iron out of circulation. Although we cannot figure out the actual amount in the absence of classified data, this must have definitely increased the need for continuous iron-working. Iron-smelting, therefore, was a full-time occupation presupposing hereditary specialization of the craft through a specific domestic group. Evidence for the existence of domestic groups specializing in metal work dates back to circa 200 BC, the period of a Tamil *Brāhmi* label referring to *kolavar* the blacksmith.[15] The heroic poems contain numerous references to a blacksmith (*kollar*) attached to an *ūr* or a chief, confirming his status as a full-time craftsman.[16] Similarly, potters (*kuyavar*) are also mentioned as a domestic group with a full-time occupation, marked by continuity.[17] The brittleness of the pots required frequent replacement, resulting in groups of *kollan* and *kuyavar* becoming separate domestic segments from the clan in the process of hereditary specialization by the turn of the Christian era.

The number of such full-time groups of hereditary occupations was greater in the headquarters of bigger chieftains called the *vēḷir*, who controlled large hills with numerous settlements. As the major redistributive pools of resources, the chieftains' settlements could support more full-time craftsmen and other functionaries who were controlled by the *vēḷir*. The bigger chieftains had hegemony over the headmen of settlements within their domain, the extent of which, though flexible, was maintained through predatory operations and forced exaction (*tiṟai*). These were mostly warrior headmen (*maṟavar*) who helped the chieftain in predatory campaigns and got a share of the booty through redistribution.

Non-craftsmen who became full-time functionaries of a hereditary nature were the warriors (*maṟavar*). Every settlement (*ūr*) needed full-time warriors since the principal mode of contemporary resource appropriation was plunder. Plunder raids were fundamental to the maintenance of the redistributive economy that characterized the lesser and bigger chieftains alike.[18] The flower symbolism associated with different kinds of raids such as *veṭci* (cattle raid), *karantai* (cattle recovery), *vañji* (chieftain's raid), and *kāñji* (defending raid) prescribed in the Tamil heroic poetics shows how instituted and frequent a plunder raid was, in those times. The poems emphasize the then hereditary nature of warriorhood through the characteristic eulogies hailing the family tradition of a warrior, normally a warrior headman (*maṟavar*).[19] In association with the *ūr* of the *maṟavar*, there existed the *kuṭis* of three others: *pāṇar* (the bards), *paṟaiyar* (who play the drum called *paṟa*), and *tuṭiyar* (who play the small drum called *tuṭi*) who seem to have lived as full-time functionaries.[20] The bards were normally attached to the headman of the respective *ūr* and they lived on gifts (*koṭai*) for singing the praise of his exploits. Many of them roamed around several settlements, disseminating stories about his heroic exploits. Often they accompanied their patron heroes to the sites of raid and obtained a share of the booty as the reward for composing eulogies. References in the poem to the *pāṇar* imparting the craft of oral compositions to their children point to the hereditary nature of the bardic profession.[21] The drummers, *paṟaiyar* and *tuṭiyar*, gave musical accompaniment to the preparations for raids (*uṇṭāṭṭu*) or predatory marches, and redistributive feasts and rituals. It appears that in the process of specialization these three groups branched off from the maṟavar as domestic segments of hereditary occupation.

The *vēḷir* chiefs represented the stage of lineage formation, as is clear in the case of Atikamān and Āy lineages, which separated them from clan ties with their people. It is evident that the resource potential varied from chiefdom to chiefdom, a few of them being relatively better-off. The exchange relations with the Gangetic valley and the Graeco-Roman world must have enabled some of these hill chieftains to secure gold, silver, horses, and other prestigious objects which they circulated as gifts to raise their own status and ranking. The house of a high-ranking vēḷir was called *koil*, as in the case of the Āy-vel. It was surrounded by *nakar*, probably consisting of different *cēris*. A *cēri* signified a site that hereditary occupation groups put together as a means to ensure the permanency of their service.[22] This would imply the existence of some kind of stratification of the society into the ruling lineage, hereditary occupation groups, and clansmen.

The stratification was much more evolved in the headquarters of the biggest category of chieftains called *vēntar*. The three ruling lineages, often mentioned as *muvēntar*, consisting of Cēras, Cōḻas, and Pāṇḍyas, had their coastal towns (*paṭṭiṇam*) and interior headquarters (*nakar*) such as Karur and Muciṟi of the Cēras, Madurai, and Kōrkai of the Pāṇḍyas, and Uraiyūr and Puhār of the Cōḻas, respectively. Commanding the resources of numerous settlements within a macro-region (*nāṭu*) through predatory control and subjugation often extending over the domains of the *vēḷir*, this category of chieftains had emerged as well-established ruling lineages without clan ties. Following perhaps the Mauryan model, some of them considered themselves to be the beloved of gods (*imayavarampan*/*vānavarampan*) and, being under brahmanical influence, were the patrons of Vedic rituals (*palyāgaśālai*, *rājasūyam vēṭṭa*). This shows a totally different ritual status in the making in contradistinction to that of the other categories of chiefs. Their resource potential was enormously high, the range of domination extensive and redistributive social relationships elaborate and complex. They were able to attract a large number of *brāhmaṇa* bards (*pulavar*) who exposed them to the Vedic, Śāstrāic, and Purāṇic means of political legitimation.[23] It is true that a few *brāhmaṇa* bards eulogized the *vēḷir* chiefs also, but by and large the majority of them took to singing the exploits of the *mūventar*. With their supreme political status and near monopoly over all cultural channels of legitimation, the *vēḷir* and the *kiḻār* were the two levels of hierarchy in descending order, although there is no evidence of a running thread of political control from top to the bottom.

The *vēntar* level of resource pooling, redistribution, and political control implied the emergence of new hereditary occupations. In the position, status, roles, and prestige within the complex redistributive relationship was only natural. References to *ēnāti* (*sēnāpati*) as a status conferred by the *mūventar* upon their trustworthy *kiḻār*, point to one clear instance.[24] The act of redistribution and gift-giving, which implies differences in terms of material possessions, amounts to allocation of differential status and roles as well.[25] However, the stratification reflected in the poems is that of a binary between the high-born (*uyarntōr*) and the low-born (*iḻipiṟappāḷar*), which seems primarily to distance the *brāhmaṇas* from the folk. The relatively flexible nature of the second category and the absence of a clear notion of stratification are evident from the lack of indicators suggesting intermediary positions. Similarly, the differentiation in terms of the objective conditions of life was also confined to the binary between those with redistributive power (*puravalar*) and their dependents (*iravalar*).

In the *paṭṭiṇam* and *nakaram* under the control of the *mūvēntar*, cēris of a new occupational group emerged. It appears that in the ports and ruling headquarters, several hereditary craftsmen and specialized functionaries drawn from the hinterlands worked and perhaps got organized into corporate bodies (*nikamam*).[26] The various industries, particularly those of textile and glass at the coastal towns, must have engaged full-time craftsmen. Who controlled these industries is not clear and the possibility of their management by foreigners is not ruled out.[27] A point to be borne in mind in this context is the nature of contemporary exchange which was an extension of the domestic mode of reciprocity, though it involved the use of gold and silver coins or bullion which functioned not as means of payment nor as a measure of value, but as valuables.[28] It is against this background that one has to examine the relatively lesser role the local merchants seem to have played in the long-distance trade of the Greeks, Egyptians, Philistines, and Arabs, and assume that contemporary harbour towns were primarily the colonies of foreign merchants. The question of chieftainly control of long-distance exchange is unclear. In the case of pearl fishing, captives are said to have been used by the Pāṇḍyas. The captives must have been employed for heavy labour in *paṭṭiṇam* and *nakaram* by the other two *vēntar* lineages also. Probably both the ruling authority and organized merchant groups (*vāṇikar*) used the labour of the servile people through coercion. What could be significant about the nature of labour processes under conditions of coercion is the formation of relations transcending kinship.

The real replacement of the kinship basis of production relations began around the *brāhmaṇa* households in the tracts of plough agriculture. A *brāhmaṇa* household represented the nucleus of a totally different unit of production vis-à-vis the *kuṭis* of *uḻavar*, which were independent production units based on familial labour drawn from the agnatic kin and affinal relatives. The produce was collectively appropriated by the *kuṭis* through the instituted practices of reciprocity and redistribution presided over by their headman (*ūr-kiḻār*) who normally had clan ties with the people (*kuṭimākkal*).[29] However, headmen without clan ties was not unlikely since the control over wetland areas was always a major attraction for the warrior headmen (*maṛavar*) who helped *vēntar* chieftains in their predatory campaigns. It appears that raids involved the capture of ūr and its redistribution among warrior headmen, which would mean the imposition of alien power. The position of the headmen of *uḻavar-kuṭi*s was, therefore, vulnerable. Nevertheless, the placement of a warrior headman on the *ūr* does not imply any fundamental change in the relations of production, since it is only a superimposition of an extraneous right of appropriation. On the contrary, the scholarly bards and Vedic priests, who also benefited from the *brāhmaṇa* institutions of redistribution and gift-giving, symbolized a radical transformation of the relations of production and conditions of labour realization. A *brāhmaṇa* household, constrained to subsist on agriculture, presupposes some permanent arrangement ensuring the required extraneous familial labour. The arrangement, implying a rupture in the existing pattern of kin labour and collective appropriation, meant the formation of a new system of relations enabling the *brāhmaṇa* to own the means of production and appropriate clansmen-labour under conditions of extra-economic coercion.

How the *brāhmaṇa* introduced non-kin labour in a society where labour and kinship were interconnected, is a vexed issue, since we do not have any clues to the exact nature of the process. Hence it is a matter of explanatory deduction based on a logical construct, rather than empirical description until direct evidence is available. The impact of this rupture was, however, confined to the premises of isolated households and their economies since the *brāhmaṇa* continued to be primarily Vedic priests with a pastoral bias during the period. However, the new system of production relations that emerged around the *brāhmaṇa* households constituted the most potential contradictory dynamic of social transformation. This becomes clear when viewed against the contradictions immanent in the aggregate of conflicting economies.

Of all the contradictions, the most striking was the plight of plough agriculture, which failed to secure its conditions of expansion. Predatory campaigns of chieftains and the resulting destruction of agriculture and agrarian settlements were strangulating it despite its status as the form of production that was superior in terms of technology and productivity.[30] That such a form of production could not dominate is the significant aspect of contradiction. It was dryland agriculture accompanied by herding that dominated the economy, as evidenced by predatory politics, the redistributive society, and heroic culture. The systemic existence of mutually conflicting economies dominated by pastoral agriculture was persistently giving rise to forces dissolving the system itself. It was not possible for the socio-economic aggregate to continue functioning as a system for a longer period with its low labour productivity and failing economic reproduction.[31] The complex redistributive system and the instituted practice of gift-giving generated the contradictory dynamic accentuating the process of kinship erosion and fissioning of clans. It is in this context that the contradictory dynamic of the new system of production which evolved in a household is considered important. Its potential as a *brāhmaṇa* alternative system of production, transcending the limitations of kin labour and as a new way of resolving the contradictions, makes it historically decisive in a dissolving social formation.

There is no direct evidence for a total crisis leading to the dissolution of the early historic Tamil society. But a disjunction is explicit in the sources, both archaeological and literary, which in their spatio-temporal contexts would have us believe that by the close of the AD third century, many of the characteristic features of the social formation had phased out. There is a marked decline in the post-third century layers of the major archaeological sites, with the exception of a couple of Buddhist centres that continued to flourish.[32] The three ruling lineages of the Cēras, Cōḻas, and Pāṇḍyas went into oblivion together with their politics of plunder, redistributive economy, and the heroic compositions of typical bardic diction. Historians have been associating this phenomenon with the inroads of a predatory people named the *Kaḷabhras* from the uplands of Karnataka, who are said to have swept through the domains of the Tamil chieftains and caused their eclipse. The *Kaḷabhra* episode, however, does not provide an intelligible explanation for the fundamental change that took place. What is to be emphasized as a social scientific explanation is the role of the contradictory dynamic of the social formation that was maturing through the years. It is not unlikely that the predatory marches of the *Kaḷabhras* accentuated the process which seemingly had deleterious effects on *brāhmaṇa* households. The hardships of the period, transmitted as dreadful memories in a few copper plates of the eighth and ninth centuries across generations of people, have allusions equating the sufferings to those of the Kali Age.

A much greater and more solid factor that stresses discontinuity is the presence of a new and radically different class of literature called the *Kīḻkkaṇakku* works and a few inscriptions belonging to the AD fourth–fifth centuries. Most of the *Kīḻkkaṇakku* works are didactical and avowedly ethical, stressing the importance of peace, loyalty, and morality. The existence of a body of literature emphasizing such values presupposes a situation where people desperately wanted them. What is significant here is their emphasis on obedience, hard work, and loyalty as the ethical postulates of an ideal society. These values as imposing pieces of advice or exhortations signify productive relations developing across fissioning clan-segments of hereditary occupations. They make sense in the context of a chaotic society straining at the leash to stabilize its new relations.

The new production relations in their institutionalized form appear in a couple of rock inscriptions roughly of the AD fifth–sixth centuries from Pulankurichchi. These inscriptions register transactions of certain tracts of land and *dēvakulams* to place them under the *brāhmaṇa* landholders of a few *brahmadēyas* and lay down the rights, privileges, and obligations of landholders, leaseholders, and actual tillers, a structure almost entirely alien to the heroic society. The records introduce two terms, *miyāṭci* and *kārāṇmai*, indicative of control over the means of production and entitlement to a share of crops respectively, the former vested with the *brāhmaṇa* households and the latter with the non-*brāhmaṇa* settlements (*mangalam*) having come into existence by the time through royal land-grants, as evidenced by the term *pirammatāyam*. The founding of *pirammatāyam*, which a century later acquired greater frequency, as evidenced by a number of copper plates registering *brahmadēya* grants, involved superimposition of the *miyāṭci* rights over the settlers of the land and transformation of the settlers (*kuṭis*) into *karalar* (leaseholder). What is striking about the process was the allocation of a new position called *kārāṇmai* to the *kuṭi* with implications of their alienation from the control of means of production.

The *brāhmaṇa* landholding, as distinguished from the communal holding known to the heroic society almost a century ago, was only a microcosm of what we see in the Pulankurichchi records. They show that institutions like *dēvakulam* and *kottam* had become land-based by this period. There are indications of other institutional formations such as *perumtiṇai* (probably an office for the appropriation of agricultural dues) and *nāṭukāppār* (the watch and ward of the agrarian locality), which are specific to an agrarian society of asymmetrical relations. In short, despite the linkage in terms of production relations, the earlier *brāhmaṇa* households and the subsequently evolved *pirammatāyam* settlements were two different entities. The disjunction between the two is not that of the two distinct sources of disparate periods blinding us about the evolutionary process, but of the two social formations: one dominated by the relations of pastoral agriculture and the other tending to be dominated by the plough agriculture. Here plough agriculture does not simply represent agriculture using the plough, which by itself hardly signifies any radical transformation, but a new system of productive relations tending to dominate the society.

The development of relations in plough agriculture towards domination of the total society was a process of the proliferation of occupational specializations and their ordering into a hierarchy. We have already referred to the emergence of hereditary occupations in the chieftains' settlements with a greater proportion in coastal towns, marketing centres, and ruling headquarters, and the trend of differential allocation of positions and roles at the instance of the highest chiefly authority anticipating the formation of a hierarchy. What began taking shape in the *brāhmaṇa* households was much more crucial for the real beginnings of the hierarchy. The permanent workforce attached to the *brāhmaṇa* households had the greatest possibility of being conceived hierarchically because of the stratifying system of production relations and the brahmanical tradition of social differentiation. The notion of hierarchy was implicit in the system of production in which the relations between two objectively antagonistic classes was fundamental. As regards the *brāhmaṇa* tradition of social differentiation, with the experience of social stratification as a part of the history of brahmanism and its theoretical abstractions into *varṇa* and sankīrṇajati as central to its legacy, there is no need of any explanation.[33] It is only natural that the *brāhmaṇa* contemporary south India, which inherited the Vedic, Śāstrāic, and Purāṇic scholarship, had the traditional perception and appreciation of their society.[34] They could have conceived the society of functionally specific families attached to their households only in terms of the hierarchy of occupations and social status implicit in the Śāstrāic explanations about *jātis*.

The brahmanical perception and appreciation of social groups would, however, just not be enough for the society to become hierarchically structured in the idiom of *jāti*. Even the existence of preconditions such as hereditary occupations, asymmetrical social relations, and differential allocations of positions would not help us to deduce the prevalence of the *jāti* hierarchy. It was the dominant position of the *brāhmaṇas* that was crucial in the operation of the *jāti* hierarchy. The tacitly recognized ritual supremacy, resource potential, social control, political influence, and cultural skills provided the *brāhmaṇas* with conditions of domination. They symbolized the authority of collective norms and took precedence over the ruling powers. Their hegemony over the communication channels and ideological structures of legitimation had made them a determinant force of political authority by the sixth century. On top of it all, their status as custodians of higher wisdom about the universe, practical knowledge about the cycles of seasons, and their calendrical measurements enabling prediction of natural changes had added to the ritual charisma of the *brāhmaṇa*s. It was this enormous potential of social control, coupled with the growing domination of the means of production which, subsuming all differential categories and groups in due course, encompassed the total society.

This is not to suggest that brahmanization of social stratification was a conscious project of the *brāhmaṇa*s. It was a historically and culturally contingent effect rather than the result of a conspiratorial scheming, though articulations of *brāhmaṇa*s as a spatio-temporally and culturally significant community were casually linked to the process. The *brāhmaṇa*s do not seem to have manipulated the political space to order the differential relations of production into the hierarchy of *jāti*s. The notion of the 'pure self' and the 'impure other', originally constituted the basis of *jāti*; it was tribal and a part of the horizontal social division of the primeval kind. The formation of *jāti*s along the domestic groups of hereditary occupations was brahmanical. In fact, even in northern India, proliferation of *jāti*s was due to the socio-economic processes and not to brahmanism, which only explained the phenomenon through the Śāstrāic idiom. This seems to be linked to the *brāhmaṇa* notion of purity and pollution as fundamental and the central point of reference for determining the relative status of each *jāti*. In short, what is brahmanical is not *jāti* but the notion of hierarchy. Hierarchy as such, however, is not merely a notional construct of brahmanism, but was derived from the objective conditions related to the forces and relations of production. The *brāhmaṇa* contribution was ideological, in which the notion of the *jāti* hierarchy acquired an institutional power, legitimizing and stabilizing the relations of production. Further, it had the specific historical context of operation at the junction of an agrarian technology and the social strategy of labour realization, necessitating institutional devices for stabilizing hierarchical stratification.

How *brāhmaṇa*s succeeded in providing the institutional devices has to be examined in the context of the culturally and historically contingent conditions of social domination which we have briefly indicated earlier. An elaborate discussion of the conditions is not within the scope of this chapter, which can only take their multiple dimensions for granted. It is their discursive aspect which we are trying to highlight here as part of a regime generally not dealt with in historical studies.[35] The emergence of brahmanism as the major discourse in the region generating knowledge about the Daksiṇāpatha, its peoples and cultures, spreading a new pattern of thinking, and transforming the local modes of social existence, constituted the historical context. It was the hegemonic form of representation involving a myriad of strategies where new forms of knowledge and power converged. The argument here is that the success of brahmanical domination and the establishment of the *jāti* hierarchy were discursively realized goals. What seems to be crucial is the discursive power of brahmanical perception through which the society came to perceive itself. The *brāhmaṇa* perception of *jātis* as hierarchically structured, happened to be acceptable as the natural social reality through this discursive process of domination. *Jāti* hierarchy was, in short, the effect of the brahmanical form of social representation which became hegemonic around the AD mid-first millennium, a temporal junction that witnessed the expansion of a technology of production and social strategies of labour realization, leading to the proliferation of hereditary occupations.

The mid-first millennium was a turning point in terms of stratification and hierarchical ordering which took more than two centuries to characterize the social aggregate. It is in the sixth century that we see the new agrarian system articulating its political control as manifested in the monarchies of the Pallava (Simhavishnu line), Pāṇḍya (Kaṭunkon line), Cōḻa (Vijayalaya line), and Cēra (Makotai line), the emergence of which was interrelated with agrarian expansion. The proliferation of hereditary occupations and their absorption into the *jāti* hierarchy were ongoing processes through new institutional agencies, of which the temple ranked foremost. Other institutional formations like service tenements, both in the domains of the temple and the king, crystallized hereditary occupations into *jāti* to hierarchy. A notable feature of the process was alienation of the *kuṭis* to the extent of total deprivation of all rights (*kuṭinīkki*), the earliest mention of which is in the Pallankoil plates of Simhavarman (circa AD 550).

The stratification later on brought in a differentiation among the *kuṭis* giving rise to a category of mere tillers (*uḻu-kuṭi*) without entitlement to *kārāṇmai*. We hear about *veṭṭikkuṭi* (*veṭṭi*/*viṣṭi*) in later inscriptions, a much more subjected group among the primary producers, indicative of the conditions of labour appropriation. This process of the agrarian structure imposing a social division of labourers and non-labourers necessitated an array of institutions in order to regulate and pre-empt class tension. Caste was perhaps the most crucial and the earliest factor that interlocked the numerous hereditary functionaries based on diverse rules of different domains.

To sum up the socio-economic processes in the region at the turn of the Christian era, the modes of stratification, remained by and large flexible despite the beginnings of hereditary occupations and allocation of differential roles and functions at the highest political level. The potential site of the emergence of non-kin labour and hierarchical stratification comprised the *brāhmaṇa* households which necessitated a permanent workforce and its order in a hierarchical form. The formation of caste was a culturally contingent effect of the brahmanical perception and appreciation of the social relations emanating from a system of production based on the expropriation of unpaid surplus labour.

NOTES AND REFERENCES

1. K. Marx, 1959, *Capital*, vol. III, Moscow, pp. 962–3; K. Marx and F. Engels, 1948, *The Communist Manifesto*, London.
2. See the discussions in Andre Béteille, 1965, *Caste, Class and Power*, California University Press, Berkley; cf. C. Bougle, 1971, *Essays on the Caste System*, D. Pocock (trans.), Cambridge; L. Dumont, 1972, *Homo Hierarchicus: The Caste System and its Implications*, Mark Sainsbury (trans.), London.
3. The different stands are studied in B. Narasimaiah, 1964–5, 'Exploration in Districts North Arcot and Salem', in *Indian Archaeology: A Review* (*IAR*); see also Exploration Reports on Shimoga (*IAR*, 1964–65) and Dharmapun (*IAR*, 1967–8); Lawrence S. Leshnik, 1974, *The South Indian 'Megalithic' Burials: The Pandukal Complex*, Wiesbaden; A. Sundara, 1975, Early Chamber Tombs of South India, Delhi; B. Narasimaiah, 1980, *Neolithic and Megalithic Culture in Tamil Nadu*, New Delhi; N.R. Banerjee, 1965, *The Iron Age in India*, Delhi; B.K. Gururaja Rao, 1972, *Megalithic Culture in South India*, Mysore; T. Balakrishnan Nair, 1977, *The Problems of Dravidian Origins: A Linguistic, Anthropological and Archaeological Approach*, Madras.
4. Rajan Gurukkal, 'Forms of Production and Forest of Change in Ancient Tamil Society', *Studies in History*, 5(2): 159, New Series.
5. A different argument is developed in Sudarshan Seneviratne, forthcoming, 'Press State Societies: Transformations in the Political Ecology of South India with Special Reference to Tamil Nadu' in R. Champakalakshmi (ed.) *State in Pre-Colonial South India*.
6. The impact of the Mauryan state over the far south has been ably discussed in M.G.S. Narayanan, 1977, 'The Mauryan Problem in Sangam Works', in his *Reinterpretations in South Indian History*, Trivandrum, pp. 83–4.
7. See *Poruḷatikāram*, 5 (*Poruḷ*) of *Tolkāppiyām* and commentator of *Iḷampūraṇam*, Madras, 1965, and Nāccinārkiṉṉiyam, Tirumali, 1948. To

Tolkappiyar, it was nothing more than a mere poetic concept. Commentators of his *Porul, Iḷampuraṇam*, and Naccinakiṇṇiyam interpreted the concept as pertaining to the 'general theme or content' and 'behaviour', respectively. Being far removed from the period of the poems, these commentators had no grasp of the original implications of the concept or of the period of the poems, and had no idea about the original implications of the concept of the anthropological context of its origins.

8. Historians have offered various interpretations to the concept of the *tiṇai*. Some have discerned a pattern of social evolution in the fivefold division and debated the actual order of the five tiṇais. See, V.R.R. Dikshitar, 1936, *Studies in Tamil Literature and History*, Madras, p. 178; Xavier S. Thaninayakam, 1966, *Landscape and Poetry*, London, p. 39; Kamil V. Zvelebil, 1960, 'Tamil Poetry 2000 Years Ago', *New Orient*, No. 5, p. 16. It signified the pattern of human evolution in world history to N. Subrahmanian, See his, 1966, *Sangam Polity*, Madras, p. 49. K. Sivathamby, agrees fundamentally with the unilinear evolutionist concept, but he rightly stresses that the tiṇais were contemporary physiographic and socio-economic reality in the light of evidence from *Āṟṟuppaṭai* literature (*Cirupanāṟṟupaṭai*, II, 143–202 and *Perumpanāṟṟuppaṭai*, II. 46–392). See, his, 1974, 'Early South Indian Society and Economy', *Social Scientist*, vol. 29, New Delhi, p. 26. See the discussions in Rajan Gurukkal, 'Forms of Production and Forces of Change in Ancient Tamil Society'.
9. In fact the term *koḻu* is mentioned in a label inscription (circa second century BC) of Anamalai, I. Mahadevan, 1966, *Corpus of the Tamil Brahmi Inscriptions*, Madras. The terms used in the poems are *nāñjil* and *mēḻi*.
10. This reminds one of the situation in a commune as explained by Marx, see Grundrisse (trans.), 1973, Nicolaus, Harmondsworth, pp. 476–7; its basic aspects such as the individual means of production, self-sustaining nature, and collective sharing are relevant here.
11. The concept of redistribution refers to the centralization of goods or rights over good and their subsequent reallocation. See K. Polanyi, 1959, 'The Economy as Instituted Process', in Polanyi *et al.* (ed.), *Trade Market in the Early Empirers*, Glencoe, pp. 243–5; Barry Hindess and Paul Q. Hirst, 1975, *Pre-Capitalist Modes of Production*, London, pp. 45–9.
12. *Akanānūṟu*, 161–4, 182, 188, 216, and 248.
13. For reference, see studies cited under note 3 above.
14. *Puṟanānūṟu*, 127–70, *Naṟṟiṇai*, 353.
15. Mahadevan, *Corpus of the Tamil Brahmi Inscriptions.*
16. *Puṟanānūṟu*, 170 and 312; *Akanānūru*, 96. *Puṟanānūṟu*, 180 mentions a blacksmith attached to a chieftain.
17. *Naṟṟiṇai*, 200, 293:2.
18. A majority of the raids were for cattle. The significance of cattle raids in the contemporary society has been adequately brought out by M.G.S. Narayana in his paper, 1977, 'Cattle Raiders of the Sangam Age; *Proceedings of the*

Indian History Congress I (hereafter *PIHC*), 38th session, Bhubaneswar, pp. 70–82.

19. *Kutinilai-uraittal* is a *turai* of songs specifically meant for extolling the tradition of warrior families. *Ēṟāṇmullai* and *Vallāṇmullai* are two other related tuṟais. See the relevant poems in *Puṟanāṉūṟu*.
20. *Puṟanāṉūṟu*, 335. Mankuṭi *kiḻār* provides a graphic picture of a settlement in the dry zone. For a different interpretation of the settlement and the people there, see M.G.S Narayanan, 1983, 'The Warrior Settlement of the Sangam Age', *PIHC*, 43rd session, Kurukshetra, pp. 102–9.
21. See the discussions in K. Kailasapathy, 1968, *Tamil Heroic Poetry*, London.
22. The term *cēris* is derived from *cēr*, meaning 'to mix', see Robert Caldwell, 1974, *A Comparative Grammar of the Dravidian or South Indian Family of Languages*, first Indian edition, New Delhi, p. 550; T. Burrow and M.B. Emeneau, 1961, *A Dravidian Etymological Dictionary*, London, p. 643.
23. A common method of legitimation is through the mention of the hero's direct association with the epic characters of events, *Puṟanāṉūṟu*, 2. Sometimes the chieftains are equated to the Purāṇic deities, see *Puṟanāṉūṟu*, 56–7.
24. *Puṟanāṉūṟu*, 167–74.
25. See the discussions in Marcel Mauss, 1954, *The Gift*, London, pp. 36–41; C.A. Gregory, 1983, *Gifts and Commodities*, London.
26. Mahadevan, *Corpus of the Tamil Brahmi Inscriptions*. A certain nikamattōr (members of *Nigamam*, a local body) of the place called Vellarai is mentioned in a label inscription of Mangulam; this obviously refers to the members of the body of merchants at Vellarai.
27. See the relevant concepts developed in K. Polanyi, 1957, *The Great Transformation: The Political and Economic Origin of Our Time*, Boston, pp. 55–63; Shereen Ratnagar, 1981, *Encounters: The Westerly Trade of the Harappa Civilization*, Delhi, pp. 231–6; and the Introduction in C. Renfrew and S. Shennen (eds), 1982, *Ranking, Resource and Exchange: Aspects of the Archaeology of Early European Society*, Cambridge.
28. Gurukkal, 'Forms of Production and Forces of Change in Ancient Tamil Society'. For a detailed discussion on the nature of Indo-Roman trade, see Romila Thapar, 1992, 'Black Gold: South Asia and the Roman Maritime Trade', South Asia, New Series, vol. XV, no. 2.
29. *Puṟanāṉūṟu*, 353, 376, 391, 396, refer to the pooling of the harvest at the chieftains' residences and its subsequent redistribution.
30. There is a detailed discussion of the problem in Rajan Gurukkal, 1987, 'Early Iron Age Economy: Problem of Agrarian Expansion in Tamilakam', in B.D. Chattopadhyaya (ed.), *Ancient Indian Economic History*, Delhi.
31. See the relevant concepts about the limitations of redistributive economy based on kinship developed in Hindess and Hirst, *Pre-Capitalist Modes of Production*, pp. 73–8; C. Meillassoux, 1972, 'From Reproduction to Production', *Economy and Society*, vol. I, no. 1; E. Terray, 1972, *Marxism*

and Primitive Societies, New York, pp. 96–8. Also see the discussions on the economic implications of kin labour in C. Meillassoux, 1973, 'The Social Organisation of the Peasantry: Economic Basis of Kinship', *Journal of Peasant Studies*, vol. I, no. I, p. 81.

32. See T.V. Mahalingam, 1970, 'Report on the Excavations in the Lower Kaveri Valley, University of Madras; and *Indian Archaeology: A Review* (1964–5). For empirical data on the post-third century decline reflected at the archaeological sites, see R.S. Sharma, 1987, *Urban Decay in India (c.300–c.1000)*, New Delhi, p. 84.
33. That the term varṇa denotes a theory rather than reality is implicit in the analysis in R. Thapar, 1984, *From Lineage to State*, New Delhi, pp. 169–171.
34. See the discussion in M.G.S. Narayanan, 1975, 'Vedic, Puranic, Sastraic Elements in Tamil Sangam Society and Culture', *PIHC*, 36th session, Aligarh, pp. 76–91.
35. The concept of discourse is borrowed from Michel Foucault, 1972, *The Archaeology of Knowledge*, New York.

14

Spread of Writing in the Tamil South and Its Social Implications*

The antiquity of the script and its use in the Tamil south is almost contemporaneous to the Aśokan *brāhmi*, the adapted characters of which appear in the region's earliest rock label inscriptions of the Jain and Ājívika caverns located on the hillocks of Ānamalai, a strategic point in the network of trade routes and premises of agrarian settlements in Madurai.[1] The purpose of cave labels on the top of the rock, catching the attention of wayfarers, was obviously to advertise the names of donors who were merchants or chieftains. Some of the menhirs on the wayside had writings on them as allusions in the Tamil heroic poems attest and a few recent archaeological findings corroborate.[2] These label inscriptions addressed themselves to wayfarers, mainly merchants, monks, and chieftains of wider cross-cultural contacts, social relations, and mobility. Long-distance merchants and monks had knowledge of the script, as a part of their occupational requirement, while that might not have been the case of chieftains and wayfarers. However, all of them must have understood what the writing meant symbolically and sometimes even literally through the oral tradition about it.[3] It is always true that more people could read than write. The evidence for the existence of the script and its use does not vouch for the presence of a literate society, for the participation of ordinary people in the written mode of communication need not be direct.[4] A literate society is the one that demands written documents as its most trustworthy proof and, therefore, the clearest symptom of its emergence is proliferation of deeds, which began in the region with the

* This chapter is a modified version of, 2007, 'Shift of Trust from Words to Deeds: Implications of the Proliferation of Inscriptions in the Tamil South', *Indian Historical Review*, XXXIV(2): 16–35.

AD seventh century. Though deeds were being produced at the turn of the fourth century itself as the epigraphs in stone and copper plates of the Pallavas prove, their proliferation occurred only a few centuries later. This chapter seeks to examine the context of the phenomenal growth of the uses of writing and interpret the social implications of the abundance of the epigraphs from a specific point of time.

The initial phase showing the presence of writing, conceived within the time frame of circa 200 BC and circa AD 300, is called the early historic period in the historiography of the Tamil south. Historians have associated the period with a social formation characterized by diverse forms of economies structured by the dominance of agro-pastoralism, involving collective appropriation through reciprocity and gifts based on kinship gradually augmenting into a system of complex redistributive relationships headed by chiefdoms of varying degrees of strength.[5] It was an ensemble of various forms of subsistence pursued by clan-based descent groups dispersed into *kuṭi*s in their settlements (*ūr*). Every *ūr* was a self-sustaining system of independent units of production (*kuṭis*) based on the familial labour of the respective clan members (*kuṭimākkal*). Each kin group had its headman (*kiḻār*) at whose instance the resources of the ūr were pooled and redistributed. This basic structure of the chiefdom under different ecosystems and productive forces acquired varying degrees of complexity. There were three categories of chiefdoms in the ascending order of *kiḻār*, *vēḷir*, and *vēntar*, the redistributive social relationships of which involved a corresponding increase in relations transcending those of kin and clan. Together they represented a wider range of economies from hunting to plough agriculture coexisting and interacting with one another. They accomplished a system structured by the dominance of the relations of pastoral agriculture.[6]

The nature of production, exchange, social appropriation, political control, and cultural practices notwithstanding, the differences in the degrees of complexity indicate that writing had a very marginal role. In the biggest chiefdom represented by the *mūvēntar* (Cēra, Cōḻa, and Pāṇḍya), some kind of differential allocation of roles, functions, and status did occur in the process of redistribution and exchange of gifts beyond clan ties.[7] Such individual differences in terms of material possessions, status, and ranking within the relatively flexible social stratification into the high-born (*uyarntōr*) and low-born (*iḻipiṛappāḷar*) were sustained by oral traditions. The economic, social, political, and cultural transactions were all governed by customary values, meanings, and parameters. Therefore, the society owed preservation of contemporary rights or privileges to conventions maintained through the oral tradition. As already noted, writing was known and had been in use for marking the personal identity of possessions and advertising donors' munificence or chieftains' might. It is not altogether accidental that we do not see in contemporary social formation any evidence for the use of writing for the production of deeds that would legitimize rights, privileges, and power. The main reason is that in early historic Tamil society, property rights, ritual status, social position, ranking, and the chiefdom level of political power were traditionally and customarily held and hence ordered and governed by the oral tradition.[8]

From the fourth century AD onwards, in the Andhra region under the Pallavas, the deed begins to appear in the form of a royal charter of the *brahmadēyas*, a public deed registering the gift of a whole village with its settlers to one or more *brāhmaṇas*.[9] What the charter bestowed upon the *brāhmaṇas* were not customary rights with precedents in the oral tradition but special rights arbitrarily created and imposed by the king, using his royal authority. Such superimpositions of non-conventional rights, privileges, and powers necessitated some concrete proof of authenticity and authority for the beneficiary to enjoy them without any opposition from the local people. This accounts for the beginnings of the use of written evidence in the form of the title deed. Each charter states where the king ordered it, when, in whose presence, and to whom, obviously by way of authentication. The entire royal officers concerned and the people going to be affected are addressed in the charter. The Mayidavoḷu copper plates of the Pallava Yuvaraja Sivaskandavarman, the earliest available charter (circa AD 305) in the Andhra region, says that it was ordered by the prince at Kanchipuram and that it was executed by the prince himself.[10] The charter concludes with punitive clauses threatening the transgressors of bodily punishments. The Hirahadagalli copper plates (circa AD 338) of the Pallava king Sivaskandavarman gives a long list of officers such as the crown prince (*rājakumāra*), the chief warrior (*sēnāpati*), provincial chiefs (*raṭṭikas*), customs officials (*madhvikas*), locality heads (*dēśādhikārs*), ministers (*amaccas*), and spies (*cancaras*) along with the affected like the free-holders of the village (*grāmabhōjakas*), the herdsmen (*vallabhas*), and the cowherds (*gōvallabhas*).[11] The charter then mentions the king himself as the executor of the charter. Both these charters invariably mention 18 exemptions (*parihāras*). These grants involved not only alienation of royal powers but also sharing of rights of the local people and superimposition of powers over their traditional rights, amounting to subordination of communities like the cowherds.

Though gift-giving played a very important role in the maintenance of the status, ranking, and authority of chieftains, it did not seem to have developed into the institution of land grants during the early historic period. However, landholdings by the *brāhmaṇas* as distinguished from the communal holdings was known to the Tamil heroic society, but it was the beginning and rights over land were yet to be evolved through the emergence of intermediaries. The *brāhmaṇa* households of the early historic period were in fact anticipatory constituents of the evolving social system that manifested itself with its institutional structures a little later, by the time of the Pulānkuṛichi rock inscriptions of the AD fourth–fifth centuries. Despite the linkage in terms of the mode of production, the earlier *brāhmaṇa* households and the subsequently structured brahmanical society were two different entities, the former as part of the social formation dominated by primitive agriculture and animal husbandry and the latter dominated by irrigated agriculture. What appears, therefore, as a disjunction between the old and new is the distance of the evolutionary process between two social formations.

The Tamil region's first major deed in stone is in the form of the two late *brāhmi*/early Vaṭṭeḻuttu inscriptions on a rock at Pulānkuṛichi in the Thiruppattur taluk of the Ramanathapuram district, dated in an unknown era but tentatively assignable to AD fourth–fifth centuries and issued by a certain king Cēntan Kūṟṟan, who is not seen in any of the known royal genealogies.[12] The deed introduces two new terms, *miyāṭci* and *kārāṇmai*, indicative of control over the landed property and entitlement to a share of crops respectively, the former vested with the *brāhmaṇa* households and the latter with the non-*brāhmaṇa* settlers (*kuṭis*). It is a fact that several *brāhmaṇa* settlements (*mangalam*) had come into existence by the time through *brahmadēya* land grants given by the early Pallavas. Though the copper plates do not mention the intermediary land rights (*kārāṇmai*) between the owner and the tiller as specified in the rock deed, one can argue that a *brahmadēya* presupposes the existence of it, since on the one side the *brāhmaṇas* were not cultivators by themselves and on the other, the villages granted were extensive. What began taking shape in the *brāhmaṇa* households was much more crucial for the real beginnings of a hierarchy. The permanent workforce attached to the *brāhmaṇa* households had the greatest possibility of being conceived hierarchically because of the stratifying system of production relations and the brahmanical tradition of social differentiation. The notion of hierarchy was implicit in the system of production in which the relation between two objectively antagonistic classes was fundamental. The AD mid-first millennium was thus a turning point in terms of stratification and hierarchical ordering which took more than two centuries to characterize the social aggregate.

The hierarchy of rights indicates a social structure almost entirely alien to the social formation of redistributive economy, predatory politics, and heroic culture that preceded it. Likewise, the political authority echoing in the deed bears no comparison with that of the predatory chiefdoms.[13] The deed, being inscribed on a huge rock in a rice-field, unfailingly caught the people's attention even from a distance. Commanding in presence, the rock as a monument of declaration of non-conventional privileges and powers was symbolically instructive to the local people, if not directly. As the deed embodied privileges and powers unfamiliar to the local people and their oral traditions, its inscription on an imposing rock and in huge characters was probably intentional rather than accidental. In fact, it was necessary for a society whose transactional relations relied entirely on the conventions and the trust of words, gradually heading for transformation into the literate mode of communication. The privileges always required documents of authority to validate and preserve them.[14] It appears that such documents were initially in the form of proclamations inscribed boldly on rock, presumably to demonstrate the rupture they make with the conventional through their non-conventional message. They must have acted as monumental signs of non-traditional impositions commanding public attention. However, there is no other rock deed of comparable significance to further substantiate the above argument, though a few pre-Pulankurichi copper plates do exist as already noted. Such copper plates invariably register privileges of exemptions relevant to the relations between the donees and the king.

It is with the sixth century that we see the new agrarian system articulating its political control as manifested in the new monarchy represented by the Pallavas of the Simhavarman III line, the Pāṇḍyas of the Kaṭunkon line and the Cōḷas of the Vijayalaya line. The *brahmadēyas* acquired greater frequency after the seventh century, as evidenced by the number of copper plate charters issued by the rulers of these lineages. The material transactions represented by land grants involving exemptions, privileges, rights, and powers acquired a phenomenal dimension during the three or four centuries that marked the emergence of the new monarchy.[15]

Founding hundreds of *brahmadēyas* and *dēvadānas* throughout the length and breadth of the region, the kings of these dynasties issued numerous copper plate charters, of which a considerable number has survived. They issued charters of land grants to the heterodox religious institutions as well, particularly to the Jain temples and monasteries, as evidenced by the copper plates registering the *paḻḻiccantam* endowments. The production of copper plate deeds with elaborate *praśasti*s and the practice of retaining them in personal custody became a regular feature in the region.[16] The deeds in stone as well as copper plates vouch for the fact that social relations were being further structured during the eighth–ninth centuries with the steady expansion of rice agriculture across the wetland.

As agrarian expansion advanced, human settlements (*ūr*) originally bound by kinship got integrated as agrarian localities (*nādu*) which subsequently acquired great political significance in the monarchical system. The role of the *jāti* in the integration of the agrarian society, whose mechanisms of appropriation were based on extra-economic coercion, was extremely crucial. The formation of agrarian localities was an ongoing process, and everywhere it accomplished a uniform structure of social relations irrespective of whether they were *brāhmaṇa* settlements (*brahmadēyas*) or *veḻḻān vagai* settlements (*ūr*). The social structure was a hierarchy with landholders (*brahmadēya-kiḻavar* in the case of *brahmadēyas* and *ūrār/nāṭṭār* in the case of *veḻḻan vagai* settlements) at the apex. Below them were intermediaries who later became leaseholders (*kārāḻar*), who were primarily the settlers (*kuṭi*), placed over the primary producers (*aṭiyāḻar*) at the bottom. Almost parallel to the leaseholders, there were many who held small strips of land as hereditary holdings (*kāṇi*) which were also tilled by primary producers. The circulation of the produce in given shares thus took a structured path through all these categories, enjoying different levels of entitlement. Those who benefited most were the landholders who were assured goods and services by the settlers in their land while the most exploited were the primary producers. As part of the social mechanisms of ensuring goods and services to the landholders through the notion of obligation (*kārāṇmai*), all artisans and craftsmen were subjected to immobility. The conditions of subjection, together with the objective reality of the producers being stripped off their produce, constituted the major contradiction in the system.

The expansion of rice-fields meant the development of relations in plough agriculture towards the domination of society which involved the spread of the system of hereditary specialization of occupations and their ordering into a hierarchy. The proliferation of hereditary occupations and their absorption into the *jāti* hierarchy were ongoing processes through new institutional agencies, of which the temple ranked the foremost. Other institutional formations, like service tenements both in the domains of the temple and the king, crystallized hereditary occupations into the *jāti* hierarchy. It is realistic to presume that the brahmadēya charters superimposed the holders' right over the collective rights of the local settlers and transformed them into leaseholders, with the tillers placed below them, and that the differentiated relation between the non-cultivating landowners and the landless tillers resulted.

The *nāṭṭār*, whom most of the copper plates mention as the local authority to have demarcated the boundary of the granted village, were the custodians of traditional rights and powers. Superimposition of powers over the rights of the various local communities and their subordination meant a non-local group's sharing of rights and powers that the *nāṭṭār* traditionally enjoyed. This is evident from the practice of notifying such affected people of the royal order. One of the main compulsions behind the affected people's acceptance of superimposed powers was fear of punishment. Transgressors were not uncommon, as the charters' punitive clauses referring to corporal punishments against transgression implies and the incidents of organized resistance mentioned as a part of the history of the gift in certain later copper plates explicitly indicate.[17] Each copper plate deed had its inception as the king's word of mouth (*tiruvāykkēḷvi*) followed by a palm-leaf transcript of it (*tirumukam*), both noted for their brevity and directness of communicative style, before it was transferred into copper plates for permanency. Early copper plates were brief too.

It is logical to presume that a charter granting rights and privileges affecting the people in a locality had been preceded by a public announcement of the grant as the king's proclamation in order to ensure the affected people's compliance. Once such orders became common and were accommodated into the local traditions, the people must have become too used to the practice to require proclamations any more. Even the practice of addressing the affected people gradually waned or disappeared completely from the charters, implying that the granting of superior rights from above was too common to have evoked any resistance. During the twilight of transition, written records began to encroach more and more upon the sphere of customs and conventions, a process that involved change in the meaning as well as function of writing. Its meaning as proof and its function as a deed were the most perceptible changes. The copper plates documenting the royal grant of rights, privileges, and obligations of landholders, leaseholders, and actual tillers indicate their function as deeds governing transactional relations of a hierarchically structured agrarian society composed of diverse categories of people grouped on the basis of their rights over land.

By the close of the ninth century, the number of epigraphs became several hundreds, which in a couple of centuries rose to several thousands, scattered all over the region and issued by the Pāṇḍya and Cōḻa kings. The epigraphs in stone register the foundation or renovation of institutions of religious importance or public utility; endowments of livestock, gold, cash, or land to the temple; transactions involving land and/or gold or money between individuals and corporate bodies like the *sabha* and *ūr* or between the corporate bodies and institutions like the temple; resolutions (*kaccam*) of the *sabha* or *ūr* or the governing bodies of the temples, relating to various issues in their respective spheres of control; royal orders (*Śrīkariyam*) or words of mouth (*tiruvākkēḷvi*) and; the heroic death of warriors in royal campaigns or local skirmishes. The copper plates are a little above fifty in all. The Velvikkuṭi plates of Neṭumjaṭaiyan mentions that it was originally meant as an *ēkabhōga* grant.[18] The Sinnamanur plates of Rajasimha and the Sivakasi plates of Vīra Pāṇḍya are *ēkabhōga* charters. The charters granting villages for the joint *bhōga* stipulate the pattern of redistribution of the land among the members of a *gōtra* or a few gotras of *brāhmaṇas*. It is explicit from the contents and context of the epigraphs that their purpose was to serve as deeds registering various conditions and agreements of transactions relating to matters such as the foundation or renovation of irrigation tanks, bunds, sluices, or temples and endowments to them, the constitutional and regulatory resolutions of the corporate bodies and royal orders being mostly of legal significance as reference documents.

Agrarian expansion, the ongoing process during the period, went on augmenting the domain of unequal rights and privileges. Correspondingly, the use of written documents was also increasing. The volume of written documents the society generated during the period of three or four centuries was amazingly large. Writing acquired an unprecedented dynamic to spread across the region as a symbol of power, legitimacy, authenticity, truth, and trust. Though the entire people were never transformed to literacy at any point in the past, the transition from orality to literacy was a common experience of all and the interactive societies as a whole had to move from memory to written accounts. This transformation cannot be described as the peculiarity of any particular period.[19] Instead, it is essential to probe into the factors necessitating the literate modes of thought and action. The knowledge about that would help us explain the proliferation of writings. The phenomenal increase of epigraphs during the period has to be examined in the light of the changes at the level of social formation, which were of a fundamental nature, as shown by studies.

Once writing became a regular aspect of socio-economic and political transactions of the times, numerous documents of an ephemeral nature such as instructions to officials and tax receipts were necessary as objects of administrative use. The number of epigraphs markedly increased and by then, the people became perhaps quite accustomed to them. Obviously, a huge number of palm-leaf records had existed. Likewise, the extant plates may be a very small proportion of the actual number that may have been several times greater when we take in to account the accidental nature of ways, contexts, and sites of their discovery. The Tamil south had become widely document-minded by the eighth century, probably four centuries before Europe. That the epigraphs in the form of deeds were intended to be preserved for posterity clearly indicates a wider use of writing in the region, which in its turn presupposes the emergence of a class-structured society of differential rights, privileges, and powers, which requires keeping documents permanently. The perpetuity of the deed is indicated often with the expression 'till the sun and moon last'. The rights and privileges of the class with a substantial political base and increasing resource control were essentially new. They were rights arbitrarily superimposed on the conventional by the political power effecting the transformation in productive functions, responsibilities, and ties. They were too non-local, disparate, and diverse to be absorbed as part of local tradition or to be sustained by social memory. The use of writing becomes essential in such a situation for recording specifications beyond the purview of conventions and traditions. Against these stipulations enhancing control over production and imposing contradictory relations of appropriation, some kind of resistance was likely, making coercion indispensable. That a political authority, capable of enforcing social acceptance of the new pattern of resource control and appropriation, makes its presence felt in the inscriptions is thus logical. Writing is symbolic of the repressive dimension of political power in the case of inscriptions carrying orders to be obeyed. Further, the spread of the use of writing as a necessary component of the administration, presupposes the rise of bureaucracy.[20]

Inscriptions with stipulations to be followed for many years, even centuries to come, became deeds of trustworthiness. The huge corpus of stone and copper plate inscriptions constitutes a landmark in the development of the use of writing for the legitimacy of enjoying privileges and powers. Each copper plate inscription was intended to be held as documentary reinforcement of the proprietary rights over land, power to control the local society, and privileges of immunity to royal impositions. The enjoyment of rights and powers in contemporary society depended on documentary evidence and it had become commonplace in the society. Deeds became indispensable for possessing anything worthwhile such as property rights and proprietary control over the people. A deed represented precision of writing and implied distrust of the spoken word. Therefore, it was imprudent for anybody holding property rights and powers to be bereft of deeds legitimizing them.

The languages used in the epigraphs of the period were Tamil and Sanskrit, clearly distinctive from each other and expected to be read in the respective languages only, as the consistent use of two different scripts indicates. Linguistically inscriptional diction, especially the diction of deeds, is different from oral diction. The Tamil diction can readily be recognized as the one based on the language of the script rather than speech. Sanskrit was used primarily in verse and had been in use as a literal language hardly ever used in speech. The composition of brahmadēya deeds is unique with their salient features such as the Sanskrit portion consisting of the genealogical prasasti and the Tamil portion of the actual grant. *Brāhmaṇas* were conscious of keeping their originality and caste exclusiveness by using only Sanskrit for their own concerns. The portion laying down rules (*kaccam*) is in Tamil presumably because they were meant not only for themselves and their dependents but also for others. We do not know whether the entire landed people such as *brahmadēya kiḻavar* and *nāṭṭār* had any knowledge of the art of writing. However, it appears that many of them must have read, for that capability was necessary for them to access deeds registering their rights and privileges in times of conflicts. Ruling class people, traders, landlords, and tenants had indeed used writing to convey matters of property rights, goods, and services. The kings, chieftains, their service personages, big merchants, and scholars in the various branches of contemporary knowledge, must have secured, in varying degrees, the skill to read and write because it was the functional necessity in their formal domains. Indeed, the possessors of land were persons familiar with the use of deeds.

While there are literally thousands of records relating to *brāhmaṇas* and temples, there are only a few relating to the *veḷḷanvagai* villages. This is not altogether accidental because the *ūrār* and *nāṭṭār* had seldom required any written instruments like deeds for holding their rights and powers, which were traditional and historically contingent and, therefore, governed by the oral tradition. They had not resorted to the institutional agency of the temple for maintaining their corporate character until a few centuries later, which also accounts for the absence of records. However, their presence in the deeds as an affected and involved group proves that they were incorporated into a system of documentation and archival trust. Once the literal mode of validation of rights and powers had become the order and royal granting of them ceased, the inscriptions on stone started tapering off as attested by the case of Kerala where palm-leaf records (*granthavaris*) came to the fore. In the Tamil region, the monarchy lasted longer, accounting for the persistence of the institution of land grants there.

A written piece of proof would not immediately excite social trust and therefore, it required not only politically endorsed authority and authenticity to establish credibility, but also coercion to ensure obedience as the punitive clauses suggest. In fact, a written document is always a product of distrust. It was hard to establish the legitimacy of a deed that seeks to authenticate non-conventional rights superimposed over the conventional. Therefore, both political and providential sanctions were inevitable. A deed was a dubious piece that necessitated a variety of ancillaries such as the witness, royal signature, official attestation, providential invocations, and penal threats. The mention of the place, the donor king, the date, the witnesses, the affected people, and the scribe, in the deed must have added to its trustworthiness. In fact, the donor, the witnesses, the affected, and the scribe were of no use for the future verification, since all of them would die away. There is lack of confidence and fear about transgression implicit in the penal as well as invocatory passages seeking the state's repressive power and providential intervention. In short, the reliability of deeds was a political creation by the dominant class and the shift of trust from words to deeds was an enforced process from above. Soon writing made it look authentic and proven as long as the document existed. The tradition of honesty about word of mouth waned and it became essential to produce written proof for a person to establish his rights.

The trust of deeds was ideological in the sense that it enabled the landlords to wield power with maximum control over resources and people with minimum resistance at the expense of the local tradition. This is not to say that deeds were conspiratorial, although this can happen, but rather a matter of spontaneity in a society of stratified agrarian relations. Briefly, this ideological legitimization was managed through the widespread imposition of Śāstraic ideas of social organization and political structuring. These ideas, often embedded in symbols and cultural practices, oriented people's thinking in such a way that they could accept deeds as trustworthy and recognize their roles in social transactions. The deed being fundamentally associated with power and power relations, which were neither a social structural phenomenon alone nor an exclusively political phenomenon, would be woven throughout all transactions. Since power is exercised in every relationship, group, and social practice, the deed, with its documentary base is strongly relied upon. Ultimately, it is the ability of one person or group to coerce another person or group that the deed provides by being in itself the authorized basis of power. The deed naturalizes, historicizes, and legalizes non-conventional rights and powers.

It appears that only kings had permanent scribes who were well versed in orthography and an official literary style. The strikingly limited number of differences in the writing style suggests that the number of scribes was not many, unlike in Europe where the beneficiaries themselves wrote them in a variety of hands. The copper plates were generally inscribed by goldsmiths as the term *taṭṭān* (the goldsmith) is given as a suffix to the names of scribes. Similarly, the stone inscriptions were carved by sculptors. It is a fact that both goldsmiths and sculptors were of lower castes, which under normal circumstances had no direct access to literacy.[21] Though the existence of users of writing among lower castes is a matter for conjecture, their insignificant status in the contemporary system of property and power relations precludes the possibility of literacy among them. Anyway, writing is a skill acquired through rigorous training, without which it is too hard for anybody to practise it all by himself, be it on copper plates or stones. Therefore, the goldsmith or the sculptor might have, presumably, inscribed over what the official scribe wrote. But the professional orthographic perfection explicit in the epigraphs seldom prompts us to believe them to have been inscribed by illiterate people. So it is more or less certain that the inscribers themselves were literate and that they were often the official scribes too. Writing being basically not an essential part of the technology of the goldsmith's or the sculptor's craft, they as scribes possessing a variety of skills and scholarship necessary for the production of deeds, were occupationally different and must have enjoyed higher social status as royal servants, despite the caste factor. The Vilaveṭṭi copper plates (circa fifth century) of Simhavarman states that the order was issued by the king and that it was committed to writing by the confidential authority (*rahasyādhikrta*).

Though the spread of writing would externalize the basis of rights and powers by preventing the people from recalling the truth from orally sustained memory, it never replaced the role of oral traditions. The use of writing was only an extension of the oral tradition. Even when writing became widespread, oral tradition continued to be the authenticator in various matters because writing was not the principal store of knowledge as yet. The wisdom of the elders was invoked wherever historical information became necessary.[22] The Velvikkuṭi copper plates mentions the donor king asking for proof in the form of the tradition of the local landholders to support the donee's claim about the history of the gift village.[23] However, it is a fact that writing would restructure people's consciousness and in the process would change and falsify it to some extent.[24] Writing and knowledge had no correspondence to each other since the former was possessed by a minority while the latter was owned by the majority through inheritance. Knowledge acquired in literacy was very narrow while it was quite broad in oral tradition, which was the veritable store of all kinds of knowledge, including vast domains of subsistence and survival strategies.[25] It included practical wisdom about the flora, medicinal plants, cycle of seasons, hierarchies of persons and things, social rules of behaviour, and rituals. Even the lower rungs in the hierarchy of labour, based on the system of hereditary occupation, were knowledgeable, specifically in their arts or crafts and generally about the environment of existence, thanks to the orally transmitted collective wisdom.

To conclude, the central argument of this chapter is that the social widening of the uses of literacy in early medieval south India, evident in the form of the proliferation of epigraphs, was necessitated by the emergence of a class of landlords with non-traditional rights, privileges, and powers that required state-sanctioned and state-protected written documents for validation. The contention is that the use of deeds was a direct consequence of certain fundamental changes in the agrarian relations by way of the rise and consolidation of the system of hierarchical relations of property and power. There were a series of interrelated and simultaneous developments such as the emergence of land as the chief form of resource and object of labour, superimposition of superior rights on the conventional, gradation of entitlements into a hierarchy, formation of temple-centred agrarian corporations, proliferation of temples and temple-centred transactions of goods and services, consolidation of a state power based on agrarian economy, and differential allocation of status and ranking based on land-rights, leading to the making of a society demanding production of deeds to prove rights and powers. In short, the rise of the inscriptional culture is not just an accidental trend of a particular period, occurring merely as a result of transplant or cultural diffusion. Writing, though its spread has always been through diffusion, required a specific historical context of socio-economic development, making the shift of trust from words to deeds essential, for its wider use in transactions and governance. The socio-economic and political processes made the execution of written contracts an inevitable component of contemporary transactions in property rights. The flood of epigraphs in the Tamil south during the early medieval period marks this shift of trust from words to deeds. The rise of the document-based society put writing to a wider use as the basis of legitimacy, authenticity, authority, and credibility on the other. The shift has to be understood as a need created by the rise of differentiated, individualized, superimposed, and hierarchical land rights and power relations, for transactions in stratified property rights depended on deeds and not on oral recollections of the elders or unwritten conventions. It was a shift articulated by the economy of brahmanical landlordism and sustained by the polity of consecrated monarchy.

NOTES AND REFERENCES

1. For a detailed discussion of the script, its use, and the contents of the label inscriptions, see I. Mahadevan, 2003, *Early Tamil Epigraphy: From the Earliest Times to the Sixteenth Century* AD, Harvard University. A discussion of the corpus of early inscriptions is given in Part III.
2. See discussions in K.R. Srinivasan, 1946, 'Megalithic Burials and Urn-fields of South India in the Light of Tamil Literature and Tradition', *Ancient India*, vol. 2, pp. 9–16. Also see R. Champakalakshmi, 1972, 'Archaeology and Tamil Literary Tradition', *Purātatva*, vol. 8, pp. 110–22. For an updated analysis, see K. Rajan, 2000, *South Indian Memorial Stones*, Thanjavur, pp. 5–12.
3. For a further discussion, see Rajan Gurukkal, 1996, 'Writing and Uses in Ancient Tamil Country', *Studies in History*, New Series, 12(1): 72.
4. I. Mahadevan thinks that literacy was widespread in ancient Tamil society. See his arguments in, 1995, 'From Orality to Literacy: The Case of the Tamil Society', *Studies in History*, New Series, 11(2): 182–6.
5. This has been discussed at length in K. Sivathamby, 1974, 'Early South Indian Economy: The *Tiṇai* Concept', *Social Scientist*, vol. 29, pp. 20–37. Also Rajan Gurukkal, 1989, 'Forms of Property and Forces of Change in Ancient Tamil Country', *Studies in History*, 5(2): 159–75. The concept of social formation is borrowed from Marx as expanded by Nicos Poulantzas. See the discussion in, 1983, *Political Power and Social Classes*, London, pp. 40–8. Also see Barry M. Hindess and Paul Q. Hirst, 1979, *Pre-Capitalist Modes of Production*, London, pp. 51–3.

6. See Gurukkal, 'Forms of Production', pp. 159–75.
7. See the details in Rajan Gurukkal, 1993, 'From Clan and Lineage to Hereditary Occupations and Caste in Early South India', *Indian Historical Review*, 20(1–2): 25–7.
8. Ancient Tamil society had a very strong tradition of oral versification pursued by the community bards called the *pāṇar*. See Kailasapathy, 1968, *Tamil Heroic Poetry*, London. Also see George L. Hart, 1979, *Poets of the Tamil Anthologies: Ancient Poems of Love and War*, Princeton.
9. The kings of the Pallava, Pāṇḍya, and Cōḻa dynasties issued brahmadēya charters in the region under study. There are thirty charters issued by the Pallavas, ten by the Pāṇḍyas, and sixteen by the Cōḻas. See for the text, translation, and historical context of the Pallava charters, *Pallava Cēppeṭukal Muppatu*, *Pāṇḍyar Cēppeṭukal Pattu*, and the Cōḻa charters.
10. See T.V. Mahalingam (ed.), 1988, *Pallava Inscriptions*, New Delhi, pp. 31–4.
11. Ibid., pp. 35–9.
12. For the first notice and historical interpretation see, R. Nagaswamy, 1981, 'An Outstanding Epigraphical Discovery in Tamil Nadu', in *Proceedings of the First International Conference Seminar on Tamil Studies*, vol. I, Section 2, Madurai, pp. 67–71. Also Natana Kasinathan, 1983, 'Pulankurichi Inscription: A Re-look', *Tolliyal Karuttaranku*, Madras, pp. 157–68. An updated text is given in Y. Subbarayalu and M.R. Raghava Varier, 1991, 'Pulankurichi Kalvettukal', *Avanam*, vol. I, part 2. pp. 57–69 and for translation and comments, see Y. Subbarayalu, 2001, 'The Pulangurichi Inscriptions', in S. Rajagopal (ed.), *Kaveri: Studies in Epigraphy, Archaeology, and History*, Professor Y. Subbarayalu Felicitation Volume, Chennai, pp. 1–6.
13. For a detailed consideration of the question of political processes of the social formation, see Rajan Gurukkal, 2002, 'Antecedents of the State Formation in South India', in R.Champakalakshmi, Kesavan Veluthat, and T.R. Venugopal (eds), *State and Society in Premodern South India*, Trissur, pp. 39–59.
14. For illustrations of the issue in various studies from different parts of the world, see W. Ong, 1982, *Orality and Literacy The Technologising of the Word*, Cambridge, pp. 33–6. Also see M.T. Clanchy, 1993, *From Memory to Written Record, England 1066–1307*, second edition, London, pp. 46–51; Rosalind Thomas, *Oral Tradition and Written Record in Classical Athens*, Cambridge, 1989, pp. 16–23.
15. See the structure and composition of the monarchy conceptualized in Kesavan Veluthat, 1993, *The Political Structure of Early Medieval South India*, New Delhi, pp. 29–69.
16. Any of the Pāṇḍya and Cōḻa plates are examples. For a detailed study of the parts, constitution, and purpose of the copper plates, see Kesavan Veluthat, *The Political Structure of Early* ..., pp. 10–11, 30.

17. See the instances discussed in Rajan Gurukkal, 1984, 'Non-brahmana Resistance to the Expansion of *Brahmadeyas*: The Early Pāṇḍya Experience, *Indian History Congress Proceedings*, Delhi.
18. See *Pāṇḍyar Cēppeṭukal Pattu.*
19. In his well-known study, Clanchy describes the spread of literacy as a peculiarity of the medieval period. See his *From Memory to Written Record,* p. 114. This cannot be described merely as a medieval peculiarity.
20. Clanchy's central contention is that lay literacy grew out of a bureaucracy. See *From Memory to Written Record,* pp. 63–8.
21. I. Mahadevan argues for high literacy in the region and among the ordinary folk even during the early historic period. See his 'From Orality to Literacy: The Case of the Tamil Society'. Clanchy produces evidence for the familiarity of even serfs with literate modes. See his *From Memory to Written Record,* p. 3.
22. Clanchy has given enough credence for the presumption. See *From Memory to Written Record,* pp. 294–6.
23. See *Pāṇḍyar Cēppeṭukal Pattu,* Madras, 1967, pp. 19–32; '... *nattanin palamai* ...' and '*nattarran palamai* ...' is the relevant expression in the plates. Grammatically, the form should have been, *nattar tam palamai* meaning the tradition of the naṭṭar. The term naṭṭar stands for the Vellala landholders.
24. For an elaboration of the concept, see W.J. Ong, *Orality and Literacy.* Also R. Finnegan, 1988, *Literacy and Orality: Studies in the Technology of Communication,* London, pp. 78–80. Also Clanchy, *From Memory to Written Record,* p. 193.
25. For details, see, Rosalind Thomas, 1989, *Oral Tradition and Written Record in Classical Athens,* Cambridge, pp. 28–31, and her, 1992, *Literacy and Orality in Ancient Greece,* London, pp. 43–4.

Section IV

The New Social Formation

15

Temples as Sites of the New Social Formation*

Being a strategic point of human convergence, any cult-spot has been a site of socio-religious interaction, plausibly a feature much more substantially true in the case of the temple with monumental structures. Several cult-spots, without being enshrined by structures, had existed at different places in ancient times and, over the centuries, underwent the process of syncretism, leading to structural transformations from the primordial to the Tantric to the *āgamic śaiva* or *vaiṣṇava* through the Jain or Buddhist types. This is a trajectory replete with evidence of the existence of cult-spots as sites of age-old socio-religious interaction. The history of such religious structures in northern India goes beyond the period under consideration if we include the Jain and Buddhist vestiges. The brahmanical temple structures there date barely beyond the AD fourth century while their counterparts in southern India date to the AD seventh century. Several huge temples had emerged in southern India during the last three centuries of the millennium. Most of these structural temples of evolved *prākārās* and elaborate rituals based on prescriptions of the āgamic texts were architectural adaptations of early Jain and Buddhist monuments. The archaeological, epigraphical, and literary evidence helps us trace the antiquity of early brahmanical temples of southern India to the AD eighth-tenth centuries.[1] On the contrary, the tradition of huge temples was largely uncommon in northern India during the AD first millennium.

Unlike elsewhere in the subcontinent, the emergence of structural temples and the formation of an agrarian society based on hierarchically

---

* This chapter is a reproduced version of, 2009, 'Temples as Sites of Social and Religious Interaction', in B.P. Chattopadhyaya (ed.), *A Social History of Early India*, (Pearson Longman: New Delhi), pp. 199–210.

structured land relations synchronized with each other as integral to a homologous historical process in southern India. The social relations began to be structured during the sixth–seventh centuries with the steady expansion of wet-rice agriculture across southern India, which was a long process of the proliferation of occupational specialization and its ordering into a hierarchy. It took a little more than two centuries for the hierarchy to characterize the social aggregate and mark a breakthrough. A perceptible feature of agrarian expansion was the proliferation of *brahmadēya* villages throughout the fertile tracts of major river valleys in the region.[2] It was a complex process of differentiation, stratification, and formation of the state manifesting as the *cakravartin* model of royal authority, represented by the Simhavarman line of the Pallavas, the Kaṭunkon line of the Pāṇḍyas, and the Vijayālaya line of the Cōḷas. Expansion of agrarian settlements through the creation of *brahmadēyas* often involved the superimposition of the superior rights of the *brāhmaṇas* over the communal holdings and the clan families of the locality. It must have been an intricate process of transformation of primitive agriculture and clan settlements into advanced agriculture and farmer settlements respectively, which simultaneously involved on the one side, the crystallization of functionally specific families into *jātis* and disintegration of the kinship ties on the other. The proliferation of hereditary occupations and their absorption into the *jāti* hierarchy were ongoing processes through new institutional agencies, of which the temple ranked the foremost.

Temples sprang up in southern India on a large scale during the period of agrarian expansion through brahmadēyas. In fact, the temple acted as the institutional means of coordination of landed households into the corporate body.

The temples studded the major agrarian localities of southern India, particularly its fertile river basins by the close of the AD first millennium. The *bhakti* movement widely spread by the Āḻvār as well as Nāyanār sects was fundamentally connected to the expansion of *brāhmaṇa* localities. The base of the bhakti movement was the temple.[3] The hymnists sang in praise of the deities of the temples, popularizing the latter. The major Vaiṣṇava temples of south India were praised by the hymnists of the AD seventh–tenth centuries.[4] The most powerful ideology that emerged during the period between the seventh and the tenth centuries centring around the temple was the bhakti or the cult of self-surrender that was institutionalized through the hymns of Āḻvārs and Nāyanārs sung in praise of the temple deities.[5] The hymns of the Āḻvārs and Nāyanārs were composed in praise of the local gods of temples whose distribution and sacred geography corresponded to the course of agrarian expansion through the institution of brahmadēyas. It gained momentum as a cult of personal gods housed in temples that grew up as the nerve-centre of agrarian settlements, both *brāhmaṇa* as well as non-*brāhmaṇa*. Nevertheless, *bhakti* spread as a movement of the temples owned and controlled by the *brāhmaṇas*. The hymns expressed an altogether new religious sensibility, an intimate devotion to the personal deity that was the characteristic feature of the temple-centred *bhakti*.

The historical context of *bhakti* was the consolidation of the contradictory agrarian relations of contemporary village society. Through the cult of complete surrender at the feet of the deity consecrated in the local temple as the final refuge, it provided an illusory solace to the harassed and the oppressed in the social system. Inventing other-worldly explanations for the social contradictions of domination and providing a psychological basis for the social acceptance of the plight of the dominated, *bhakti* glossed over the material reality of the conditions of oppression. The *bhakti* hymns of the Āḷvārs and Nāyanārs portraying the enslaved and bonded status of the devotees to their deities, in fact, mirrored the way the subjected and exploited lived their relation with their oppressive conditions of existence. This homology between the ideology of the *bhakti* hymns and contemporary social reality is further illustrated through their capacity of containment, which is evident in the articulation of the dissent and protest of the lower orders. Voices of dissent against the hegemonic existed within the mystifying cult of *bhakti*. Since it was a social formation of contradictory relations, involving the tension of subjection and exploitation, voices of protest were inevitable, but they functioned as a strategy of containment that pre-empted and foreclosed the chance of a radical dissent. With the manifestation of the *bhakti* cult as a temple-based movement in the eighth and ninth centuries, the enunciation of the dominant ideology of the agrarian society was complete.

The temple-centred *bhakti* movement is a clear illustration of how the temple functioned as a site of socio-religious interaction. It brought an integrated nexus of sacred geography, the wide terrain of the temple-centred agrarian societies of southern India between Kanchi and Kanyakumari, which the hymnists popularized as seats of *tirupatis* (holy shrines), through their songs in praise of temple deities. The *bhakti* movement systematically enhanced the popularity and extent of the agamic religion by using the temple site. Apart from the movement of the hymnists, the temple had other institutional vehicles for the dissemination of *bhakti* or the feeling of devotion. The institution of *māpāratapaṭṭattānam* (the *bhaṭṭa* of the Mahābhārata) emerged for reciting and explaining the Mahābhārata stories. The sculptures and paintings of the temple formed another effective medium for popularizing Purāṇic stories and inculcating bhakti in different sections of the society.[6] Music and dance were equally powerful media for the diffusion of the *bhakti* ideology. There were full-time dance-drama professionals called *kūttar* attached to the temple, whose performances effectively circulated the ideology of *bhakti* and helped the profuse spread of socio-religious ideas and institutions. In addition to all these, the commanding presence of the structural temple as the principal focal point and nerve centre of the village excited bhakti in the minds of the people. The glorious festivals and ceremonies of the temple added vigour and colour to *bhakti* and attracted the populace to its fold.

Bhakti, or the cult of personal devotion, was not the sole channel of social attraction and interaction of the temple. Among the various other sources of its social interaction were the numerous rituals, ceremonies, and entertainment associated with it. The daily rituals and occasional ceremonies had drawn the local society to the temple as their patrons, for the rituals and ceremonies increased the people's religious merit and devotion. The institution of endowments was another major channel of the temple that facilitated socio-religious interaction. The temple was richly equipped for conducting routine and special rituals, celebrating auspicious days of festive occasions, and maintaining its numerous functionaries. This is borne out by many hundreds of thousands of inscriptions sparsely distributed in the numerous temples of southern India.[7] Institutions like the *śālās* and *ghaṭikas* with *caṭṭas* and *bhaṭṭas* attached to the temple received separate grants for their maintenance. The temple grew as a huge repository of valuables like gold and as a custodian of a large extent of productive lands through the institution of endowments.

The temple became a landed magnate of the time and acquired the central place in the realm of the agrarian economy and socio-religious life towards the end of the first millennium AD. It enjoyed a lot of revenue from the land owned and controlled by it. A lot of revenue reached the temple by way of *rakśābhōga,* the dues exacted for the protection it offered to the local people, *daṇḍam* (fine) it imposed on the defaulters, and *prāyascittam* (remorse) it received from the guilty. The resource strength of the temple was commendable enough to easily organize the local society into a stable system of institutions, groups, and relations suitable for better production. There are epigraphical evidences of affluent temples of southern India indulging in high-level construction work and carrying out productive enterprises such as big irrigation projects and large-scale land-improvement schemes. The temple had specifically constituted committees or departments called *vāriyams* to look after such enterprises. Several inscriptions refer to committees of irrigation tanks (*ērivāriyam*), agrarian fields (*kaḻani-vāriyam*), and garden land (*tōṭṭa-vāriyam*).

The various endowments, especially those in the form of livestock, land, and gold facilitated the temple's role as a site of extensive social interaction. Perhaps the most widespread category of endowments is the one instituted for the permanent lamp (*tirunontāviḷakku*) in the temple, and livestock constituted the most common form of wealth connected with it. The livestock reached the temple in specified numbers, as neither dying nor growing old (*cāvā mūvā*) implying that the endowment was permanent, ensuring the quantity of ghee required to keep the lamp burning continuously. Several hundreds of inscriptions in the numerous temples register the institution of the perpetual lamp through the endowment of livestock. In a society where the production of fire was considered rare magic, the institution of a perpetual lamp in the temple served the purpose of the sustenance of fire for the local people. The livestock wealth endowed to the temple was entrusted with the headmen of pastoralists (*iṭaiyar*) or livestock dealers (*manṛāṭiyar*) who undertook to provide the specified amount of ghee to the temple. It is obvious that both these headmen as well as the dealers had, in their turn, assigned the livestock to the pastoralists, probably giving rise to a cattle fiefdom with the temple at the top of the hierarchy.

The land endowments of the temple included crown land held by the ruling aristocracy (*cērikkal*), land owned by the *brāhmaṇas* (*brahmasvam*), land occupied by merchants, and the leases (*kārāṇmai*) held by the temple functionaries. Most of the land was endowed to the temple permanently and with absolute rights. In contemporary society, all rights over land were hereditary and ownership of land meant a system of relations among a host of inherited rights, and any holders could pledge their rights for borrowing loans. Many people borrowed money (both gold and silver as coins or bullion) from the temple on the security of the rights over land. The endowments and the various transactions brought the temple different kinds of land rights, both superior and subordinate, such as those of the owner of all revenues from land, protector with all political rights, and temporary revenue ownership with kārāṇmai rights.[8] Being an institution, it was not possible for the temple to manage the various forms of ownership except by redistributing them among the members of the temple corporation (*sabha*). The *sabhaiyar* were not cultivators by themselves and, therefore, they had to redistribute the land in their turn to the *kārāḷar* and the *kārāḷar* to *kuṭikal.* Thus, the land rights transferred as endowments or securities were the ownership from the donor to the temple, the rights to cultivate from the latter to the *kārāḷar* and from the *kārāḷar* the right of occupation to artisans, craftsmen, and tillers.

The lands endowed were leased out to the *kārāḷar* who undertook to pay *pattam* (land dues). An official called *pāṭṭamāḷumavan* collected the land dues on behalf of the temple corporation. This elaborate system of distribution and redistribution of land rights, with the temple as its nucleus, provided an integrated organization of economic activities.[9] The land endowment, which reached the temple in large numbers, was divided among the members of the various *gaṇa*s (trusts) constituted by the *ūrāḷar.* Each endowment was entrusted to a *gaṇa,* the members of which shared it equally and leased it out to the *kārāḷar.*[10] The *kārāḷar* were made responsible for providing the requirements of the specified temple rituals, and endowments were made for their maintenance. This shows how the dues from the *kārāḷar* could provide a definite and regular resource-base for the perpetuation of the specified rituals and ceremonies in the temple. The link thus established between the land dues and the performance of a ritual in the temple, not only underlines the obligations of the *kārāḷar* to the temple but to some extent implies the trust reposed on them by the temple corporation. If there was a default, the *kārāḷar* was liable to pay double the amount of the original dues. In extreme cases, they had to forfeit their *kārāṇmai.* The *kārāṇmai* right seems to have been hereditary. In certain cases, the land was leased out to the *kārāḷar* nominated by the donor and in other cases it was stated that the land leased out once should not be given to any other person. The records of certain temples indicate restrictions on the *kārāṇmai* rights of the individual *brāhmaṇa ūrāḷar.* Sometimes, the members of the temple's executive committee were prevented from becoming the *kārāḷar*s of temple land.

Thus, the temple was discharging a land redistributive function through which it gave away only subordinate rights like *kārāṇmai* and *kuṭimai* (occupation rights) to the *kārāḷar* and *kuṭikal* (the artisans and craftsmen) respectively, while it retained the *ūrāṇmai* (proprietary rights) in the hands of the members of the sabha. The net effect of the redistribution was transference of a lot of land from the ruling families and aristocracy to the *brāhmaṇas* and subordination of a huge number of intermediaries, artisans, craftsmen, and tillers to the temple. It established in the descending order the *ūrāṇmai* enjoyed by the *ūrāḷar* (proprietors), *kārāṇmai* possessed by the *kārāḷar,* and the *kuṭimai* held by the kuṭikal.

The temple corporation redistributed the gold accumulated through endowments and fines mainly by using it is a medium of exchange and measure of value for purchasing new land. The temple lent it out at interest to procure more land and revenue as well. Also, it used gold as a means of payment to reward the higher rungs of temple servants. Land provided an effective form of investment for the temple's huge stock of gold. There are instances of purchase of land by the temple with gold that was being used as a medium of exchange in contemporary land transactions. The different weights of gold with established ratio-proportions and fineness served the purpose of money in the financial transactions of the temple. The practice of lending gold out at interest to those who mortgaged their lands to the temple was common in those days and it enhanced the agrarian control of the temple, for the borrower invariably had to mortgage his land to the temple. The loan was given, generally, to the landed group alone. Land mortgage involved alienation of the *kārāṇmai* rights and part of the revenue rights over the mortgaged land by way of the stipulated rate of interest for the gold loan. The loans were seldom paid back and, in effect, the gold lent out by the temple remained a permanent investment for acquiring agrarian wealth and land rights.

Functioning as a site of barter exchange in the local society, participating in the transactions and stipulating conditions for them, the temple standardized the inter-commodity exchange rates. Certain records refer to a stable gold-paddy exchange ratio too, which was owed to the temple. The stability of the gold–paddy exchange ratio over the last two centuries of the AD first millennium in the transaction economy of the temple seems to be suggestive of the rate of gold influx and productivity growth as commensurate with their demand growth rate. The prevalence of regular inter-commodity exchange rates and the non-fluctuating gold-paddy ratio of the time seem to indicate the absence of monetization in the economic transactions of the temple society. Generally two units, *kāṇam* and *kaḷancu,* were used to indicate the measure of gold in contemporary records of south Indian temples. Sometimes, the payments to and from the temple were made in different units of gold. It was always laid down in the records that the gold used in transactions should be of a given quality ensured by the specified heat and fineness.[11] The records of south India indicate the general prosperity of merchants and their consolidation into the corporation during the period. But in spite of the prevalence of the money economy of the trading corporations and royal issues of the Pallavas and Cōḻas, the rural transactions in south India generally remained non-monetized because of the localized character of rural settlements.[12] This seems to be particularly true of Kerala where, except for the few references to the coins noted above, there is no evidence of the issue of coinage by the state.[13] Some scholars have pointed out that the royal coins of south India, being of higher denominations of gold and silver, their entry into ordinary transactions was unlikely. But there are references to a large number of copper coins of the Cōḻa period. In Kerala, however, there is no evidence of coins of lower denominations either.

The dearth of coins and the primarily localized nature of production seem to have promoted the practice of payment in kind as the usual system in the temples. This system led to an economically dependent social organization based on ties from the lowlier groups to the higher as a need-satisfying device. All the artisans and craftsmen or professional castes were settled in the temple-centred village to ensure their services to the temple and the village proprietors. The implication is that the temple-centred rural society, with the system of service tenure, a standardized inter-commodity exchange ratio, and insufficiency of coins as the features of a closed economy, became a relatively self-sufficient local unit.[14]

We have seen how the temple functioned as the site of economic transactions in the hinterland. The focus here is on the nature of the society that flourished around the temple. The temple's relation with the society was fundamentally the same as that of a landed chief to his landed intermediaries, other subordinates, and tillers. The temple had a significant role in the integration of its society. In the process of integration, it exerted a great deal of influence in the organizational and institutional aspects of the society. The temple employed a large number of people in its various fields under the system of service tenure. The records of Thanjavur reveal that the Rajarājēśvara temple alone employed more than six hundred people, excluding the numerous scholarly, spiritual, and secular personages, for its various services at prescribed rates of reward.[15] Generally, the temple servants were paid under the system of service tenure and the rewards normally took the form of shares of land with the rights for life, called as *virutti* or *jīvitam.* The *āgamic* instructors, the narrators of the Mahābhārata, the priests, the secretaries, the accountants, the drummers, the dancers, the musicians, the dancing girls, the singers, the dramatists, the watch and ward, sweepers, and various other functionaries were paid their rewards in the form of virutti or *jīvitam.*[16]

The localization of agrarian activities under the institutional supervision of the temple resulted in the establishment of an elaborate agrarian order and in an unprecedented expansion of agriculture. Through its land control, the temple harnessed landed intermediaries, leaseholders, and actual tillers into an integrated whole. The parts of the whole can be grouped as the *brāhmaṇa* and the non-*brāhmaṇa* orders. The development of various land rights through the redistribution of resources by the temple went hand-in-hand with the formation of power groups in the society. They had great control over land as owners of their individual holdings and corporate custodians of temple holdings. They were the proprietors of the agrarian village. As learned *brāhmaṇas* and the priestly class they enjoyed a very high socio-ritual status. The secretary of the temple known as *madhyastha* in Tamil Nadu and *potuvāl* in Kerala represented a powerful component, second only to the *sabhaiyar*.[17] In the early phase, they seemed to have formed a part of the community of *brāhmaṇas*. Similarly *vāriyar*, literally a member of a *vāriyam* (committee or department), was a *brāhmaṇa* too. However, the later records and ethnographic accounts show that in Kerala both *potuvāl* and *vāriyar* were endogamous castes of the Sūdra *varṇa* (fourth *varṇa*). The term *vāriyar* is used to mean the member of *vāriyam* in the other parts of south India also, but there it denotes a category of *brāhmaṇa varṇa*.[18]

Below the *brāhmaṇa* functionaries were the large group of non-brahman functionaries like *cākkaimār*, *naṭṭuvan*, *kāndarppikar*, *uvaccakal*, and *tēvaraṭiyāḷ*. In the lowlier orders were the gatekeepers, sweepers, and other menial servants. The male dancers of the temple were called *cākkaimar* who performed *kūttu* (dance-drama), which involved dancing, acting, and storytelling in the temple theatre. The terms *kāndarppikar* and *naṭṭuvanār* appear in certain records of the time along with *nankaimār* or *tēviṭiccikal*. It appears that *kāndarppikar* were instrumental musicians of the temple who played music for the dance (*nāṭya*) of the *nankaimār*. It is interesting to note that the term *kāndarppikar* literally means 'the people of *Kamadeva*'. The term *naṭṭuvan* means the dance instructor who was appointed by the temple to train the *nankaimār* in the art of dance. The drummers, dancers, and musicians formed a large group of temple functionaries drawn from the non-*brāhmaṇa* people. The drummers were called *uvaccakal* in contemporary records.[19] *Koṭṭikaḷ* was another term frequently used for referring to them. The temple dancing maid or courtesan is referred to in the south Indian temple records as *tēvaraṭiyāḷ* and as *nanka*, *tēvaṭicci*, and *kūttacci* in the inscriptions of Kerala.

Apart from the professional castes, the temple had a lot of non-specialized workers who performed the functions of menial servants. They were *aṭikkumavar* (sweepers), *viṛakiṭumavar* (suppliers of firewood), *ilayiṭumavar* (suppliers of plantain leaves), *vāyirkkalanirkkumavar* (gatekeepers), *arikūttumavar* (rice-pounders), *viḷakkeṭukkumnambi* (the lamp-attender), and *aṭakkainalkumavar* (distributor of areca nuts). It seems that the temple had different types of sweepers like *akattaṭikkumavar* (those who swept the holy courtyard of the temple) and *ecciliaṭippan* (those who swept the dining hall). These functionaries did not seem to have formed themselves into profession-labelled castes, since various sub-castes of the temple functionaries indulged in these kinds of services. For instance, in the Kerala temple the sweeper of the holy courtyard was a *vāriyan*.[20] Most of the temple property and the individual holdings of the *brāhmaṇas* were leased out to *kārāḷar* who were primarily of the non-*brāhmaṇa* order.

In addition to the employees directly associated with the daily rituals of the temple, there were a few artisans and craftsmen (*kammāḷar*) who were settled within the limits of the temple-centred village and obliged to render their services to the temple as well as the village. Inscriptions refer to *taccar* (carpenters), *kalavāṇiyar* (potters), *vāṇiyar* (oil-mongers), and *vaṇṇār* (washermen), brought to settle in the temple-centred society. The *pulayar* and *ceṛumar,* who were the actual tillers, constituted the base of the society. They were the most servile group, purchased and sold as goods and transacted along with the land.

It appears that all service in the temple had a relatively high and appreciable socio-ritual status, thanks to their consecrated character. As usual there was an internal hierarchy of functionaries graded according to ritual status on the one side and material status on the other. The *brāhmaṇas* functioned as sabhaiyār in the caste corporation, as *paraṭaiyār* in the executive committee of the temple, as *gaṇattār* in the endowment trusts called *gaṇam,* as *tantri,* the *āgamic* instructor of the temple, *bhaṭṭa,* the Vedic teacher or the professor of Mahabharata, and *santi,* the priest of the temple. All these services had a hierarchy of ritual and material status. In other words, some sort of inequality prevailed among the *brāhmaṇas* themselves on the basis of their different roles in the temple services. The tantrī (*āgamic* priest) as well as the *vaidika* (Vedic priest) headed the hierarchy of ritual status. Often it corresponded in the case of material status as well. However, high ritual status never presupposed a high material status. For instance, the priest of the temple who had a high ritual status, seldom had a corresponding material one. The internal inequality among the non-*brāhmaṇa* functionaries was also two fold as in the case of *brāhmaṇa* functionaries, that is, the inequality of ritual and material statuses.

It appears that the differences in the material position of the temple servants were determined by their private holdings of land and not by the rewards from the temple. Not much disparity seems to have existed in the remuneration of the temple functionaries of southern India. Some temples had the practice of obtaining the approval of the servants on the emoluments fixed for their services in the temple by allowing them to be present when the sabhā took the decisions concerned.

The temple was the site for various contestations too. The contestations of regional political powers were carried forward to the temple so that they were a source of religious merit and legitimization. The major ruling dynasties turned to the temple and its ritual procedures for divinization of kingship. The ruling dynasties of southern India had not emerged fully out of the moorings of tribal lineages and required various means of legitimization. Of the manifold ideas and institutions of the divinization of royalty, the temple ranked foremost. The Pallavas were the first to go through the process of restructuring and, hence, the first to seek deliverance from the tribal moorings through the divinization of kingship. The Pāṇḍyas, Cōḻas, and Cēras followed the same strategies of legitimization. The deity in the temple was a prototype of the sovereign in grandeur, paraphernalia, and the idealized iconic representation of the reigning king.[21] The daily rituals in the temple and practices in the palace were homologically linked and it is significant to note that the *āgamic* texts consider rājopacāra in the palace and *dēvōpacāra* in the temple are the same. There is a well-known saying in Tamil that seeing the king in his royal attire is seeing the deity (*tiruvuṭal mannarē kkāṇal tirumālē enṟum*). So, naturally, the royal conflicts, predatory campaigns, and belligerent marches had their repercussions on the temple. The temple was the site of contestation for various social groups, cults, and sects of contemporary society. It was the site of compromise for the competing and conflicting landlords of the locality, for it was under the temple's umbrella that they coalesced into an oligarchy. In short, the temple was the most influential mediating force for all the competing and coalescing constituents of contemporary power structure. It was a site for contradictory social relations to release the tension embedded in them. As the sacred space of the larger society, the tensions of all social segments were carried forward to it. It absorbed and ameliorated them with its ideological power. It reminds us of the social functions of feudal Europe's religious institutions of seigniorial jurisdiction that commanded total obedience from the lowlier orders to the top under the threat of sedition. The temple could ensure such an unconditional submission and allegiance under its unseen pressure of ideological coercion. In short, the temple embodied the totality of relationships in contemporary local society.

The temple was linked with all the other social institutions through relationships of transactions in everyday life. In the process, it modified or augmented or crystallized the various social institutions. The institution of caste that the temple augmented and crystallized through its social transactions deserves special mention in this context. The system of service tenure followed by the temple in paying its functionaries tagged land rights to services. This practice acted as the basic incentive for hereditary specialization of services, for it enabled the retention of the land assigned for the service as family property. The *virutti* and *jīvitam* tenure of land made several services of the temple hereditary as a historically contingent strategy for preserving the right over land. Once the functionaries began to serve the temple as workers of hereditary specialization, they began to be labelled by the name of their professions, which turned into caste suffixes over the years. The caste system to a great extent, thus, owed the proliferation of sub-castes to the social transactions of the temple and contemporary system of land tenure. This was true in the case of royal services too. Numerous artisans and craftsmen were settled on temple land to ensure their services to the temple as well as its settlement. These people were granted the right to settle down in the temple's landed property, which they were bound to reciprocate through their arts or crafts. Thus, they also became groups of hereditary occupations under the incentive of land rights. Further, the contractual obligation not only led to the localization of their services but also subjection of themselves to the servile position of bondsmen of the temple. As usual, they were also graded according to their birth and occupation and were accommodated into the *varṇa–jāti* complex. Just as any of the major caste, the caste of artisans or craftsmen evolved its own sub-castes and separate hierarchy. The actual tillers of the soil, who were purely landless, constituted the lowest stratum. In short, the temple working as an institutional force had accelerated the crystallization of the caste-based stratification.

The temple was a theatre of all arts in itself with its grand monumental structure, architecture, sculptures, paintings, and other decorative features besides the various cultural practices, such as music and dance. The architecture and sculpture of the royal temples of the Pallavas, of the numerous *dēvadāna*s and *brahmadēya*s in the age of the Pāṇḍyas and early

Cōḷas bear testimony to it. Of the several paintings, the frescoes of the early Cōḷa times rank the foremost.[22] The temple theatre has gone down in history with lasting contributions to the institutionalization and standardization of instrumental music, dances, and dramatic literature. The variety of drums, their standardized playing, the dance-dramas like *kūttu* and *kūtyāṭṭam,* and the few dramatic compositions in Sanskrit are examples that have survived to our times. Great poets and dramatists like Saktibhadra, widely renowned for his *Āscaryacūṭāmaṇi* that has survived only in excerpts, and Kulasēkhara for his *Subhadrādhananjayam* and *Tapatīsamvaraṇam,* had rendered rare professional perfection in the temple theatre of the eighth–ninth centuries. A variety of amusements entertained the temple society during festive occasions and ceremonies. The elaborate festivals and ceremonies of the temple for their own colourfulness and ritualistic grandeur, too, were sufficiently attractive to the local society. This context of large-scale social convergence involving enormous chances of economic transactions often made the temple an urban spot within the village. It had become a township by the ninth–tenth centuries.[23]

With all these socially significant aspects in their historical context, the temple brought the local people as a whole in closer interaction and provided an effective platform for socio-economic and religious transactions among the people of a system of unequal relations. The temple provided an atmosphere of consecrated communion of competing and conflicting social groups to coalesce. Helping the people to live out the contradictions inherent in the socio-economic system through a religious life–world of contentment, it guaranteed a sort of collective solidarity.

NOTES AND REFERENCES

1. The historical details are scattered in the various volumes of *South Indian Inscriptions* (Archaeological Survey of India) and *Travancore Archaeological Series* (Travancore Archaeological Department). For a comprehensive history, see Nilakanta Sastri, 1929, *The Pandyan Kingdom,* London; *The Colas,* vols I and II, Madras, 1935 and 1937, respectively; A. Appadorai, 1936, *Economic Conditions in Southern India,* vols I and II, Madras; and C. Minakshi, 1977 (1938) *Administration and Social Life Under the Pallavas,* Madras. For the historical details about Kerala, see M.G.S. Narayanan, 1996, *Perumals of Kerala,* Calicut, pp. 197–222. For an outline of the general socio-economic processes, see Rajan Gurukkal, 1992, *The Kerala Temple,* Sukapuram.
2. The socio-economic functions of the temple, particularly the agrarian aspects, though discussed at length by Sastri and his contemporaries, the interconnection between the emergence of the temple and the

socio-economic processes was highlighted in the works of Burton Stein and his fellow researchers. See B. Stein (ed.), 1972, *Essays on South India,* New Delhi. There is a substantial body of published and unpublished literature on the subject. For a comprehensive account, see B. Stein, 1980, *Peasant State and Society in Medieval South India,* New Delhi; B. Stein (ed.), 1978, *South Indian Temple: An Analytical Study,* New Delhi. Also, N. Karashima, 2001, *History and Society in South India,* New Delhi.

3. For a detailed illustration, see Kesavan Veluthat, 1979, 'The Temple Base of the Bhakti Movements in South India', *IHC,* Waltair. Also M.G.S. Narayanan and Kesavan Veluthat, 1989, 'The Bhakti Movement in South India', in S.C. Malik (ed.), *Dissent and Protest in Indian Tradition,* Shimla.
4. See *Nālāyiradivyaprabandham.*
5. For a discussion of the socio-economic implications of the bhakti ideology, see Narayanan and Veluthat, 'The Bhakti Movement in South India'.
6. A large number of such sculptures are found in the Pallava and Pāṇḍya cave temples and the Cōḻa structural temples of Tamil Nadu. For some of these representations see R. Champakalakshmi, 1970, '"Bhagavatha" scenes in Pallava and Cola Sculptures', *JIH,* vol. XLII (1 and 2): 159–70. Also see her 'New Light on the Cola Frescoes of Tanjore', *JIH* Golden Jubilee Volume, 1973, pp. 349–59. In Kerala, with the exception of one or two panels depicting such stories, there are no stone sculptures. The present wooden sculptures in certain old temples were executed, perhaps, in imitation of earlier representations.
7. See the volumes of *South Indian Inscriptions,* Archaeological Survey of India, New Delhi; *Travancore Archeological Series,* Travancore Government Publications; and *Epigraphia Carnatica,* Mysore.
8. See the discussion in Gurukkal, *The Kerala Temple.*
9. Karl Polanyi, 1956, *The Great Transformation: The Political and Economic Origin of Our Time,* Boston. It was Burton Stein who tested the hypothesis of temple-centred resource-redistribution in the context of medieval south Indian temples. See his, 1961, 'State, the Temple and Agricultural Development: A Study in Medieval South India', *EPW* Annual No., vol. XIII, February 1961, p. 187. For a study of the resource redistribution in early Tanjore, see George W. Spencer, 1968, 'Temple Moneylending and Livestock Redistribution in Early Tanjore', *IESHR,* vol. 3, pp. 277–92. For a recent analysis of the temple-centred redistribution of medieval south India, see A. Appadurai and C.A. Brecknridge, 1976, 'The South Indian Hindu Temple: Authority, Honour and Redistribution', *Contributions to Indian Sociology,* New Series, Vol. 10, pp. 187–211.
10. M.G.S. Narayanan, *Perumals of Kerala,* pp. 109–11.
11. '...*Cūṭu muriyum varuvitu...*' is the phrase generally used in south Indian inscriptions to mean the prescribed heat and fineness. See for instance No. 218 of 1911.

12. See B.D. Chattopadhyaya, 1977, *Coins and Currency Systems in Early South India,* New Delhi, p. 303. Also D.N. Jha, 1974, 'Temples as Landed Magnates in Early Medieval South India, c. AD 700–1300', in R.S. Sharma (ed.), *Indian Society: Historical Probings,* New Delhi, p. 207.
13. See P.L. Gupta, *Early Coins of Kerala,* also M.G.S. Narayanan, *Perumals of Kerala,* p. 162.
14. The features of closed economy in medieval Europe have been discussed by Henry Pirenne, 1967, *Economic and Social History of Medieval Europe,* the chapter on money, London, pp. 108–18. Also Marc Bloch, 1967, *Feudal Society,* London, vol. I, p. 67.
15. A. Appadurai, 1936, *Economic Conditions in Southern India, AD 1000–1500,* Madras, pp. 275–6.
16. C. Minakshi, *Pallavas,* p. 199. Also see M.V. Krishna Rao, 1936, *The Gangas of Talakad,* Madras, p. 155 and Nilakanta Sastri, 1924, *Pandyan Kingdom,* London, p. 238.
17. *TAS,* vol. IV, p. 8.
18. T.V. Mahalingam, 1967, *South Indian Polity,* Madras, pp. 345–57; Minakshi, *Pallavas,* p. 127.
19. They are found in the temple inscriptions of the Pallava, Pāṇḍya, and Cēra periods. See, for example, no. 152 of 1916 and *SIL,* vol. I, p. 108.
20. Gurukkal, *The Kerala Temple,* p. 54.
21. See discussions in Rajan Gurukkal, 1987, 'From Royalty of Icons to the Divinity of Royalty: Aspects of Vaisnava Icons and Kingship in Medieval South India', in Ratan Parimoo (ed.), *Vaiṣṇavism in Indian Arts and Culture,* New Delhi, pp. 119–24.
22. See R. Champakalakshmi, 1973, 'New Light on the Tanjore Frescoes', *Journal of Indian History,* Golden Jubilee Volume.
23. For a detailed analysis of the urban processes of the temple complex, see R. Champakalakshmi, 1996, 'Urbanization from Above: Tanjavur, the Ceremonial City of the Cōḷas', in her *Trade, Ideology and Urbanization* (*South India 300 BC to AD 1300*), New Delhi, pp. 425–37.

16

The Formation of Caste Society in Kerala

Historical Antecedents*

The earliest known social formation of Kerala, as in the Tamil region, dates back to the times of ancient heroic Tamil anthologies generally assumed to have belonged to 300 BC and AD 300, when the deep south as a whole remained a single culture zone called Tamilakam. It was a semi-tribal system combining unevenly developed multiple forms of subsistence such as hunting and food gathering, animal husbandry, primitive cultivation, plough agriculture, and primitive commodity production, fast shedding its tribal mooring to emerge as a peasant society.[1] Plough agriculture was the superior form of production in terms of technology and productivity, but it was yet to become the dominant form as evidenced by the superstructure characterized by the juridico-political hegemony of predatory chieftains, incessant plunder raids, the institution of redistribution, and the ethos of heroic ideas, passions, values, rituals, and customs which were entirely uncongenial to the development of plough agriculture. Though it was more or less a self-locked system, it generated, while functioning, a series of contradictions which subsequently acted as the transforming forces. By and large, it represented a social formation of undifferentiated economy and non-stratified relations. This chapter seeks to explore the mechanisms and processes of the widening of economic differentiation, formation of a class structured society, and the cultural practice of caste-based social stratification.

---

* This chapter is a reproduced version of, 1994, 'Formation of Caste Society in Kerala: Historical Antecedents', in K.L. Sharma (ed.), *Caste and Class in Indian States*, (Rawat Publications: Delhi), pp. 395–410.

The primordial social formation as understood from the clues of heroic poems, popularly known as Sangam literature, was not a system of relations based on caste. By and large, it was not an altogether simple society with no differentiation at all, but the differentiation was of a flexible nature. *Brāhmaṇas* seem to have enjoyed the highest socio-rural status and maintained a brahmanical ritualistic domain of caste exclusiveness by distancing themselves from other people as the purest. The heroic Tamil anthologies refer to both the *brāhmaṇas* and gods as *uyarntōr*.[2] *Tolkāppiyam*, a grammatical treatise, which the traditional Tamil scholars ascribe to the period before the anthologies, describes the Tamilian counterpart of the *varṇa* system consisting of *antaṇar, aracar, vaṇikar*, and *vēḷāḷar* as the four varṇas.[3] But modern historians and linguists alike, consider it a later work, probably of the AD fifth or the sixth century, and moreover, aracar, vaṇikar, vēḷāḷar actually do not correspond to the *kshatriya, vaisya*, and *sūdra* ranks of the varṇa system.[4] Some scholars have tried to show that there existed in Tamilakam an entirely different set of four castes, nothing to do with the traditional four varṇas. As already pointed out earlier contention is based on a poem which states that there were no *kuṭis* excepting those of the *tuṭiyar, pāṇar, paṟaiyar*, and *kaṭampar* in the land.[5] The term *kuṭi* is often taken to denote caste, which is an unwarranted translation, and actually the term denotes settlement. In this context, it denotes settlements of clans such as the tuṭiyar (people with a kind of drum called *tuṭi* as their magico-religious symbol), pāṇar (people composing and singing bardic poems), paṟaiyar (people with a kind of drum *paṟai* as their magico-religious symbol), and kaṭambar (people with the *kaṭambu* trees as their totem). The poet does not speak of the general situation in Tamilakam and what he describes is the feature of a specific locality in the land.

The question whether the ancient society of Tamilakam had a caste-based stratification or not has to be better scrutinized against the background of contemporary economic processes. We understand from the anthologies that the relatively undeveloped forms of subsistence such as hunting, animal husbandry, primitive agriculture, fishing, and salt manufacturing were essentially adopted by the groups that had clan ties. The anthologies mention clannish groups like *kānavar* and *vēṭar* taking to hunting and primitive cultivation; *iṭaiyar* doing animal husbandry; *valayar* or *mīnavar* taking to fishing; *paratavar* undertaking salt manufacturing and *umaṇar* its distribution; and *uḻavar* taking to plough agriculture.[6] All the forms of production were based on kinship ties of the agnatic or affinal type, within which were submerged the division and specialization even of plough agriculture. Though there were certain specialists in arts and crafts such as *taccar* (carpenters) and *kollar* (blacksmiths), there is nothing to show that they constituted themselves as groups outside clan ties. The functional and transactional relations of the people, by and large, did not generate any rigid stratification of an institutional nature, leading to the break-up of kinship. The authority structure too was submerged in kinship and we do not find a ruling class totally alienated from the masses although the former had a lineage identity.[7]

However, the growth of economic differentiation and the disintegration of kinship were ongoing processes in contemporary society. Regular plunder raids and booty redistribution among people outside the clan ties too were causing economic differentiation. Sometimes the booty included productive lands and their redistribution among people outside the clan caused the disintegration of kinship as the base of production.[8] This was particularly crucial when productive land was given away to *brāhmaṇas* who were entitled to a share of booty as reward for performing rituals, composing eulogies to chieftains, and functioning as preceptors. It gave rise to a new system of production relations transcending the framework of kinship. This would suggest that although a full-blown institutional manifestation of caste was yet to surface, there existed in the society a potential nucleus anticipating the formation of castes. There was the *brāhmaṇa* household that signified the new system of production relations. The novelty of the system was that it involved the relation between *brāhmaṇas* and tillers who were non-cultivating landholders and cultivating landless people, respectively. It was a relation involving two objectively antagonistic classes.

The *brāhmaṇa* land as an independent unit of production required working families attached to it to ensure a permanent labour force. So naturally, several families belonging to clannish groups must have permanently resorted to production as well as other essential functions. It is quite reasonable to presume that the beginnings of the crystallization of functionally specific families into castes took place in the localities of *brāhmaṇa* households. It is possible that those families distinguished themselves from the rest of the population, as associated with a unit of production, supreme both ritually and economically. Also, they must have differentiated themselves from one another with their tribal norms of purity and pollution. However, the germination of the concept of the *jāti* system must have existed in the localities of *brāhmaṇa* households during the days of the anthologies, but the number of *brāhmaṇa* households in Tamilakam was not large enough for the *jāti* system to characterize the society.

The social formation in the period of the anthologies seems to have undergone a total crisis during the fourth and fifth centuries of the Christian era, which was a logical culmination of the contradictions in the formation, accentuated by more extensive predatory marches, migrations, and the entailing disintegration of the kinship ties in production.[9] Though the *brāhmaṇa* household economy suffered a temporary set back in the wake of the crisis, subsequently it thrived vigorously as the alternative mode of production.[10] An important feature of this development was the emergence of large *brāhmaṇa* villages, which meant the virtual extension of the new system of production relations to a larger society, and the emergence of the *jāti* system as a concomitant development.

During the seventh, eighth, and ninth centuries, the *brāhmaṇa* villages, the *brahmadēyas*, proliferated all over Tamilakam as a result of royal grants of land to *brāhmaṇas*. The expansion of irrigated agriculture as well of the new system of relations was the outcome of the dissolving semi-tribal system and the process involved the superimposition of *brāhmaṇa* proprietorship over many a communal land tract, integration of several clannish groups, and the formation of new social relations, the latter being particularly relevant to the present discussion. As already noted, the process of the formation of functionally specific groups with some sort of caste identity could be related to the permanent association of certain communal kinship units with the labour processes of the expansion of the *brāhmaṇa*-headed agrarian economy. The evolving relations in a society headed by *brāhmaṇa* were primarily based on the nature of the functional association of producers, artisans, and craftsmen. Their grading on a hierarchical scale depended on the kind of entitlement each group had regarding the sharing of the surplus.[11] This entitlement was determined by each group's relation with the means of production, particularly land. *Brāhmaṇas* were the proprietors of land, but they often leased their large farms out to a group of people, who emerged as a class of intermediaries between the *brāhmaṇas* and peasants. So what was crucial in the social relations of the period was the separation between the primary producers and the full-time non-producing functionaries, such as administrators and warriors, who were entitled to the lion's share of surplus through their managerial and protective functions. The group, entitled to a higher share of surplus, distanced themselves from the people directly associated with the labour processes and this superior class-position formed the basis of caste hierarchy.[12] In short, it was the hierarchy of entitlement to the surplus that provided the real foundation of the caste structure in the *brāhmaṇa*-headed agrarian society of south India.

The proliferation of *brahmadēyas* corresponded to the emergence of temples in south India and each *brāhmaṇa* village became temple-centred, with the temple acting as the headquarter of the agrarian village. The land system and service-tenancy became widespread in the temple-centred villages. Through royal land grants, private land endowments, gifts of gold, and other forms of resources by devotees, the temple became a fabulously rich institution.[13] Being a landed magnate by itself, it commanded a large society of people as its dependents and functionaries.[14] With *brāhmaṇas* as its material and ritual custodians at the top, various groups of people hierarchically structured on the basis of their entitlements to the temple-resources in the middle, and the group of primary producers at the base, the temple signified a gamut of social relations into which the principles of caste were introduced for the first time in a full-fledged form. The formation of a hierarchy was a natural consequence of the system of social differentiation, based as it was on varying levels of ritual status positions in the orbits around the *brāhmaṇas*.

The period from the eighth to the AD twelfth century, the earliest documented phase in the history of Kerala, saw the proliferation and consolidation of temple-centred agrarian villages headed by *brāhmaṇas*.[15] We do not know the exact process of the brahmanical colonization of Kerala and as a reasonable hypothesis it can be suggested that the colonization was the result of a large-scale exodus of *brāhmaṇas* from Andhra through Tamil Nadu and Karnataka.[16] Unlike the rest of south India, Kerala has no copper plate characters registering grants of land to *brāhmaṇas* and there is nothing to show that any of the *brāhmaṇa* settlements here originated as a *brahmadēya*. It seems that the *brāhmaṇa* settlements in Kerala grew on their own. Traditional sources indicate that there were originally 32 *brāhmaṇa* settlements in Kerala and now it remains historically true in the light of temple epigraphs.[17]

The establishment of these early settlements must have taken place during the seventh and eighth centuries. As evidenced by the very first epigraph of Kerala from a temple, the early *brāhmaṇa* settlements had started growing further into subsidiary settlements by the beginning of the ninth century. The evidently long processes of social formation since the days of the anthologies down to the ninth century therefore, can only be extrapolated conjecturally. The waterlogged and marshy landscape ecosystem of Kerala necessitated extensive mobilization of hard labour for the reclamation of agrarian fields. This presupposes a long period of large-scale labour mobilization for reclaiming the productive land out of a relatively inhospitable landscape ecosystem. The labour force must have been recruited from the clan families living along the red soil hill-slopes beside the marshy wetlands, who cultivated millet and highland paddy. In the process, they got attached to the land on a permanent basis under the institution of bonded labour, probably enabled by the persuasion of their headmen by the *brāhmaṇas*, who were already recognized for their scholarship, tradition, and charisma. The *brāhmaṇas*' ideological coercion was a very significant factor of leavening influence. Their Vedic, epic, Purāṇic, and Śāstrāic ideas and institutions were effective devices of social control and domination. It is reasonable to presume that the instituted relations of labour realization by the *brāhmaṇa* laid the foundation of a stratified society based on an objective antagonism between the landlords and tillers.

The system of production relations evolved in the primordial *brāhmaṇa* households had, in due course, acquired a higher institutional and organizational manifestation as evidenced by the set up of huge temple-centred *brāhmaṇa* villages of the ninth to tenth centuries. The thirty-two *Brāhmaṇa* villages became well-established in the fertile tracts best suited for paddy cultivation by the period. With the agrarian activities centralized under the temple, managed by a corporation of *brāhmaṇa* landlords, each village signified an elaborate agrarian order.[18] The *brāhmaṇa* landlords held almost all agrarian tracts as individual holdings (*brahmasvam*) and collective holdings (*dēvasvam*) and exercised proprietary control over the settlers in the village.[19] Just as an ancient *brāhmaṇa* household had its required functionaries around it, a temple-centred *brāhmaṇa* corporation had all the required functionaries settled in the village itself. By and large, it was a self-sufficient unit with all necessary goods and services. The process of localization often involved the bringing and settling of various functional groups on the village land. Once so settled, they all became attached and obligated to the village, that is, to the landlords. All the functionaries enjoyed one or the other type of rights over the village land: the intermediaries enjoyed the *kārāṇmai* (tenancy), while the artisans and craftsmen had the *kuṭiyāmai* (occupancy). In short, a temple-centred *brāhmaṇa* village was the corporation of *brāhmaṇa* landlords with the people associated with them as landed intermediaries, tenants, artisans, craftsmen, and tillers. The process of integration of a large number of such functionaries was evidently complex and the process of their absorption into a hierarchy of caste was all the more complex. However, we are able to draw certain inferences and insights out of the temple records of the period.

The temple-centred nature of the society and economy led to the formation of groups, classes, and castes under the institutional influences and directions of the temple. The status of the temple as a landed institution and as a repository of gold and other valuables, enabled it to wield a great deal of social control. Through its control over land, it harnessed landed intermediaries, leaseholders, artisans, craftsmen, and tillers into a society that can very well be called a temple society. The pooling of wealth in the temple as endowments and its redistribution among the functionaries in the temple society led to the formation of power groups even among *brāhmaṇas* themselves.[20] Those *Brāhmaṇa* landlords who were members of the village corporation (also called *sābha)* were the most powerful in this society. As the custodians of the temple wealth and the proprietors of the village, they had the highest economic status, and as the most learned priests they enjoyed the highest socio-ritual status too. They constituted the *āgamic* specialists as well as Vedic priests, but there were other exceptional cases of *brāhmaṇas* also who had equal land control without enjoying agamic rights and Vedic scholarship.[21] However, the rich agamic specialists gradually emerged as a separate group called *tantrikal,* as distinguished from the other *brāhmaṇas*. There were *paṭṭakal (bhaṭṭas* or *Brāhmaṇa* scholar*), cāttirar (caṭṭās* or armed *Brāhmaṇas),* and *śānti* (temple priest) among the *brāhmaṇas*, who received *virutti,* the land-lease as reward for their services in the temple. *Caṭṭās* and *bhaṭṭas*[22] had a relatively better economic status when compared to that of the temple priest, whose ritual status was higher. The interesting thing to be noticed is the formation of an internal differentiation among *brāhmaṇas* themselves, based on the nature of land control. During the later period, the differentiation became almost as sharp as that between castes and we find the major landlords among *brāhmaṇas* identifying themselves as *ādhya* as distinguished from others who were called *āsya.* Similarly, in relation to the nature of land control or the nature of entitlement to the produce caused a hierarchical division among the non-*brāhmaṇa* order also.

Potuvāl and *vāriyar* are the two most important functional categories in the non-*brāhmaṇa* order.[23] *Potuvāl* was the common man, the *madhyastha* between the custodians of the temple and the devotees for all their transactions with the temple, who acted as the secretary of the temple. As a functionary shouldering managerial and executive responsibility, the potuvāl was relatively close to the *brāhmaṇas* and received *virutti* land as reward for his service to the temple. Anyone who was a member in any of the temple committees (*vāriyams),* could be called a *vāriyar.* However, there is a specific functional group referred to in the temple inscriptions as *vāriyar* by profession and not by virtue of membership in any *vāriyam*. Members of this group were also given *virutti* land as a reward for their services in the temple. These two are now names of two separate castes in Kerala. It is obvious that both the *potuvāl* and *vāriyar* were two functionally specific groups attached to the temple. Their functions became hereditary since the reward was in the form of the service tenure called *virutti*. These groups of hereditary professions gradually, by virtue of their improved economic status and association with the *brāhmaṇas* in the affairs of the temple, distanced themselves from others through rules of marriages and inter-dining to constitute two endogamous caste groups. In the same manner, the drummers, dancers, and musicians of the temple constituted separate caste groups. The drummers of the temple are referred to in the inscriptions as *koṭṭikal* or *uvaccakal*, and these names as such do not seem to have survived as caste names. Their modern caste name is *mārār*. The dancers of the temple are referred to in the epigraphs as *cākkaimār* (male dancers) and *nankaimār* (dancing girls).[24] *Cākkiyār* is a caste name now in Kerala and *nangyār* is the name given to the female members of the *cākkiyār*. All these functionaries were paid in land as *virutti* which, as already shown, led them to become hereditary professional groups and subsequently endogamous castes. These castes are generally called the *āntaraḷa-jāti*, the caste between the *brāhmaṇas* and the other non-*brāhmaṇas*.

They are also called the temple castes suggestive of their origins. Most of the temple lands and the individual *brāhmaṇa* holdings were leased out to *kārāḷar*, who were primarily from the non-*brāhmaṇa* order. The caste that later came to be called the *nairs* seems to have been the foremost among them. Forming the major part of the *kārāḷar*, this caste represented the second dominant factor in the temple-centred agrarian society. It was from this caste that the *sāmanta* chieftains emerged. It seems that the majority of military recruits were from among this caste. This class of intermediaries in land, with the rank and entailing privileges of the nobility, owing allegiance only to the *brāhmaṇa* landlords, succeeded in asserting themselves in the temple society. The relations of the women of this caste with the *brāhmaṇas* through a peculiar material institution called *sambandham*, added to its ritual status.[25] This caste of *kārāḷar*, on the basis of the nature of land control it wielded, gave rise to several divisions in it. Some of them, in course of time, eventually became part of the ruling aristocracy and differentiated themselves from the rest of the nairs by adopting a kshatriya title like '*varma*'. A few others on the basis of land control achieved through high military positions differentiated themselves as *paṇikkar* and similarly, yet another group distinguished themselves as *menon* on the basis of better land control and their ritual status acquired through their association with the *brāhmaṇa* landlords as the latter's accountants.

In the same manner, the artisans and craftsmen also became caste groups through their attachment to the temple society. These people were settled at the fringe of the temple-centred villages and were obliged to render their services to the temple as well as to the landlords. Inscriptions refer to groups such as *taccar* (carpenters), *kollar* (blacksmiths), *kalavāṇiyar* (potters), *vāṇiyar* (oil mongers), and *vaṇṇār* (washermen). They were brought to the temple village to settle to ensure their services.[26] They enjoyed occupancy rights over village land and this constituted the material incentive for them to be hereditary professional groups, with no other alternative occupation as they were caught up in a social milieu of immobility and functional obligations. They were more or less the bondsmen of the temple village where they were settled.

At the base of the temple society was the actual tillers who constituted the most servile group and their only privilege was *aṭiayma* (servility). They were attached to agricultural lands and were transacted along with land as goods.[27] As a caste, they are called *pulayar,* probably a tribal name, and *ceṛumar,* the lowest people. All the people distanced themselves from the pulayars or ceṛumars and soon this class of primary producers metamorphosed into a polluting caste, a process that need not be explained here.

It is to be noted here that the temple society and the *brāhmaṇa* villages were confined only to a small area in Kerala, that is, in the fertile wetlands. We do not have any archival records highlighting the situation in non-*brāhmaṇa* villages. However, since the *brāhmaṇa*-headed agrarian villages were the units of the dominant mode of production of the period, the relation evolved was characteristic to the society as whole. There are indications in certain records that in the non-*brāhmaṇa* villages also, agrarian relations and the land system remained the same.[28] The situation in non-agrarian tracts must have been different, and the society there may not have been stratified on the principle of castes. We have evidence in the ninth-century Syrian Christian copper plates for the existence of certain caste groups and the land tenure system in the market town of Quilon.[29] The plates mention the grant of certain caste groups like *i̤ḻavar* (toddy-tappers), taccar, vēḷāḷar (agricultural people), and vaṇṇār to the Tarsa church. It actually registers a grant of lands required by the functionaries of the church. The above mentioned castes were the settlers of the granted land and they were to serve the church and its people according to certain conditions. As the grant was made by the local ruler, the land originally must have been the *cērikkal* property (crown-land), and the alienation of the caste groups suggests that in the crown's lands also, the relations of production were in tune with the caste system. In short, the cērikkal as well as market towns had the same land system as the *brāhmaṇa* villages and their functionaries were caste groups too. It may be said that the Kerala society witnessed the formation of caste groups all over the agrarian region during the ninth and tenth centuries.

What emerges is a hierarchical structure of entitlements to varied rights over land institutionalized by service tenements. The highest right tacitly recognized was the king's suzerainty (*koima*). As recognized and exempted from taxes by the king, the *brāhmaṇa* land (*brahmasvam*) and temple land (*dēvasvam*) enjoyed autonomous rights of the landlord. The local rulers (*nāṭūvāḷis*) and probably other non-*brāhmaṇa* landlords had their proprietary control over their hereditary lands. Below the ownership of landlords was the leaseholder's right (*kārāṇma*), while the artisans and craftspeople were entitled to occupy the land (*kuṭiyāma*) by way of reward for their service to the settlement. At the base were the tillers attached to land, a people of bonded servitude and immobility. These varied entitlements in the hierarchy superimposed in the ascending order were tightly bound through ties of dependence and protection besides relations of exploitation and subjection. People in every stratum were locked up in a system of hereditary service obligation and land-related reward. Those enjoying these varied entitlements in the hierarchical order began the practice of undertaking their vocations on a hereditary basis primarily for retaining the land rights as their family property. As people of hereditary occupations, they began to be called by the name of their vocations. These occupation names subsequently became caste names, a process indicating their transformation into endogamous castes.

To sum up, the earliest identifiable social formation of Kerala was a combination of several simple unevenly evolved economies largely incapable of generating division and specialization of labour leading to the divergence of kinship and the formation of castes. However, one of them, the *brāhmaṇa* household economy, required a permanent association of full-time function-specific families and hence involved relations cutting across kinship. This, under the incentive of the security of labour rewards, might have led to the formation of hereditary occupation groups. Hereditary occupation groups gave rise to occupation-labelled people, who in the course of time turned into endogamous castes. Formation of castes acquired greater dimensions in the wake of agrarian expansion through the establishment of *brahmadēyas* and *dēvadanas*. As a pivotal institutional agency of the *brāhmaṇa* lords with their extensive agrarian activities, the temple played a crucial role in the multiplication of services and rewards in land. The institution of reward by land, integrated with the service-tenure under the agrarian system of the times, was responsible for the emergence of hereditary professional groups on a large scale. With *brāhmaṇas*, the community of the highest ritual status as the point of reference, the various functionaries permanently attached to the *brāhmaṇa* village acquired a relatively graded differential status depending upon the nature and extent of each one's service-tenure. A higher service-tenement meant a better economic status and proximity to the *brāhmaṇas*, implying a higher ritual status. Such a system of status differentiation in terms of economic as well as ritual values was instrumental to the transformation of hereditary functionaries into an endogamous caste hierarchy. The system of service-tenure under the king and the local rulers also gave rise to hereditary offices, generating castes and sub-castes with economy and royalty as determinants of status hierarchy. Its extension into non-*brāhmaṇa* villages, and even to market towns, is attested by records. In short, caste appeared as an institutional manifestation in the hierarchically structured agrarian society in which services were paid for in the form of land rights.

NOTES AND REFERENCES

1. Rajan Gurukkal, 1987, 'Forms of Production and Forces of Change in Ancient Tamil Society', *Studies in History*, 5(2): 159–75, n.s.
2. *Puṛanānūṛu* (*Pn.*) 221; *Patiṛṛuppattu* (*Prp*) 1: 35; 3: 9 refer to *Brāhmaṇas* as *uyarntōr*. *Iḷipiṛappāḷar* is referred to in *Pn.* 82: 3; 170: 5; 287: 2; 289: 10; 363: 14.
3. *Tolkāpiyam; Porul.* 625–6; 635. It is mentioned in the text that *antaṇar* wore the sacred thread, carried the *karakam* (vessel containing holy water for ceremonial ablutions), the *mukkōl* (trident-like staff), and the *manai* (wooden plank to serve as seat). The aracar had the royal paraphernalia, the vaṇikar wore a garland on their shoulder and a flower on their head, and the *vēḷāḷar* carried their weapons and the totemic garland. For details, see N. Subrahmanian, 1966, *Sangam Polity*, Bombay, pp. 258–60. Also M.G.S. Narayanan, 1987, 'The Vedic Puranic Sastraic Element in Tamil Sangam Society and Culture', in K.M. Srimali (ed.), *Essays in Indian Art, Religion and Society*, New Delhi.
4. The concept of *varṇa* has to be understood as the Śāstraic abstraction of contemporary *jāti* experiences of the northern India. For dealings on the caste system in detail, see C. Bougle, 1971, *Essays on the Caste System*, D. Pocock

(trans.), Cambridge. Also L. Dumont, 1972, *Homo Hierarchicus*, (tr.) London. As regards the questions of origins see the scientific observations in Romila Thapar, 1984, *From Lineage to State*, New Delhi, pp. 18–20.

5. *Pn.* 335 by Mankuti kilar.
6. *Naṟṟiṇai* (*Nar.*) 142; 303; 331; 372; 338. *Ainkuṟunūṟu* (*Aink.*) 47; 48; 111; 195. *Akanānūṟu* (*An.*) 60; 65. *Pn.* 33; 73; 82 are examples. See the discussions in K. Sivathamby,1974, 'Early South Indian Society and Economy; the *Tiṇai* Concept', *Social Scientist,* no. 29, pp, 20–37. Also see S. Singaravelu, 1966, *Social Life of the Tamils: Classical Period,* Kuala Lumpur, pp. 32–7.
7. Anthologies refer to the three major ruling lineages *(muvēntar),* the Cēra, Cōḻa, and Pāṇḍya besides the minor ones called the *vēḷir*. But none of these seems to have completely freed themselves from the nexus of the clan ties.
8. *Pn.* 297 describes a warrior chief telling his fellow warriors that he would not accept the arid gram-growing tracts as rewards for fighting, but would take only paddy fields. This would suggest that the capture of productive land was a major attraction for warrior leaders participating in the raids. For a substantial analysis of the question, see M.G.S. Narayanan, 1982, 'Warrior Settlements in the Sangam Age', *PIHC.*
9. The AD fourth century witnessed the climax of the crisis in the form of a large-scale predatory march by the marauding *Kaḷabhras,* who swept over the region under all the three ruling lineages of Tamilakam. Brahmins were reminded of the evils of *kaliyuga* by the sufferings in the wake of *Kaḷabhras*' aggression. The implications of the Kali Age in the context of northern India have been ably interpreted as a transitional crisis of a social formation. See R.S.Sharma, 1982, 'The Kali Age: A Period of Social Crisis', in S.N. Mukherjee (ed.), India: *History and Thought, Essays in Honour of A.L.Basham,* Calcutta, pp. 186–203. Also B.N.S. Yadava, 1978–9, 'The Accounts of the Kali Age and the Social Transition from the Antiquity to the Middle Ages', *Indian Historical Review,* v(1&2). The interpretation holds good in the context of the fourth–fifth century Tamil society too. See Rajan Gurukkal, 1984, 'Agrarian System and Socio-political Organisation under the Early Pandyas', unpublished PhD dissertation, Jawaharlal Nehru University, New Delhi, pp. 76–80.
10. See Gurukkal, 'Agrarian System and Socio-political Organisation', p. 76.
11. It recalls the pattern of resource-sharing in the medieval European society. See R. Rodolsky, 1951, 'The Distribution of the Agrarian Product in Feudalism', *Journal Economic History,* XI(3): 247–9. Also P. Anderson, 1974, *Lineages* of *Absolutist State,* London, p. 401.
12. See the caste and class identity question ably discussed in Claude Meillassoux, 1973, 'Are There Castes in India?', *Economy and Society,* 2(1): 89–111.
13. For details see Burton Stein, 1960, 'The Economic Function of a Medieval South Indian Temple', *Journal of Asian Studies,* 19(2): 163–76. Also *The South Indian Temple* edited by him, New Delhi, 1977. The economic position of

the temple is well brought out in N. Karashima, 1896, 'Land Donations to Hindu Temples in Medieval South India', *Journal of Asian and African Studies*, Tokyo.

14. D.N. Jha, 1974, 'Temples as Landed Magnates in South India, c. AD 700–1300', in R.S. Sharma (ed.), *Indian Society: Historical Probings*, New Delhi.
15. The details are given in Rajan Gurukkal, 1980, 'The Socio-economic Milieu of the Kerala Temple: A Functional Analysis', *Studies in History*, 11(1).
16. The problem has been elaborately considered in M.G.S. Narayanan, 1972, 'Political and Social Conditions of Kerala under the Kulasekhara Empire', unpublished doctoral dissertation, Kerala University.
17. Kesavan Veluthat, 1976, *Brahmin Settlements in Kerala*, Calicut.
18. Gurukkal, 'The Socio-economic Milieu of the Kerala Temple'.
19. Ibid.
20. Ibid. The concept of redistribution is borrowed from Karl Polanyi, 'The Economy as Instituted Process', in Karl Polanyi, Conrad M. Arensberg, and Harry W. Pearson (eds), *Trade and Market in the Early Empires*, Glencoe, pp. 243–6. But the concept is used only to explain the niceties and the central perspective is that of the mode of production concept formulated by Marx. The insights of E. Terray and M. Godelier are also made use of. See E. Terray, 1975, *Marxism and 'Primitive' Societies*, New Delhi and Maurice Godelier, 1977, *Perspectives in Marxist Anthropology*, Cambridge.
21. The Manur inscription of the Pāṇḍya period and the Uttaramcrur inscription of the Cōḻa period prescribe Vedic and Agamic scholarship as one of the essential qualifications for the *Brāhmaṇa* landlords to become members of the *sabha*. See discussions in K.A. Nilakanta Sastri, 1975, *The Colas*, Madras, pp. 495–6.
22. Reference to armed *brāhmaṇa* learning martial arts and scholarly *brāhmaṇa*.
23. Gurukkal, 'The Socio-economic Milieu of the Kerala Temple'.
24. Ibid. Also see 'Proliferation and Consolidation of the Temple Centred Social Hierachy in the Cera Period', *Journal of Kerala Studies*, VI(III and IV): 333–46.
25. Sambandham was a system of concubinage by the *Brāhmaṇas* with the Nair ladies. But it acquired the status of a loose marriage since among the Kerala Brhmans (*namputiris*), only the eldest male son was entitled to marry from the same community. Thus all the junior members of the family were forced to have sanbandham alliances with the Nairs.
26. Gurukkal, 'The Socio-economic Milieu of the Kerala Temple'.
27. Ibid.
28. An inscription recently recovered from Cembra in north Malabar sheds light on the socio-economic process in a non-*Brāhmaṇa* village. It is a coastal village with tracts generally unsuitable for paddy cultivation owing to the tidal flow of saline water into the fields. Such areas were inevitably avoided by the *brāhmaṇas*. Still, it appears that the relations of production were more or less the same in this village too.

For details of the inscription see, Raghava Varier, 1985, 'Cambra Lightitangal' (Mal.) *Vijnanakairali*, 16(2), pp. 84–98.

29. See the text of the inscription given in M.G.S. Narayanan, 1972, *Cultural Symbiosis in Kerala*, Trivandrum, Appendix IV.

17

Aspects of the Reservoir System of Irrigation in the Pāṇḍya Country*

This chapter pertains to certain aspects of the early reservoir system of irrigation in the Pāṇḍya country, the southern districts of modern Tamil Nadu, in the AD seventh to tenth centuries as tentatively made out from archaeological, epigraphic, toponymic, and ethnographic source materials of a fragmentary nature. It seeks to understand who executed, owned, controlled, and maintained the irrigation sources, mainly the reservoirs and associated distributive infrastructures during the period under review. The period is noted for the wider utilization and effective management, technological, and institutional aspects of the reservoir system of irrigation all over Tamil Nadu in general and the region under study in particular.

The reservoir system of irrigation in the Tamil south and Sri Lanka had its beginnings in the use of small tanks, probably by the iron-using people of the megalithic tradition, whose subsistence, according to some archaeologists, was based on irrigated agriculture.[1] Nevertheless, planned and systematic utilization of over-ground water sources for irrigation was unlikely in the dry zone agriculture of the Tamil south and Sri Lanka during the Iron Age proper, say between circa 1000 BC and circa AD 300, for the people in those centuries were primarily millet farmers in the red-soil tracts of dry agro-climatic conditions.[2] Primordial techniques of utilization of over-ground water sources for irrigation might have continued from early times, but their improvement and extension could have happened only at least three centuries later. Knowledge of irrigation techniques alone does

* This chapter is a modified version of, 1986, 'Aspects of the Reservoir System of Irrigation in the Pāṇḍya State', *Studies in History*, 2(2)" 155–62.

not imply their extensive use, for it requires hierarchical social relations, structures of control, institutions of domination, and other facilities of the process of agrarian expansion. It is the nature and extent of utilization and the systematized mode of management of the technology that determine it.[3] It is the nature of the utilization and management of water resources that indicates the potential for expansion. In about the AD fifth century the onset of the process, relations, structures, and institutions of agrarian expansion began in the Pallava region from where, in the next century, they began to expand further south in the Pāṇḍya region. The period from the seventh to the tenth centuries witnessed the consolidation of organizational and institutional facilities compatible with the best application of the technology of agriculture in general and irrigation in particular, all over the Pāṇḍya country, studded by peasant settlements of temple-centred *brahmadēyas* and *ūrs*. Both the perennial and inundation techniques of irrigation were extensively used in suitable areas in the Pāṇḍya country, where the cultivation of paddy and sugarcane had to depend almost entirely on rain-fed reservoirs from the seventh century onwards. The records show that the major irrigation projects in the region were carried out during the seventh to the eighth centuries, the period that witnessed an unprecedented expansion of wet-rice agriculture.

A reservoir is a depression with embankments at required points, often covering an area of one to two or more kilometres, harvesting and preserving rainwater and water from perennial sources like streams and rivers, for later use, primarily for agriculture. The reservoir system was fundamental to the irrigation practices of the early Tamil region and the dry zone of Sri Lanka in general and the Pāṇḍyan state in particular, as a part of the landscape ecosystem without perennial rainfall, due to alternation between droughts and monsoons.[4] The modern districts of Madurai and Ramanathapuram, the major dry zone of the Pāṇḍya state, are full of rain-fed reservoirs of the past. Often the reservoir was constructed by taking advantage of the landscape of mounds and depressions, mostly across a slope enabling easy collection and storage of run-off water. Small tanks (*kuḷam*) and wells (*kiṇaṟu*) were other storage structures that facilitated irrigation in small fields and household gardens. The reservoir (*ēri*) system consisted of the huge water storage structures with embankments (*maḍagu*), several sluice systems (*tūmpu* and *kumiḻi*) at suitable points for releasing water through the conduit to the main distributive channels (*peruvāykāl*), and sub-channels (*ciṟuvāykāl*).

RULING CLASS PATRONAGE

The epigraphical evidence vouches for the fact that the execution and renovations of all major irrigation facilities were part of the responsibility of the king and the ruling aristocracy, while the task of their maintenance was the responsibility of the local bodies of landlords and merchants. The earliest epigraphical evidence known so far, attesting irrigation works in the Pāṇḍya region, is the Vaigai bed inscription of Cēntan Arikesari's fiftieth year (circa AD 720).[5] The epigraph registers the event of the construction of a *maḍagu* (sluice) and the excavation of a *kāl* (channel) from the Vaigai river by the Pāṇḍya king Cēntan Arikēsari. The record mentions that the *maḍagu* was named Arikesariyan, obviously after the name of its founder. There is a reference in the same record to the closing of a channel, probably gone out of use. The area irrigated through the new channel seems to have being part of Paruttikkuṭi-*nādu*, which is referred to in the inscription towards its end. This is obviously a royal irrigation project completed under the auspices of the Pāṇḍya king. That the sluice was constructed and a channel excavated right on the Vaigai river at a site close to the royal capital, accounts for the direct involvement of the king. There are not many specific inscriptional references to royal irrigation projects after Arikesari's period. Nevertheless, there is a stock expression in all the copper plates, praising the king to have caused the construction of many reservoirs (*eṇṇiṛanta taṭākangngal*). We have no detailed inscriptional references to irrigation projects in the Pāṇḍya country till the time of Srimara Srivallabha (circa AD 811–57). An epigraph probably of the reign period of Srimara Srivallabha, found inscribed on a rock in the village of Ramanathapuram (Dindigal), speaks about the excavation of a reservoir by a local chief, namely, Nakkan Puḷḷan alias Parāntaka Paḷḷi Vēḷān, a military chief in the service of king Parāntaka Neḍunjaḍaiyan (circa AD 767–811), as the title suggests. As the work was not finished during his time, his son Puḷḷan Nakkan undertook to complete it. The reservoir was named Puḷḷan-ēri.

An unpublished inscription on a stone bund (*maṭaikkāl*, also called *kanmay*) of the reservoir of Cinnakkollappaṭṭi in the Sattur taluk, dated in the eighth year of Srimara Srivallabha (circa AD 819), registers the renovation of certain bunds and sluices built by a certain Eṭṭi Cāttan, the *kiḷavan* (literally, the elder, meaning the headman or the local chief) of Iruppaikkuṭi, an agrarian locality in the taluk.[6] The inscription is a record of the said chief's achievements in executing several irrigation projects. The first irrigation project mentioned in the inscription is the renovation of a collapsed mud bund (*maṭai*) on Perumkuḷam, the major reservoir in the agrarian settlement called Cāttanūr (Sattur). In the inscription, the chief is mentioned to have rebuilt the old collapsed mud bund in granite. The chief is praised in the same inscription for rebuilding in bricks two more bunds (maṭais) made of mud, the Ponnān-maṭai and Pūnkuṛi-maṭai, besides the one called Cennir-*maṭai* on the reservoir, namely, Putukkuḷam.

Two inscriptions of Eṛunkkankuṭi allude to the various projects of this chief.[7] One record says that in the sixteenth year of Srimara Srivallabha's reign, the chief dismantled an old bund on the reservoir called Karumkuḷam (Sattur) and reconstructed it with a strong foundation of stone and constructed a new one, raising the bank west of the mud bund and east of the reservoir.[8] He renamed the reservoir Kiḻavan-ēri. The other record dated the eighteenth year of the same king, enumerates his various projects.[9] He is said to have excavated a reservoir at the agrarian village called Ten-Veḷiyankuṭi (Sattur) and called it Kiḻavan-ēri. At the village called Māranūr (Sattur), he dismantled and rebuilt an old bund on Perunkuḷam, renaming the reservoir as Kiḻavan-ēri. Likewise, he dismantled and rebuilt a bund on the reservoir called Vaḻḻaikkuḷam, which he also renamed Kiḻavan-ēri and cut channels with troughs for the flow of water at the locality called Iruppaikkuṭi (Sattur). On the same reservoir he connected two bunds, called *Kan-maṭai* and Pattan-maṭai to strengthen the capacity of the reservoir. On the reservoir called the Tirumāl-ēri in the same village, he is mentioned to have repaired a collapsed stone sluice and constructed it with the help of a 'string-line' (*nūliṭṭeṛuvitta* is the expression in the inscription), which is an indicator of the improvement in the techniques of construction.[10] The technique ensuring precision implies the notion of right angles too, which helps secure vertical exactness too. The reference is to the craft of masonry involved in the use of a string (*nūl*) in paving the stones along the line, ensuring that they are laid exactly straight.

The chief's achievements enumerated in the inscription include renovation of the old bunds on the reservoirs, namely, Neri-maṭai-ēri, Aracan-kuḷam, Cen-kuḷam, and Māran-ēri (Sattur). On the reservoir called Pallikkuḷam, he dismantled the old bund and built a new one with a sluice, and renamed the reservoir Kiḻavan-ēri. In the same inscription, his renovation of the bund on Perunkuḷam in the village called Cāttanūr, is mentioned with names of the channels of the reservoir. Here the sluice is mentioned to have been paved with stone and connected the other two maṭais at Perunkuḷam, that is, Ponnān-maṭai and Pūnkuṛi-maṭai, with each other. He is praised to have built a bund with a stone sluice on Perumkuḷam, the major reservoir of the village called Āḷankuṭi. The inscriptional enumeration shows that in Kummanamangalam, he had excavated a reservoir called Kiḷavan-ēri. He is said to have opened a reservoir called Tirunārāṇan-ēri at Srivallabhamangalam, a *brahmadēya* created by the king Srimara Srivallabha. It is mentioned that its sluice was built straight in a 'string-line'. The record winds up saying that these and other similar projects were executed by him in Irunjola-nādu so that his name would last as long as the moon and sun endure.

Parāntaka Vīranārayaṇa is praised in the Dalavaypuram copper plates as the builder of many tanks.[11] At the village of Nilaiyur, on the southern side of a stone sluice called paḻḻa-maṭai, the name of this king has been found recorded.[12] A Srivillipputtur inscription of Rajasimha's seventh year (circa AD 915) records the decision of the *mahānāḍu*, renaming the bund and channel of the reservoir in Parankuśapputtūr as Aruḷākkip-perumaṭai and Aruḷākkipperumkāl, after a certain Mūri-Aruḷākki, the *kiḻavan* of Amma-nāḍu obviously in honour of his services.[13] A record of Anaimalai, belonging to the time of Cōḻa Parāntaka registers the improvement of the tank of the *ūruṭaiyan* of Naracinka-*mangalam* by Arunuti Kaliyan alias the *ūruṭaiyan* of Marutūr in Puramkarampai-nāḍu.[14] He is mentioned to have raised the banks of the reservoir, lengthening and deepening it to irrigate the fields of Naracinkamangalam (Madurai) by a certain Arunuti Kaliyan alias the ūrutaiyan of Marutur in Puramkarampai *nāḍu* (Palani).[15] The record mentions that the expense for the project was met out of *iṛai-kāval*, the lump sum obtained on tax-dues. The reservoir was renamed Kaḻiyan-ēri. The Rajacinkap-perumkuḷam, alluded to in the larger Cinnamanur plates was evidently excavated under the auspices of king Rajasimha.[16]

The survey of epigraphical evidence shows that the irrigation activities of kings were confined to Madurai, the capital or core area of the Pāṇḍya state and the Vaigai river, the main perennial water source there. It is significant to note that the major irrigation projects of localities were carried out by the chieftains. However, the leadership of the king is explicit. Praising the king as the 'founder of many reservoirs' though a stock expression in copper plates registering royal charters of land grants to *brāhmaṇas* is not altogether a conventional inscription, along with many other virtues. Both the primacy of irrigation and the royal involvement in providing it are tacitly recognized facts. The local chieftains who enriched their localities with irrigation projects were granted higher political status by the kings. The Eṛukkankuṭi inscription enumerating the projects of Eṭṭi Cāttan, says that Srimara Srivallabha honoured the former by conferring the status of the *kiḻavan* of Iruppaikkuṭi. This shows that providing irrigation facilities was indeed the state's responsibility, though not in a centralized form as in the case of 'hydraulic despotism'.[17] The 'hydraulic despotism' thesis has no relevance here, since the upkeep and maintenance of irrigation sources such as reservoirs and distributive facilities like sluices and channels was the responsibility of the local chieftains. The chieftains were not merely officials of the king, but were local rulers of a relatively autonomous status as heads of ruling lineages. Neither is there any evidence of perpetual subjugation of localities by the king nor of villages by chiefs through the construction and maintenance of irrigation sources and control of their distributive systems. The kings and chiefs expropriated only a small share of agricultural surplus and part of even that was often redistributed as endowments to local temples.

The revenue interest of the ruling class is quite evident in the special administrative interest shown in agricultural development through the extension of irrigation facilities in the state. There are many instances of the purchase of barren lands by the chieftains and endowing them to temples after providing irrigation facilities. They cannot be understood merely as actions of devotion or charity but as strategic actions of developmental implications too. Pūvanan Paṛaiyan, who purchased a barren plot in the periphery of the *brahmadēya* called Iḻankoikkuṭi in Muḻḻi-nādu, caused a reservoir to be excavated in the land.[18] Tennavan Sri Tonkap-Pallavaraiyan purchased an uncultivated stretch of land and caused a water channel cut to ensure irrigation before endowing the purchased land to the Sucindram temple.[19] Generally, such projects of the chieftains increased the control of irrigated lands by the temples, virtually by their *brāhmaṇa* custodians who in turn enhanced the socio-cultural and political status of the ruling aristocracy.

DISTRIBUTIVE ARRANGEMENTS

The reservoir system of irrigation involved a well established convention of distributive arrangement ensuring conflict-free water management, based on consensus and rationalized prioritization of user needs. Located at points suitable for the flow of water under the force of gravity, the distribution under normal conditions was according to the sequence of users as determined by the sequential points of the flow (*pōkumuṛai*). Contrary to this, another arrangement in the distributive system was based on the order of urgency of the user's need (*muṭṭumuṛai*). This arrangement is obviously indicative of the lean season when the water level lowered in the reservoir, demanding rationalization and prioritization of water consumption.[20] Those who required out of turn emergency distribution of water to the field were called *muṭṭukkaṛar*, and catering to their needs was an accepted common practice of every village (*ūrpotuvāna muṭṭumuṛai*). The fields of the *brāhmaṇa* landlords as well as those of the temple were privileged to receive water during the first turn (*munmuṛai*) itself. Every field had its own turn (*tanmuṛai*) and stake to a certain fixed quantity of water measured in terms of time (*nāḻikai*).

The distributive arrangements were not always local, for huge reservoirs (*perumkuḷam*) existed together with big channels (*perumkāl*) irrigating several villages. Every agrarian village had a network of channels (*vāykkāl*) to supply water in each field, leading from the village reservoir (*ūrkkuḷam*) or the big channel of the locality (*nāṭṭupperumkāl*) connected to certain huge reservoirs that were either rain- or river-fed. The Tirukkuṛunkuṭi inscription of Parāntaka Neḍunjaḍaiyan's fourth year shows that the huge reservoir called Vāsudēva-ēri and certain minor reservoirs like Arak-kulam and Nakkan-eri-kulam belonged to Vaikunṭa-valanāḍu, a larger *brahmadēya* in Nāṭṭāṟruppōkku (Nanguneri).[21] The Velvikkuṭi plates show that the granted village, Velvikkuṭi, was on the bank of the reservoir called Kalantaik-kuḷam.[22] A Vijayanarayanam inscription refers to a channel called Paramēśvara-vāykkāl, passing through the *brahmadēya* called Vijayanarayana Caturvēdi mangalam.[23] The Daḷapatisamudram inscription of Parāntaka Neḍunjadaiyan's forty-first year (circa AD 808) mentions the Perumkuḷam of Perumpaḻanji and its sluice-pit, Velvik-kumiḻi.[24] Another main reservoir of the village and its channel find mention in the same record. From two Sucindram inscriptions it is learnt that Alaik-kāl, Marutakuna-vāykkāl, and Tiruvenkata-vāykkāl were the channels carrying water to the *dēvadāna* lands of Nripasekharavalanallūr.[25] Aruḷākkipperumaṭai and Aruḷākkipperumkāl are mentioned in a Srivillipputtur epigraph as the chief sources for irrigation. Sriparantakanallur, also called Vamadevamangalam, a *brahmadēya* in Māṭakkuḷakkīl (Madurai) mentioned in the Kīḻmāttūr inscription, had a reservoir called Kōn-ēri as its chief irrigation source. Individual plots of land used wells for irrigation. The Daḷavāypuram plates allude to the irrigation of fields with the water impounded in wells attached to them.[26] Wells were attached to fields mainly to supplement irrigation from reservoirs.

A Sāḷaigrāmam record alludes to an order by Srimara Srivallabha permitting the *dēvadāna* lands of Varaguṇīśvaram to be irrigated by Kuḻuvānai-ēri, which was situated at Kuḻuvāṇainallūr in Tuvvūrk-*kūṟṟam*, according to two Kaḻukumalai inscriptions.[27] Sriparantakanallur alias Vāmadēva-mangalam a *brahmadēya* in Māṭakkuḷak-kiḻ mentioned in a Kīḻmāttūr inscription had Kōn-ēri as its chief irrigation source.[28] Individual plots of land had used wells for irrigation. These epigraphic references show that the rights, privileges, and claims over water were well stabilized and commonly agreed upon by the local landlords. By and large, it was a conflict-free distributive system, thanks to the united and institutionalized existence of landlords with a corporate character as exemplified by the bodies of *ūrār/nāṭṭār* and *brahmadēya-kiḻavar*.

UPKEEP AND MAINTENANCE

Regarding the details of the upkeep and maintenance of the irrigation systems, there is very little information in the inscriptions of the Pāṇḍya period. It is known from the Pallava inscriptions that the village reservoirs and sluices were looked after by committees like *ērivāriyam* and *kalinka-vāriyam* respectively, the committees specifically constituted by the *sabha*. Such specialized committees are not referred to in the Pāṇḍya records. Nevertheless, it is indicated in the records that the everyday maintenance of irrigation sources and distributive infrastructures provided by the kings and chieftains was bestowed upon the corporate local bodies of landlords, namely the *sabha* and *nāṭṭār* in the *brāhmaṇa* and non-*brāhmaṇa* villages, respectively. These bodies of landlords were oligarchic corporations of *brāhmaṇas* and *vēḷālās* who enjoyed proprietary rights over agrarian fields, intermediaries, artisans, and craftsmen besides the landless peasant workforce, some of whom were subjected to a servile status. The sabhas and ūrs expropriated the unpaid surplus labour through the most subjecting institution of labour realization called *veṭṭi*, derived from *visti* or bonded labour. There are references to *veṭṭi* and *vēdanai* in a few inscriptions.

The Sinnamanur inscription of the forty-sixth year of Srimara Srivallabha (circa AD 857) alludes to two resolutions (*kaccam*) by the sabha of Arikesarinallur regarding the operation of a sluice under its jurisdiction.[29] The record mentions that the supply of water through the channel called Srikanṭa-*vāykkāl* was to be made according to the resolution engraved on the sluice. Unfortunately, the sluice has not survived to our times and so the inscription giving details of its operation is also lost. The Srivillipputtur inscription of Vira Pāṇḍya's fourteenth year (circa AD 960) alludes to an undertaking by the *mahāsabha* to maintain the reservoir attached to the land purchased and endowed by a certain Satrubhayankara Mūvēndavēḷān alias Velan Paranjoti.[30] It was also undertaken that the reservoir would be repaired if any damages occurred. It is obvious that the Pirammadēya-vāykkāls and their reservoirs in *brahmadēyas* were administered by the *sabha*. It is clear from the Ambasamudram inscription registering the endowment of Pūvanan Paṛaiyan, that the manual work of irrigation in the fields was done by a servile group.[31] Such specialized committees are referred to in the records of the Pallavas.[32] The tūmpu inscription at Peryaminakshipuram reservoir seems to specify some land which was probably set apart for the maintenance of the *tūmpu*.

Sometimes more than one agrarian locality depended on a reservoir. So it is obvious that the irrigation system of the period had a system of collective management. We have already seen that the local chiefs were usually the patrons of irrigation projects. Royal projects were very few and the irrigation system involved only small-scale works which could be carried out locally. There was no centralization in the management and administration of the contemporary irrigation system. It appears that the local chiefs and other prominent landholders who were the patrons of the various irrigation projects had some control over the irrigation sources. Generally, there was no royal interference in the administration of local irrigation systems unless disputes occurred between the agrarian villages on irrigation rights. Usually the corporate bodies of landholders, the *nāḍus* and *ūrs* managed the irrigation systems in their areas. The larger irrigation networks common to two or more villages must have necessitated their collective administration, upkeep, and maintenance by the *nāḍu*.

There is no doubt that by and large the irrigation systems of the period were locally owned and managed, so, collective management was generally practised. Usually the *sabhas* and *ūrs* seem to have managed the irrigation systems in their areas. The irrigation systems involved only small-scale maintenance works which could be locally carried out. There is no evidence of state interference in the management of local irrigation sources unless some disputes occurred between agrarian villages on irrigation rights. The Sāḷaigrāmam inscription cited earlier as referring to an order by king Srimara Srivallabha permitting the Varagunisvaram temple to irrigate the *dēvadana* lands from the reservoir called Kuḻuvāṇai-ēri (Paramaguṭi), signifies the context of a conflict resolution. The order of the king was obviously meant for settling some disputes between the temple and the *ūr*. The inscription ends with a preventive statement by the king that the *ūr* should not obstruct the temple from using the reservoir. The reservoir villages were largely heterogeneous, often confined to a hierarchy of multiple castes.

WATER CESS

About the irrigation taxes too, the records contain very little information. Who owned and controlled the reservoirs, sluices, and canals is the question central to any attempt at understanding the nature of water cess that had been in vogue in the Pāṇḍya country. As already noted, the kings and chieftains were involved in executing construction of reservoirs, periodic repairs, renovation, and maintenance of embankments, installation of sluices, excavation of canals, and other infrastructures of irrigation. Apart from the tacit recognition of the fact that traditionally everything in the kingdom belonged to the king, there are a few direct indications in the epigraphs to the royal ownership and control of major irrigation sources. The inscription from Salaigramam referring to an order of Srimara Srivallabha, clearly shows that the king was the ultimate authority to decide the irrigation rights of any village over its irrigation sources, obviously at critical points of conflicts.[33] The inscription contains a royal order giving sanction to the *dēvadāna* of Sāḷaigrāmam to irrigate through a specific channel, probably the one close to the *dēvadāna* fields.

Theoretically, therefore, it goes without saying that the kings and chieftains had exacted by way of cess or rent, some amount of the produce from the fields benefited by the facilities of irrigation. Though the rate and tenure are not clear, there are a few inscriptional indications of the prevalence of the institution of water cess. For instance, the last line of the Ramanathapuram rock inscription, probably of the period of Srimara Srivallabha (circa AD 811–57) seems to specify one *paṭakku* of paddy as cess for each field irrigated by a particular channel.[34] Likewise, the above Salaigramam inscription registers the royal order reducing *dēvadāna* taxes. Inscriptions would have us believe that a lot of royal taxes on *dēvadānas* and *brahmadēyas* were diverted to the temples by way of endowments.

The chieftains must have received a share of the produce as water cess too, over and above the usual periodic revenue (*puravuvari*) from productive fields, although we do not have any inscriptional evidence. Inscriptions are mostly from the *dēvadānas* and *brahmadēyas* possessed by *brāhmaṇas*. Though we do not have much inscriptional evidence, it is certain that non-*brāhmaṇa* villages or peasant villages known as *vēḷānvakai* villages held by the prominent local households (*nāṭṭār*) had to pay water cess to the chieftains and kings who had their formal agency (puravuvari-*tiṇaikkaḷam*) for revenue exaction.

TECHNOLOGY

Remains of bunds and sluices of the period indicate the technical skill involved in the reservoir system of irrigation. The position and depth of the sluices demonstrate adequate knowledge of the architects in choosing the most suitable points and ascertaining the correct sill level. They knew the place where the banks were to be raised for storing the maximum quantity of water. The amount of water stored depends primarily on the quantity of precipitation which flows freely on the surface of the ground. The extent of the area which is drained into the water source is also very important. All the surviving reservoirs of the period show that the architects had a thorough understanding of these factors.

A number of granite sluices (*kartūmpu*) of the period are found in several big reservoirs. Some of them carry label inscriptions, mostly relating to their installation. The stone sluices were installed by royal personages and local chiefs, as already noted. The *tūmpu* inscription at the Peryaminakshipuram reservoir registers the foundation of a *kartūmpu* constructed by a certain Kasivākara *taṭṭān* (goldsmith) of Arikulakesarinallur.[35] The tūmpu (see Fig. 17.1) was a single valve system operated without any devices for mechanical advantage.[36] As shown in the picture, the sluices consisted of two granite pillars installed in the reservoir on either side of the sluice mouth. The pillars varied in height, according to the depth of the reservoirs. The distance between the two pillars was about one to one-and-a-half metres. The pillars were connected to each other by a series of cross-slabs from the base of the sluice to the top. Each cross-slab had a hole in the centre with a diameter of about five to eight inches. The base of the system was a rectangular enclosure built in granite on the bed of the reservoir. It had a rectangular opening of one to two feet. The stone above the opening had a long aperture and the stones on either side of the opening had slots, obviously for the movement of the shutter-plank. It appears that through the series of holes in the cross-slabs, a wooden rode lowered to the sluice mouth. The edge of the rode must have been connected to a shutter-plank lowered through the long aperture so as to cover the opening of the sluice. The operation of the system was quite simple. The sluice mouth could be opened by lifting the rode. This lifting was not difficult since a little opening would cause enough upward thrust from the flow of water for the shutter-plank to move up easily. The sluice opened into an underground conduit which led water to a well called *etirakkiṇaṛu*, built outside the embankment. Unlike ordinary wells, the *etirakkiṇaṛu* was constructed upwards from ground level. It had openings at its base in the channels running in various directions. The flow of water through the channels required no contrivance since it worked on gravitational force. For lifting water from the wells attached to fields, they must have depended on the various types of *piccotah* systems based on human and animal power. In certain types, simple contrivances like adding weight at the effort point of water-lifts, were used for mechanical advantage.

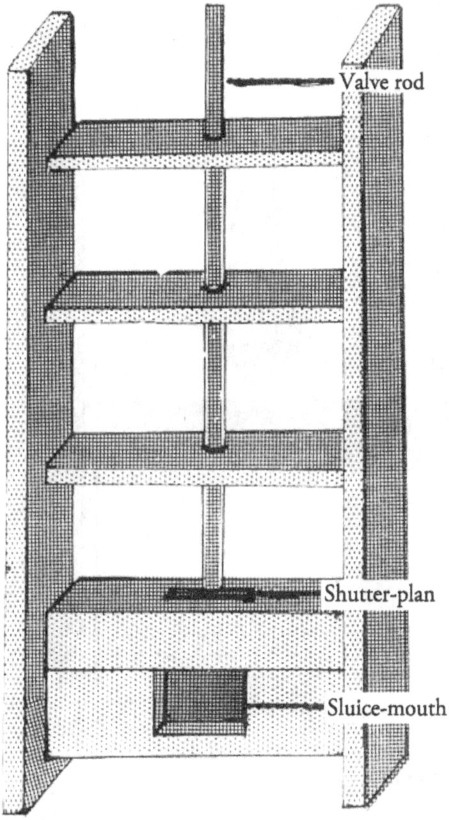

Figure 17.1 The single valve system—*tūmpu*

The sluice pit, ***kumiḻi***, was another system for the regulation of the flow of water from the reservoir. In this case, the sluice mouth (*vāy*) is a pit, also enclosed, and with a circular opening on the surface. The rode lowered through cross-slabs in the system must have been connected to a global stone or wood that acted as the shutter (Fig. 17.2). The post lifts the stone shutter open whenever necessary, taking advantage of the upward thrust of the water that starts escaping as in the previous system. Here the difference was in nature of the valve of the sluice. In the case of the *tūmpu* system, water from the reservoir flowed into the sluice from the side, and in that of the *kumiḻi*, from above. The *tūmpu* opened at the side whereas the *kumiḻi* opened from above.

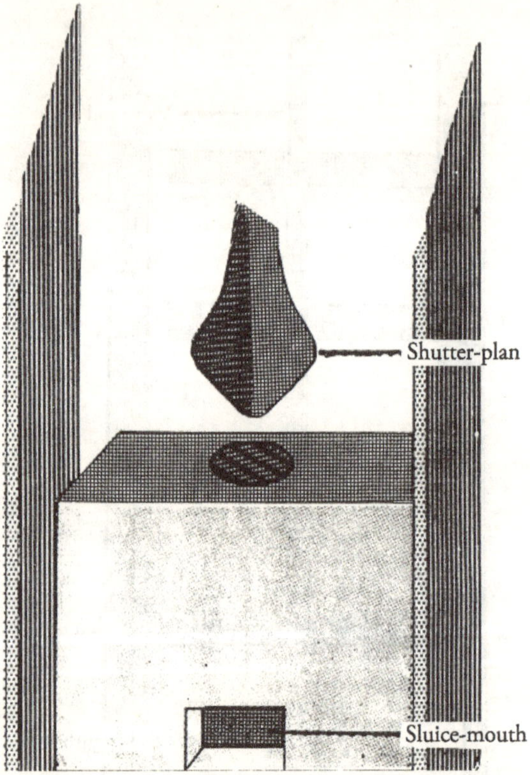

Figure 17.2 The *Kumiḻi* system

The *tūmpus* in the reservoirs were generally installed quite far from the embankments, which meant that those who operated them often had to swim across or resort to conveyances like a small boat to reach them. The positioning of the sluices off the shore has been viewed as an attempt to check the surreptitious operation of the sluice by water thieves.[37] It appears that the actual purpose was different. The *tūmpus* are installed at points of maximum depth where water would be available even during the peak of summer. The reservoir would be increasingly shallow towards the embankments, making the installation of sluices there meaningless. For better outflow of water from the reservoir, sluices had invariably to be at the points of maximum depth which would, naturally, be considerably far from the embankments. Theoretically, sluices are to be installed at points of maximum depth ensuring availability of water even in peak summer and enough pressure for water to flow out. So their positioning off the bank has to be viewed as indicative of the contemporary technical know-how in fixing the correct sill level.

Over a period of about four centuries reviewed here, the historical development of irrigation related construction technology seems to indicate a trajectory of shift from the primeval to the evolved and standardized. Generally, the embankments were made up of mud during the entire period. However, after the primeval phase of the construction of embankments characterized by the use of mud, there appears a trend of preference to laterite and rubbles at vulnerable points. At points of outlet systems ashore, the use of rubble seems to have slowly given way to bricks during the eighth century. Throughout the ninth and tenth centuries, the construction of sluices in reservoirs and the outlet systems at vulnerable points on the bunds, becomes distinct for the use of granite instead of mud, rubble, and laterite. Most records of the periods which deal with irrigation works, refer to the rebuilding or remodelling of bunds and sluices with stone. The project of Eṭṭi Cāttan, the *kiḻavan* of Iruppaikkuṭi, which we have already discussed in detail, provide enough examples of this. The use of chiselled blocks of stone instead of rubble, as well as the practice of precise paving and piling based on the string-line method instead of the tradition of randomized mud and rubble packing, clearly indicate technical advancement. This is not to suggest that there was phasing out of one technology and the arrival a new one in any pure form. Always, there was continuity and change as well as an overlap and coexistence of the old and the new technological practices. The record enumerating the projects of the chief (*kiḻavan*) of Iruppaikkuṭi gives instances of replacement of mud and rubble with bricks, and bricks with chiselled granite stone constructions straight in the string line (*nūḻitteṛuviṭṭa*). The Ramanathapuram inscription of the early ninth century mentions that chiselled stone was used for the construction of the sluice on the reservoir called Puḻḻan-ēri.

The distribution patterns of reservoirs vouch for the fact that the architects were knowledgeable about the 'cascade system', meaning linking up of a series of reservoirs together for effective storage and sustainable distribution of water for irrigation.[38] The reservoir system of the past had involved a lot of insightful, practical, and normative knowledge about water harvesting, storing, and distribution feasible in the ecological, socio-economic, and cultural environment. Systematized over centuries and an age-tested inheritance from generation to generation, the technology of water conservation and management was a sustainable outcome of the need for an economical and rational system of water management, involving even reuse that must have helped the peasants in passing through difficult times during the droughts. Water from the upper parts of the cascade was used and reused several times before it reached the outlet. The cascading system had operated as an ideal rainwater harvesting technology and had worked as a soil moisture and groundwater-maintaining technology as well.

SOCIAL RELATIONS

It is crucial to examine the structure of contemporary social relations in order to understand the sustainability of irrigation technology, which rests on the compatibility of relations through which the technology effectively operates and develops. At the core of social relations of the period were productive relations of contemporary agriculture involving specialization of arts and crafts, stabilized by a hierarchy of entitlements to the produce. Landlords, who were not cultivators by themselves, occupied the apex of the hierarchy and the landless cultivators, the bottom, separated by a few intermediaries. The hierarchy was in the process of consolidation through the caste system that was slowly heading towards rigidity, with those at the base forming the most subjected caste of bondage forcibly deployed for hard labour. It appears that the institutional form of labour realization was closer to that of the bonded workforce attached to the productive land.

The hard labour involved in the operation of the contemporary technology of irrigation was expropriated from a category of bonded workforce, *veṭṭi*, a term derived from *viṣṭi*. *Cennīr-veṭṭi* is the expression used in Tamil inscriptions to refer to the workers subjected to irrigation labour. Almost as a pair, *veṭṭi* and *vedanai* figure in inscriptions to mean workers under bondage and servitude. *Vedanai* literally means pain. In the specific context of forced hard labour, the literal meaning is not out of place. The term occurs sometimes in the general context of unbearable taxation as well in several inscriptions in which the metaphorical meaning is pertinent.

AFTERWORD

As an afterword, the problem of the limited and fragmentary nature of the source material for the study is to be stated at the outset. Nevertheless, from the available archaeological, epigraphic, toponymic, and ethnographic data, we are able to formulate certain tentative ideas about who the founded the major irrigation systems and how they worked. It is clear from the inscriptional sources that the kings and chieftains were the founders of all major irrigation sources. It helps us assume that the reservoirs and sluices were locally owned and managed by the corporate bodies of landlords such as *ūrs* and *brahmadēyas*, that is, the prominent *brāhmaṇa* landlords of the brahmadēyas and *dēvadānas* on the one side and the prominent non-*brāhmaṇa* landlords of *vēḷānvakai* villages. They settled all the everyday matters of the upkeep, maintenance, and operation of the irrigation facilities. The king interfered only in times of disputes and for granting new rights. Often the same irrigation sources were depended upon by several villages, resulting in their management and maintenance being collective and institutionalized. The inscriptional and archaeological evidence shows a linear development of technology from the primeval to the evolved over a period of about four hundred years. The remains of reservoirs and distributive infrastructures indicate the irrigation technology involved, knowledge about cascading, and the correct sill level, respectively. The relations of irrigation works were part of the agrarian hierarchy and the instituted practice of labour realization. The hard manual labour relating to the operation of sluices and maintenance of reservoirs was realized from a category of workforce in a position of bondage through structures of control and institutional domination.

Table 17.1 Irrigation sources mentioned in Pāṇḍya epigraphs

Irrigation Source	*Village/Division*	*System*	*Reference*
Aruḷākki-perumkāl	Parānkuśapputtūr Villipputtur, Rd.	Canal	Newly discovered
Iṭaikkuḷam	Perumpaḻanji, Nāṭṭāṟṟuppōkku, Nāngun-ēri	Tank	S.I.I. XIV. 40
Kalandaikkuḷam	Cinnamannūr, Periyākuḷam, Md.	Tank	S.I.I. III *Pt.* IV LSP
Kiḻavan-ēri	Māranūr Perumkuḷam, Rd.	Tank	S.I.I. XIV. 44

Contd

Table 17.1 Contd

Irrigation Source	*Village/Division*	*System*	*Reference*
Kon-ēri	Kiḻmattur, Madurai, Md.	Tank	S.I.I. XIV. 86
Kuluvanai	Perumpaḻanji, Nāṭṭāṟṟupōkku, Nangun-ēri, Tn.	Well	S.I.I. XIV. 40
Kuḷuvāṇai-ēri	Sāḷaigrāmam, Paramaguḍi, Rd.	Tank	EI. XXVIII 17 A 17 B
Māranūr perumkuḷam	Māranūr, Eṛukkan-*kuṭi*, Sattur, Rd.	Tank	S.I.I. XIV. 44
Marutaguna-vaykkal	Nripasekharanallur, Agastisvaram, Sucindram, KK.	Canal	KK. 1968/212
Māṭak-kuḷam	Madurai, Kiḻmāttūr, Md.	Tank	S.I.I. XIV. 86
Mūlai-vāykkāl	Perumpaḻanji, Nāṭṭāṟṟupōkku, Nāngun-ēri, Tn.	Sluice	S.I.I. XIV. 40
Nakkan-ēri	Tirukkuṛunkuṭi, Nāṭṭāṟṟupōkku, Nāngun-ēri, Tn.	Tank	S.I.I. XIV. 19
Nāṭṭup-perumkāl	Vepu-*nadu*, Tn.	Canal	PCP. SP
Nāṭṭup-perumkāl	Panai-*nadu* Sivakasi, Tn.	Canal	PCP. SP
Nāṭṭup-perumkāl	Eli-*nadu*, Tn.	Canal	PCP. SP
Paramēśvara-vāykkāl	Vijayanarayanam, Nāṭṭāṟṟuppōkku, Tn.	Canal	S.I.I. XIV. 17
Perumkuḷam renamed as Aruḷākkip-peruma-ṭai, Parānkusapputtūr	Parānkuśapputtūr, Villiputtur, Rd.	Tank	Newly discovered
Perumpaḻanji perumkuḷam	Perumpaḻanji, Nāṭṭāṟṟupokku, Nāngun-ēri, Tn.	Tank	S.I.I. XIV. 40
Rājacinkap-perumkuḷam	Sinnamannur, Periyākuḷam, Md.	Tank	S.I.I. III. *Pt.* IV LSP
Srīkanta-vāykkāl	Arikesarinallur, Periyākuḷam, Sinnamannur, Md.	Canal	S.I.I. XIV. 78

Contd

Table 17.1 Contd

Irrigation Source	*Village/Division*	*System*	*Reference*
Vaigai-matagu	Madurai, Māṭakkuḷakkīl, Md.	Canal	EI, XXVIII, 4
Varamoli-ēri	Sāḷaigrāmam, Paramaguḍi, Rd.	Sluice	EI, XXVIII, 17 A & 17 B
Vasudēva-ēri	Tirukkuṛunkuṭi, Nāṭṭāṟṟupōkku, Nāngun-ēri, Tn.	Tank	S.I.I. XIV. 19
Velvik-kumiḻi	Perumpaḻanji, Nāṭṭāṟṟupōkku, Nāngun-ēri, Tn.	Sluice	S.I.I. XIV. 40
Vāsudēva-ēri	Sāḷaigrāmam, Paramaguḍi, Rd.	Tank	EI, XXVIII, 17A
Vīranārāṇam-ēri	Nalaiyur, Melur, Md.	Tank	KK. 1941/224 S.I.I. V. 405 406

Note: LSP = Larger Sinnamanur Plates; SP = Sivakasi Plates; Md. = Madurai, Rd. = Ramanathapuram; Tn. = Tirunelveli; KK. = Kanyakumari.

NOTES AND REFERENCES

1. It is the proximity of tanks to a few megalithic sites that forms the basis for the conjecture. See R.E.M. Wheeler, 1941, 'Brahmagiri and Chandravalli Excavations', *Ancient India*, no. 4, pp. 180–310. Also Gururaja Rao, 1972, *Megalithic Culture of South India*, Mysore, pp. 298–300. For more details showing the proximity, see K. Rajan, 2008, *Ancient Irrigation Technology*, Thanjavur, pp. 13–15.
2. The grave goods of the culture actually points to a stage of hunting, food-gathering, and subsistence farming. See Rajan Gurukkal, 1989, 'Forms of Production and Forces of Change in Ancient South India', *Studies in History*, 5, n.s., 159–75.
3. Certain relevant issues are highlighted in D. Ludden, 'Ecological Zones and the Cultural Economy of Irrigation in Southern Tamil Nadu', p. 4 and n. 7.
4. See R.L. Brohier, 1934, *Ancient Irrigation Works in Ceylon*, Government of Sri Lanka, Colombo. Also E.R. Leach, 1959, 'Hydraulic Society in Ceylon', *Past and Present*, Oxford. Also his 1976, *Science and Civilization in China*.
5. For the text, its translation, and other basic details see *Epigraphia Indica* (*EI*), XXXVIII, part I, pp. 27–9. The editor had ascribed the inscription to Centan. However, recent epigraphical studies have clarified the fact that the inscription belonged to Arikēsari, the son of Cēntan. That the

irrigation sluice is named as Arikēsariyan after the title of Arikēsari, further substantiates it.

6. The text of the inscription has been published in *Āvaṇam*, 1990.
7. For the text of and comments on the inscription, see *South Indian Inscriptions* (SII), XIV, nos 43–4.
8. See *SII*, XIV, no. 43.
9. Ibid., no. 44.
10. Ibid.
11. See, 1967, *Pāṇḍyar Cēppeṭukal Pattu* (*PCP*), Madras, pp. 95–115.
12. See *Annual Report of South Indian Epigraphy* (*ARE*), no. 223, 1941.
13. Ibid., no. 285 of 196–6.
14. *SII*, III, part III, no. 106.
15. Ibid.
16. *PCP*. line l. 144–5, pp. 147–59.
17. The concept of hydraulic despotism is formulated in K.A. Wittfogel, 1957, *Oriental Despotism: A Comparative Study of Total Power*, Yale. Also its criticism in Irfan Habib, 1962, 'An Examination of Wittfogel's Theory of Oriental Despotism', *Enquiry*: Old Series, no. 6, pp. 54–73.
18. *SII*, XIV, no. 56.
19. See 1968, *Kanyakumari Kalveṭṭukal* (*KK*), no. 224.
20. There is no consensus about the meaning of the term *muṭṭumuṭai*, for the context of its occurrence in inscriptions is not enough to assert anything clear. Nonetheless, there is no semantic ambiguity about the term either. It is a word for shortage and hence a metaphor signifying the situation of urgent need for something lacking. For a discussion of the different semantic interpretations of the term, see K. Rajan, *Ancient Irrigation Technology*, pp. 61–2.
21. *SII*, XIV, no. 19.
22. *PCP*, pp. 19–32, line, 120.
23. SII, XIV, no. 17.
24. Ibid., no. 40.
25. *KK*, nos 212 and 224, 1968.
26. *PCP*, pp. 95–115, line 212–13 and 219.
27. *SII*, XIV, no. 91.
28. *SII*, XIV, no. 86.
29. Ibid., no. 78.
30. *SII*, XIV, no. 91.
31. Ibid., no. 56.
32. Specialized committees are referred to in the records of the Pallavas. See C. Minakshi, 1977, *Administration and Social Life under the Pallavas*, Madras, p. 131. Also, T.M. Sreenivasan, 1968, 'Irrigation and Water Supply in South India, upto 1300 AD', unpublished MLit thesis, Madras University; S.Y. Krishna Swamy, 1968, 'Major Irrigation Systems of Ancient

Tamilnadu', *First International Conference Seminar on Tamil Studies*, Kuala Lumpur, pp. 451–3.

33. *SII*, XIV, no. 78.
34. *SII*, XIV, no. 26: '.... *Ūrk(ku)ḻattukkīḻtalainīrpātukāllōrō vayal patakku nel....*' is the passage. It has been interpreted as 'each field irrigated by the village reservoir was sowable with a patakku of paddy'. See *EI*, XXXII, part VI, p. 269.
35. The text of this inscription was copied and read with the help of Y. Subbarayalu and N. Vedachalam. "*itarkku tiṛappu nilan ......araikkāl cei.*" This portion of the record is partly damaged.
36. The *tūmpus* are often covered by almost half their heights with silt. At an old reservoir called Cēntan-ēri, obviously named after Māran Cēntan, near Tirumanikkam in the Tirumangalam taluk, we explored a tūmpu of 19 feet height. Its sluice was covered by silt. The tūmpu at Nattam in the reservoir called Ēḻumaṭakkanmai, in the Nattam taluk has been covered mostly by silt. The reservoir is now a paddy field. One can identify the place as a reservoir only from the place name and the remains of the tūmpu. The distance between the two pillars is about one to one-and-a-half metres.
37. See R.A.L.H. Gunavardhana, 1984, 'Intersocietal Transfer of Hydraulic Technology in Precolonial South Asia: Some Reflections Based on a Preliminary Investigation', *South Asian Studies*, 22(2): 126.
38. Madduma Bandara C.M., 1985, 'Catchment Ecosystems and Village Tank Cascades in the Dry Zone of Sri Lanka: A Time-Tested System of Land and Water Management', in J. Lundqvist, U. Lohm, and M. Falkenmark (eds), *Strategies for River Basin Management*, Linkoping, Sweden; Panabokke, C.R., 2000, *The Small Tank Cascade Systems of the Rajarata: Their Setting, Distribution Patterns, and Hydrography*, Colombo.

Index